The Ulama in Contemporary Islam

PRINCETON STUDIES IN MUSLIM POLITICS

Dale F. Eickelman and James Piscatori, Editors

Diane Singerman, *Avenues of Participation: Family, Politics, and Networks
in Urban Quarters of Cairo*

Tone Bringa, *Being Muslim the Bosnian Way: Identity and Community
in a Central Bosnian Village*

Dale F. Eickelman and James Piscatori, *Muslim Politics*

Bruce B. Lawrence, *Shattering the Myth: Islam beyond Violence*

Ziba Mir-Hosseini, *Islam and Gender:
The Religious Debate in Contemporary Iran*

Robert W. Hefner, *Civil Islam: Muslims and
Democratization in Indonesia*

Muhammad Qasim Zaman, *The Ulama in Contemporary Islam:
Custodians of Change*

The Ulama in Contemporary Islam

CUSTODIANS OF CHANGE

Muhammad Qasim Zaman

PRINCETON UNIVERSITY PRESS

PRINCETON AND OXFORD

COPYRIGHT © 2002 BY PRINCETON UNIVERSITY PRESS

PUBLISHED BY PRINCETON UNIVERSITY PRESS, 41 WILLIAM STREET,

PRINCETON, NEW JERSEY 08540

IN THE UNITED KINGDOM: PRINCETON UNIVERSITY PRESS,

3 MARKET PLACE, WOODSTOCK, OXFORDSHIRE OX20 1SY

ALL RIGHTS RESERVED

LIBRARY OF CONGRESS CATALOGING-IN-PUBLICATION DATA

ZAMAN, MUHAMMAD QASIM.

THE ULAMA IN CONTEMPORARY ISLAM: CUSTODIANS OF CHANGE /

MUHAMMAD QASIM ZAMAN.

P. CM. — (PRINCETON STUDIES IN MUSLIM POLITICS)

INCLUDES BIBLIOGRAPHICAL REFERENCES AND INDEX.

ISBN 0-691-09680-5 (CLOTH : ALK. PAPER)

1. ULAMA. 2. SCHOLARS, MUSLIM. I. TITLE. II. SERIES.

BP185 .Z36 2002

297.6'1—dc21   2002020127

BRITISH LIBRARY CATALOGING-IN-PUBLICATION DATA IS AVAILABLE

THIS BOOK HAS BEEN COMPOSED IN SABON TYPEFACE

PRINTED ON ACID-FREE PAPER. ∞

WWW.PUPRESS.PRINCETON.EDU

PRINTED IN THE UNITED STATES OF AMERICA

3   5   7   9   10   8   6   4   2

ISBN-13: 978-0-691-09680-3 (cloth)

ISBN-10: 0-691-09680-5 (cloth)

For Shaista, Zaynab, and Mustafa

Contents

FOREWORD   ix

ACKNOWLEDGMENTS   xiii

Introduction   1

I
Islamic Law and the 'Ulama in Colonial India:
A Legal Tradition in Transition   17

II
Constructions of Authority   38

III
The Rhetoric of Reform and the Religious Sphere   60

IV
Conceptions of the Islamic State   87

V
Refashioning Identities   111

VI
Religiopolitical Activism and the 'Ulama:
Comparative Perspectives   144

Epilogue
The 'Ulama in the Twenty-First Century   181

NOTES   193

GLOSSARY   259

BIBLIOGRAPHY   263

INDEX   287

Foreword

THROUGHOUT THE MUSLIM-MAJORITY world, advancing levels of education, greater ease of travel, and the rise of new communications media have contributed to the emergence of a public sphere—some call it the "street"—in which large numbers of people, and not just an educated, political, and economic elite, want a say in political and religious issues. The result has been increasing challenges to authoritarianism and fragmentation of authority.

Many of the emerging new voices and the leaders of such movements claim to interpret basic religious texts, and they work in local or transnational contexts to shape religious movements intended to improve the human condition. However, like their counterparts in Poland's solidarity movement and the liberation theology movements in Latin America, these new intellectuals and interpreters often lack theological and philosophical sophistication. Such leaders have often succeeded in capturing the imagination of large numbers of people, nonetheless.

Other spokespersons represent a darker side of the fragmentation of authority. Usama bin Laden and his associates in al-Qaʿida, including the Egyptian physician Ayman al-Zawahiri, are no match for Thomas Hobbes, Martin Heidegger, or Muhammad Iqbal. They have, however, emerged as the leaders of a tiny but lethal minority, and their interpretations of religious texts are heard throughout the world.

Fascination with understanding these new interpreters has deflected attention from the role in the Muslim world of the ʿulama, religious scholars with intensive training in religious texts and jurisprudence who have long sustained widespread respect as the guardians of the Islamic religious tradition. Such was their influence that successions of colonial regimes, including the British, French, and Dutch, vigorously sought to circumscribe their influence and curtail financial support for the institutions of religious learning in which they were trained. Autocrats throughout the Middle East, Central Asia, and Southeast Asia likewise sought to silence or co-opt them.

The ʿulama, often misleadingly portrayed as guardians of tradition who play a diminishing role in modern societies and who endeavor to ignore or disqualify anything new, nonetheless play a vital, albeit changing, role in the societies in which they participate. *The Ulama in Contemporary Islam: Custodians of Change* offers a highly readable assessment of that role. Zaman focuses intensively on the role of the ʿulama in British India and its successor independent states, India and Pakistan, but he also compares their changing role in South Asia with that of their counterparts in

Iran, Saudi Arabia, Egypt, and elsewhere. He shows that the religious and social views of the 'ulama have as much disparity as the views of religious modernists, Islamists, and secularists. He also demonstrates how Islamic tradition in general, and interpretations of Islamic law, the *shari'a*, in particular, are a process shaped through ongoing discussion and debate, rather than a fixed content.

On the shifts in the context of 'ulama discourse and practice during precolonial, colonial, and postcolonial rule and after the introduction of print technology, Zaman suggests that the critical question is not whether the authority of the 'ulama has increased or decreased, but "how that authority is constructed, argued, put on display, and constantly defended." Here as elsewhere, Zaman raises seminal questions that offer fresh perspectives on Islam in South Asia and on ideas of religious authority elsewhere in the Muslim world and in other religious traditions.

The Ulama in Contemporary Islam is the first work to look comprehensively at the 'ulama and their institutions of learning in both the colonial and postcolonial contexts, as well as at the subtle and nuanced relationships between what the 'ulama say and do and the changing contexts of religiopolitical activism. In colonial India, the British saw precolonial Islamic and Hindu law as "uncertain, unsystematic, and arbitrary"—a characterization that might be equally applied to British colonial rule—so they sought to codify it. The results often were ironic. As Zaman shows, the 'ulama altered shari'a rules even after British-inspired codification. They also managed to subtly shape British efforts to "reform" (which in practice meant to control and regulate) the system of *madrasa* (mosque university) education. A major consequence of British rule was to redefine the function of the 'ulama, creating the idea of religion as a "specialty" in which the 'ulama had a particular authority in linking Islam's past with the present and increasingly contributing to senses of community that transcend local social contexts.

Earlier scholars have suggested that the 'ulama turned away from issues of state and society during the colonial period and shifted their focus to personal moral qualities. *The Ulama in Contemporary Islam* indicates how this interpretation has deflected attention away from the growth of radical sectarianism that has characterized Pakistani religious life in the last three decades and from the rise of such movements as the Taliban in Afghanistan. As Zaman indicates, religiously sanctioned violence and the growing lists of martyrs contribute as much—though in a negative way—to a sense of community in both rural and urban contexts as do mosques, religious schooling, religious texts, and shared social background and economic interests.

This highly original book offers fresh insight into the role of Islamic religious scholars in the modern world. It will shape for years to come how we understand religious tradition, sectarianism, religious knowledge and its carriers, and the diverse ways in which religious arguments are created and disseminated. Zaman's accessible style and persuasive comparison of religious developments in South Asia with other parts of the Muslim world make this book a significant port of entry for anyone wishing to understand Islamic religious tradition and the modern social and political contexts in which it is elaborated and reproduced.

Dale F. Eickelman
James Piscatori

Acknowledgments

I HAVE INCURRED many debts of gratitude while working on this book over the past several years. A generous fellowship funded by the Rockefeller Foundation and awarded by the Triangle South Asia Consortium's Residency Program in South Asian Islam and the Greater Muslim World at Duke University and the University of North Carolina, Chapel Hill, provided me with the initial opportunity to begin sustained work on this project. Later, a fellowship funded by the Lilly Endowment at the National Humanities Center, Research Triangle Park, North Carolina, enabled me to bring this book to completion in the inimitable environment provided by the Center. I am also grateful to Brown University for much support, especially in the form of a sabbatical leave, a grant from the Faculty Development Fund, and research support from the Robert Gale Noyes Endowment.

At various stages in the research and writing of this book, many people have shared their wisdom and expertise with me, offering valuable advice, insight, and encouragement. Among them, I would especially like to mention Charles J. Adams, Engin D. Akarli, Zafar Ishaq Ansari, Arthur F. Buehler, Richard M. Eaton, Dale F. Eickelman, Carl W. Ernst, Marc Gaborieau, Mahmood Ahmad Ghazi, David Gilmartin, Sumit Guha, Wael B. Hallaq, Bruce B. Lawrence, Seyyed Vali Reza Nasr, and John F. Richards. I should also like to thank John P. Reeder, Jr., and other colleagues at Brown University's Department of Religious Studies for their encouragement, and Gail Tetreault and Kathleen Pappas for their assistance. None of this work would be possible, however, without the crucial assistance I have received from library personnel at a number of places, above all at Brown University, the National Humanities Center, Duke University, Harvard University, and the Islamic Research Institute, Islamabad. I thank all of these institutions and individuals, especially the late Ahmad Zafar of the Islamic Research Institute.

An earlier draft of the entire book was read with exemplary sensitivity and thoroughness by Bruce Lawrence and David Gilmartin, both of whom, along with Carl Ernst, have been sources of crucial support over many years. Part of the title of this book is also based on a suggestion from Lawrence. The very helpful feedback provided by Dale Eickelman and Muhammad Khalid Masud has made this a better book than it would have been without the benefit of their advice. Mary Murrell, my editor at Princeton University Press, has expertly guided this book through the various stages of review and publication; I am deeply appreciative of her interest in this project and of her wise counsel all along. I also wish to thank Sara Lerner for her supervision of the production process, and Carolyn Bond for her superb work in copyediting the manuscript.

Portions of the research on which this book is based were presented at conferences and as lectures at Duke University; the University of North Carolina, Chapel Hill; the School of Oriental and African Studies, University of London; École des hautes études en science sociales, Paris; Fondation maison des sciences de l'homme, Paris; Institut d'études politiques, Paris; Harvard University; McGill University; the Carolina Seminar in Comparative Islamic Studies, North Carolina; the National Humanities Center; and the Watson Institute for International Studies, Brown University. I wish to thank the organizers of these conferences and lectures for inviting me to present my work, and the participants for their comments and questions. I also thank Cambridge University Press for permission to include here revised versions of material I have previously published as the following articles: "Sectarianism in Pakistan: The Radicalization of Shi'i and Sunni Identities," *Modern Asian Studies*, vol. 32, no. 3 (July 1998); "Religious Education and the Rhetoric of Reform: The Madrasa in British India and Pakistan," *Comparative Studies in Society and History*, vol. 41, no. 2 (April 1999); and "Arabic, the Arab Middle East, and the Definition of Muslim Identity in Twentieth Century India," *Journal of the Royal Asiatic Society*, third series, vol. 8, no. 1 (April 1998). With grateful acknowledgment to the publisher, I also draw on material published in "Nation, Nationalism, and 'Ulama: Hadith in Religiopolitical Debates in Twentieth Century India," *Oriente Moderno* vol. 21, no. 1 (2002).

My family has been the source of much strength and comfort during the long gestation of this book. I am most grateful to them, but above all to Shaista Azizalam, for the love, patience, and understanding without which it would have been difficult and perhaps impossible to bring this work to completion. It is to Shaista, and to our children, Zaynab and Mustafa, that I dedicate this book.

A Note on Transliteration and Spelling

With the exception of the ' to signify the Arabic letter *'ayn* (as in " 'Uthmani" or "shari'a") and ' to represent the *hamza* (as in "Qur'an"), diacritics are not used in this book. The *hamza* itself is only used when it occurs within a word (as in "Qur'an") but not when it occurs at the end (thus "'ulama," rather than "'ulama'"). With the notable exception of the term "'ulama" (singular: "'alim"), the plural forms are usually indicated by adding an *s* to the word in the singular, as in "madrasas" (rather than "madaris") or "fatwas" (rather than "fatawa"). In the interest of consistency, the spellings of Arabic and Urdu words, and of Muslim names, follow the convention used for Arabic consonants by the *International Journal of Middle East Studies*.

The Ulama in Contemporary Islam

Introduction

IT HAS OFTEN BEEN ASSUMED that in the face of massive and
unrelenting changes in the modern world, the traditionally educated
Muslim religious scholars, the *ulama* (singular: *'alim*),[1] have become
utterly redundant, a mere relic of the past, as it were, and therefore of
little interest to anyone seriously interested in understanding contemporary Muslim societies. Not very long ago, a somewhat similar attitude
was common towards the role of religion in public life as a whole, though
movements of religious revival, and not just in the Muslim world, have
forced a major rethinking of such attitudes in recent years. The religiopolitical activism of the college- and university-educated, the professionals
and the urban bourgeoisie—the "Islamists," as they are often called—has
now come to receive extensive attention; and thanks to their leadership
of the Iranian revolution of 1979, so have the Shi'i 'ulama. But old assumptions have remained rather more entrenched in the case of the 'ulama
of the *Sunni* Muslim world. The "new religious intellectuals"[2] emerging
in the Muslim public sphere undoubtedly merit close attention, and the
contemporary Islamist movements continue to be in much need of sober
analyses. The emphasis on relatively new and emerging intellectuals and
activists should not, however, obscure the significance of a community of
religious scholars that has existed in Muslim societies for more than a
thousand years and, in recent decades, has also witnessed a resurgence of
great moment.[3] As increasingly prominent actors on the contemporary
scene in Muslim societies, the 'ulama—their transformations, their discourses, and their religiopolitical activism—can, indeed, only be neglected
at the cost of ignoring or misunderstanding crucial facets of contemporary
Islam and Muslim politics. The processes and consequences of social and
religious change as they have shaped, and been shaped by, the 'ulama are
the subject of this book. The book focuses primarily on British India and
Pakistan, but does so in a comparative framework, with extensive and
sustained consideration of religious and political trends in a number of
contemporary Muslim societies.

The challenges and consequences of modernity have no doubt hit the
'ulama hard. Mass higher education and the impact of print and other
media have made deep inroads into the 'ulama's privileged access to authoritative religious knowledge,[4] even as the "reflexivity" of modernity,
that is, the need to constantly adapt existing forms of knowledge, institutions, and social relations to relentless flows of information, poses severe
challenges to the credibility of their discourses.[5] The modern bureaucratic
state seeks to bring all areas of life under its regulation. And the trans-

formative forces of global capitalism grow ever more relentless in undermining culturally rooted identities and social relations. How have the 'ulama responded to these challenges, to the fragmentation of their authority, to the rapidly changing world around them?

To the French sociologist Olivier Roy, "the 'Islamic political imagination' [of the 'ulama] has endeavored to ignore or disqualify anything new. . . . The atemporality of the mullahs' and ulamas' discourse is striking to this day. History is something that must be endured; whatever is new is contingent and merits only a *fatwa* from time to time."[6] On this view, the 'ulama are the representatives par excellence of a religious tradition that is stagnant and, for all their glosses and commentaries on the texts that comprise this tradition, essentially anachronistic in the modern world. Their "status" might vary a great deal, ranging anywhere between a certain approximation to the social position of "Westernized intellectuals" on the one hand and the "lumpen-intelligentsia" on the other;[7] but there is little evidence to temper the "atemporality" of their discourse or action.[8]

Yet the 'ulama have not only continued to respond—admittedly, with varying degrees of enthusiasm and success—to the challenges of changing times; they have also been successful in enhancing their influence in a number of contemporary Muslim societies, in broadening their audiences, in making significant contributions to public discourses, and even in setting the terms for such discourses. In many cases, they have also come to play significant religiopolitical activist roles in contemporary Islam. The 'ulama's institutions of learning have grown dramatically in recent decades. In Pakistan, there were less than 150 *madrasas* at the time of the establishment of the state in 1947; according to certain recent estimates, there are at present more than 2700 in the Punjab, the most populous of Pakistan's four provinces, alone. The number of madrasa students in the Punjab has increased from 24,822 in 1960, to 81,134 in 1979, to 249,534 in 2001; that is, their number has multiplied by more than ten since 1960 alone.[9] In several other contemporary states, both where Muslims constitute a numerical majority and where they are a minority, the 'ulama in recent decades have grown increasingly prominent in society and politics. The case of Iran is, of course, the most striking example of the 'ulama's successful leadership of a revolutionary movement. But in Egypt too, where the millennium-old university, the Azhar, continues to be one of the most prestigious centers of Islamic learning, a new generation of politically activist 'ulama has made its presence felt in the public arena. 'Ulama in Saudi Arabia, in India, in Afghanistan, in the southern Philippines, and elsewhere in the Muslim world are a crucial part of the changes sweeping through these societies in increasingly significant, often unprecedented ways.

The 'Ulama and the Islamic Religious Tradition

"No categories require more careful handling these days," the ethicist Jeffrey Stout observes, "than *tradition* and *modernity*."[10] Not long ago, contrasts between "tradition" and "modernity" were a convenient shorthand way of explaining what particular societies had to get rid of in order to become part of the modern world. Increasingly, however, such dichotomous constructions have given way, in academic writing at any rate, to a recognition that "tradition" is not a monolithic entity any more than "modernity" is; that appeals to tradition are not necessarily a way of opposing change but can equally facilitate change; that what passes for tradition is, not infrequently, quite recent vintage; and that definitions of what constitutes tradition are often the product of bitter and continuing conflicts within a culture.[11]

With such caveats, can the concept of tradition be rescued from the role Western modernization theorists of an earlier generation[12]—or Muslim modernists, for that matter—assigned to it? Can it serve as an analytical tool in examining some of the competing discourses and conflicts in the Muslim public sphere, in listening to debates on issues of religious authority, in trying to understand how perceptions and imaginings of the past shape articulations of identity in the present? As a way of introducing some of the themes of this book, I propose to explore briefly the meaning and implications of this concept, both to show how we might try to understand major trends in contemporary Islam with reference to it and to suggest its relevance for our understanding of the 'ulama, the Muslim religious scholars who are the subject of this book.

Historian of religion William Graham has argued that "traditionalism" ought to be seen as a defining feature of Islamic thought. This traditionalism consists, he says, "not in some imagined atavism, regressivism, fatalism, or rejection of change and challenge," but rather in the conviction that "a personally guaranteed connection with a model past, and especially with model persons, offers the only sound basis . . . for forming and reforming one's society in any age."[13] The traditionalism Graham considers characteristic of Islam is rooted in styles of authenticating the statements attributed to the Prophet Muhammad (or statements about his conduct and teachings as reported by his companions) by affixing to each of these statements a chain of transmission that goes back to him or to one of the other early authorities. Western scholars have usually characterized these discrete statements (*hadith*) as "traditions" of Muhammad. But the traditionalism of which Graham speaks is something broader in scope and significance: it is the recurrent effort by Muslims to articulate authority and evaluate claims to such authority by positing and reaffirming a connectedness to the past. Graham acknowledges that anchoring authority in efforts to establish a link with the past is not unique to Muslims, but he argues that this effort is nowhere more pervasive than in Islam, and that it is institutionalized here to an unparalleled degree. For instance, the emphasis on "a personally guaranteed connection to a model past" has, for centuries, remained the fundamental principle of validating the transmission of religious knowledge; it underlies genealogical claims to social standing; it is at the heart of the Shi'i belief in the authority of the rightly guided and infallible *imam*s; and it is the basis on which institutionalized Sufism, with its lineages of masters and disciples, rests.[14]

Yet, while Graham shows how "traditionalism" informs religious authority in Islam, he does not give much attention to the concept of tradition itself.[15] For that, we must turn to the moral philosopher Alasdair MacIntyre, whose conception of tradition, especially as mediated to Islamicists by the anthropologist Talal Asad, offers a potentially fruitful way of approaching and understanding Muslim institutions and discourses in the complexities of their development, change, and continuity.[16]

To MacIntyre, tradition is, quite simply, "an argument extended through time in which certain fundamental agreements are defined and redefined in terms of two kinds of conflict: those with critics and enemies external to the tradition who reject all or at least key parts of those fundamental agreements, and those internal, interpretative debates through which the meaning and rationale of the fundamental agreements come to be expressed and by whose progress a tradition is constituted."[17] Traditions may be more or less successful in asking new questions or satisfactorily answering old ones, in meeting the challenges posed to their adherents and in adapting to change; but what remains key to their constitution as traditions is a history of argument and debate over certain fundamental doctrines in shared languages and styles of discourse.[18]

The intellectual positions held by the adherents of a tradition can only be understood, MacIntyre insists, in the context of that tradition. There are no texts, theses, or conceptions—of justice and rationality, for instance—in themselves; they exist, and can be evaluated, only as part of this or that tradition, and so far as their criteria for evaluation are concerned, the different traditions are "incommensurable."[19] For all the disagreements within a particular tradition, there remains a broad agreement on which differences are the critical ones and how, or within what limits, to argue over them. There is, however, no such agreement *between* traditions, and even to understand a rival tradition presupposes that one be immersed in the language of that tradition. This position is at the heart of MacIntyre's quarrel with contemporary liberalism.

The view that texts and authors can be approached, translated, and evaluated according to some universal principles of rationality is a liberal myth, MacIntyre believes, and one characteristic of "modernity, whether conservative or radical."[20] To him, this view is deplorable, but not only because it leads us to gravely misunderstanding traditions other than our own.[21] The liberal view also underlies a hegemonic discourse where intellectual positions from other traditions are decontextualized in translation and those at odds with liberalism are rendered innocuous by being recast as "debates within liberalism, putting in question this or that particular set of attitudes or policies, but not the fundamental tenets of liberalism. . . . So so-called conservatism and so-called radicalism in these contemporary guises are in general mere stalking-horses for liberalism: the contemporary debates within modern political systems are almost exclusively between conservative liberals, liberal liberals, and radical liberals."[22]

MacIntyre's notion of the incommensurability of traditions has been criticized for its many perceived inadequacies, as indeed has his conception of tradition itself. Critics have observed, for instance, that if a tradition were so utterly incommensurable as he supposes, one could not comprehend *any* of its ideas; yet MacIntyre's own writing about other traditions intelligibly and at length seems to suggest otherwise.[23] Rival traditions, even in MacIntyre's sense, do, in fact, often share many basic assumptions;[24] conversely, certain disagreements *within* what MacIntyre characterizes as a single tradition of liberalism are so fundamental as to qualify for his label of incommensurability.[25] Liberal critics have also discerned authoritarian implications in MacIntyre's views of tradition and of tradition-centered criteria of rationality, fearing that "MacIntyre is in the grip of a world view promulgated by authority rather than reason [and] . . . is using this view to justify perpetuating authority at the heart of human life and, indeed, at the heart of human reason."[26] MacIntyre has not answered all his critics to their satisfaction. And he has continued to not only insist on tradition-specific criteria of moral valuation but increasingly to write self-consciously in a way that foregrounds his own commitment to a particular tradition—Roman Catholicism, specifically Thomism.[27] Yet he has also continued to affirm the possibility, in principle at least, of debate and interaction with other, rival traditions. His condition is, however, that one be willing and able to learn "the language of the alien tradition as a new and second first language"[28] in order for such interaction to be possible, and that only then can one tradition seriously try to remedy its weaknesses by creative engagement with a rival.

We need not, however, agree in all respects with MacIntyre to see the relevance of his concept of tradition for our purposes here. Drawing on the work of MacIntyre, Talal Asad has underlined the relevance of the concept of tradition, as a "discursive tradition," to the study of Islam. To Asad:

A tradition consists essentially of discourses that seek to instruct practitioners regarding the correct form and purpose of a given practice that, precisely because it is established, has a history. These discourses relate conceptually to *a past* (when the practice was instituted, and from which the knowledge of its point and proper performance has been transmitted) and *a future* (how the point of that practice can best be secured in the short or long term, or why it should be modified or abandoned), through *a present* (how it is linked to other practices, institutions, and social conditions). An Islamic discursive tradition is simply a tradition of Muslim discourse that addresses itself to conceptions of the Islamic past and future, with reference to a particular Islamic practice in the present.[29]

This discursive tradition is constituted and reconstituted not only by an ongoing interaction between the present and the past, however, but also by the manner in which relations of power and other forms of contestation and conflict impinge on any definition of what it is to be a Muslim. Such a view of Islam, Asad suggests, helps avoid essentialist constructions that strive to judge all facets of Islamic thought, ideals, and practice in terms of how they relate to (or, more often than not, fail to relate to) Islam's foundational texts, even as it seeks to steer clear of the temptation to reduce the variety of religious and cultural expression to different, local "islams."[30]

But if Islam *in general* ought to be approached as a "discursive tradition," I would argue that particular facets of this tradition can also be viewed in a broadly similar way. The *shariʿa* is the preeminent example of a tradition and, indeed, of a discursive tradition. Often translated as "Islamic law," the shariʿa is more accurately characterized, as the anthropologist Brinkley Messick has argued, as a "total discourse," viz., a set of institutions and practices that pervaded and shaped varied aspects of people's lives in premodern Muslim societies (see chapter 1).[31] But many other facets of the intellectual and religious history of Islam are also discursive traditions in their own right. Classical Islamic historiography, for instance, has its own "continuities of conflict"[32] even as it also reveals a broad consensus on how, say, the earliest history of Islam is represented—a consensus that baffles and exasperates modern historians as they try to reconstruct Islam's origins. This historiography, too, is a tradition, shaped by arguments within the earliest community as well as by disputations with outsiders.[33] One might similarly characterize institutionalized Sufism or the career of Hellenistic philosophy in Muslim societies as discursive traditions. The etiquette, styles of argumentation, and modes of transmitting knowledge that informed Islamic higher learning, and the institutions with which such learning was often associated, comprise another example of a multifaceted Islamic tradition—a tradition whose modern transformation is the subject of this book.

Though Asad does not say so, the concept of tradition is helpful not only in studying the history of discursive practices but also in tracking and understanding the significance of the *ruptures* in that history. No rupture is greater in the history of Islam than that brought about by the impact of Western modernity. As Marshall Hodgson observed at the end of his magisterial history of Islamic civilization, modern Western societies have managed to retain a much deeper, more coherent, and more integral relationship with their traditions than have Muslim societies: the former are far more "traditional" in this sense than the latter. In the Western philosophical tradition, for instance, "from the Scholastics to Descartes to Hume to Kant to Hegel to Hüsserl to the Existentialists, the philosophical dialogue has been continuous. By and large, the old books continue to be read, and some of the same terms continue to be used, even if in transformed contexts."[34] Alasdair MacIntyre would no doubt respond that, so far as Western intellectual history is concerned, what we have is not one continuous tradition but several "incommensurable" ones. Moreover, the notion that one can approach the "great books" without much attention to the particular traditions in which they are embedded is, for MacIntyre, a characteristic liberal fallacy.[35] Yet Hodgson's point here is different: in question for him is not the issue of *how* the classics of the Islamic intellectual and religious tradition are to be studied, but whether, with the rupture that modernity has entailed, those reared in modern, Westernized systems of education retain any significant link with the tradition such classics once constituted.

The rupture with the past has also meant sharper divisions within Muslim societies. Those schooled in modern secular institutions have often continued to regard Islam as an important, even fundamental, part of their identity, but typically in a very different way from how the 'ulama have done so. Two of what might very broadly be characterized as the major intellectual and religiopolitical trends that have successively emerged in the Muslim world since the late nineteenth century—modernism and Islamism—have both been largely rooted in modern, Westernized institutions of education.[36] Modernist Muslim intellectuals have sought, since the nineteenth century, to find ways of making Islam compatible with what they have taken to be the challenges of the modern age. And their proposed reforms have encompassed virtually the entire spectrum of life in Muslim societies. The intellectual vigor with which these reforms were proposed, and the success with which they have been carried through—often in alliance with the postcolonial state—has varied from one Muslim society to another, as have the precise ways in which different thinkers among these modernists have viewed the Islamic intellectual and religious tradition and defined themselves in relation to it. More often than not, however, the effort has been to retrieve the teachings of "true" Islam from the vast and oppressive edifice that centuries of "sterile" scholasticism, "blind" imitation of earlier authorities, and the "intransigence" of the religious specialists had built. In general, the modernist project is guided by the assurance that once retrieved through a fresh but "authentic" reading of the foundational texts, and especially of the Qur'an, the teachings of Islam would appear manifestly in concord with the positions recommended by liberal rationalism.[37]

In terms of cultural authenticity and religious authority, however, as well as in view of the failed promises of liberal, socialist, and nationalist regimes, the cost of the effort to find a concordance between Islam and Western, liberal rationalism has, seemed too high to many in the latter half of the twentieth century. These "Islamists," as they are often called in Western scholarship, are typically also products of modern, secular educational institutions but are drawn to initiatives aimed at radically altering the contours of their societies and states through the public implementation of norms they take as "truly" Islamic. To them, such norms need no justification in terms of Western liberal thought; the sole rationale for their implementation is that they express the will of God. Yet, while the Islamists position themselves towards Western thought and institutions in ways that are starkly different from the Muslim modernists, Islamist activists and intellectuals are themselves nothing if not modern, and as historian of religion Bruce Lawrence has argued, they are inconceivable in any but the modern age.[38] This is so not only because they rail against the epistemological assumptions of Western Enlightenment rationalism and the ideologies based on such assumptions, or against the overarching powers of the nation-state, or against global capitalism—all of them part of the experience of modernity.[39] Nor is it only because they are dexterous in their use of modern technology in disseminating their oppositional message.[40] They are also modern in that their intellectual positions are often formulated in terms heavily indebted to the discourses of the modern age. For instance, in his conception of social justice, Sayyid Qutb (d. 1966), one of the most influential Islamist thinkers of the twentieth century, is far more indebted to modern Western ideas than he is to the Qur'an.[41] And as political theorist Roxanne Euben has observed, Qutb's "reification of Islam, the understanding of social systems in terms of dynamic, social processes, the incorporation of an idea of progressive (if contingent) historical change . . . the dialectical vision of history, and the very concept of modern jahiliyya [a new paganism]" all exemplify the influence of the modern world against which Qutb was so vociferously preaching.[42]

Modernists and Islamists differ very considerably *within* their ranks in their attitudes to the Islamic tradition. Contemporary Arab modernist thinkers like the Moroccan Muhammad ʿAbid al-Jabiri (b. 1936) and the Egyptian Hasan Hanafi (b. 1935) have delved deeply into the Arab-Islamic "heritage" (*turath*) to discover the roots of the intellectual, social, and political malaise of the modern Arab world and, in Hanafi's case, to explore ways of selectively mustering the resources from this heritage in the service of an intellectual and political revival.[43] Muhammad Shahrur (b. 1938), a widely read Syrian civil engineer who calls for a radically new reading of the Qurʾan, rejects sources of law other than the Qurʾan and the normative example of the Prophet (*sunna*). He is sharply critical of the premodern jurists for misunderstanding the legal import of the Qurʾan and seems more indebted to the natural sciences in his "contemporary rereading" of the Qurʾan than to premodern Islamic exegetical or juristic discourses.[44] By contrast, Fazlur Rahman (d. 1988), a Pakistani modernist thinker, while sharply critical of the ʿulama, emphasizes a sustained constructive engagement with the "historic formulations of Islam—juristic, theological, spiritual" in the course of reinterpreting Islam in the modern world.[45]

Islamists likewise display widely different orientations in their attitude toward the Islamic tradition. The radical Islamist Shukri Mustafa (d. 1977), whose "Society of Muslims" advocated a complete withdrawal from the existing iniquitous society (hence its designation by the Egyptian media as the "Society of Excommunication and Emigration") was contemptuous of much of classical and medieval Islamic learning, arguing that one needed little more than a dictionary to explicate any possible complexities in the otherwise plain words of God.[46] On the other hand, the Egyptian Islamist ideologue Sayyid Qutb acknowledged that there was much to value in the writings of the medieval jurists and scholars[47] even as he insisted that Islam does not countenance any "priesthood" that would mediate between ordinary human beings and God.[48] And Abuʾl-Aʿla Mawdudi (d. 1979), the influential Pakistani Islamist thinker was often (though not invariably) even more laudatory than Qutb of the riches of medieval Islamic civilization:

> If . . . people earnestly and dispassionately study the achievements of their ancestors in the field of jurisprudence . . . [t]hey will come to know that during the last thirteen centuries, their forefathers had not been engaged in fruitless controversies: on the contrary, they have left a very vast and priceless treasure of knowledge . . . for the posterity. They have built for us quite a considerable portion of the edifice; and what a folly it would be if, out of sheer ignorance, we insist on demolishing what has already been built and start constructing all anew.[49]

While there are varying attitudes towards the Islamic intellectual and religious tradition within the ranks of the modernists and the Islamists, what is often shared among them is a certain sense that one does not *necessarily* need that tradition to understand the "true" meaning of Islam,[50] and that one certainly does not need the 'ulama to interpret Islam to the ordinary believers. That authority belongs to everyone and to no one in particular. So far as the rich and varied history of, say, classical and medieval exegesis or medieval legal debates or premodern theological speculation are concerned, most modernist and Islamist intellectuals—even those who might, in principle, acknowledge a certain attachment to that tradition—usually have only the most tenuous of links to it. This remains true even when certain older discursive modes—for instance, commentaries and study circles—are retained.[51] For if the goal is, for example, to study the Qur'an not in the light of the long record of agreements and disagreements about how to read it, but as if "the Book had been revealed *to us*, as if it had come for our own generation . . ., and as if the Prophet had died only recently after bringing this Book to us"[52] then such formal continuities as those constituted by the commentary or the study circle can barely conceal the reality of the fundamental rupture with the past.[53]

The 'ulama, as I show in this book, are hardly frozen in the mold of the Islamic religious tradition, but this tradition nevertheless remains their fundamental frame of reference, the basis of their identity and authority. They differ widely in the extent of their actual acquaintance with this tradition. As the cases of the Egyptian reformer Muhammad 'Abduh, and the later rector of al-Azhar university, Mahmud Shaltut, suggest, moreover, boundaries between the 'ulama and "modernists" can become blurred, just as they sometimes do between the 'ulama and the Islamists.[54] Yet, in general terms, it is a combination of their intellectual *formation*, their *vocation*, and, crucially, their *orientation* viz., a certain sense of continuity with the Islamic tradition that defines the 'ulama as 'ulama; and it is this sense of continuity that constitutes the most significant difference between them and their modernist and Islamist detractors.[55]

What makes the 'ulama of the modern world worth studying is not merely that they have continued to lay claim to and self-consciously represent a millennium-old tradition of Islamic learning, however. Their larger claim on our attention lies in the ways in which they have mobilized this tradition to define issues of religious identity and authority in the public sphere and to articulate changing roles for themselves in contemporary Muslim politics. The 'ulama's tradition is not a mere inheritance from the past, even though they often argue that that is precisely what it is. It is a tradition that has had to be constantly imagined, reconstructed, argued over, defended, and modified. All this has entailed highly significant changes in the world of the ʿulama, and it is some of these changes—which constitute a critical part of the history of modern Islam, even though they have not always been adequately recognized as such—that this book seeks to explicate.

The ʿUlama in This Study

With the aim of explaining the religious transformations of the ʿulama in the modern world, this study focuses primarily on the traditionally educated Muslim religious scholars of British India and Pakistan during the nineteenth and twentieth centuries. It examines, in particular, one highly visible and influential strand among the ʿulama, viz. those belonging to the "Deobandi" sectarian and doctrinal orientation. This orientation is associated with a madrasa founded in a small north Indian town called Deoband in the United Provinces (now Uttar Pradesh) in 1867. Thousands of other madrasas—all called Deobandi, though often without any formal affiliation with the parent madrasa—share the same doctrinal orientation, which is emphasizes the study of law and of the traditions attributed to the Prophet Muhammad (hadith), as well as a self-consciously reformist ideology defined in opposition to existing forms of "popular" Muslim belief and practice. Within modern South Asian Islam, the "Deobandis" distinguish themselves not only from the Shiʿa but also from other Sunni rivals such as the "Barelawis" and the Ahl-i Hadith, both of which also emerged in India in the second half of the nineteenth century. Though these three movements are united in their reverence for the teachings of the Prophet, their interpretations of the sources of religious authority differ markedly. The Barelawis affirm the authority not just of the Prophet but also of the saints and holy people, whom they revere as sources of religious guidance and vehicles of mediation between God and human beings. It is against such a vision of shrine and cult-based Islam that the Deobandis have preached. The Ahl-i Hadith, for their part, deny the legitimacy not just of all practices lacking a basis in scriptural texts, but even of the classical schools of law, stringently insisting on the Qurʾan and hadith as the exclusive and directly accessible sources of guidance.[56] Besides differentiating themselves from each other, the Deobandis, the Barelawis, the Ahl-i Hadith, and the Shiʿa are all opposed to the Ahmadis, who profess belief in Mirza Ghulam Ahmad (d. 1908) as a prophet after Muhammad. This Ahmadi belief contravenes the doctrine that Muhammad was the last of God's prophets, and the Ahmadis are therefore regarded as heretical by most other Muslims.[57]

All of these movements, including the Ahmadi, are products of a time of great ferment in the history of Muslim India. How Muslim scholars have historically positioned themselves in regard to the ruling authorities has varied considerably in different Muslim societies, but until the onset of colonialism, the ruling authorities were, for the most part, at least nominally Muslim. That was no longer the case in late-nineteenth-century India. But it was not only the loss of Muslim rule that posed serious problems to Muslim identity. Colonialism was itself the product of fundamental social, political, intellectual, and technological transformations in the West, and colonial rule was the medium through which new ideas, institutions, and forms of knowledge based on these transformations confronted Muslims as well as other colonized peoples—in India as elsewhere. Religious movements such as the aforementioned, as well as emerging forms of Muslim modernism, were ways of responding to a world that was becoming increasingly, and rapidly, unfamiliar. Initiatives aimed at revival and reform were nothing new in the history of Islam; but beginning in the late nineteenth century, the perceived challenges to existing institutions, practices, and traditions were more urgent and the responses to them more varied. The movement associated with the madrasa of Deoband was one response to these challenges.

The work of Barbara Metcalf on the early history of Deoband has done much to evoke the reformist concerns of the 'ulama associated with this orientation. Metcalf demonstrates that Muslim response to colonial rule was not exclusively in terms of adaptation to Western norms and institutions. As illustrated by the Deobandi 'ulama, the Muslim response also took the form of systematic recourse to facets of the Islamic religious tradition in striving to affirm Muslim identity in a hostile and unfamiliar environment. For their part, the 'ulama themselves underwent—even inaugurated—important changes in this process: for instance, nineteenth-century Indian Islam saw a new emphasis on the study of hadith; the 'ulama adopted the technology of print, which, together with their use of the vernacular Urdu language as the medium of their reformist discourses, enabled them to reach ever new audiences; they founded new madrasas as a means of resisting some of the threats that colonial rule represented—though these institutions were themselves indebted to the organizational model of colonial schools. Above all, the Deobandi orientation represents to Metcalf a certain interiorization of Islam, an emphasis on the reform of the believer as an individual: the 'ulama "fostered a kind of turning away from issues of the organization of state and society, toward a concern with the moral qualities of individual Muslims."[58]

Metcalf's work remains extremely important for the early history of Deoband. But she stops at the end of the nineteenth century, which means that the better part of the history of Deobandi 'ulama remains largely outside her purview. There are, however, certain other limitations to Metcaff's pioneering work as well. It is largely a study of the "social milieu" of the 'ulama, and much less so of their thought and their discourses, and it is based far more on the biographies of the first generation of Deobandi 'ulama than it is on the 'ulama's own varied and extensive writings.[59] While such biographies are obviously an important resource in understanding the contours of the milieu to which these reformist scholars belonged, the 'ulama's world of learning can hardly be evoked without reference to what they regarded as their most important intellectual and religious concerns or what they themselves wrote in the pursuit of these concerns. Thus it is telling, for instance, that there is barely more than a passing reference to the considerable energy that the Deobandi 'ulama expended writing commentaries on classical collections of hadith. The implication of this neglect is not merely that a critical facet of the 'ulama's discourses is thereby lost from view. What is also lost is a sense of how religious authority is constituted through the discursive medium of the commentary, why it has been important for the 'ulama to retain this discursive medium, how they have fashioned their discourses at many levels simultaneously, and what impact the technology of print has had on the 'ulama and their authority (see chapter 2). Furthermore, while Metcalf repeatedly emphasizes the 'ulama's effort to anchor their reformism in an orientation to the Islamic religious tradition of the past, what that tradition consisted of or how it informed the modern 'ulama's discourses remains unclear at best.

That the 'ulama wanted, in the immediate aftermath of the establishment of British rule in India, to focus on *individual* reform, on inculcating a renewed sense of *personal* religious responsibility as a way of coping with new challenges, is a central argument of Metcalf's work. Important as it is, however, this argument doesn't provide an adequate frame of reference in which to understand the public and political dimension of the activities of Deobandi 'ulama in the twentieth century. That the work stops at the beginning of the twentieth century partly accounts for this, of course, but Metcalf's focus on the interiorization of reform also suggests a sharpness and narrowness of focus on the personal as opposed to the public or political that is not always borne out by the often-fluid world of the 'ulama she has studied, a focus that becomes increasingly less convincing as the twentieth century progresses. Her account of Deobandi reformism hardly prepares one for the radical sectarianism in Pakistan in the last quarter of the twentieth century—a development in which the Deobandi 'ulama have been central players (see chapter 5); nor does it contribute anything to our understanding of the Taliban of Afghanistan in the last years of the century, many of whom were the products of Deobandi madrasas in Pakistan and remained closely allied to the Deobandi orientation.

The present study builds on the work of Metcalf on the Deobandi 'ulama, as well as on studies of Islam and the 'ulama in other Muslim societies.[60] This is not a "comprehensive" history of the 'ulama in the modern world, however, nor even of the Deobandi 'ulama. I seek only to illuminate what I consider the more important facets of religious change as they relate to the 'ulama, and I examine them here with reference to the Deobandi 'ulama of British India and Pakistan. The context and trajectories of social, political, and religious change are often different in other modern Muslim societies. My source material, analysis, and conclusions pertain in the first instance to the 'ulama of modern South Asia, but wherever possible, I have tried to show parallels and contrasts with traditionally educated religious scholars elsewhere (see especially chapter 6). No such broadly comparative study has been attempted so far, but it is crucial that a beginning be made, not only because all major Muslim societies have their own 'ulama who often define their identity and stake out their claims to authority in broadly comparable ways but also because the modern transformations of the 'ulama and their increasing contemporary prominence can be appreciated more clearly once they are viewed in a larger, global context. Besides being the first book to study the 'ulama of contemporary Islam in a comparative framework, the present work is also the first to study *both* their discourses and the significance of their religiopolitical activism in their multifaceted relationship; it is also the first work on South Asian Islam to examine the 'ulama and their institutions of learning in both the colonial and postcolonial contexts. In examining how the 'ulama have fared in responding to the challenges of a rapidly changing world, I seek to shed new light on religious and political thought in modern Islam. But I hope also to illuminate how a more nuanced understanding of religious and political trends in contemporary Islam can emerge when the 'ulama are firmly integrated into the broader picture.

The first chapter examines some of the changes that the shari'a underwent in colonial India. Unlike much of the scholarly work on Islamic law, I focus here not on how the shari'a was gradually replaced by modern, Western legal systems, but rather on the 'ulama's discourses on the shari'a during colonial rule. Though often neglected by scholars of Islamic law, this is not only an important part of the modern history of Islamic law but also critical to any understanding of how the 'ulama have viewed and responded to a world that was rapidly changing around them.

Issues of religious authority are at the center of this book's overall concerns, but they are especially the subject of the next two chapters. Chapter 2 focuses on the discursive form of the commentary to examine how religious authority is articulated in its terms, as well as through other kinds of texts, and what the technology of print has meant for the ways in which this authority is conceived or configured. Chapter 3 is concerned with colonial and postcolonial governmental discourses on the need to "re-form" the education imparted in madrasas. Such efforts have often been seen by the 'ulama as encroaching on their authority, but some of these initiatives came from within the ranks of the 'ulama and, as such, point to contention within the scholarly community. More importantly, how-ever, the contention over what needed to be reformed and how it should be reformed has led to a novel view whereby the 'ulama have often seen religion as occupying a distinct sphere in society, and they have defended their own authority in terms of such a view. The history of this idea is the subject of the third chapter.

The construction and defence of religion as a distinct sphere in society has proceeded, in Pakistan, alongside the 'ulama's own calls for making the state "truly" Islamic. Yet the latter project also threatens to compro-mise the former, and it is this tension that I explore in chapter 4. More broadly, this chapter seeks to explicate what the 'ulama mean when they call, as they often do, for an "Islamic state." Islamist formulations on the Islamic state have received considerable scholarly attention, but, once again, the 'ulama's political thought has continued to be much neglected. This chapter examines how the 'ulama debated the issues pertaining to the implementation of the shari'a—a central concern of all discussions on the Islamic state—and it shows how a comparison of the contemporary 'ulama's political thought with that of the Islamists sheds considerable new light on their competing notions of the state.

In chapter 5, I consider various facets of the religious and political activ-ism of the 'ulama in Pakistan, demonstrating how, in the last quarter of the twentieth century, a remarkable configuration of social, political, and religious factors at the local, national, and transnational levels has led to the articulation and radicalization of new religious identities under the leadership of the 'ulama, especially of the lower-ranking 'ulama. Among the factors I examine as contributing to this new activism are the emer-gence of a new middle class supporting the growth of mosques, madrasas, and sectarian organizations; the strong impact of the Iranian revolution, which led to heightened tensions between the Sunnis and the Shi'a of Pakistan, as well as to new avenues of patronage for the 'ulama of both communities from Middle Eastern regimes; and, finally, Pakistan's active involvement in supporting the Afghan struggle against the Soviet occu-pying forces. Many Pakistani 'ulama and their madrasas played an active role in this struggle—a role that contributed to, and continued after, the rise of the Taliban in Afghanistan. This examination of the 'ulama's activ-ism is extended in chapter 6 to incorporate examples from Egypt, Saudi Arabia, India, and the southern Philippines. The purpose here is to under-stand why certain important facets of this activism emerged when they did, in the last quarter of the twentieth century, how it relates with other—

Islamist—trends, and how the 'ulama are to be situated in larger discussions of "political Islam."

In each chapter, my analysis proceeds with reference to one or more key figures within the ranks of the 'ulama. Many of these figures remain little known to students and scholars of Islam, yet their lives, activities, and thought illustrate with particular vividness some of the transformations that the 'ulama, Islam, and Muslim societies have undergone in the modern world.

I

Islamic Law and the 'Ulama in Colonial India: A Legal Tradition in Transition

MODERN SCHOLARSHIP has often viewed the premodern Islamic legal tradition as a highly rigid structure, defined in opposition to the social and political institutions of society, and resistant to change once its fundamental principles and doctrines had been articulated in the first centuries of Islam. Once the age of formative legal development came to an end, Muslim jurists became, in this view, increasingly resistant and even outright hostile to possibilities of legal innovation. *Ijtihad*—the jurist's systematic exertion of his knowledge and faculties of reasoning to arrive at legal rulings on matters not explicitly regulated by the foundational texts—was now a thing of the past. Adherence to the legal doctrines as already agreed upon by the school of law (*taqlid*) was to be the order of the day, signifying little more than "blind imitation" of earlier authorities and hair-splitting casuistry. Despite certain mechanisms through which legal rules continued in effect to be added to it, the corpus of Islamic law appears in this narrative to have been largely stagnant through much of the Middle Ages, and it was only with the impact of colonial rule that the dead weight of the shari'a was gradually dislodged to make room for the emergence of new legal systems in the Muslim world.[1]

Almost all of the guiding assumptions of this conventional view have been called into serious question in recent work on the history of premodern Islamic law.[2] That juristic discourses were not mere theory divorced from actual practice, but shaped, and were shaped by, the evolving needs of Muslim societies has now been persuasively demonstrated by a number of scholars.[3] Wael Hallaq has shown, moreover, that there never was a definitive consensus among medieval jurists on the inadmissibility of ijtihad, and that major figures in the history of Islamic law continued in fact to claim the ability for creative adaptation, rethinking, and expansion of the legal tradition.[4] This, however, is not to deny the hold that the idea of taqlid had over the minds of many jurists. In the course of the development of the schools of law, legal thinking was indeed supposed to have reached a level of maturity and a degree of comprehensiveness that required preservation rather than radical departures; and it was held that the further development of a school ought to take place *within* these perimeters by adhering to the authority of the earlier masters. As Sherman Jackson has argued in examining the work of the thirteenth-century Maliki jurist al-Qarafi (d. 1285), taqlid was critical not only to assuring a continuing link with the past, which in turn was a central feature of how authority was constituted; it was also the basis of endowing a particular school of law with an important measure of autonomy. By insisting that the adherents of a certain school of law were to be governed by the agreed-upon doctrines of that school rather than, say, by the dictates of the ruler, the jurists were in effect restricting the right of the state to meddle with the life of the people beyond what they saw as the proper and limited scope of state authority.[5]

Yet even taqlid does not signify the opposite pole to creative legal thinking, as the conventional scholarly view would have it.[6] While the theoretical distinction between taqlid and ijtihad, between the *muqallid* and the *mujtahid* (one who practised taqlid and, conversely, the one qualified to practice ijtihad), was a sharp one, the practice exhibited many different shades of gray. The jurists recognized several categories of ijtihad—for example, ijtihad within the framework of the fundamental principles agreed upon by the founders of one's school of law, or ijtihad on a particular matter but not necessarily on others. With the passage of time the practice of ijtihad acquired an aura of great prestige and authority, and even leading jurists were often reluctant to claim the conceit of being mujtahids. Yet whether they did in fact lay claim to this ability or not, and whether or not they actually characterized as ijtihad their continuous search for and articulation of new rulings on sundry legal issues, the discourses of even late medieval jurists bear ample testimony to continuous legal adaptation and even innovation—that is, in effect, to the continuing practice of ijtihad. Their legal advances might be couched in the rhetoric of taqlid itself, but they are no less significant for being such.

Even when new rulings were not, in fact, articulated, there was often considerable flexibility in the selection and application of a particular ruling from the range and diversity of existing legal options. Within the framework of adherence to the authority of a given school considerable flexibility was still ensured in the actual practice of the law. In her study of the *mufti*s' (jurisconsults) responsa and court records from Ottoman Syria and Palestine in the seventeenth and eighteenth centuries, Judith Tucker has shown how the law, in practice, was much more flexible than the legal texts in which it was set out. In interpreting these texts the muftis often took account of how the circumstances of a particular case might help mitigate the severity of the jurists' theoretical prescriptions. These muftis, for the most part, were not "creative" thinkers in the sense of people seeking to rewrite the law, as it were, or produce intellectual breakthroughs in their interpretation of the law. They continued to remain strongly committed to the established doctrines and the authoritative texts of their schools. Yet their interpretation of these texts often showed considerable ingenuity and flexibility. For instance, though bound in principle to follow the prescriptions of their own school of law, Ottoman Hanafi judges occasionally transferred their own jurisdiction on a given matter to a Shafi'i or Maliki judge if those schools were more likely to guard the interests of the plaintiffs than the Hanafi school.[7]

Even in the first half of the nineteenth century, the widely influential Damascene Hanafi jurist and mufti Ibn 'Abidin (d. 1836) had insisted that the mufti must always take account of the peculiar circumstances and customs of the time in his juristic responsa: "[T]he rigidity of the mufti and the qadi [judge] in following [only] the apparent meaning of the reported text (*zahir al-manqul*), while neglecting custom (*'urf*) and context (*al-qara'in al-wadiha*), and his ignorance of the [actual] circumstances of the people necessarily entails the loss of numerous rights and [results in] injustice for numerous people."[8] In fact, Ibn 'Abidin went so far as to acknowledge that much in the corpus of the law as articulated by the great jurists of the past was itself based on custom and that those jurists would have enunciated their rulings differently if they had lived at a different time.[9] This recognition not only justified taking changing local custom into account but, more fundamentally, argued for a flexible relationship with the existing juristic tradition.

We do not have very much by way of documentary records of the activity of the *qadi* in precolonial India, compared with, for example, the same in the Ottoman lands.[10] It is therefore difficult to know precisely how different the situation in India may have been from that described by Tucker for Ottoman Syria and Palestine. Yet there are strong indications that in India, too, the interpretation of the shari'a remained subject to considerable flexibility. The effectiveness of the qadi, and the functions assigned to him, seem to have varied from one time and place to another in Mughal India.[11] It was the military governor who often determined the scope of those functions;[12] and the shari'a was hardly the only source of legal rights in precolonial Muslim India.[13] But the shari'a was a crucial part of the legal system—a part, however, whose significance, and indeed whose very presence, may elude us if we insist too strongly on trying to discover it in the landscape as a fixed codelike entity rather than as a dynamic but unevenly distributed element of precolonial India's judicial discourse and practice.[14]

Much work needs to be done to determine the ways in which the shari'a norms were implemented or how they mingled and interacted with other sources of right in Mughal India. Such an examination is beyond the purview of the present study. Yet a glance at what is undoubtedly the most famous of precolonial India's legal compendia, the *Fatawa al-Hindiyya*

(or *Fatawa-i 'Alamgiriyya*, as this work is better known in South Asia) is
instructive. The compilation of this monumental work scarcely needed
any justification except that the pious emperor Aurangzeb 'Alamgir (r.
1685–1707)—perhaps best known for his controversial efforts to implement aspects of Islamic law in his realm—had willed it. Significantly, however, the justification that was in fact offered concerned precisely the need
to make judicial practice *less varied* and more firmly entrenched in the
opinions of the best and most widely accepted authorities in the Hanafi
school of law.[15] "The standard books and treatises of this discipline [of
law] . . . deal, in some cases, with only some of the [legal] problems, and
most of them encompass differing reports and conflicting proofs"; at a
loss for the most authoritative views, many have strayed from the "light of
the sunna towards the fires of mere whim."[16] Much of this is undoubtedly
stylized rhetoric with which the compilers of the *Fatawa al-Hindiyya/
'Alamgiriyya* (hereafter *'Alamgiriyya*) underlined the significance of their
own venture and the sagacity of this project's royal patron; and it is unlikely that this work was able to finally harmonize the legal practice of
the shari'a in late Mughal India.[17] Irrespective of its own success or failure,
however, the *'Alamgiriyya*'s lament regarding the diversity of legal opinions in the "standard texts" is evidence of flexibility in the legal practice
of the time when this work was compiled.

Despite their apparent mandate to reduce the fluidity (or uncertainty)
of legal opinions, even the compilers of the *'Alamgiriyya* did little to try
to harmonize the diversity of opinions in the Hanafi legal tradition. A
variety of differing opinions are routinely noted in this compilation—as
indeed in manuals of *fiqh* (Islamic law) generally[18]—giving the judges as
well as the muftis considerable choice in dealing with the cases brought
to them.[19] It was in the presence of such divergences of opinion (*ikhtilaf*)
that the jurists found the freedom to adjust the law and its application to
changing times. Thus in a section of its "Book of the Judge's Etiquette"
("*Kitab adab al-qadi*") entitled "The Sequence of Proofs according to
Which [the Judge Is] to Act," the *'Alamgiriyya* notes the view that should
clear guidance from Abu Hanifa and his "companions" (viz., his two
principal disciples, Abu Yusuf and Muhammad al-Shaybani) not be available, and should the latter-day scholars (*al-muta'akhkhirun*) be in disagreement on the matter, the judge ought to himself choose among the
conflicting views of the latter. Furthermore, "In case even the latter-day
scholars have nothing to say on the matter, [the judge] exercises ijtihad in
accordance with his considered opinion (*yajtahid fihi bi-ra'yihi*), provided
that he understands the precepts of the law (*wujuh al-fiqh*) and has con-
sulted on the matter with [other] jurists."[20]

The *'Alamgiriyya*'s own recommendations to the judges seem to suggest, then, that despite the jurists' oft-repeated commitment to the most

authoritative views within the Hanafi school of law, the actual practice of the shari'a in precolonial India, as indeed elsewhere, allowed for considerable flexibility in determining how that law would be implemented. Indeed, despite its professions to the contrary, the 'Alamgiriyya itself relies far more on the works of the latter-day scholars than it does on the founders of the Hanafi school of law.[21] The socio political context in which the shari'a functioned underwent drastic change with the onset of British colonial rule, however, and therefore so did conceptions of the shari'a. While the new legal systems that have emerged in Muslim societies during colonial rule have received considerable scholarly attention,[22] the 'ulama's discourses on the shari'a under colonial rule have been little studied. In what follows, I examine some of the ways in which these discourses evolved under British colonial rule in India.

Colonial Constructions of the Law and the 'Ulama

In 1765, when the British East India Company acquired the authority to collect and administer the revenues of Bengal, Bihar, and Orissa, the supervision of the judicial administration also passed on to British officials. While initially the qadis continued to administer justice under the Company's supervision, a series of measures from 1772 onwards gradually set up a new judicial system with distinct "civil" and "criminal" courts as well as courts of appeal. The role of the qadis increasingly became one of assisting British judicial officials, and later the position was abolished altogether.[23] Regulation II of 1772 did provide, however, that "in all suits regarding inheritance, succession, marriage and caste and other usages or institutions, the law of the Koran with respect to Mahomedans, and those of the Shaster with respect to the Gentoos [Hindus] shall be invariably adhered to."[24] And muftis and pandits continued, until 1864, to be attached to the British courts to advise the judge on matters of personal law.

Yet even as they sought the help of Hindu and Muslim jurisconsults in discovering and interpreting the law, British officials felt considerable misgivings about administering justice in this manner. "Pure Integrity is hardly to be found among the Pandits and Maulavis, few of whom give opinions without a culpable bias, if the parties can have access to them," noted Sir William Jones (d. 1794), the preeminent Orientalist of the late eighteenth century and a judge under the East India Company. "I therefore always make them produce original texts," he said, "and see them in their own Books."[25] On another occasion Jones noted that he could "no longer bear to be at the mercy of our pundits, who deal out Hindu law as they please, and make it at reasonable rates, when they cannot find it ready made."[26] Though specifically concerned with the Hindu pandits, this statement seems to equally reflect his judgment of the "Maulavis." Jones sought therefore to create a "complete Digest of Hindu and Mohammedan laws," especially on contracts and succession,[27] which would make dependence on "Pandits and Maulavis" unnecessary, or at least provide "*a complete check* on the *native* Interpreters."[28] Such a digest would also provide an authentic, authoritative, and *fixed* code of the law according to which the courts would then act.[29] While *The Digest of Hindu Law on Contracts and Succession* was later published by Jones's successor, H. T. Colebrooke,[30] no comparable work for Muslim law appears to have been published. Instead, certain works of law that were regarded by Muslims of India as among the more authoritative now came to be invested with almost exclusive authority as the basis of judicial practice in British courts, so far as Muslim personal law was concerned. These works included the *Hidaya* of al-Marghinani (d. 1196–97);[31] the *Kitab al-Fara'id al-Sirajiyya* of Siraj al-din Muhammad al-Sajawandi (fl. end of the twelfth century),[32] which Jones had himself translated into English; the *Durr al-mukhtar* of 'Ala al-din al-Haskafi (d. 1677);[33] and the *Fatawa-i 'Alamgiriyya*.

British legal scholars and judicial officials were aware that works such as the foregoing were by no means the only ones that were regarded as authoritative in India. William Morley's history, *The Administration of Justice in British India* (1858) for instance, gives a long catalogue of the "Muhammadan law-books," with particular attention to works in use in India, often with valuable information on the date, during the early nineteenth century, when the technology of print first made them more widely available.[34] In the spirit of the search for the "complete digest" and the fixed and authoritative code, however, only a small body of works came to be recognized as *the* sole and unchanging repository of Muslim law. In this way, not only would the British avoid dependence on the local legal scholars, but the alleged arbitrariness of the scholars' juristic constructions could be restrained.

To the colonial officials, the very character of precolonial law and legal practice was uncertain, unsystematic, and arbitrary. Their own judicial practice was not always very different, as historian Radhika Singha has argued with reference to early colonial Bengal, and judicial discretion in fact played a large role in how particular crimes were punished by British officials. Yet when not practiced or recommended by themselves, it was precisely such discretion that appeared to them as little better than sheer arbitrariness.[35] And it was this and other perceived failings of the indigenous legal systems that the British venture in the codification of the law was intended to finally remedy. Thomas Babington Macaulay, who played a pivotal role in shaping the Indian Penal Code of 1862, had characterized the guiding principle of the colonial code in terms that made the contrast with the arbitrariness of the Hindu and Muslim law explicit: "The principle," he stated in 1833, "is simply this; uniformity when you can have it; diversity when you must have it; but, in all cases certainty."[36] The last vestiges of Islamic criminal law ceased to exist with the Penal Code of 1862. The letter of the shari'a was now to be implemented exclusively in the realm of the laws of personal status (pertaining mostly to marriage, divorce, children, and inheritance) for Muslims.

Yet even in matters of personal status, the application of the shari'a under colonial rule was in fact far from uniform. In the Punjab, for instance, a system of customary law, defined—in matters of inheritance, for example—in opposition to shari'a norms, governed the rural populace. This customary law, which varied from one agricultural "tribe" to another, was not merely "recognized" by the British but, in a real sense, was developed by them to serve as the cornerstone of colonial administration in the province.[37] In other regions of the colonial realm and in diverse aspects of the law, custom or political expediency often dictated how or what shari'a norms would be given legal effect even in matters that were supposed to be governed by those norms.[38] For all the accommodations and contradictions of the legal system that evolved in colonial India, however, the rhetoric of a rationalized law that applied uniformly to Muslims, and that was embodied in a small number of fixed and authoritative texts, remained powerful. This "Anglo-Muhammadan law," as it came to be known, was premised, inter alia, on the notion that to try to resolve legal issues by going beyond the "authoritative" texts to earlier sources on which these texts were themselves based would violate the well-established interpretations of these texts and consequently violate accepted forms of legal thought and practice. As the Privy Council observed in 1897, it was not for the courts to "speculate on the mode in which the text quoted from the Koran . . . is to be reconciled with the law as laid down in the Hedaya and by the author of the passage quoted from Baillie's Imameea. . . . It would be wrong for the court on a point of this kind to put their own construction on the Koran in opposition to the express ruling of commentators of such great antiquity and high authority."[39]

How did this colonial legal discourse of authority, as embodied in a few fixed texts, affect the 'ulama's conception of the shari'a? The appeal to the commentators of "great antiquity and high authority" would surely have resonated with the 'ulama, who, with the exception of the Ahl-i Hadith (the people/partisans of hadith), were committed to following the stipulations of their own earlier authorities (taqlid). Yet, as already noted, taqlid did not necessarily signify blind adherence to earlier authorities or texts; and even those who claimed to be practicing only taqlid did have means at their disposal to decide among alternative options on particular

taklid·
immitation
of law

matters. While it is possible to see the Privy Council's recognition of the commentators' "high authority" as reflecting the 'ulama's own views on the matter, it is no less likely that the British insistence on this authority created a more constricted and stringent literalism for the 'ulama as well.[40] The practice of taqlid was no doubt part of the basis on which a new and more thoroughgoing literalism now came to be adopted by the 'ulama. The challenge of the Ahl-i Hadith, who were vociferous critics of taqlid and insisted on basing their religious norms and practice not on the prescriptions of the schools of law but only, and directly, on the Qur'an and the sunna/hadith, forced the Deobandi 'ulama to also close ranks behind the practice of taqlid. The Deobandi sensitivity to the Ahl-i Hadith challenge is indicated by the polemics they engaged in with the Ahl-i Hadith and by the large commentaries on classical works of hadith written specifically to refute them (see chapter 2). Yet while both the Deobandis and the Ahl-i Hadith were themselves products of the colonial context—products of the effort to provide authoritative religious guidance to a community whose religious and cultural identity was seen as gravely threatened in the changed world of colonial rule—there were more direct colonial pressures that we also need to take into account to understand some of the shari'a's transformations.

The notion that Islamic (or Hindu) law was arbitrary, that "pure integrity [was] hardly to be found" among the native scholars, that they made up the law as they pleased, must have exerted pressure on those scholars to demonstrate that their laws were in fact predictable, certain, and unchanging. Traditionally educated Muslim and Hindu scholars worked for colonial officials like Jones and were long associated with colonial courts, so that British colonial conceptions of the certainty of the law undoubtedly shaped indigenous discourses as well.[41] Not only would the certainty of the law—making the indigenous scholars "produce original texts," as Jones said, and verifying their rulings "in their own Books"—conform to colonial conceptions of a law worth the name; it would equally undergird the authority of the indigenous informants. In reality, the 'ulama did show themselves willing to accommodate changes when compelled by circumstances to do so, or when it suited their interests to do so; and even in colonial India, the taqlid of their own school of law could be foregone on occasion, as we shall see. However, the *rhetoric* of adhering to, and representing, an invariant corpus of the law was also crucial to their religious authority in colonial India, and the British conception of the invariance of the law doubtlessly contributed something to the way this authority was articulated.

If the rhetoric of an invariant law was one factor militating towards an increasingly inflexible conception of the shari'a on the part of the 'ulama, the radical change in the administration of Islamic law was the other and, no doubt, the more powerful one. A new judicial system was being put in place from the late eighteenth century onwards. Ever since the time of William Jones the colonial officials had striven to reduce their dependence on indigenous guides, and Jones's project of codifying the law was motivated, as we have seen, by the same concern. With a codified law, or with the availability of certain texts that had the authority of a legal code, one would no longer need the indigenous legal guides—the muftis and the pundits, whose position was abolished in 1864—to help the court in its rulings.[42] For if it was merely a matter of applying the rulings contained in certain legal classics and commentaries of "great antiquity and authority," as the Privy Council had stated in 1897, then surely *anyone* trained in the British legal system could do so. One did not need someone trained specifically in Islamic law. For the 'ulama, however, this development meant that there would be only a highly truncated link with the Islamic legal tradition of old: the new "Anglo-Muhammadan law" was decidedly not the 'ulama's legal tradition but a hybrid of certain legal classics and English common law. It also meant that the 'ulama themselves were not part of this development. Historically the most distinctive aspect of their vocation, the interpretation of the law, was effectively being removed from them.

The 'ulama could continue to function as muftis, of course, as they had for centuries. Indeed, in colonial India, this function registered certain important changes: from the late nineteenth century, fatwas were often given on the authority of a particular madrasa, such as the madrasa of Deoband, rather than on that of a single jurisconsult; fatwas were issued in larger numbers than had been the case earlier; and the technology of print enabled the madrasas to disseminate their fatwas more widely and, in many cases, to begin publishing influential compilations of them.[43] The degree to which muftis and judges worked together varied considerably in different premodern Muslim societies. In fourteenth-century North Africa, as studied by David Powers, muftis often played an important role in advising the qadis on some of the more intractable problems brought to the courts.[44] In the court cases reviewed by Judith Tucker for eighteenth-century Ottoman Syria and Palestine, on the other hand, the responsa of the muftis do not seem to have been prominent in the qadis' deliberations.[45] But even when the muftis did not necessarily shape the actual judicial practice, the muftis and the judges had been part of the same intellectual universe, products of the same legal tradition. This was no longer the case in colonial India. And what added insult to injury was that these colonial judges, administering the Anglo-Muhammadan law, were not even required to be—and, for the most part, were not—Muslims.

The texts according to which a ruling was to be made might be at hand, but it was very hard for the 'ulama to countenance the possibility that a judge who was not himself Muslim, let alone one not trained in Islamic law, could legitimately arrive at such a ruling. The taqlid of the Hanafi legal position on matters, say, pertaining to divorce could be relaxed in favor of a position from the Maliki school of law; but even to rule according to a different school it was a Muslim judge that one needed. If a Muslim judge was not to be found, then, the Deobandi 'ulama insisted, abiding by the strict letter of the law was the only option a devout believer had. The full force of the stringency of the law was thus at hand in colonial India. Consider the following two fatwas, issued by the madrasa of Deoband on matters relating to the dissolution of marriage (faskh):[46]

1. *Question*: Hinda was married by her uncle to Zayd while she was a minor. Upon reaching legal majority, she expressed her displeasure with this marriage and, in the presence of a few men, stated her refusal to accept it. Has her marriage contract become annulled (faskh) because of this refusal, or not?

Answer: According to the *Durr al-mukhtar* and al-Shami,[47] Hinda does have the right to have her marriage annulled immediately after attaining legal majority. However, without the judgment of a qadi (*qadi shar'i*), her marriage contract will not be annulled. The *Durr al-Mukhtar* requires "the qadi's verdict for annulment"; and as al-Shami has it: "if she chooses annulment, that cannot take place without a judicial verdict." Consequently, since at this time there is no Islamic judge, the marriage contract in question will not be annulled; for Hinda cannot annul her marriage contract on her own, and she cannot marry anyone else unless her [first] husband has divorced her.[48]

2. *Question*: A woman used to have her regular menstrual cycles like other women, but for a year now these cycles have ceased. Her husband has divorced her. How long should her waiting period ('idda) last? Will it be reckoned by months or by menstrual cycles? If the latter, then must she wait till the time she has despaired of further menstruation (*sinn-i iyas*)? The woman is extremely poor and lacks any means of financial support [hence the urgency for her to remarry]. Explain and be rewarded [by God]!

Answer: One learns from the chapter on 'idda in the *Durr al-Mukhtar* and the *Radd al-muhtar* that, according to the Hanafis, it would be necessary [in this case] to wait until the time that the woman has despaired of further menstruating by reason of age. According to the Malikis, however, the waiting period [in this situation] is nine months; or, according to a more authoritative [Maliki] opinion, it is one year after divorce. Acting on this view is allowed in a circumstance of necessity. [However, I] say that the following matters ought to be considered before [this Maliki view can be adopted]. First, she should receive medical treatment; only if such treatment does not restore her menstrual cycles should the [Maliki] position be followed; the "necessity" [for following that position] is based on this [unsuccessful treatment]. Second, in order to act on this [Maliki] view, the verdict of a qadi is required. A Muslim judge, even if appointed by an infidel king, is acceptable as a shar'i judge. Consequently, a petition should be given to the government to empower a Muslim judge to decide on this matter; that Muslim judge may then allow the woman to remarry after having passed her waiting period, as laid down in this fatwa. This is the way to act [on this matter]. Third, in case the waiting period were begun according to this [Maliki] view, and her menstrual cycle happens to start before the end of the year, then the waiting period would be observed from the time of the [commencement of the] menstrual cycle. And God knows best. 9 Dhu'l-qa'd, 1325 A.H. [December 14, 1907].[49]

Those issuing these fatwas were clearly aware that the practice of Islamic law had become dysfunctional in British India. Without a qadi, even relatively simple matters such as the dissolution of a marriage or the determination of the "waiting period" could not be resolved. Even when, in principle, the Hanafi mufti was willing to allow recourse to the Maliki school of law on a particular matter, he would immediately point out that a Muslim judge was still required to decide according to the Maliki position—as the above fatwa on menstruation illustrates. As in the case of menstruation, the Maliki school also stipulated a much shorter period of time for which a woman was required to wait for her "missing" husband before she could remarry; the Malikis required four years in such cases, whereas the Hanafis stipulated that the woman wait till the end of the "natural" lifespan of ninety years! Again, the Hanafi muftis of colonial India claimed that they were willing to countenance the adoption of the Maliki position *provided* a qadi was available to actually dissolve the marriage according to the Maliki law.[50] These muftis sometimes suggested that the person seeking to dissolve an undesirable marriage might have recourse to the principalities outside British India (such as the Muslim-ruled princely state of Bhopal), which still had qadis.[51] Moreover, they pointed out, if the judge were a Muslim even if the appointing authority was itself non-Muslim, the former's decision should be valid;[52] but there could be no recourse without a Muslim judge. Muslims were encouraged to lobby the government for the appointment of qadis well-versed in the shari'a (or at least Muslim judges who would be bound to act according to the guidance of the 'ulama),[53] but in the meanwhile the muftis insisted that the stipulations of the legal texts were to be unrelentingly followed in the most literal sense.

Why were the 'ulama of the late nineteenth and early twentieth centuries prepared to impose extreme hardship on Muslim individuals through their inflexibility? The 'ulama's position, or predicament, perhaps ought to be seen not just in terms of the law's invariance—a rhetoric much indebted to colonial pressures—but also with reference to the long tradition of person-to-person transmission of learning in Islam and the idea that religious texts can be properly understood only by those who are "authorized" (*ijaza*) to interpret them. The latter idea obviously means that it was not enough to designate certain texts as "authoritative" for purposes of judicial practice, as the colonial legal system had done; the validity of that practice also required that the right people interpret those texts, and for non-Muslims to presume to do so was intolerable. In the colonial context, when Islam and the Muslims were politically subdued and the colonizers and the colonized viewed one another with serious misgivings, the Muslims could not be certain of how the British would implement the law even when they claimed to base their decisions on Islamic legal sources. The consequences of entrusting Islamic law to non-Muslims were thus unforeseen and potentially undesirable. (Similar fears were to be at the heart of the agitation, in late-twentieth-century postcolonial India, against the meddling of a Supreme Court comprised of Hindu judges in Islamic personal law, as I discuss in chapter 6.)

Less favorably to the 'ulama, one might argue that they hoped to bring pressure on the colonial administration for the appointment of qadis by willingly heightening the personal and social cost that the absence of such judges entailed for ordinary Muslims. This, furthermore, was a situation that afforded them one more opportunity to enhance their own influence and authority: Muslims were to adhere patiently to the law as expounded by the 'ulama and the muftis; and for all the harsh rigidity of the law, the 'ulama saw themselves as the only people to whom a Muslim ought to legitimately turn. Given, moreover, that it was women rather than men who experienced the hardship entailed by the 'ulama's refusal to accept non-Muslim judges, the male Muslim elite was conceivably more willing to tolerate that harshness precisely because they were not its primary victims. As reconceptualized with all its rigidity in the colonial context, maintaining the invariance of the legal tradition was evidently seen as a greater good than protecting individual welfare. As Lata Mani has argued with reference to the colonial and indigenous Bengali middle class discourses on widow burning (*sati*), "[t]radition was . . . not the ground on which the status of woman was being contested. Rather, the reverse was true: women in fact became the site on which tradition was debated and reformulated. What was at stake was not women but tradition."[54] The same, mutatis mutandis, could be said of the 'ulama.

Yet, if the 'ulama were willing to tolerate the heavy cost of trying to safeguard Islamic law from non-Muslim judges, that cost proved too heavy for many ordinary Muslim women: their hardship was, for them, reason enough to renounce Islam itself. Though the Hanafi school of law does stipulate certain circumstances under which a wife can seek divorce, there are considerable limitations on her ability to do so. The husband's impotence is grounds for divorce. And, as seen in a fatwa quoted earlier, a minor married by someone other than her father or grandfather can, on coming of age, renounce her marriage;[55] but that required the decree of a qadi, who was usually not at hand in British India. A judge's decree was also required if a woman whose husband was missing were to remarry. Hanafi law also allowed the woman to initiate the termination of the marriage by foregoing her dowry (*mahr*), but that presupposed the husband's prior agreement. Finally, apostasy—her own or that of her husband—was believed to dissolve the marriage contract. The "dominant" view (*zahir al-riwaya*) among Hanafi jurists had been, however, that the apostate-wife had to be forced to both reconvert to Islam and to remarry the same spouse.[56]

In British India, until 1939, while apostasy was recognized as valid grounds for the dissolution of the marriage contract, as Hanafi law maintained, it was not considered the court's function to force the wife to reconvert to Islam and remarry her former spouse—as the Hanafis also required. Consequently, a number of Muslim women, especially in the Punjab, apostatised in order to rid themselves of undesirable husbands. As legal historian Muhammad Khalid Masud has shown, this situation greatly alarmed the 'ulama.[57] Precisely at a time when they were engaged in reinvigorating the community's religious identity in the context of colonial rule, Muslim personal law was, ironically, being invoked to sanction apostasy from Islam.

In this situation, Mawlana Ashraf 'Ali Thanawi (d. 1943), one of the most prominent Deobandi scholars of the time, stepped forth to argue for a reinterpretation of Hanafi law by pointing to three views among Hanafi jurists on the matter of the dissolution of marriage through apostasy. The "dominant" view held that though the marriage is dissolved on the wife's apostasy, she is to be forced to convert back to Islam as well as to remarry her previous husband. A second view, attributed to some Hanafi jurists of Central Asia, is that apostasy has no effect on the woman's marital status. The third and most extreme view is that the woman loses her freedom on account of apostasy, turning into her former husband's slave girl. Given that the "dominant" view was no longer workable in colonial India—since Muslims did not have the authority to coerce an apostate-woman to reconvert to Islam and remarry her former husband—Thanawi argued that the second view now ought to be adopted: apostasy should have no effect on the marriage contract, thus ceasing to be an option for women wishing to have their marriage dissolved.[58]

Thanawi also argued for replacing certain provisions of Hanafi law with less stringent ones of the Maliki school. In extreme circumstances, Hanafis were to be allowed recourse to the Maliki position that a woman whose husband had disappeared could have her marriage dissolved and might remarry after a wait of four years—rather than waiting for the expiry of the "natural" human lifespan, as required by Hanafi law. Further, in the absence of a qadi, as in British India, a committee of righteous Muslims could exercise some of the qadi's functions, including dissolution of the marriage of a missing person. These views were articulated for Thanawi in fatwas he solicited from leading Maliki jurists of Medina;[59] and an extensive effort was made in India to seek the support of other Hanafi scholars for this selective adoption of Maliki positions.[60] Thanawi's arguments for these changes in Hanafi law, along with the Maliki fatwas and the endorsements by other Indian 'ulama, were set forth in a treatise entitled *al-Hila al-najiza li'l-halilat al-'ajiza* (The consummate stratagem for the powerless wife). As laid out here, these arguments became the basis of a campaign organized by the Deobandi 'ulama's political organization, the Jam'iyyat al-'Ulama'-i Hind (on which more later), to seek changes in the law regulating the dissolution of marriage in British courts. This campaign culminated in the Dissolution of Muslim Marriages Act (1939), which, with minor changes, continues to be in effect in both India and Pakistan.[61]

Ironically, however, this Act did not meet the most basic of the 'ulama's demands: Muslim judges, let alone those well-versed in the shari'a, were not provided to settle matters of personal status, and the 'ulama were to continue to voice this demand not only in the remaining years of British colonial rule but also in post-independence India.[62] The act did, however, close the door to the use of apostasy as a means of annulling a marriage: it was now easier to end an undesirable marriage, and apostasy was no longer recognized by the courts as achieving that end. In this respect, then, the Act represented a victory for the 'ulama. But it was also significant for them in certain other ways. Thanawi's initiative had shown that the 'ulama had the resources within the Islamic legal tradition to bring about necessary change.[63] Certain less authoritative opinions already existed within the medieval handbooks which could now serve as the basis for combating the threat of apostasy; and the adoption of a position from another school of law—in this instance, the Maliki school—was itself a practice attested from earlier times. The scope of the law was being expanded in a changed milieu even while upholding the authority of the legal tradition, not by undermining or rejecting it. The 'ulama had, moreover, demonstrated considerable unity of purpose within their ranks in seeking to close the door to apostasy. And the fatwas that Thanawi had sought from Maliki 'ulama of the Hijaz no doubt served as a symbolic demonstration of the Indian 'ulama's ties with scholars elsewhere and, indeed, of the membership of the Muslims of India in a larger global community. Thanawi's initiative had underscored both that the Islamic legal tradition was not subject to quick changes based on mere whim *and*, conversely, that it could be changed in particular circumstances. Also underscored was the assertion that such change was to be brought about legitimately only through the Islamic religious specialists, the 'ulama.

Thanawi had also argued that should Muslims fail to find a Muslim judge, there was another Maliki legal doctrine to be invoked to dissolve a marriage: in circumstances of extreme need, a committee of righteous individuals (*jama'at-i muslimin*) could assume the authority of a qadi and pronounce the divorce as the latter would have done. Though Thanawi had written the *Hila al-najiza* several years before the Dissolution of Muslim Marriages Act of 1939, his position here obviously remained relevant even afterwards, given that that Act had failed to provide for the sort of judges the 'ulama had wanted. Though there is no data on whether or how extensively such committees were constituted, the idea at least suggests a mechanism to escape some of the effects of colonial rule on the practice of Islamic law. It also suggests an effort to extend the influence of the 'ulama. Thanawi had insisted that the committee in question ought to be constituted of people who were righteous as well as locally influential, and that it ought to include, or at least be guided by, religious scholars.[64] If no religious scholar was locally available, the committee was to write to 'ulama and muftis elsewhere to have them guide its decision.[65] The message here was clearly that the 'ulama were indispensable to the guidance of the community, and equally, that *at their hands*, the shari'a remained responsive to the needs and welfare of the people. As Thanawi asserted at the outset of his treatise, if Muslims fail to secure their demands for qadis, the fault is their own, not that of Islam; the latter could scarcely be blamed for the condition in which Muslim women found themselves in colonial India.[66]

Late Colonial Politics and the 'Ulama

The shari'a, as we have seen, underwent significant transformations in colonial times. Taqlid, of course, predated colonialism by centuries, but under the pressures of colonial rule it acquired a new salience and an unprecedented rigidity. Moreover, as Nathan Brown has argued with reference to the changing conceptions of the shari'a in the Middle East, the link between the juristic discourses and the judicial and educational institutions through which these discourses had historically been articulated was severed under the impact of colonial rule: the shari'a now came to be increasingly seen as "content" rather than "process."[67] This conception, according to which the shari'a is essentially akin to a fixed legal code rather than an ongoing discursive tradition, is central to the conception of an "Islamic state" (see chapter 4). Yet, as we have seen, it remained possible to alter and expand the contours of shari'a rulings even in colonial times. When convinced that there was no way but to change, the 'ulama could "discover" resources within the juristic tradition to legitimize the required change. In doing so, as Masud has observed, Thanawi had moved with great care: he had worked with leading muftis on this project and had sought the fatwas from Maliki jurists in the Hijaz;[68] the latter fatwas were published verbatim (in Arabic) in his treatise to lend added authority to his proposal, and the names and endorsements of leading Deobandi 'ulama of India were made part of the treatise to similar effect.

Other discourses of the 'ulama in late colonial India, however, evince a more vigorous invocation of the "flexibility" of Islam than Thanawi's example suggests. This is brought out most strikingly in the context of a major political controversy in which one of Thanawi's Deobandi colleagues, Mawlana Husayn Ahmad Madani (d. 1957), was a central figure. In the 1930s, when Thanawi was seeking provision for the dissolution of Muslim marriage to close the door to the apostasy of Muslim women, Madani was the principal of the madrasa at Deoband as well as the most visible leader of the Jam'iyyat al-'Ulama'-i Hind. This 'ulama organization had been founded at the end of World War I to lead the campaign against the threatened dismemberment of the defeated Ottoman empire at the hands of the victorious Allied forces.[69] As we have noted, the Jam'iyya had spearheaded the campaign for the Dissolution of Muslim Marriages Act of 1939; Madani himself had worked closely with Thanawi on *al-Hila al-najiza*.[70] The politics of the two luminaries of Deoband were different, however. Thanawi was a retiring man, devoted to Sufi practices, scholarship, and preaching. He disliked active participation in politics, through it is believed that he supported the emerging demand for a separate homeland for the Muslims of India. He died, however, four years before the establishment of Pakistan. Madani, on the other hand, had an active political career as the leader of the Jam'iyya and as a strong supporter of the Hindu-dominated Indian National Congress, which led the struggle for Indian independence. Like the Congress, Madani was opposed to the partition of India, and it is this position and the attendant controversy that I want to briefly examine here. At the heart of the controversy, which raged during the decade immediately preceding the partition and independence of India, was the question of whether the Muslims of India constituted a separate nation, as argued by the "modernist" Muslim leaders who were to lead the movement for Pakistan, or were part of the same nation as the non-Muslim peoples of South Asia. The position of the so-called "nationalist" 'ulama—viz., Madani and his followers, who opposed the demand for a separate state for the Muslims of India and sided with the Indian National Congress in demanding an undivided free India—has been illuminatingly examined by Peter Hardy and Yohanan Friedmann.[71] My interest here is not in Madani's political thought but rather in the implications of the nationalist position for these 'ulama's understanding of the shari'a.

Madani argued that while the Muslims of India were a distinct religious entity among the religious communities inhabiting the subcontinent, they were part of the same "nation" (qawm) as their Hindu compatriots. A nation was not constituted by ties of faith; such ties were the basis of a milla, which denotes a religion, a religious law, and a faith-based path as well as the community of those who follow it.[72] Differences of religion are immaterial to the constitution of a qawm, just as they are central to a milla. But even as a milla, the Muslims of India were not a distinct entity, for they were part of the universal community of Muslims, and it was unacceptable for one segment of this universal community to define itself in territorial terms to the exclusion of Muslims elsewhere.

The prophets depicted in the Qur'an as preaching to their people belonged, Madani argued, to the same qawm as did their infidel audiences.[73] The same understanding of the term emerges from the sunna and the hadith,[74] and the Prophet himself had created in Medina a "nation" that comprised Jews as well as Muslims.[75] The term umma, though used in common parlance for the Muslim community, can refer to other communities as well; and as the case of the umma created by the Prophet in Medina illustrates, Muslims and non-Muslims could share membership in it.[76] The view put forth by Madani was guided not only by the desire to see the Hindus and the Muslims struggle together against British imperialism, however. It seems to have been no less inspired by pan-Islamic ideals that would not countenance any subdivisions within the global Muslim community. That Hindus and Muslims could not form a single nation was to him as insidious a notion as the idea that the Muslims of India were separate from the global Muslim community.[77] In both notions he saw the handiwork of British colonial machinations, intended only, he believed, to keep the Indians as well as the Muslims divided.[78]

Though so threatened by British colonialism, Islam was, for Madani, a religion resourceful and flexible enough to meet all changing needs and circumstances. His position on this matter is emphatic:

> Islam comprises the principles that underlie the rectitude of doctrinal, practical, and moral matters. It is the means not only for reforming the individual, but also for the regulation of the collectivity in its particular (household) and

general (political) dimensions. It sheds light on all necessities of life, and it provides for all sorts of regulation. We must now consider whether Islam—being constituted of principles regulating individual and collective life, and pertaining to the relations between the Creator and the created as well as to relations among the human beings themselves—allows, on the basis of shared residence, race, color, and language, a shared nationalism with non-Muslims. [Does it allow a nationalism] whereby to defeat the enemy and to seek and promote common political, economic, commercial, agricultural, and military goals? [Does Islam allow] such extensive interaction as long as there is no threat to its basic principles? To the extent that we have studied the foundational texts of the shari'a, it seems clear to us that, depending on the given situation, [such interaction] is at times obligatory, at other times recommended, at yet others permissible, at others reprehensible, and in certain circumstances it is forbidden.[79]

Madani goes on:

The view that Islam is an inflexible religion is beyond my comprehension. To the extent that I can understand its laws, [Islam] can live together with non-Muslims in the same country; it can be at peace with them; it can enter into treaties with them, as well as in commercial transactions, partnership, tenancy, the exchange of gifts, loans, trusts, etc. [Muslims] can interact with them, participate in matters of joy and grief, and dine with them. . . . A Muslim can enter into and live in the unbelievers' lands of unbelief and the "abodes of war." . . . There are countless laws and principles governing social order in Islam that reveal its consideration for and tolerance of others and that are not found in other religions. . . . This is the meaning of [Islam's] flexibility (lachak). But this flexibility does not imply weakness, nor a willingness to make false and forbidden acts matters of acceptable practice.[80]

Madani was severely criticized by many leaders of Muslim opinion in the late 1930s and 1940s for being too subservient to the Indian National Congress and for showing a complete lack of understanding of the dangers Muslims would face in a Hindu-dominated India. Muhammad Iqbal (d. 1938), the widely influential modernist poet and philosopher, was among such critics, as was the Islamist thinker Mawlana Abu'l-A'la Mawdudi (d. 1979). Against Madani's view that Muslims and non-Muslims could be part of a single "nation" defined by territorial and other ties, Iqbal argued that religion was the sole basis of Muslim nationhood: "[A]ccording to the Quran, it is the religion of Islam alone which sustains a nation in its true cultural or political sense. It is for this reason that the Quran openly declares that any system other than that of Islam must be deprecated and rejected."[81] Given its all-encompassing claims on the life of its adherents, Islam could not be relegated to the status of a privatized religion, and to yoke together different religious communities could only mean the destruction of those communities.[82] Western ideas of nationalism had misled Madani, Iqbal said, and it was ironic that, while "[f]ormerly, the half-Westernised educated Muslims were under the spell of Europe[,] now the curse has descended upon religious leaders. . . . Circumstances have forced the present-day ulema to say things and interpret the Quran in a way which could never have been the intention of the Prophet and the Quran."[83] Most shocking perhaps is Iqbal's comparison of Madani's support for nationalism to the belief of the Ahmadi sect that their leader, Mirza Ghulam Ahmad (d. 1908), was a prophet—a belief that is the basis for the Ahmadis' being generally considered heretical by other Muslims. According to Iqbal, in both cases something new was being added to Islam that did violence to its basic principles:

> The upholders of the idea of nationalism . . . say that, in view of present-day needs, it is necessary for the Muslim community to take up a position in addition to what the divine law has prescribed and defined for them for all time to come in the same way in which the Qadiani [Ahmadi] view, by inventing a new prophethood, directs the Qadiani thought into a channel which ultimately leads to the denial of the perfection and consummation of prophethood in Muhammad.[84]

Mawdudi, for his part, ridiculed Madani for being so obsessed with bringing about the end of British colonial rule as to be utterly oblivious of the dangers that a Hindu-dominated India would pose to Muslim religion and culture after the end of British rule.[85] Madani, he said, had little understanding of what nationalism meant; he seemed to be thinking more in terms of a "confederation" (*wifaq, tahaluf*) of different, autonomous nations in an independent India,[86] but this is not what the Indian National Congress meant when it spoke of a united nation for India. Madani was conflating these two very different conceptions and, in doing so, was pushing the Muslim community along a path of destruction.[87]

That Madani's notion of "united nationalism" was, in fact, predicated on the assumption that the Muslim community would retain full religious and cultural "autonomy" within the state is not an unfair reading of it, as Peter Hardy has also noted.[88] Such a view not only betrayed an insufficiently sophisticated understanding of the potentialities of the modern state—*any* modern nation-state—in affecting and regulating the lives of its citizens; the rise of Hindu nationalism in the late 1980s and the 1990s also cast its long shadow over that view. Yet despite the importance of this issue, my concern here is not whether Madani and the nationalist 'ulama were right or wrong in the approach they advocated for the Muslims of India, but only to note that for all the rigidity with which the shari'a was seen in colonial India, at least some scholars could still insist on its "flexibility" and could adopt positions that seemed shocking, even perverse, to many of their contemporaries. Unlike Thanawi's careful demonstration of how his proposed solution to the problem of dissolving unwanted marriages in the colonial context had roots in the medieval legal tradition, Madani does not explicitly invoke juristic discussions on whether Muslims could continue to live among non-Muslims in non-Muslim lands. Such discussions do exist, however, and though it is impossible to know how well-acquainted Madani was with them, it is not unlikely that they exerted some influence on him.

Since the first centuries of Islam, jurists have discussed the question of the legal status of Muslim minorities living in non-Islamic states and territories. As Khaled Abou El Fadl's survey of the juristic discourses on Muslim minorities shows, the developed positions of the different schools of law date from the twelfth century, that is, from the time that jurists were confronted with the presence of substantial Muslim populations in non-Muslim lands.[89] With some exceptions, the Maliki jurists adopted the most uncompromising position on the question, insisting that Muslims who, because of conversion or conquest, find themselves in non-Muslim lands must migrate to a Muslim territory.[90] Other schools of law were more tolerant of the idea that Muslims might legitimately reside in a non-Muslim land as long as they were able to practice their religion openly there. The Hanafis and the Shafiʿis believed that a territory that had once been part of the *dar al-Islam* ('the abode of Islam') continued to be so even after it had fallen into the hands of the non-Muslims, as long as the Muslims were still able to practice their religion in that territory.[91] The presence of Muslims in non-Muslim lands might in fact be beneficial, and "might at times [even] be either recommended or obligatory" if, for instance, the continued Muslim residence and public practice of their faith in non-Muslim lands could become the means of calling people to Islam there.[92] The 'nationalist' ʿulama did entertain hopes of the further spread of Islam on the Indian subcontinent.[93] And Madani was clearly echoing the idea that Muslim residence in non-Muslim lands was recommended or even obligatory when, in the passage quoted in full earlier, he noted that "depending on the given situation, [interaction with non-Muslims] is at times obligatory, at other times recommended, at yet others permissible, at others reprehensible, and in certain circumstances it is forbidden."[94]

The reasoning on which Madani's political stance was based reveals a view of Islam that, ironically, is less reified than that of the modernist Iqbal. This is ironic both in light of the hardening of the shariʿa in the colonial context, as we have seen, and also because neither the scholarly nor the popular—let alone the Muslim modernist—perceptions of the ʿulama generally associate much flexibility with the ʿulama's view of the world. Madani was evidently drawing on premodern juristic discourses in formulating his position on united nationalism, but there is no evidence that these discourses necessarily constrained him in the choices he made. Other 'ulama made different choices when they broke with the Jam'iyyat al-'Ulama'-i Hind in 1945 to create the Jam'iyyat al-'Ulama'-i Islam, which, unlike the former, supported the demand for Pakistan. While Madani's position was premised on the conviction that Muslims as a whole comprise a single global community, which ought not to be divided into Muslim territorial states, his opponents among the 'ulama regarded the existence of a Muslim state necessary for the preservation of Islamic culture and identity. We have an opportunity to consider the refutation of Madani's ideas by a leading Deobandi scholar in chapter 2, where I examine how religious authority is articulated through the commentary—a medium of discourse that has long been part of the culture of the 'ulama.

But Madani's position also illustrates a larger point that appears in different guises in subsequent chapters: the 'ulama's identification with the Islamic religious and juristic tradition is the basis of their claims to religious authority, but it does not preclude their adaptation to changing needs—their own or those of the societies in which they operate. The ways in which the modern 'ulama have sought to preserve or enhance their influence in society, and the positions they have espoused in doing so, are not reducible to a single or necessarily coherent vision: for example, insistence on the need to preserve the shari'a unchanged can exist simultaneously with affirmations of its remarkable flexibility and adaptability; or, as we will see later, the 'ulama's calls for an "Islamic state" exist side by side with their ambivalence towards the state. Yet it is precisely by expressing themselves in many different ways, and in terms of multiple discourses, that the modern 'ulama have asserted their presence and their role in society; this is how they have often defined and defended their religious authority. That authority has been articulated in many different ways, including the age-old yet evolving tradition of writing commentaries.

II

Constructions of Authority

ONE OF THE MOST DISTINCTIVE facets of premodern 'ulama culture was the articulation of discourses through the medium of the commentary. Medieval works of law were "open texts," the very "internal discursive construction" of which required constant interpretation and commentary.[1] The discursive form of the commentary was, in fact, one of the principal means (the other was the fatwa) through which the law was not only elaborated but also expanded and modified to meet the exigencies of changing times. Commentaries allowed scholars to preserve the identity and authority of their school of law, their legal tradition, while simultaneously providing them with the means to make sometimes important adjustments in that tradition. As Baber Johansen has argued in examining mechanisms of legal change in medieval Hanafi law, different levels or "layers" of juristic discourse, existing side by side and not necessarily in complete harmony with one another, served the crucial function of allowing the jurists to retain earlier, authoritative school doctrines while also modifying those doctrines in practice: "While the early tradition is upheld in the textbooks for teaching purposes and as a yardstick by which to measure the unity of the legal system, new solutions are widely accepted in other literary genres like the commentaries (*shuruh*), the *responsa* (*fatawa*) and the treatises on particular questions (*rasa'il*)."[2]

The commentary was not only a major medium through which an evolving juristic thought found expression, but also a means of expounding the meaning of Islam's foundational sources, the Qur'an and the hadith. It was equally critical to disciplines such as philosophy, with Muslim philosophers making some of their most significant contributions in the form of commentaries on ancient Greek works.[3] Nor, indeed, is there anything peculiar about the significance of the commentary in the world of medieval Islamic learning, for the continuing dialogue with authoritative texts, and with past and present generations of scholars, that the commentary made possible was equally characteristic of the Jewish, Christian, Confucian, Hindu, and other religious traditions.[4]

Yet those looking at earlier societies from this side of the Enlightenment have, not infrequently, seen in the commentary all the marks of intellectual decadence and sterile scholasticism. Edward Gibbon's characterization of Roman intellectual life as one of "blind deference" to authorities of the past, of "cold and servile imitations," with "a cloud of critics, compilers, and commentators darken[ing] the face of learning"[5] expresses a view of the commentaries that has long resonated with students of medieval societies. Such views are no less common in modernist perceptions of medieval Islam. For instance, Fazlur Rahman, a more astute student of medieval Islamic intellectual history than perhaps most other Muslim modernists, repeatedly laments the "sterile commentarial literature" of the later Middle Ages, even as he acknowledges that "a great deal of ingenuity lies buried in these generally ponderous and repetitive works."[6]

That medieval commentaries are often regarded as hollow and "sterile" demonstrations of intellectual virtuosity, rather than as cultural productions that served any really "useful" purpose, does not mean, however, that as a discursive form the commentary itself is necessarily in disrepute. Two of the most influential Sunni Islamist thinkers of the twentieth century, Sayyid Abu'l-A'la Mawdudi of Pakistan and Sayyid Qutb of Egypt, wrote major multivolume commentaries on the Qur'an.[7] Qutb's commentary, *In the Shade of the Qur'an*, may, according to Johannes Jansen, "actually be the most widely translated and distributed Islamic book of all time."[8] The modernist Syrian exegete, Muhammad Shahrur, has also employed commentary as the vehicle for proposing a radical rereading of the Qur'an and a reconceptualization of Islamic law.[9] Ayatollah Khumayni's lectures titled "Islamic Government," which he delivered before advanced madrasa students while in exile in Iraq and which later became the basis of revolutionary Iran's new constitution, advance their arguments by way of commentary on verses of the Qur'an and on traditions attributed to the Prophet and the Shi'i imams.[10]

Barbara Metcalf has drawn attention to the importance of hadith for the reformist movements of nineteenth-century India.[11] The Ahl-i Hadith, as we have noted earlier, argued that the Qur'an and hadith provided sufficient guidance to the believers and that one ought to base one's conduct on their teachings directly, rather than as mediated (and, they held, distorted) by the various schools of law. But the Deobandis, who did insist on the authority of their Hanafi school of law, and indeed on taqlid concerning matters agreed upon by this school tradition, also gave a new and, in the Indian context, unprecedented salience to the study of hadith in their madrasas. Hadith had, of course, been studied in precolonial Indian madrasas, but the Deobandis instituted the practice of studying (or, more exactly, "reviewing") all six of the Sunni canonical collections of hadith in the course of a single year; this practice has come to serve in Indian and Pakistani madrasas as the capstone of a student's advanced madrasa training.[12] Yet, while Metcalf repeatedly emphasizes the importance of hadith as a central feature of the 'ulama's training and of their discourses, she tells us little about what sorts of work the 'ulama were actually writing and publishing on hadith.

Though it is hard to know it from Metcalf's work on the early history of the Deobandi 'ulama, South Asian 'ulama have continued to write ambitious commentaries throughout the nineteenth and twentieth centuries.[13] The commentaries that I consider in this chapter are the sort of "elitist" works that only a handful of the leading 'ulama have produced. There is little evidence of such works among modern Sunni 'ulama outside South Asia, though several of those produced in South Asia have been published, in some cases repeatedly, in the Middle East.[14] Yet these writings suffice to illustrate a significant and continuing intellectual tradition. Many of these writings are, no doubt, "ponderous and repetitive," but they serve important functions for the 'ulama even when they appear to us as "sterile." What are these functions? How has the technology of print affected the commentaries? How do such works relate to the 'ulama's other writings? And how do their writings help construct their religious authority?

The Commentary as Polemic

Scholars from among the Ahl-i Hadith were at the forefront of those writing and publishing on hadith in the late nineteenth and early twentieth centuries.[15] The adherents of this movement had some affinity with the Wahhabis of the Arabian peninsula and, like the latter, admired the work of Ibn Taymiyya (d. 1328); the Ahl-i Hadith were also influenced by the works of two eighteenth-century scholars, al-Shawkani (d. 1839) of Yemen and Shah Wali Allah (d. 1762) of northern India, both of whom had contributed significantly to the study of hadith and had emphasized the necessity of ijtihad.[16] Conscious of the need to demonstrate their own competence and authority, to show the authenticity of their understanding of the true faith, and, not least, to forge ties with religious scholars of the Middle East, many of the more prominent scholars of the Ahl-i Hadith often wrote in the Arabic language.[17] Undoubtedly the most prolific of these was Siddiq Hasan Khan (d. 1890), the Azhar-educated husband of the ruler of the princely state of Bhopal in northern India.[18] In addition to his own writings on hadith, Qur'an exegesis, law, and a vast body of sectarian, polemical literature, he also arranged for many classical works of hadith—including the *Fath al-bari*, Ibn Hajar's (d. 1449) classic commentary on al-Bukhari's (d. 870) *Sahih*, and al-Shawkani's (d. 1839) *Nayl al-awtar*—to be published and widely disseminated.[19] He is reported to have had agents in Cairo, Alexandria, Beirut, Jeddah, Constantinople, and other important intellectual centers of Islam who were responsible for introducing and disseminating his own works (and those published under his auspices) throughout the Muslim world.[20] Whole-hearted use of the possibilities created by print did not, however, compromise his admiration for more traditional feats of memorization. Thus he is known to have instituted a prize for anyone who would memorize the monumental *Sahih* of al-Bukhari, as well as prizes for memorizing other works; and indeed there were still people who were able to lay claim to this distinction.[21]

Though the compulsions inherent in print meant that the classical works of hadith (whose printing was sponsored by patrons such as Siddiq Hasan) would be available to all scholars and not just to those of a particular sectarian persuasion, much effort was expended on "appropriating" such classics by demonstrating how they supported one's viewpoint and contradicted that of one's rivals. The writing of commentaries on early collections of hadith was, and continues to be, a favored means of such polemical exchanges. The *Tuhfat al-ahwadhi*, an Arabic commentary by the Ahl-i Hadith scholar Muhammad 'Abd al-Rahman Mubarakpuri (d. 1935) on the hadith collection of al-Tirmidhi (d. 892)[22] is not only an effort to elucidate the meaning of the Prophetical traditions in al-Tirmidhi's *Jami'*, but equally a demonstration of how the Hanafis have frequently gone astray in their understanding of hadith.[23] Such polemics, and more fundamentally, the writing of commentaries as such, were often facilitated by the fact that increasing numbers of classical works—printed in India or the Middle East—were becoming available to the 'ulama for the first time. Classical commentaries such as Ibn Hajar's *Fath al-bari* not only brought with them a wealth of new and exciting information with which to advocate or attack a viewpoint; they also served as models to be emulated, and—in the imagination of at least some of those writing their own monumental commentaries—perhaps even surpassed.

Undoubtedly the most ambitious response to the Ahl-i Hadith from the Deobandis, in their self-appointed role as the defenders of the Hanafi school of law, is a monumental, twenty-one-volume commentary, the *I'la al-sunan* (The exaltation of the normative practices [of the Prophet]) by Mawlana Zafar Ahmad 'Uthmani.[24] This is not a commentary on a particular classical collection of hadith; rather, it pertains broadly to Prophetical traditions on legal issues (*ahkam*) in general. The primary motivation for writing this work was to demonstrate, against the charges of the Ahl-i Hadith, that the legal doctrines of the Hanafi school were in fact solidly based in traditions of the Prophet rather than in mere "opinion" (*ra'y*) or analogical reasoning. But the space afforded by this massive commentary also lent itself, in the two decades it took to complete it, to the settling of many other scores. Of these, the most striking is 'Uthmani's refutation of "united nationalism," which he undertakes in the form of a short treatise embedded in the twelfth volume of the *I'la al-sunan*, and it is on this treatise, completed in 1939, that I would focus here.[25] This controversy, which I have touched on in the previous chapter and consider at greater length in the following pages, had nothing to do with the Ahl-i Hadith. Rather, it pitted certain Deobandi scholars against others from the same school on a hotly contested issue in late colonial India. That a polemical work dealing with a controversy of great moment and urgent relevance to the political life of the Indian Muslims should be part of a supposedly arcane genre of scholarly discourse—the commentary—strikes one as odd and anachronistic. But there are important rhetorical strategies at work in this choice, no less than in certain other aspects of this treatise, all of which illustrate not only something of the 'ulama's mode of argumentation but also the construction of religious authority through the commentary.

The author of the *I'la al-sunan*, Zafar Ahmad 'Uthmani, was the nephew of Ashraf 'Ali Thanawi, who, as we saw, had played an active role in responding to the crisis precipitated by the incidence of apostasy in colonial India. 'Uthmani was educated at madrasas in Deoband, Thana Bhawan, and Saharanpur in the United Provinces and later taught at similar institutions in Rangoon (Burma), Dacca (East Bengal, later East Pakistan/Bangladesh), and Ashrafabad (Sind). He was among the founders of the Jam'iyyat al-'Ulama'-i Islam and later remained active in Pakistani politics as one of the national leaders of this organization. He died in 1974.[26]

Nowhere in his short treatise refuting the idea of united nationalism does 'Uthmani actually mention the most famous of its proponents and his fellow Deobandi, Mawlana Husayn Ahmad Madani. Yet to anyone familiar with Madani's writings on this subject, there can scarcely be any doubt that it is his views that are meant to be refuted here, often in the form of a point by point rebuttal. As in the *I'la al-sunan* as a whole, the text of select Prophetical traditions is quoted at the top of each page, with the lower and usually the greater portion of the page given to a commentary on the issues raised by one or more traditions. The commentary has a life of its own, however, and though the traditions chosen for inclusion are related in some way to the themes emphasized in the commentary, every single tradition is not specifically or necessarily commented on, nor is its relevance to the commentary itself always explicitly brought out.

'Uthmani takes united nationalism to mean that

> there is complete mixing (*ikhtilat*) between the people of different religions—
> Muslims and unbelievers—to the extent that none of them has a culture or
> community distinct from those of the others. Indeed, they are all united in
> their religion [*din*], either through the creation of a religion which is a com-

posite of the different religions, or in that the religion has no trace in anything but one's inner [scil., private] life, and outwardly [scil., in public] they are like one nation [*qawm*].[27]

A united nationalism would be unobjectionable to the shari'a, 'Uthmani holds, if the majority of the nation's members were Muslims, so that *their* law defines the law of the land and the culture of the non-Muslim minority is gradually "erased" (*yanmahi*). But a unified nation in which the non-Muslims form the numerical majority would, by the same token, signify the destruction of Islam, its laws, and its rituals, and it is therefore forbidden from the viewpoint of the shari'a.[28] In the upper, textual portion of the commentary, a number of traditions are adduced to underline that the only legitimate mark of distinction between people is "piety" rather than such "pagan" (*jahili*) bases of identity as kinship ties, race, or color.[29] These traditions 'Uthmani takes to signify that there is no basis for a shared community or nationhood except religion, and that the only way in which Muslims and non-Muslims might legitimately cooperate is if Islam is the dominant religion.[30]

'Uthmani then cites and comments on a number of Prophetical traditions that warn against intermingling with people of other religions. Many of these traditions are derived from the well-known polemical work titled "The Necessity of Following the Straight Path in Opposition to the Inhabitants of Hell," by Ibn Taymiyya (d. 1328), the famous Damascene jurist of the Hanbali school of law.[31] But while he refers repeatedly to Ibn Taymiyya, 'Uthmani's concerns are, in fact, quite different. Ibn Taymiyya sought, in his own work, to combat what he saw as the continuing attraction of Muslims to non-Muslim and especially Christian rituals—an attraction exercised by the presence of non-Muslims *in Muslim lands*.[32] 'Uthmani, on the other hand, is worried about the pressures to which Islamic culture and identity would be exposed under non-Muslim rule. What links the two works is the argument, implicit in 'Uthmani's use of Ibn Taymiyya's diatribe, that if Muslims are exposed to non-Islamic (and un-Islamic) ritual practices in a land dominated by Muslims, then, *a fortiori*, they would be far more vulnerable if the state itself is dominated by those who are not Muslim.

Having already defined united nationalism in a way that it must entail the loss or privatization of a religious identity, the Prophet's admonition that "whoever imitates a people is to be reckoned as one of them" becomes, in 'Uthmani's hands, a direct and stinging refutation of the nationalist position. He repeatedly emphasizes that this position must eventuate in the destruction of the foundations of Islam.[33] Distinguishing Muslims from unbelievers (including "the People of the Book") is, indeed, one of the "fundamentals" of the shari'a.[34] And anyone who denies the importance in Islamic law of maintaining sharp boundaries between Muslim and non-Muslim—he says in a thinly veiled allusion to Madani—is neither a competent scholar of Islamic law nor even a proper Muslim.[35]

The directive to maintain a distinctive Muslim identity extends to all areas of Muslim life. Following Ibn Taymiyya, 'Uthmani cites traditions that warn not only against participating in the rituals of the non-Muslims—the central concern of Ibn Taymiyya's aforementioned work[36]—but even against learning their languages. The issue of language is, in fact, given special attention in 'Uthmani's treatise, very likely because language was among the more controversial issues of communal politics in British India. Since the nineteenth century the Muslims of north India had used Urdu rather than Persian as the principal language of culture and communication. Though many among the more learned 'ulama often wrote in Arabic—the language of 'Uthmani's I'la al-sunan as well as of many a commentary written in the late nineteenth and the twentieth centuries—it was in Urdu that they more commonly wrote.[37] From the late nineteenth century, the Muslim religious and political elite had waged a continuous struggle against those Hindu leaders who held that Hindi (or "Hindustani"), written in the Devanagiri script, rather than Urdu, written in the Arabic script, should be the officially recognized language for purposes of administrative business; and the safeguarding of the Muslim language—and its attendant culture—was at the forefront of the issues that the demand for a separate Muslim state sought to resolve.[38]

The issue of language is also given particular attention by 'Uthmani because unlike, say, the proscription of non-Islamic rituals, the traditions on language use needed to be adequately "translated" into the contemporary Indian context for their relevance there to be fully intelligible. Statements attributed to the Prophet, to the second caliph, 'Umar b. al-Khattab, and to other Companions of Muhammad, as cited by 'Uthmani, command the learning of Arabic and caution against speaking or developing an expertise in Persian or other languages.[39] The Arabic language, 'Uthmani writes, is "a mark of Islam,"[40] and it is among the "great afflictions" of the Indian Muslims that they abandoned this language, first to adopt Persian and then to evolve the Urdu language. Yet in an interesting move, 'Uthmani goes on to equate the religiocultural status of Urdu in the context of India with that of Arabic in the first centuries of Islam, and to apply the warnings against Persian in the traditions he has cited to Hindi in the contemporary context. Urdu is the language, he says, in which Muslim religious and cultural heritage—exegesis, hadith, law, and the teachings of the pious forbears is now preserved; in the Indian context, it is the language most closely associated with Arabic as well as with Islam in India. Against the efforts of the Indian National Congress, then, the

Muslims of India must preserve this language even as the 'ulama ought to continue promoting the Arabic language in and through their madrasas.[41]

Having critiqued, to his satisfaction, the position of those propounding a united nationalism, 'Uthmani turns to the question of how methods of nonviolent protest and civil disobedience might be evaluated with reference to the sunna of the Prophet. He does not specifically name Mohandas K. Gandhi, the most famous proponent of such methods and one of the most visible figures with whom the "nationalist" 'ulama were allied in their anticolonial struggle. 'Uthmani's highly uncomplimentary language leaves little doubt, however, that it is indeed Gandhi who is meant here.[42] He does not object to either the legitimacy or the possible political effectiveness of nonviolent methods of protest and civil disobedience. Rather, it is to the effort of the "nationalist" 'ulama to find a precedent for such methods in Prophetical sunna that he takes strong exception.[43]

As 'Uthmani presents their argument, his opponents claim that during the Meccan period in the earliest part of Islam's career the Prophet and his Companions patiently bore all persecution at the hands of the pagans without responding to it in kind, and that this stance prefigures contemporary forms of nonviolent struggle through which oppressive political authority might be challenged and eventually undermined. But 'Uthmani retorts that if the Prophet had really intended the patient bearing of hardship in Mecca as a potentially efficacious nonviolent struggle against the Meccan establishment, he would not have migrated to Medina at all to begin a new phase in which he did have full recourse to the use of force. 'Uthmani anticipates the argument of his opponents that nonviolent struggle was the preferred path for the Prophet *before* he gained political authority, with the implication that Gandhian nonviolence was in accord with the sunna in the colonial context, but he remains unimpressed by this defense. For Gandhian nonviolence is the prescribed course of action at *all* times, he notes, and it is thus very different from the way the Prophet was forced to act while in Mecca.[44]

From 'Uthmani's viewpoint, in their effort to find a Prophetical precedent for nonviolent struggle the "nationalist" 'ulama are in danger of representing the Prophet's own example (viz., his recourse to the use of violence as a possible option while in Medina) as undesirable. If Muslims imbibed the creed of nonviolence in their schools, he says, they would become admirers of nonviolent Brahmins, and such heroes of Islam as 'Umar and 'Ali and Khalid b. al-Walid (all Companions of the Prophet and all associated with celebrated military victories) would cease to appeal to them: Islam would seem to be founded on bloodshed, and Hinduism on love and mercy, and they would be convinced of the latter's superiority over the former.[45]

Islam, 'Uthmani insists, is indeed a religion of peace and forgiveness, but it is also a religion of strength and force. The reason why the Prophet did not respond with force to the Meccan pagans was not because he was pursuing a nonviolent strategy; it was simply because he and his followers did not have the means to resist oppression. He used force as soon as he had the means in Medina to do so; and even in Mecca, the more powerful of his Companions (notably 'Umar) did not refrain from challenging the pagans because, unlike most of the other Muslims, these Companions were strong enough not to fear reprisals for such public defiance.[46]

Basing himself on certain reports in the early *Sira*-historiography, 'Uthmani notes that, while in Mecca, the Prophet was offered political leadership if only he would refrain from condemning Meccan deities and threatening norms of tribal solidarity. The demand, 'Uthmani says, was not that he give up his religion or even that he stop calling others to it. "The [pagan] people (*qawm*) offered him obedience, by way of recognizing him as their king, if only he would establish a united nation (*qawmiyya muttahida*) of himself and them. [Such a nation would signify that] no one interferes with anyone else in one's religious affairs, condemns them, or deems them misguided, or finds fault with their religion; everyone is to be regarded as equal in the freedom of conscience and faith. Yet [the Prophet] refused [any deal] and sought only to 'perfect the light of God, however much the unbelievers might dislike that.'"[47] In this refusal of pagan ministrations by the Prophet, 'Uthmani believes, lies "the strongest of proofs in refutation of united nationalism, which the foolish people (*sufaha'*) of our times[48] seek to base on the Qur'an and the sunna."[49] He concludes this treatise by noting that he has been blessed in a dream with the vision of the Prophet, who gave him the glad tidings that Islam would soon dominate over the unbelievers; and he ends by praying that this dream may soon come true.[50]

The brief treatise by Zafar Ahmad 'Uthmani, and the large commentary in which it is embedded, raise a number of important issues. There is, first of all, the issue of audience. The *I'la al-sunan* was written in the Arabic language, which means that it was primarily intended for an 'ulama audience and perhaps also for an audience outside the Indian subcontinent. The choice of language also suggests an effort to demonstrate scholarly religious authority. The Ahl-i Hadith often wrote in Arabic for the same reason, and a work which, for all its other objectives, was conceived as a response to them could scarcely concede mastery of Arabic to the opponent. Significantly, colonial observers seem to have contributed towards heightening the importance of Arabic as a mark of cultural authenticity and authority. G. W. Leitner, the first principal of the Government College of Lahore (established in 1864), saw Arabic as one of the "classical languages of India," and founded a weekly "Arabic journal for the maulavis" just as he founded one in Sanskrit "for the [Hindu] Pandits."[51] And W. D. Arnold, who in 1856 was appointed as the first director of public instruction in the Punjab, thought that "Urdu is as offensive to a learned Arabic scholar as vernacular English in connection with English subjects would have been to a scholar of the age of Erasmus."[52] Yet English officials also complained that most Indian Muslim scholars lacked the ability to converse or properly write in the Arabic language.[53] Writings in Arabic thus not only met the needs of sound polemics; they also may have conformed to perceived colonial criteria of religious authority.

That 'Uthmani's treatise on united nationalism is embedded in a monumental Arabic commentary on hadith points to another function it seems implicitly called upon to perform: the treatise not only refutes Madani's position but does so by laying claim to the authority and learning of the 'ulama and by seeking to wrest the mantle of that authority from the nationalist 'ulama. Madani's views on united nationalism had been attacked before—by the poet and philosopher Muhammad Iqbal, and by Mawdudi. Yet for all the severity of his criticism, Iqbal came from a modernist, Western educational background, as did most other Muslim political leaders who had attacked Madani's position. Mawdudi, for his part, was a journalist and an Islamist thinker, but he too did not have a formal madrasa education, and he neither claimed nor was usually recognized to be one of the 'ulama. Husayn Ahmad Madani, on the other hand, was one of the most prominent 'ulama of his time. In this context, 'Uthmani's critique of united nationalism becomes a major alternative voice of authority within the ranks of the 'ulama—a voice that seeks to be heard more clearly by them precisely because it comes from within.

This effort to wrest authority away from a leading scholar also reveals the political dividedness of Muslim community. And such divisions could only make it more vulnerable to the dangers inherent in being exposed to a non-Muslim majority and a state dominated by that majority. Notably, 'Uthmani does not explicitly link his fears about the future of the community to divisions within the community. Nor, for all these fears, does he explicitly call for the creation of a separate Muslim state. That demand was yet to be formally made by the leadership of the Muslim League, though the idea that Muslims ought to have their own homeland was already being much discussed at the time 'Uthmani wrote his treatise in 1939.[54] Though it was not articulated, 'Uthmani's arguments as outlined above do, in any case, seem to point towards the idea that the only viable way in which the future of the Muslim community can be secured—against the threat of external domination as well as of internal dissension—is for Muslims to have a state of their own.[55]

Talal Asad's definition of "orthodoxy" as "not a mere body of opinion but a distinctive relationship—a relationship of power,"[56] elucidates well 'Uthmani's conception of the Muslim community as essentially a political entity, whose survival requires power and political domination. This conception has obvious similarities to Muhammad Iqbal's critique of Madani, briefly noted in chapter 1, though Iqbal and 'Uthmani arrive at this position differently. Unlike Iqbal, 'Uthmani seems concerned to salvage the generality of the 'ulama by showing how some of them (Madani and the "nationalists") diverged so much from the Islamic tradition as to be disqualified to speak authoritatively as 'ulama at all.[57] 'Uthmani's critique of Madani is thoroughly and self-consciously imbued with the intellectual culture of the madrasa, the milieu in which it originated: It not merely invokes the Qur'an (as does Iqbal) and hadith (which, in this context, Iqbal doesn't) but, as we have seen, proffers its argument in the form of the "traditional" medium of a commentary on hadith; it enlists to its cause the authority of the Arabic language, the "mark of Islam"; and it adduces classical authorities, such as Ibn Hisham's classical biography of Muhammad, collections of hadith, other commentaries on these collections, and of course Ibn Taymiyya's aforementioned work. Much of 'Uthmani's treatise is occupied, in short, with the effort to demonstrate that the weight of the Islamic religious, historical, and juristic tradition is emphatically on *his* side.

Yet for all of 'Uthmani's polemical interest in obscuring the fact, tradition—broadly conceived—is also the ground on which Madani's position was articulated.[58] Madani's views also had some basis in medieval Hanafi discussions on the question of Muslim minorities, as we observed in chapter 1. 'Uthmani's fears about the consequences of Muslim residence in a Hindu-dominated India appear much closer to the stringency of the medieval Maliki position on Muslim minorities than they do to the view of the Hanafi jurists.[59] This unacknowledged departure from the Hanafi juristic tradition is ironic because, as already noted, 'Uthmani's polemic against united nationalism is part of a larger work whose very rationale is the defense of Hanafi jurisprudence in terms of hadith. But if 'Uthmani's view on the position of Muslim minorities is not in accord with the overall premodern Hanafi position on the matter, the Hanafi conception of what Baber Johansen has characterized as the "territorial concept of law" does seem to resonate in his polemic against united nationalism. The Hanafis held that it was the territorial jurisdiction of the state that defined the rights of those inhabiting it. A Muslim's person and property were inviolable if he or she resided in a Muslim territory; but a Muslim state did not extend its guarantees to Muslims residing outside its territories. Conversely, non-Muslims residing in a Muslim state were entitled to the same inviolability of person and property as its Muslim inhabitants. Muslim political and military power was essential to any guarantees of security, but such guarantees extended only as far as did the state's territorial reach.[60] While Madani's advocacy of united nationalism was premised on the conviction that Muslims as a whole comprise a single global community (umma), which ought not to be divided into Muslim territorial states, 'Uthmani seems to follow the territorial concept of Hanafi law in regarding political power necessary for the preservation of Islamic culture and identity. Though he does not explicitly say so, 'Uthmani's position implies that the world-wide Muslim community offers no guarantee for the survival of the Muslims in a Hindu-dominated India; nor indeed does the existence of Muslim states elsewhere in the world provide any such guarantee.[61]

We have examined a small portion of 'Uthmani's commentary at some length in order to illustrate a mode of argumentation and rhetorical strategies not uncommon in works of this genre. Other segments of this commentary, or other commentaries, would illustrate similar or different modes of argumentation, depending on the subject matter in question and the concerns of the commentator. There is a discursive style that commentaries might be said to broadly share—elaborating viewpoints; refuting rival positions (though not necessarily *contemporary* positions); and situating texts, authors, and communities within a genealogy. It is such things, rather than merely that a text is being expounded by writing another one on its basis, that make commentaries part of a tradition and, conversely, help constitute a tradition through them. But while they are part of an ongoing tradition, commentaries are also produced in a precise historical context that defines many of their specific concerns, *even when* the commentator seems only to be engaging with a long-standing debate within the school rather than (as in case of Zafar Ahmad 'Uthmani's treatise) with a "burning issue" of the time. In colonial India, even the choice of language might have been defined by the context in which the commentator was writing. While many commentaries have been, and continue to be, written in (or translated into) Urdu, and while commentaries had been written in Arabic earlier as well,[62] the colonial context gave a new impetus to demonstrations of virtuosity in the Arabic language. 'Uthmani's decision to write in Arabic was no mere continuation of an age-old practice but a strategic choice. As noted earlier, it was dictated in part by the need to respond to the Ahl-i Hadith in the same coin; in part by the need to bolster his own credentials against fellow travelers like Madani; in part by British colonial expectations of what it meant to be an 'alim; and, not least, by a desire, heightened by new technology and better communications, to find an audience in the greater Muslim world.

To take a different example in illustration of the last point, consider the following justification for a new edition of Shabbir Ahmad 'Uthmani's

(d. 1949) *Fath al-mulhim bi-sharh Sahih al-imam Muslim* (An inspiring
beginning in the explication of the *Sahih* by the imam Muslim), an Arabic
commentary, first published in 1933, on the canonical collection of hadith
by Muslim b. al-Hajjaj (d. 875): "This book, though well known among
the scholars and students of the Indian subcontinent, has remained unknown elsewhere. The reason [for this neglect] was the small number of
copies published, which disappeared within a few years, as well as the
lithographic print [of the first edition] . . . , which does not accord with
modern sensibilities."[63] Muhammad Taqi 'Uthmani, author of the words
quoted here and vice-president of the Dar al-'Ulum, another Deobandi
madrasa of Karachi, had edited and reissued this commentary in a grace-
ful new edition to "accord with modern sensibilities." And he also wrote
an erudite three-volume *takmila*, or supplement, to "complete" the commentary Shabbir Ahmad had begun.[64] This supplement, which really is
an independent work, not only serves to establish Taqi 'Uthmani as a
major contemporary exegete; it also demonstrates, once again, how contemporary concerns can influence a commentary. The *Takmila* was published in Pakistan at a time when there was much discussion about "Islamization" and the implementation of Islamic laws—a subject examined at
some length in chapter 4. Though discussions about the penalties sanctioned in the Qur'an (*hudud*) or about the position and functions of a
judge are, of course, nothing new in commentaries and in other works,
Taqi 'Uthmani's discussion of such topics clearly reveals a present-minded
concern in the context of the debates in Pakistan.[65] But they are relevant
not just in Pakistan. The commentary itself announces its availability at
locations in Saudi Arabia, where discussions on the implementation of
the shari'a would obviously have a certain market.

The "Presence" of the Master

Commentaries also served purposes other than what we have observed
so far. Many of the commentaries published in the early twentieth century
were based on the lectures of noted teachers of hadith as transcribed by
their "star" pupils. The *Lami' al-darari 'ala jami' al-Bukhari* (The stream-
ing light on the comprehensive [collection] of al-Bukhari) a posthumous
two-volume commentary on the canonical hadith collection of al-Bukhari, is based, for instance, on the lectures of Rashid Ahmad Gangohi (d.
1905), one of the founders of the Deoband madrasa.[66] These lectures were
compiled by one of his students, Muhammad Yahya Kandhlawi, with
further glosses added by the latter's son, Muhammad Zakariyya (d.
1982), himself a famous scholar of hadith.[67] There is little in Rashid Ahmad's commentary, or in the 'introduction' (*muqaddima*) and glosses of

Muhammad Zakariyya, to distinguish it from other works of its genre. On no account can the *Lami'* be considered to add significantly to what was already known, or even widely accepted, about the meaning of the traditions in al-Bukhari's canonical collection. Yet we would fail to understand the function and significance of the *Lami'*, as indeed those of many other writings produced in the same milieu, if we focused exclusively on the "contribution" of this work to the field of hadith.

Part of the reason why the 'ulama in modern Muslim societies have not been much studied, as opposed to the jurists and theologians of premodern Islam, is surely that in terms of intellectual significance the former are deemed not comparable to the leading figures among the latter, and therefore not especially deserving of serious intellectual engagement. That may well be so, though too often the point seems to be assumed rather than demonstrated. But even if this were true—and it is not my intention to investigate or dispute the point here—intellectual significance is not the only or in all cases the best yardstick by which to understand a culture or tradition. Likewise, to measure the significance of a work by the amount of controversy it arouses, or the polemics and refutations it generates[68] would be little better than the journalist's standard for determining what counts as "newsworthy." What makes a work like the *Lami'* unique, for those who compiled and published it, is not its intellectual acumen, nor simply the religions merit of writing down the words of the pious.[69] This commentary, like many others, also purports to preserve the "presence" of a highly revered master, and it is this fact among others that justifies and, indeed, requires that his disciples labor on it. Timothy Mitchell has written of the ambivalence premodern and early modern Muslim scholars often felt towards the written word, in that the author's words could travel without him and thus could be in danger of being misconstrued; and Francis Robinson has suggested that the 'ulama's insistence that all texts be read under the guidance of a scholar rather than on one's own was their way of continuing earlier forms of authoritative learning, to which they wanted to see even printed texts conform.[70] Leaving aside the question of this alleged ambivalence towards the written word, it is clear that a text such as the *Lami'* decidedly seeks to make the master, Rashid Ahmad, present to the readers of his commentary: through the preservation of Rashid Ahmad's lectures, his *dars* (course of study), during one given year, he becomes part of such *durus* in the madrasa in all subsequent years. Students of hadith can continue to "hear" his lectures, and if there is any doubt about the master's presence, or his ability to continue "authorizing" transmissions of hadith, his preprinted certificate of authorization (*ijaza*)—which was duly made part of the commentary—ought to dispel it.[71] That the text would be studied with and by (actual or prospective) scholars seems taken for granted; that the master is once again part of this study circle is what bears emphasis here. Even more important, thanks to this new mode of the printed book, he can, in principle, be part of as many *simultaneous* study circles as there are printed texts enshrining his words.

But it is not only Rashid Ahmad's presence, or his personal authority, that is perpetuated through this commentary. Muhammad Yahya, who wrote down the lectures; his son Muhammad Zakariyya, who added an introduction and glosses to the commentary; and Abu'l-Hasan 'Ali Nadwi (d. 1999), the former rector of the Nadwat al-'Ulama' of Lucknow and the most influential Indian religious scholar of his generation (see chapter 6), who added a short biography of Muhammad Zakariyya to it, are all part, in varying measures, of a select group that this commentary helps to constitute, celebrate, and link both with the earliest generations of Islam, and with other scholars of all times engaged in the venture of transmitting similar materials. Each scholar, dead or living, shares some of the lustre of the others and adds some of his own authority to this company.

The *I'la al-sunan* which we examined at some length earlier in this chapter, is informed by a similar rhetoric. The commentary is "by" Zafar Ahmad 'Uthmani, but its title page gives equal space to the author's name and to that of Ashraf 'Ali Thanawi, "in the light of [whose] teachings" this work is said to have been written. Among Deobandis, Thanawi is regarded as one of the most eminent religious scholars of all times; and given that 'Uthmani's commentary is viewed as having been commissioned by Thanawi and written under his guidance, it is scarcely surprising to see that a biographical notice of the latter is not only included at the outset of this commentary but is more detailed than and precedes that of the author's.[72] Another name that appears on the title page of the first volume is that of the aforementioned Mawlana Muhammad Taqi 'Uthmani, who has edited the most recent edition of this work. And finally, there is an "encomium" by a leading Saudi-based Syrian scholar, Shaykh 'Abd al-Fattah Abu Ghudda (d. 1997), on whom more will be said presently.[73] Again, each name reinforces the others in constituting a living and authoritative tradition.

To take yet another example, the *Fayd al-bari 'ala Sahih al-Bukhari* (The grace of the Creator on the *Sahih* of al-Bukhari) is a commentary on the canonical hadith collection of al-Bukhari, which is based on the lectures of Mawlana Anwarshah Kashmiri (d. 1933), a major Deobandi scholar of the early twentieth century. Kashmiri taught for many years at the madrasa of Deoband but was later forced to leave due to disagreements with the madrasa's administration. He then went to Gujarat, where the patronage of Gujarati merchants enabled him to establish a madrasa, the Jami'a Islamiyya, in Dabhel, as well as a research institute affiliated with the madrasa.[74] His Gujarati patrons also included those settled in

South Africa, and it was with some assistance from Indian Muslims in South Africa, and especially from the Jam'iyyat al-'Ulama' of Johannesburg (an offshoot of the Jam'iyyat al-'Ulama'-i Hind), that his lectures on al-Bukhari were posthumously published.[75] The work was published in Egypt, and it was seen through the press by Muhammad Yusuf Banuri (d. 1978), a student of Kashmiri. This student later founded a major Deobandi madrasa of his own in Karachi and distinguished himself as one of the leading Pakistani 'ulama.[76] A work like the *Fayd al-bari* again preserves the master's presence, but it also illustrates some other ways in which the 'ulama have articulated their religious authority. "Licenses" (ijaza) from prominent Indian and Middle Eastern scholars authorizing Kashmiri to narrate hadith from them are reproduced in the Introduction to this commentary, as are the chains of transmission through which those scholars were themselves authorized to transmit hadith—elaborate chains of transmission of which Kashmiri is now also shown to be a part.[77] But there is more. In his introduction to this work, Banuri provides a broad-ranging survey of hadith scholarship from the first centuries of Islam to the present in a way that culminates in modern Indian scholars: "When, from the middle of the tenth century of the Hijra [sixteenth century A.D.], the sciences of hadith were overtaken by weakness in the Arab lands, and the eternal sunna of Allah—as expressed in His statement, "and if you turn away, [He] would replace you with a people other than you . . ."— came true, this privilege [of attending to hadith] passed from the people of these [Arab] lands to its [new] carriers and trustees in the lands of India."[78] Banuri then to lists the principal South Asian scholars and commentators of hadith from the sixteenth century down to his own mentor, Anwarshah Kashmiri.

Such claims are not mere wishful thinking. As John Voll has shown, an Indian scholar, Muhammad Hayat al-Sindi, was prominent among teachers of hadith in the Hijaz in the eighteenth century and may have exerted some influence on Muhammad b. 'Abd al-Wahhab, the founder of the Wahhabi puritanical movement.[79] Another Indian scholar of much greater repute during the eighteenth century was the Yemen-based Murtada al-Zabidi, coveted teacher and transmitter of hadith and the author of a commentary on al-Ghazali's *Ihya al-'ulum al-din* and, most memorably perhaps, of the *Taj al-'arus*, "the largest Arabic lexicon in the classical tradition."[80]

While Banuri's claims about the prominence of Indian hadith scholarship are not without foundation, the facticity of these claims is not the only interesting thing about them. Such claims also had a particular function in the context of colonial rule. Banuri's teleological rendition of the history of hadith scholarship not only highlights how Deobandi 'ulama saw their own intellectual genealogy but no doubt was meant to under-

score the 'ulama's claims to leadership of the Muslim community in colonial India. At the same time, it betrays a thinly veiled desire to find, or
rediscover, broader audiences in the greater Muslim world. This work as
well as others discussed earlier also illustrate, once again, the significance
of the discursive form of the commentary in pursuing such goals. The
commentary links generations of scholars past and present; it is a means
through which claims to authority are staked within a school and against
other schools or sects; it creates networks of scholars; and, even for those
who would not necessarily be reading the commentary in question, it
establishes the credentials of a particular scholar or of the scholarly community to which he professes allegiance. Perhaps most important of all,
however, it is a medium through which at least part of the leading 'ulama's
intellectual work gets done. Commentaries are not necessarily responsive
to the changing conditions of their times. Yet, as we have seen, they *can*
be so responsive, and in significant ways. Zafar Ahmad 'Uthmani's choice
to engage with an important political controversy of the day through a
commentary was not dictated by his inability to think of a better way of
disseminating his message. The medium was as critical to his message as
was its content, for in effect it represented an effort to enlist the authority
of the Islamic juristic tradition to support the position he was putting
forth against the "nationalist" 'ulama like Madani.

Multiple Audiences

Recent work on the impact of print on Muslim societies has been much
concerned with debating how conceptions and structures of religious authority may have been altered, and a new era of religious change inaugurated, through this technology.[81] Some scholars have emphasized the role
of print in enabling the 'ulama to reach wider audiences than could ever
be conceivable in a manuscript age. Though print threatened to undermine the age-old styles of person-to-person transmission of knowledge,
and conceptions of authoritative transmission associated with those
styles, what the 'ulama gained was not only a new, effective, and—compared to the costs of the manuscript age—relatively inexpensive medium
to reach and influence new audiences, but also broad access to religious
classics that were hitherto available only to a select few but would now
undergird new movements of revival and reform in their societies.[82] While
acknowledging these aspects of the impact of print, other scholars see
the adverse effect of print on the 'ulama's religious authority as more
noteworthy. Precisely because religious classics had become accessible,
often through translations into the vernacular, the special claims of the
'ulama as the guardians and authoritative interpreters of religious texts

came to be disputed. As Francis Robinson has put it: "Increasingly from now on any Ahmad, Mahmud or Muhammad could claim to speak for Islam."[83]

Whether the authority of the 'ulama increased or decreased by virtue of the technology of print has considerable bearing on our understanding of the processes of religious change in modern Islam, of course, yet this way of formulating the question obscures more than it illuminates. Print and other new media no doubt have strong "democratizing" tendencies;[84] and there can be little doubt that the 'ulama's authority has come under severe pressure and unprecedented challenges in an age of mass higher education and modern technologies. "New religious intellectuals" are not indebted to the 'ulama for their own understanding of Islam, nor do they acknowledge the 'ulama's superior claim to that understanding. But while all of this is true in practically all Muslim societies, what is often over-looked is that the way in which the 'ulama themselves articulate their discourses is not monolithic. The critical question, then, is not whether their authority has increased or decreased, but how that authority is con-structed, argued, put on display, and constantly defended.

The commentary is one of the many media through which authority is articulated, though as we have seen, this medium itself allows for many different formulations of authority. That this age-old and elitist medium has continued to exist in a democratizing age of print and other media is a point worth underscoring. But it is equally important to stress that even earlier forms of person-to-person transmission of learning have also per-sisted in the world of new media.[85] Instructive, in this regard, is the career of a prominent Syrian scholar, 'Abd al-Fattah Abu Ghudda, who was briefly mentioned earlier in this chapter.[86] Abu Ghudda had received his higher education at al-Azhar in Egypt, from whose College of Shari'a he had graduated in 1948. He also taught at the Azhar, at the Shari'a College of the University of Damascus, and later at the Imam Muhammad ibn Sa'ud Islamic University of Riyadh, in Saudi Arabia.[87] He was a prominent member of the Muslim Brotherhood in Syria and had spent some time in prison in 1966, before moving to a life of exile in Saudi Arabia.[88] Abu Ghudda's reputation as a scholar rests on his critical editions of numerous works of law and hadith. These include works by scholars of different schools of law, though he was himself an avid partisan of the Hanafi school.[89] It was his interest in South Asian writings on hadith and law that drew him to the scholars of this region. He published and introduced to the Arab world a number of works by modern South Asian 'ulama including several writings on hadith by 'Abd al-Hayy Laknawi (d. 1886), one of the most prolific of the Indian 'ulama of the nineteenth century;[90] a polemical treatise against the Ahmadis by Anwarshah Kashmiri;[91] and an elucidation of the "principles of the study of hadith" by Zafar Ahmad

'Uthmani—a work that also serves as one of the two prolegomena to the latter's commentary, the *I'la al-sunan*. Abu Ghudda also wrote an encomium to this commentary.[92]

But alongside his publishing activity older forms of transmitting learning continued. Abu Ghudda's biography, published shortly after his death by one of his students, is really an extended list not just of his writings but also, and especially, of his teachers and numerous students. The biographer lists the names of scholars from Saudi Arabia, Turkey, Iraq, Yemen, Syria, Sudan, Egypt, Morocco, India, and Pakistan who had authorized him to narrate hadith from them;[93] lists of those authorized *by* him are even more expansive, and again straddle the Muslim world.[94] Given that Abu Ghudda was not only a traditionally educated 'alim but also maintained close ties with the Islamist organization the Muslim Brotherhood, his circles of hadith transmission were wider than those of many other 'ulama. Thus the list of those authorizing him to narrate hadith includes not just prominent 'ulama but also the leading Pakistani Islamist ideologue, Mawdudi.[95] Besides indicating an expansion of the circles of hadith transmission beyond the 'ulama, this also suggests how politics and patronage impinge on such matters: it was not only a broadly shared Islamist ideology that brought the two men together (closer, in fact, than Mawdudi, a Pakistani, was to the Pakistani or Indian 'ulama) but also the Saudi state, which was a patron of both Mawdudi and Abu Ghudda, and indeed of many of the Pakistani and Indian 'ulama.

If oral transmission and printed commentaries on hadith exist side by side in the culture of the 'ulama, so too, increasingly, do works produced for a broader, more "popular" audience. Print allows the new religious intellectuals to compete with the 'ulama for religious authority and to add their own distinctive voices to what Eickelman and Anderson have called the "religious public sphere."[96] It also allows the 'ulama to present their own merchandise in that same sphere.

Islamist intellectuals like Mawdudi and Qutb have written commentaries for ordinary educated Muslims, and some of the 'ulama have done the same. The influential and widely read Urdu Qur'an commentary, *Ma'arif al-Qur'an* ('Knowledge of the Qur'an') by Mufti Muhammad Shafi' of the Dar al-'Ulum of Karachi originated in a radio program in which he regularly expounded the meaning of the Qur'an for ordinary believers.[97] Muhammad Manzur Nu'mani (d. 1996), an Indian religious scholar, likewise wrote an extensive Urdu commentary on hadith that is explicitly described as intended for "ordinary-educated, Urdu-reading Muslims."[98] Muhammad Zakariyya, a renowned teacher of hadith at the Mazahir al-'Ulum madrasa of Saharanpur in India and the glossator and publisher of many commentaries on hadith, is also the author of a number of tracts written for the guidance of the ordinary Muslims. Collected and published in a single volume entitled *Tablighi nisab* (The curriculum for prose-lytizing)—later changed to *Fada'il-i a'mal* (The merits of [virtuous] prac-tices)—these tracts were written to undergird the reformist message of the Tablighi Jama'at, a proselytizing movement that began in India in the 1920s and which now has operations worldwide. Through selections from hadith and edifying anecdotes from the life of Muhammad and, especially, the lives of Muhammad's Companions, these texts aspire to present a model of orthodox and orthoprax Islam that all readers are called upon to emulate and put into practice.[99] The writings of Sayyid Abu'l-Hasan 'Ali Nadwi are typically addressed to ordinary Muslims, both in India and in the Arab world. These writings, all of which are intended for general audience, include biographies of Muslim scholars and reformers; a five-volume autobiography; and books on the contribu-tion of India to Islamic civilization, the position of Muslims in contempo-rary India, and the role of the Arabs in Islamic and world history.[100]

Manzur Nu'mani is also the author of a popular book in Urdu, *What Is Islam? (Islam kiya hai?)*. First published in 1949, by 1978 this book had been printed in 70,000 copies in India and, according to the Indian publisher, perhaps in similar numbers in Pakistan;[101] by the late 1990s it had been reprinted thirty-eight times by its original publisher, as well as translated into several languages.[102] The sources of religious authority to which appeal is made here are exclusively the Qur'an and the hadith, especially the latter, and it is in their terms that such matters as basic beliefs and practices; social and moral conduct; the need to variously serve the interests of religion; and prayers of supplication, and forgiveness, and so on are described. Divided into twenty lessons, the book contains "by the grace of God, the essence of the entire religion." By following the teachings presented here, "an ordinary person can become not merely a good Muslim, but, God willing, a perfect believer (*mu'min-i kamil*) and even a saint (*wali*)."[103] As Eickelman and Piscatori have argued, such works exemplify the "objectification of Muslim consciousness," whereby "religion has become a self-contained system that its believers can de-scribe, characterize, and distinguish from other belief systems."[104] Many such works are written by the new religious intellectuals, but, as Nu'-mani's example illustrates, 'ulama are active contributors to writings of this genre as well.

Several madrasas publish monthly magazines, and these typically ad-dress a general audience. Many among the 'ulama have also regularly contributed articles on Islamic themes to widely circulating magazines and newspapers. The daily *Jang*, Pakistan's most widely circulating Urdu newspaper, began an "Islamic page" in 1978 to which religious scholars have regularly contributed. In particular, Mufti Muhammad Yusuf Ludhi-anawi, a leading scholar affiliated with the Jami'at al-'Ulum madrasa of

Karachi wrote for many years a weekly question-and-answer column called "Your Problems and Their Solution." Ludhianawi here acted as what Brinkley Messick has called a "media mufti," giving religious guidance on all sorts of issues in a highly simplified style.[105] These and other writings were later compiled and published as a seven-volume work under the same title and for a similar target audience.[106] With some hyperbole, the publisher introduces this work as follows:

> "Your Problems and Their Solution" is the best-loved serious column in the *Jang* newspaper. It is the first thing to be read every Friday. God has granted it a popularity such that hundreds of thousands of people not only await it eagerly but consider it a necessary part of their lives. It has brought about revolutionary change in the lives of countless people. Thousands of people have molded their lives according to the life of the Prophet.[107]

Yusuf Ludhianawi and Manzur Nu'mani are among the 'ulama who have also used the technology of print in the service of forging new and radicalized sectarian identities, as I discuss in chapter 5. The writings by 'ulama intended for a general audience of believers in South Asia, in the Arab world, or elsewhere, are too numerous and varied to discuss here, even in terms of a schematic typology. That the 'ulama write and publish extensively, but often separately, for both a learned, 'ulama audience—at home and abroad—and the general public clearly shows, however, that generalizations about the adverse impact of print on the 'ulama's influence and authority are suspect.[108] Print has not heralded a "priesthood of all believers" in Muslim societies, as the printing of the Bible in the vernacular is supposed to have done in Protestant Europe.[109] Even the Tablighi Jama'at, which, according to Barbara Metcalf, "explicitly proclaims that any Muslim can be a preacher, not only the 'ulama,"[110] does not encourage its supporters to read much beyond Muhammad Zakariyya's handbook, the *Fada'il-i a'mal*.[111] In general, the 'ulama compete—not unfavorably—for a popular audience with new religious intellectuals, but they have also continued to write for an elite audience of religious specialists. Distinctions between a general and a specialized audience, between exoteric and esoteric matters, have a long history in Islam, which may be left aside here. It is worth noting, however, that the technology of print has easily adapted to such distinctions, enabling the religious scholars to assert their ability to speak to different audiences at different levels—and even in different languages.

Different kinds of texts help constitute authority in different ways and can exist simultaneously with each other. So too can somewhat different conceptions of the shari'a, as we saw in chapter 1. That different texts performed distinct functions in, say, the medieval Hanafi school, as noted at the outset of this chapter, is an important reminder that simultaneity of discourses, or their articulation at different levels, is, in itself, no novelty for the 'ulama. Nor, of course, is there anything novel about the form of the commentary itself. What does, however, serve as a register of change is the question why a "traditional" medium such as the commentary continues to be cultivated, or the precise functions it is called upon to undertake, or the meaning it holds for those associated with its production and publication, or the ways in which it relates to other discursive forms. In all these respects, the commentary is not only a mark of an ongoing tradition; it also has facets of change inscribed on it.

III

The Rhetoric of Reform and the Religious Sphere

THIS CHAPTER, like chapter 2, examines issues of religious authority, but the focus shifts here from the 'ulama's ways of constituting that authority to their ways of defending it. There is no better lens through which to examine this than the contestation over the "reform" of the 'ulama's institutions of learning, the madrasas. The modern state, colonial as well as postcolonial, has everywhere shaped "traditional" institutions and practices, not infrequently altering them beyond recognition, if not shaping them out of existence. The use of the state's resources has been variously legitimated by ideologies of modernization, efficiency, utility, rationality, overcoming a static tradition, and so forth. The targets of such initiatives have been as varied as the initiatives themselves, including but not limited to the family, law, education, the economy, and religion. These arenas were not, of course, thought of as necessarily distinct or separate from each other in many a premodern society, though in the course of state-sponsored "reform" they have typically come to be conceived of as such.

The madrasa attracted much reformist attention from colonial and postcolonial modernizing governments during the nineteenth and twentieth centuries, with the most important and best-documented reform being that of the Azhar of Egypt.[1] Initiatives towards governmental regulation of the 'ulama began in the early nineteenth century with Muhammad Ali's confiscation of vast amounts of charitable land (*waqf*) that had supported the Egyptian madrasas and the 'ulama. Other efforts at governmental control of the Azhar took place at the end of the nineteenth century and in 1911, in 1930, and especially after the Free Officers' coup of 1952. The most thoroughgoing of these reforms was that of 1961,[2] when the Azhar was placed under the control of the Ministry of Endowments and the Shaykh al-Azhar became an appointed official of the government through whom other appointments and dismissals were effectively controlled. The reforms of 1961 also made a number of secular colleges (notably those of medicine and engineering) part of the Azhar, thus radically altering the character of this institution. There was considerable opposition to each of these initiatives, but it is significant that each time the ruling elite were largely able to carry through the reform, gradually but significantly curtailing the autonomy of the Azhar's 'ulama.

Nor were the Egyptian ruling elite unique in their ability to carry out extensive reforms of such institutions. In Tunisia, for instance, the governmental attack on the preeminent Islamic institution of learning, the Zaytuna, was radical and thoroughgoing. The Tunisian Islamist Rached al-Ghannouchi describes the assault on the Zaytuna at the end of the French colonial rule in these striking terms:

> Bourguiba [who became president when Tunisia gained independence] came in as a conqueror and . . . he began striking religious institutions, the institutions which were the very life of Tunisia. At this period, everything revolved around the University of Zitouna: traditional craftsmanship, Tunisian literature, all thought. Up to a certain point, all of Tunisia was produced at Zitouna. So this brutal blow against these institutions constituted a blow at the social, economic and cultural structure of all of Tunisia.[3]

In Morocco the major institutions of traditional Islamic learning (the Qarawiyyin and the Yusufiyya) were restructured by the French in the 1930s; after independence, and especially in the 1960s, they were subjected to further reorganization, as Eickelman has shown, in order to incorporate them into Morocco's educational mainstream.[4] Asking why the "effective collapse" of traditional Islamic education in Morocco "[did] not result in any major concerted action, or reaction, on the part of men of learning,"[5] Eickelman offers a number of overlapping explanations. For one thing, he notes, the Moroccan religious elite were not directly threatened by colonial rule. The French colonial system in Morocco had tried with some success to co-opt this elite, helping them to maintain their privileges in society and thus reducing their antagonism to the changes around them.[6] Another explanation, according to Eickelman, is the religious elite's "highly restricted sense of social responsibility." "There was no expectation in Morocco that Islamic men of learning should constitute an ideological vanguard, even in times of social upheaval."[7] Yet another explanation is the continued appeal of the 'ulama to many of the more conservative segments of society—an appeal that the older 'ulama sometimes took for granted, thus not feeling the need to actively resist the changes taking place in society. It is, Eickelman suggests, not so much the waning of such appeal as the gradual disappearance of the older men of learning who can persuasively count on it that underlies the decline of traditional learning in Morocco.[8]

The consequences of imposing governmental reform have sometimes been unpredictable, as the example of Egypt illustrates in chapter 6. But so far as the project of reform itself is concerned, whether the 'ulama tried to resist it, as in Egypt, or not, as in Morocco, the ruling elite in many

Sunni Muslim states were often able to effectively and extensively exert their control over the religious institutions. The Indian subcontinent represents an important variation on this pattern, however, as I hope to demonstrate in this chapter with reference to British India and Pakistan.

The debate over madrasa reform in the South Asian context does more than illuminate a dimension of the modern history of the 'ulama, however. It is also a debate in which issues of religious authority are central. More importantly, it has provided an important basis for the emergence of new conceptions of religion. Initiatives towards reform, no less than the opposition to them, have fostered the view that religion occupies a distinct sphere in society. Such a conception of religion is distinctly modern, so far as Muslim societies are concerned. Yet it is striking that this conception is favored by many 'ulama, that is, by the very people who often deny in principle that matters religious comprise, or that they are limited to, a separate, or separable sphere of life.

Madrasa Reform: British Perceptions, Categories, Initiatives

In their effort to understand and regulate the systems of education prevalent in India, to relate them to their own ideas of how education ought to be imparted and to what end, and to reform the local systems in view of their own perceptions, British colonial officials routinely invoked what to them were familiar and often self-evident concepts and categories. These were not peculiar to colonial analyses of the educational systems in India, though we shall consider them here only with reference to education. The significance of these categories lies not only in their defining the British understanding of Muslim (and Hindu/Sanskrit) education, but also, and especially, in their subsequent influence both on the 'ulama and on initiatives by successive governments in Pakistan to reform the madrasa.

The most important of the categories that have shaped all discussion of the madrasa, as indeed of many other institutions of Indian society, is the notion of "religion." As Talal Asad has argued, developments in modern Europe and especially the impact of the Enlightenment led not merely to the subordination of religion to the state, or the confinement of the former to the sphere of "private" life, but also to "the construction of religion as a new historical object: anchored in personal experience, expressible as belief-statements, dependent on private institutions, and practiced in one's spare time. This construction of religion ensures that it is part of what is *inessential* to our common politics, economy, science, and morality."[9]

In India the British constantly encountered situations and institutions where no clear distinctions between the religious and the secular/nonreligious were made. To many, this situation was reminiscent of Europe's own medieval history, where such distinctions were frequently blurred, often to the advantage of the Church. For all the horrors that this parallel suggested, viewing India as dominated or determined by religion meant that the Indians could be seen as not only different from post-Enlightenment Europeans, but also inferior to the colonial rulers, and therefore in need of their enlightened governance and liberating reform.[10] There was, however, much ambivalence concerning whether all life was *in fact* governed by religion in India or, conversely, Indians only thought (or were made to believe by a devious religious elite) that it was. Either way, it was imperative for sound practical administration, and in the interest of reform and "improvement," to make a distinction between the religious and the nonreligious—the "personal" and the "public" or "general."

Such distinctions were commonly made in the British handling of the Muslim pious endowments (waqf),[11] and no less so in matters of education. In government schools a policy of religious neutrality was adopted, which meant excluding all formal instruction in religion from the school curriculum[12]—suggesting that religion could be confined to a definite sphere. Conversely, if "indigenous" education was perceived to be suffused with a religious ethos, then reform meant, among other things, taking education out of the religious sphere. The first Director of Public Instruction in the Punjab had little doubt about how to effect a separation of the religious and the secular. "I [have] ordered all village schools to be removed from the precincts of mosques and other buildings of a religious character," he wrote in June 1858. "Native subordinates informed me that no other buildings were available. I then ordered that the schools should be closed rather than held in such buildings. . . . I [have also] directed the disuse of all books of a religious character in the schools."[13]

The madrasas were, of course, regarded as religious institutions and for that reason, especially in the aftermath of the Mutiny of 1857, many were abolished or their existence was effectively jeopardized.[14] Yet many also continued to be administered or financially supported by the government. And familiar distinctions between religious and secular learning continued to be invoked in colonial analyses of the madrasas, as in the analysis of other educational institutions. Even in institutions defined as religious, British policy favored the patronage of what was deemed secular learning. Thus "indigenous religious schools . . . . [were] entitled to a grant from the Government . . . so long as they teach secular subjects in a satisfactory manner."[15] However reform was conceived, the distinction between the religious and the nonreligious was central to that project.[16] As we shall see, this distinction has remained a constant theme of all discussion on the reform of the madrasa; it is, however, a modern distinction, with little precedent in earlier Muslim societies.[17]

Medieval Muslim scholars often distinguished between the "traditionally transmitted" (*naqliyya, manqulat*) sciences—such as morphology and syntax, Qur'anic studies, hadith, law (fiqh), principles of jurisprudence (usul al-fiqh), and theology—and the "rational" (*'aqliyya, ma'qulat*) sciences, for example, logic, philosophy, astronomy, arithmetic, and medicine. The rational sciences too might be studied in madrasas, whereas the study of the "transmitted" or, for that matter, any other sciences was not confined only to these institutions.[18] The standing of the sciences relative to one another was frequently discussed, and many scholars were opposed to the study of such "foreign," rational sciences as Aristotelian logic and philosophy; there were also complaints that the sciences that are worth studying "for their own sake," such as Qur'an, hadith, and law, were sometimes given less attention than ancillary disciplines like morphology and syntax, which were meant only to assist in the study of the former.[19] Yet debates on madrasas as representing, and guarding, the "religious" sphere in society, on what is "purely religious" in the curriculum of the madrasa, and on religion as occupying a distinct sphere in society—discussions that have continually occupied reformers of the madrasa in the nineteenth and twentieth centuries—are eminently modern debates with little precedent in medieval Islamic societies.

Another fundamental category of colonial analysis in matters of education was the criterion of "useful" instruction. The English Utilitarians were most emphatic in invoking the notion of useful learning, though not unique in their commitment to it. Addressing the question of the allocation of funds by the East India Company for the advancement of education in India, the influential Utilitarian thinker and historian James Mill (d. 1836) had written in February 1824:

> The great end should not have been to teach Hindoo learning, or Mahomedan learning, but useful learning. . . . In professing, on the other hand, to establish Seminaries for the purpose of teaching mere Hindoo, or mere Mahomedan literature, you bound yourself to teach a great deal of what was frivolous, not a little of what was purely mischievous, and a small remainder indeed in which utility was in any way concerned.[20]

In his evidence before the Punjab Education Commission of 1884, however, G. W. Leitner—a Hungarian Orientalist and the principal of the Government College of Lahore—provided the following somewhat sarcastic illustration of education in government schools in terms of "useful learning":

> After leaving the middle school, a boy . . . knows arithmetic, Urdu and Persian, if not a little English, all of which may be said to be "useful" to him, whilst he has acquired some information regarding history, geography, and elementary science, which, also, cannot be affirmed to be "useless." He has also learnt the elements of mensuration, which is a "practical" acquirement for him, especially if he wishes to become a sub-overseer, overseer, or engineer. He has also, if he has studied English, read Cunningham's Sanitary Primer, and if he has practised the lessons contained in it, that knowledge too is "practical."[21]

Leitner notes that by the time a student completes high school, "he has more information [but] . . . is rather less suited for a 'useful' and 'practical' career, than when he passed the middle school. His distaste to all physical exertion, except to that of the pen, has grown, and he is more unwilling than before to return to his father's shop."[22]

Given constructions of "usefulness" such as James Mill's, the religious sciences studied in madrasas were scarcely useful, which meant that it was deemed inappropriate for the East India Company to support such institutions at all, or without first reforming their "inefficient" condition. But many British officials of the early nineteenth century had a different view of "useful learning." They did not of course deny the usefulness of English and the European arts and sciences, but they affirmed the value of "Oriental" learning and the need for its patronage by the British. The disagreement between the "Orientalists" and the "Anglicists" over what constituted 'useful' knowledge was settled in the 1830s in favor of the 'Anglicists';[23] the notion of useful knowledge continued, however, to define British approaches to problems of education in India and their negative perception of madrasa education. Nor was this concept of useful knowledge peculiar to India. A Society for the Diffusion of Useful Knowledge had been established in England by Lord Brougham in 1823 to reform and educate English people of the lower classes—a venture with which James Mill was also associated—and a branch was established in Calcutta in 1839.[24] The influence of this Society and its work was also seen in the Middle East, where it was mediated, in part at least, through British India.[25]

The notion of "useful knowledge" (al-'ilm al-nafi') also figures prominently in the discourses of medieval Muslim scholars, where it refers, among other things, to knowledge that assists in salvation and is consequently used to facilitate virtuous acts.[26] As an early Muslim mystic put it with some emphasis:

> The best of things is knowledge. And what is sought from knowledge is its usefulness [or benefit: naf'uhu]; so if it does not benefit you, then carrying

dates is better than carrying knowledge. The Messenger of God sought refuge from it and said: "I seek refuge in You from knowledge which is not useful"; and he said, "the best knowledge is that which is useful". Knowledge can be gained from the creatures (*min 'ind al-makhluqin*), but usefulness is not gained except from God. The usefulness of knowledge consists in obedience to God; His obedience is its usefulness. Useful knowledge is that with which you obey Him. Knowledge that is not useful is what you disobey Him with.[27]

The very activity of imparting or receiving knowledge was also frequently described in medieval texts as "useful," or as a "benefit" (*naf',* *fa'ida, mufid*).[28] The modern 'ulama's defense of madrasa education as "useful," however, even as it inverts the Utilitarian scale of priorities, is far more indebted to the Utilitarian discourse of "useful learning" than it is to the medieval vocabulary of naf', fa'ida, and al-'ilm al-nafi'. The useful learning that the colonial officials spoke of left little room for religion in general, let alone for the learning acquired in the madrasa. It was precisely in awareness of, and response to, this challenge that the 'ulama appear to have argued for the usefulness of madrasa education and, as we shall see, for religion as occupying a distinct sphere in society. But there is another sense too in which madrasa learning and the 'ulama's vocation had become "useful" in the colonial context. Now that political power had been lost and Muslim identity itself was at stake, religious education was a critical means of safeguarding that identity. To the 'ulama, the usefulness of such education could scarcely need a better justification.

British initiatives for reform were limited to those madrasas that had either been established by them, such as the Calcutta Madrasa founded by Warren Hastings in 1781, or that they financially supported. Even among the latter, however, not all madrasas were reformed, or reformed in the same measure. Colonial policies were often confused and contradictory, the more so because of the hesitation with which they were implemented,[29] and education was no exception. Though the idea of reform remained paramount, precisely how it was conceived or carried through varied at different times or in the case of different madrasas. The reform of the Madrasa-i A'zam of Madras, found in a "very inefficient condition" according to the Education Report of 1858–59, may be taken to represent one end of the spectrum:

> The amount of useful instruction imparted was extremely limited. The business of the Institution, like that of its namesake at Calcutta, was teaching the Arabic and Persian languages, and the doctrines of the Mahommedan religion. All this has been altered. An efficient Master has been placed at the head of the School; and the teachers, generally, have been replaced by more competent ones.[30]

The "namesake at Calcutta" was treated less severely, however. The Calcutta Madrasa had begun by following the Dars-i Nizami, a list of texts the study of which was already in vogue in most other madrasas of the subcontinent.[31] But only a decade after the madrasa's inception, the first of several efforts at reform was already thought necessary and, among other things, changes were introduced into the curriculum. A major reorganization was also effected in 1850, when the Madrasa was divided into two separate departments, the Arabic (or Senior) Department and the Anglo-Persian (or Junior) Department. The latter was modeled on other "Anglo-Vernacular" government schools, and was termed "a complete success" in government reports.[32] Much ambivalence continued, however, to characterize efforts to reform the former—to substitute "a more modern and rational system of instruction in the Arabic language and in the principles of Mahommedan Law for the antiquated and faulty system of the Indian Moulovies."[33] There was resistance to radical reform from the Muslims and, more decisively perhaps, from many British officials themselves. Though some saw the madrasa as not merely useless but also politically subversive,[34] government support for it continued. So also did uncertainties about reform. The "Moulovies" were occasionally reminded that the Madrasa was a "Government Institution . . . and it is the Government and not the Professors who are responsible for the nature of the education given to its Mahommedan subjects therein."[35] Yet the Calcutta Madrasa (and in particular its Arabic Department) was usually exempted from having to teach the "useful" subjects that were introduced in most of the other government madrasas of Bengal.[36]

British ambivalence on the question of reform seems to have been due primarily to two factors: lingering uncertainties—despite the success of the Anglicists against the Orientalists—about the "usefulness" of Oriental learning; and apprehensions that drastic measures of reform might provoke a hostile reaction on the part of Muslims.[37] In 1873, the government of Bengal even took the initiative (to the dismay of many, including some modernist Muslims)[38] of establishing three new madrasas, to "realise the Muslim ideals of liberal education." Lest this measure be seen as a reversion to the discredited Orientalist stance, it was emphasized that "the encouragement of the study of oriental literature for its own sake was a very subsidiary part of the plan."[39] These new institutions were, in all likelihood, "reformed" madrasas, where "useful" instruction was to be imparted together with the teaching of authoritative Islamic texts. Teaching such texts was deemed desirable, if only because it appealed to "Muslim ideals" and was worth patronizing for that reason.

British administrators were aware of the prestige that many madrasas enjoyed,[40] and they were conscious that drastic changes, even in madrasas that they had themselves established, provoked deep resentment. For all their uncertainties about the utility or efficacy of Oriental learning, more-over, British administrators saw themselves as preserving "tradition," not doing away with it.[41] In case of madrasas they established or took over and administered, "reform" usually meant adding "useful" learning to the Islamic sciences taught in the madrasas, not—as at the Madrasa-i A'zam of Madras—reforming Oriental learning right out of existence in these institutions. The extent to which this was implemented varied, which meant that, as in Bengal, a spectrum of reformed, semireformed, and unreformed government madrasas, in addition to those that the government neither recognized nor supported, existed side by side, posing a constant challenge to the energies of the government committees periodically constituted to suggest ways to reform them.[42]

Reform and the 'Ulama in British India

The texts studied at present in most madrasas of India and Pakistan comprise what is known as the 'Dars-i Nizami,' a corpus whose introduction in madrasas is attributed to the influence of Mulla Nizam al-din Muhammad (d. 1748), the founder of the Farangi Mahall family of scholars in Lucknow. Many of these texts were being taught in Indian madrasas long before Nizam al-din's time, however, and several others were added long after his death.[43] The texts themselves were, in most cases, composed between the ninth and eighteenth centuries, largely by scholars of Iranian, Central Asian, and Indian origin. The contents of the Dars-i Nizami were subject to considerable fluidity until after the middle of the nineteenth century. Only in the latter half of the nineteenth century, and, as Farhan Nizami has suggested, possibly in response to a certain measure of influence exercised by Western styles and institutions of education in British India, did the Dars-i Nizami acquire a more or less standardized form that was widely adopted as a "curriculum" by madrasas of the Indian subcontinent.[44] Madrasas have continued, however, to differ in their versions of this curriculum, which has scarcely been impervious to change even after its standardization in the late nineteenth century.

The institutional setup of the madrasas also underwent change in the late nineteenth century. Deoband—and soon madrasas everywhere in the Indian subcontinent—"emulating the British bureucratic style for educational institutions, came to have, besides a fixed curriculum, separate classes for students of different levels, a well-defined academic year, annual examinations, and networks of affiliated schools.[45] With the exception of the madrasas' new and increasing concern with the study of hadith, the texts studied in this new institutional setup have remained largely those that were part of the Dars-i Nizami in its earlier forms. The primary concern at Deoband—and most other madrasas—has always been the conservation of the classical Islamic texts and sciences as studied in madrasas, not textual innovation.[46]

Unlike Deoband, however, the movement of the Nadwat al-'Ulama', launched towards the end of the nineteenth century to bring Muslim religious scholars of various persuasions together, concerned itself from the outset, self-consciously and even ostentatiously, with the reform of the madrasa.[47] In the view of the Nadwa's founders, the revival of the Muslim community depended on infusing the ranks of the 'ulama with fresh vigor, and on broadening the scope of their activities and their role in the Muslim community. To achieve these goals, it was deemed imperative to reform the prevalent styles of learning, for the existing madrasas were seen as lacking in intellectual creativity and as equally indifferent to changes in Muslim societies and to the challenges facing them.[48] As Mawlana Muhammad 'Ali Mongiri, one of the founders of the Nadwat al-'Ulama', emphasized at the annual session of 1896, the Nadwa's proposed curriculum sought to produce religious scholars capable of providing guidance and leadership to the community in a wide range of spheres: in law and theology, in *adab* (belles lettres), in philosophy, and in "matters of the world."[49] As part of the initiative to unite the 'ulama, it was proposed to have all the existing madrasas adopt the curriculum that the Nadwa promised to devise. It was not long before it became clear, however, that not many among the 'ulama were willing to merge their differences into a common curriculum or to accept the Nadwa's reformers as arbiters of their differences.[50] Consequently, the founders of the Nadwa established a new madrasa (the Dar al-'Ulum) of their own, where at least, if nowhere else, they could hope to experiment with their reforms.

Those associated with the Nadwa have frequently complained of a duality in the system of education in South Asia "between the old and the new, the religious and the secular," a duality they trace to colonial rule in India.[51] Yet even as they lamented this compartmentalization and pledged, in striving for a new curriculum, to do away with it, the Nadwa's founders often spoke and wrote in terms that presupposed precisely the same distinctions. Religion or matters religious continued to be defined as a distinct sphere, albeit one that was assigned the first importance. The early leaders of the Nadwa were also keen to allay all British suspicions about this institution by insisting on its strictly apolitical character. This entailed presenting the Nadwa as an exclusively 'religious' forum. It also meant laying claim to exclusive representation of the Muslim community in all matters religious. As Mawlana Shibli Nu'mani (d. 1914), a major Muslim intellectual who was prominent among the leaders of this movement, suggested at the annual session of 1912, the Nadwa ought to become the voice of the entire nation *in religion*, at a par with the All-India Muslim

League, which sought recognition as the representative of the Muslims' political interests.[52] Abu'l-Hasan 'Ali Nadwi (d. 1999) has likewise noted that the basis of the movement that culminated in the establishment of the Nadwat al-'Ulama' was "purely religious," unlike that of many other, contemporary reformist movements.[53]

In discussing the establishment of a new madrasa under the aegis of the Nadwa, Shibli Nu'mani lamented that "there is not even one *purely religious madrasa* in the whole of India, no institution worthy of being considered the 'great madrasa' in terms of its all embracing concern [with the religious sciences] and its grandeur."[54] The implication here seems to be that the existing madrasas were spending far more time teaching the "ancillary sciences" like morphology and syntax, or the "rational sciences" like logic and philosophy, rather than the "purely religious sciences," such as hadith, law and legal theory, and the Qur'an and its exegesis. The madrasa of Deoband and its affiliates had tried to redress this perceived imbalance by emphasizing the study of hadith in its curriculum, but the Nadwa wanted to go further. Striking here is the sense, which the 'ulama of the Nadwa had possibly imbibed from colonial analyses of educational and other institutions, that religion was a distinct sphere of life. They denied that religion was a "private" matter, divorced from "public" life, yet they had little trouble speaking of a "purely religious" institution, and of the "religious" sphere as clearly distinguishable from all others.

Paradoxically, however, the founders of the Nadwa also attacked the madrasas from another perspective that is quite incompatible with the one just outlined. The existing madrasas were out of touch with the world in which they existed, it was said; hence they were incapable of providing leadership to the community. "A major reason for the decline in the 'ulama's influence in the country," Muhammad 'Ali Mongiri wrote, "is the popular perception that they have withdrawn into their cells and know nothing about the state of the world, so that in worldly matters their guidance is entirely unworthy of attention."[55] In this view, even if the madrasas were academically sound—which they were deemed not to be— and even if they were "purely religious" institutions, they would still not be fulfilling what was required of them. In fact, to be "purely religious" was precisely what a madrasa ought not to be if it was to meet modern challenges to Islam. In its initial years, therefore, the Nadwa sought to bridge medieval and modern disciplines—a goal whose implications bitterly divided the leaders of this movement and, as it turned out, was never to be achieved.[56]

The ambivalence in the Nadwa's goals points, among other things, towards an inability to arrive at an acceptable definition of "religion" and of the means to "reform" it.[57] At issue in the enterprise of devising a new curriculum was nothing short of determining what an "Islamic educa-tion"—and, by extension, "Islam" itself—signified, how to teach it, and how to make that education "useful" to the Muslim community.

As in the reports and recommendations of British policy makers on education, there was much in the Nadwa's reformist rhetoric on "useful" education.[58] The reformers of the Nadwa did not all mean the same thing by "useful" education, though all agreed on its ultimate goal of creating a new generation of 'ulama fit to lead the Muslim community. Other attri-butes of a useful education, as enunciated by the Nadwa's leaders, are also worth noting. Learning to write and converse in the Arabic language, which was said to be beyond the abilities of most graduates of the Indian madrasas, was another accomplishment the Nadwa sought. Graduates of its curriculum were to be not only aware of modern challenges to Islam, but also able to defend Islam against them and to actively engage in prose-lytization. An intimate knowledge of Arabic was to assist them in these purposes as well as in establishing a rapport with scholars elsewhere in the Muslim world; the Arabic language would also serve as the basis of the study of literature (adab), a subject "the neglect of which was tanta-mount to neglecting the religious sciences."[59] Much emphasis was laid, too, on "moral" instruction, of which the study of certain classical Sufi texts was to be a medium.[60] Finally, there was recognition that some prac-tical skills ought to be imparted to students so that they would be able to earn a respectable living.[61]

In general, not just the notion of useful education but also the idea of what such usefulness consists in show the influence of colonial analyses—and perhaps also the desire to make the Nadwa's education *look* useful to colonial authorities. The emphasis on "moral" instruction, which British officials thought was lacking in Indian systems of education;[62] on litera-ture, which in government schools had come to substitute for formal in-struction in religion;[63] on practical skills; on fostering a generation of 'ulama who would be more in touch with and hence, according to British notions, more "representative" of the people;[64] on bridging medieval and modern education; and, not least, on an intimate knowledge of Arabic, which to many colonial officials was a "classical language of India" and hence a mark of cultural authenticity, are all interpretable as responses to ideas much in vogue in late-nineteenth-century British India.

The existing madrasas had served as the foil against which the Nad-wa's goals were defined. But there was serious disagreement over the extent to which it was appropriate to break with those madrasas' prevail-ing intellectual styles. To have many a religious scholar agree that the choice of texts and subjects needed revision was one thing; to have a consensus on precisely what changes were to be brought about and how was quite another. That the 'ulama would agree to substitute the books that they had studied for long and from whose mastery they derived their religious authority proved to be an unrealistic expectation.[65] (The authority of many of these works had, if anything, only increased in colonial India, as we saw in chapter 1.) The Nadwa had initially aspired to have a reformed curriculum introduced in *all* the madrasas; but even in its own Dar al-'Ulum, a century after the movement of the Nadwat al-'Ulama' began, change has only been partial and it has been controversial. Aristotelian logic and philosophy came to be given much less importance than they were in other madrasas; and scriptural exegesis, hadith, history, and Arabic literature are prominent in the curriculum.[66] Yet key texts in law and legal theory, theology, and even logic and philosophy (which had especially been the object of criticism by the Nadwa's founders)[67] have remained substantially the same as those in other madrasas.[68] In general, the Nadwa's curriculum has continued to be very much under the shadow of the Dars-i Nizami. Contrary to the rhetoric of some of the Nadwa's founders, even the teaching of English and the question of the students' exposure to Western learning have also remained thorny and divisive issues.

The Nadwat al-'Ulama's reformism points to fissures within the ranks of the 'ulama. But more importantly, the gradual loss of this reformist zeal underlines just how important it has been for the 'ulama to hew closely to what they take to be their tradition, rather than to be seen as departing from it. Those associated with the Nadwa had wanted to unite the 'ulama on a new platform and themselves to become the voice of this united "community of scholars." But they wanted to do so by *distancing* the madrasas from some of their traditional practices. For instance, they deemed the study of commentaries, instead of the "original" works of the "ancients" on which these commentaries were based, to be detrimental to creative thinking; and they sought to replace many madrasa texts with other, more "useful" ones. The Dars-i Nizami curriculum, which the Nadwa's moving spirits had wanted to reform, was itself an evolving entity, of course, and this no doubt gave some justification to their reformist project. Even so, the texts that comprised this curriculum were centuries-old. The idea that reform would mean dispensing not only with many of these texts but also with the discursive practices associated with them was disquieting, and it did not sit well with the other 'ulama.

Some years before the founding of the Nadwa, Shibli Nu'mani had undertaken a journey to Constantinople, Egypt, and Syria, during which he had keenly observed the cultural and especially the educational life of the people in these lands. He was a firm advocate of madrasa reform, as his active association with the Nadwat al-'Ulama' shows. But what he had seen at madrasas in Constantinople and at the Azhar in 1892 had not impressed him at all. In fact, he had become convinced that Indian madrasa education, even under colonial rule, was far superior to that found in the Middle East. On madrasa education in Constantinople, he commented:

> What constantly spoiled all my happiness during these travels was the degra-dation of this education. This issue is also being much discussed in India at present, and the decline of traditional education (ta'lim-i qadim) is often lamented. But my regret is of a different sort. For when those educated in the modern systems lament the decline of traditional education, they are not re-ally lamenting but rather only ridiculing and condemning it. Although I like the new education, and like it with all my heart, I am also a strong supporter of traditional education. I believe traditional learning is absolutely essential for the preservation of Muslim nationhood (qawmiyyat). But to see the use-less and meaningless way in which this education is imparted is deeply dis-tressing. In India, I could console myself with the thought that this sorry state is only natural where governmental protection and patronage are lacking; but to see this condition in Constantinople, Syria, and Egypt was extremely painful.[69]

To other 'ulama, however, the sort of reform that Shibli and the Nadwa advocated threatened to divest the madrasa of its identity—which was the more critical to preserve in the interest of the Muslim community's collective identity, as Shibli himself believed. From the beginning, there was pressure on the Nadwa's Dar al-'Ulum to draw close to the other 'ulama if its graduates were to be recognized *as 'ulama*. If being one of the 'ulama meant that one was reared on certain texts, then to deny the authority of those texts or to replace them with others, as was partially attempted at the Nadwa, was to be marginalized in the structures of au-thority sustained by reverence for such texts. During the nearly one hun-dred years of the school's existence, scholars of the Nadwa have often looked for alternate sources of influence: the Tablighi Jama'at, a respected proselytizing movement with a worldwide network; Sufism; and, perhaps most distinctively, recognition in the Arab world. But they have also suc-ceeded remarkably well in minimizing their differences with the other 'ulama and so to become (and thus to be recognized as) one of them. And, as I discuss in chapter 6, there is no better illustration of this than the career of Abu'l-Hasan 'Ali Nadwi, who served for many years on Deo-band's board of directors, and was, at the time of his death in 1999, the most widely respected of the Indian 'ulama.

The Nadwat al-'Ulama's rhetoric regarding the need to reform the ma-drasa curriculum has no parallel among nongovernmental reformist ini-tiatives in British India. Yet the question of madrasa reform has continued to be much discussed in both post-independence India and Pakistan and in terms not dissimilar to those familiar in British India. Governmental initiatives at reform, typically backed by monetary inducements and the promise of official recognition leading to further education and government employment, are often fiercely resisted by the 'ulama; and madrasas continue to be ranged, in fact if not always officially, on a spectrum comprising the reformed, the semireformed, and the unreformed.

The stakes for keeping the madrasas "unchanged" would seem to be much higher in India than in Pakistan. In a Hindu-dominated state whose secular credentials were questioned by many Muslims long before the political prominence of Hindu nationalism, madrasas are seen by many Muslims as a guarantee of the preservation of their religious and cultural identity. It is in madrasas, and often nowhere else, that their children can hope to learn the Urdu language, whereas the modern schools are seen by many as threatening, not only because they expose children to Western learning but also because of the "objectionable" Hindu, and anti-Muslim, content of many textbooks taught in them. And, in any case, lower-class Muslims are often too impoverished to keep their sons at school and need to have them assist in their trade or craft.[70]

Conversely, as we will see in chapter 4, Pakistan's successive constitutions have assigned Islam a prominent place in public life, and many among the 'ulama have remained active in the effort to define an Islamic identity for Pakistan. Yet in Pakistan as well, the 'ulama's vision of how an Islamic identity is best preserved is closely tied to the institution of the madrasa. Much of the discussion on the madrasa in Pakistan has revolved around government initiatives towards madrasa reform, and it is these initiatives and the reactions to them that I now propose to discuss.

Madrasa Reform in Pakistan

Pakistan did not inherit most of the better-known madrasas that had been active in the colonial period—and many of which have continued in existence in post-independence India. One notable exception was the Calcutta Madrasa, which, as its historian says, "migrated" to Dhaka at the time of the partition.[71] Significantly, this "migration" was also a partition for the Madrasa itself along lines in keeping with familiar categories of colonial analysis. Thus it was decided in August 1947 that of the two departments that comprised the Madrasa, the Anglo-Persian department, which had borne the brunt of government reforms and experiments in "usefulness," would stay in Calcutta, while the Arabic department, concerned more directly with the medieval Islamic sciences, would move to Dhaka in what was to become East Pakistan (now Bangladesh).[72] It was thought fitting perhaps that only the "purely religious" side of the Madrasa ought to become part of a state established in pursuit of the Muslim community's Islamic aspirations.

The subsequent history of the Calcutta Madrasa does not occupy us here. While other prominent madrasas of British India did not "migrate" to Pakistan, religious scholars associated with many of them did; together with scholars native to the areas that comprised Pakistan, they came to play a considerable role in the religious and political life of the newly established state, fostering, *inter alia*, the growth of many new madrasas. The modern school system has everywhere come to dominate education, yet the madrasas have not only survived but shown a quite remarkable growth during the more than half-century of Pakistan's existence.

Of the various government efforts to reform and regulate the affairs of madrasas,[73] I focus on two here. The first dates to the early 1960s and the second to the late 1970s. Before examining these efforts, however, a third major initiative, launched in 2000 by the military government of General Pervez Musharraf (1999–), ought to be mentioned. This initiative—still underway as this book went to press—preceded the U.S.-led global War on Terrorism in the aftermath of the September 11, 2001 terrorist attacks in New York and Washington, D.C. (see chapter 5), but it has become especially urgent and energetic in the context of these attacks.[74] There already are indications that the rhetoric accompanying this latest government venture in madrasa reform will continue, in many ways, to echo motifs and themes we shall encounter in the following discussion of the earlier efforts at regulation. The precise contours and scope, let alone the outcome, of the current initiative are far from clear, however, and any judgement about its significance seems premature.[75] I therefore leave it aside here, to focus on the two major initiatives that preceded it.

In both the early 1960s and the late 1970s, reports comprising recommendations on madrasa reform were produced by committees that included some prominent religious scholars, though bureaucratic officials outnumbered the 'ulama in the first committee and were marginally fewer than the 'ulama in the second; neither committee was headed by a religious scholar.[76] Some of the major issues with which policy makers and reform committees had grappled in British India continued to be prominent in both reports, while certain other themes were conspicuously new. Of the latter, the single most important theme—a refrain throughout these two reports—is the assurance of Pakistan's continuing commitment to Islam. As the *Report* of 1962 puts it, "No doubt it was Islam which gave birth to Pakistan and more than anything else it is Islam which will guarantee its future greatness. The importance of religious education is therefore obvious in a country like Pakistan."[77]

Yet a nagging uncertainty about precisely what religious education means, or worse still, what is religious in the education imparted in madrasas, continues to persist. The *Report* of 1962 explains that it refers to religious learning (Deeni Uloom [*sic*]) and nonreligious learning (Duniavi [literally: worldly] Uloom [*sic*]) "only as convenient expressions and not . . . to convey the impression that Duniavi Uloom are something outside religious education." Yet repeated reference to "basic Islamic studies," "strictly religious subjects," and to the need to expunge "unnecessary nonreligious subjects from the existing syllabus" suggest just the opposite: that is, the positing of a basic dichotomy of the religious and the secular, not just in society but in the madrasa itself.[78] In the *Report* of 1962, "reform" seems to mean primarily two things: to restore the purity of religious learning to the madrasa by eliminating all that is perceived as unnecessary, nonreligious, or both; and, at the same time, to introduce "essential non-religious disciplines comprising modern knowledge"[79] into its curriculum. The latter is of course the "useful" instruction that colonial initiatives at reform so assiduously sought. The *Report* does not do away with the dichotomy between the religious and the nonreligious, but rather reinforces it. The sphere of the nonreligious stays intact in the madrasa, with the only (though for the reformers, fundamental) difference that "essential" nonreligious disciplines are to occupy the space that is to be vacated by the "unnecessary" nonreligious ones.

The *Report* of 1962 does not deny that the religious disciplines are "useful," but only that everything usually taught in the madrasa is "religious." Logic and philosophy are subjects of particular emphasis in the Dars-i Nizami curriculum of the madrasas. In the past, these disciplines were considered crucial to the study of legal theory and jurisprudence (usul al-fiqh) and of theology (*'ilm al-kalam*);[80] and expertise in them helped make many of the other disciplines accessible, for madrasa texts even on morphology and syntax, rhetoric and disputation, often presume an intimate acquaintance with logic. The *Report* of 1962 recommends, however, that logic and philosophy be "drastically cut down," for "frankly speaking these are not essential in achieving the objective of religious education."[81] That objective apparently consists in making ordinary people, who are "generally religious-minded, though they have very little knowledge of Shari'ah," better acquainted with Islam.[82] But inculcating "true religious values" presupposes that those charged with the task are themselves possessed of it, and that, in turn, requires that religious learning must be based only on "undisputed sources of knowledge." For the latter alone would assure both the usefulness of the madrasa's learning and the fact that it will indeed be properly religious.

Medieval Arabic "rational sciences" are, in short, deemed to deserve less attention than they have received in the past, while Qur'anic studies, hadith, and early Islamic history are deemed to require greater emphasis.[83] Other implications of exercising this criterion of "undisputed sources" are not stated. But given that much of what is taught in the madrasa is considered to be *not* based on such sources, it can hardly escape notice that in purifying the sphere of religious learning, the recommendations of the *Report* also restrict that sphere; and to the extent that this is so, the sphere of modern knowledge is enlarged in the madrasa. In general, the *Report* reveals with admirable clarity how the modernists and the 'ulama differ in their attitude towards the medieval intellectual and religious tradition and, ultimately, in their view of what defines whether something is religious or not. Whatever does not appear directly to derive from the foundational texts, the "undisputed sources," is to the former not religious at all. To the 'ulama, on the other hand, the Islamic tradition means not just those sources, but a broad spectrum of texts, techniques, and sciences that collectively and, in their evolution, cumulatively comprise the heritage with reference to which the 'ulama define themselves. A reified essentialism is often far more in evidence in modernist reformism than it is in the discourses of the 'ulama.

The concern to precisely define and thereby delimit the sphere of the religious accords with the strong distrust of the religious elite characteristic of the Ayub Khan era during which the *Report* of 1962 was produced. That concern is much less in evidence in the *Report* of 1979. The latter is a part of the campaign of "Islamization" launched by General Muhammad Zia al-Haqq early in his eleven-year rule (1977–88). Courting the support of the religious scholars was a major concern of Zia ul-Haqq's policy, and the *Report* of 1979, produced by a committee he had appointed to review the state of the madrasas and suggest reforms regarding their functioning, leaves little doubt about the regime's efforts to co-opt the 'ulama. The *Report* credits the madrasas with preserving Muslim identity in British India,[84] and goes on to describe their position in Pakistan as that of "an anchor which holds the entire society together."[85] Yet, no less than earlier governments, Zia al-Haqq's regime sought to bring madrasas under government supervision, even as it paradoxically disclaimed any intention to "interfere" in their affairs. It was not without reason that many sceptics saw some incongruity between the government's initiatives to reform madrasas and, especially, to integrate them into the mainstream of education,[86] and its disclaimers about involvement in the madrasas' own matters.

The rhetoric justifying the integration of the madrasa into the educational mainstream—a major concern of the *Report*s of 1962 and 1979, as indeed it was of the reform committees in British India—has had many expressions, but it is perhaps best illustrated with reference to the *Report* of 1962. In terms with which the 'ulama could have had little quarrel, the *Report* of 1962 begins by characterizing Islam as an all-encompassing religion, which it takes to mean that religious education ought to "cover

all aspects of human life."[87] Such a conception of Islam seems to contrast
sharply with the effort to define and restrict the sphere of religion, which
we noticed earlier. But the contrast is apparent only. That Islam regulates
all aspects of life, this-worldly as well as otherworldly, only supports the
case for the reform of the madrasas: for reform alone would enable the
ʿulama to better participate in modern life, to play an active role in matters
of the world, as Islam itself enjoins upon them. The ʿulama should not,
moreover, have anything against the introduction of the modern sciences
in madrasas, since Islam recognizes no distinction between the religious
and the nonreligious. But precisely because the latter is the case, not only
should the modern disciplines be made part of the madrasa education,
but (a point only implied) the madrasa should itself be integrated into the
general system of education.

Neither the *Report* of 1962 nor that of 1979 actually says that madrasas should therefore cease to exist, but both do recommend that religious education be somehow brought within, and be regulated by concerns similar to those of, the general stream of state-sponsored education.
Whether the sphere of religion is so delimited as to create greater space
for the modern disciplines, or conversely, is so extended as to become
indistinguishable from other areas of life, the independence of the madrasa and the authority of its ʿulama seem to be called into question or,
at least, to be reshaped in ways that are not of the ʿulama's choosing.
Even the *Report* of 1979, which offered the ʿulama many perquisites (financial aid to madrasas, scholarships and various other amenities to students, government recognition of the degrees awarded by madrasas and
hence the prospect of government employment) should they consent to
the reform of their madrasas and was generally more favorable to them
than any government initiative before or since, was nevertheless a challenge to their autonomy.

Reform and Religious Authority

Though few ʿulama have failed to perceive the challenge to their autonomy, few were as strident in their response as Mawlana Muhammad
Yusuf Ludhianawi (d. 2000) in his detailed critique of the *Report* of 1979.
Though the ʿulama of different sectarian orientations (and even of the
same orientation) sometimes differ in their criticism of the governmental
initiatives, I confine myself here to some aspects of the Deobandi critique.
On the other hand, the following is not limited to works written specifically as rejoinders to the reports of the reform committees; this discussion
also considers some of the other views expressed in defense of the madrasa

but without the immediate provocation of any impending government-sponsored reform.

Taking it as a given that the system of education established in India by the British was meant to undermine Muslim identity and culture, and that it remains largely intact in Pakistan, Ludhianawi argued that to integrate madrasas into this educational system could only mean destroying Islam itself: the government of an Islamic state would thereby achieve what the British never could![88] The madrasas are the "defenders of the religious sciences" in society, he said; their integration with the state-sponsored system of education would signify nothing but to "prevent them from their *purely religious services* and to subordinate them to [literally: make them the servants of] the modern [Western] sciences."[89] Though in other contexts what we might characterize as Islam's "worldliness"—encompassing life in all its fullness—is a major theme in the 'ulama's religious discourse, it becomes necessary to deemphasize this 'worldliness' in the face of the madrasa's reform. In Ludhianawi's view, the madrasas guarantee the preservation of religion in society. That is, there is a separate and independent sphere of religion to be so preserved; and only the independence of the madrasas can assure its continued existence.

Ludhianawi's critique of the *Report* of 1979 makes explicit an issue that is central to all discussion of madrasa reform: the question of religious authority. Any attempt at reform that is perceived to threaten the identity and the authority of the 'ulama is by definition suspect. The *Report* of 1979 had attempted to devise a curriculum that would be acceptable equally to all sectarian affiliations—to the Deobandis, Barelawis, and Ahl-i Hadith among the Sunnis, as well as to the Shi'a; the establishment of a national board of madrasas was also visualized, and all sects were to have equal representation on it. But if the authority of a religious scholar is based, in part at least, on his sectarian identity and on his ability to appeal to (and foster) that identity in his audience, then a "mixed" or hybrid (*makhlut*) curriculum can scarcely be acceptable. Further, as Ludhianawi put it, any "equality" between the sects is conceivable only "in the purely worldly sphere; but no convergence is possible from the point of view of religion."[90]

The *Report*'s insistence that madrasas open themselves to the modern sciences and, more generally, that religious education be integrated into the educational mainstream, was likewise unacceptable, but not only because the latter is a legacy of the British and therefore detrimental to Islam. For a "mixed" curriculum, with something from both the religious and the modern sciences, will not produce men who "combine the medieval and the modern. . . . [Rather], the products of such a system would be useless equally for religion and the world."[91] What the reform seeks to create is not 'ulama, Ludhianawi concluded, but "only loyal government servants."[92]

That government reform diminished a madrasa's standing in society had already been clearly recognized in British India. Though "reformed" madrasas of British Bengal had the privilege of government recognition, which meant that they might receive financial support and that their graduates were eligible for government service as well as for admission to government educational institutions, they were seen, even by the official reforming committees, to lack the prestige or authority that the "unreformed," nongovernment madrasas enjoyed. Thus even as the Harley Committee of 1915 had insisted, for instance, that only by being reformed could madrasas "play their part in the various activities which go to make up the public life of India," it had also recommended that the Calcutta Madrasa "be reserved for studies *on the orthodox lines* . . . [and] the kind of teaching which made the madrasahs in Upper India centres of Islamic learning for the whole of India."[93]

In British India, it may not have taken much imagination for the 'ulama to see government initiatives to reform madrasas as a conspiracy to undermine Islam and do away with the 'ulama. In post-independence India, likewise, government-sponsored efforts to reform the madrasas are often seen, and resisted, as threats to a beleaguered Muslim community and its identity.[94] And as Ludhianawi's criticism of the *Report* of 1979 shows, similar suspicions have continued to be expressed in Pakistan as well.[95] He had no doubt that the content of the proposed reform subverted the purpose of the madrasa and the position of the 'ulama, and he is not alone in such suspicions. The 'ulama have often defended their madrasas by pointing to the prestige, influence, and authority of some of the most distinguished religious scholars educated in them. If madrasas can produce such scholars, then, the argument goes, there can hardly be anything wrong with their system of education; and those who insist on changes in the curriculum can have no purpose but to undermine the madrasa, to prevent the role this institution has historically played in the life of Muslims.

The justification for reform offered by government committees is thus turned on its head: it is not by undergoing reform but rather by resisting it that madrasas can continue to play the role they have in Muslim societies of the past.[96] That reform can and does connote a variety of things in modern Muslim societies comes out strongly here. Many religious scholars, as well as madrasas like Deoband, are "reformist" in the sense of seeking change in existing styles of religious belief and practice. It can be argued, in fact, that their claim to religious authority is rooted, in part at least, on their reformist credentials. But reform in this context does not mean striking out on a new, uncharted path; rather, it signifies changes that would bring religious doctrine and practice, as interpreted by these reformers, into conformity with whatever is conceived of as "true" or "original" Islam—the Islam of the pious forbears. Reform in the sense of actively integrating "modern" with "classical" knowledge is suspect to many, however, for it is perceived as undermining the unity and integrity of madrasa education and as devaluing the credentials of those trained in it. Such sentiment is of course not peculiar to the Indian subcontinent. Shaykh 'Abd al-Rahman al-Shirbini, the rector (1905–9) of Egypt's al-Azhar, had argued, for instance, that that institution had been established "for nothing but the preservance and propagation of *religion and the religious sciences.*" He demanded of the government therefore to "leave it as it is—as a fortress of religion. . . . If reform is sought at all, then let it be limited to [better arrangements for] the health, comfort, and good food for the students. As for [modern] philosophy and the modern sciences, let the government introduce these in its own numerous colleges."[97]

Notwithstanding al-Shirbini's reticence, the Egyptian government did carry through large-scale changes in al-Azhar, as we noted at the beginning of this chapter. The 'ulama of India and Pakistan have sometimes pointed to experiments with madrasa reform in other Muslim countries as the reason why scholars of any standing have ceased to appear in those societies; conversely, madrasas of the Indian subcontinent, thanks to their having resisted reform, can still boast of many distinguished scholars.[98] In question here is not only the problem of religious authority—those reared on a hybrid (religious/nonreligious) education would not be "real" 'ulama—but also the issue of "useful" knowledge. In a book on "the syllabus and the system (*nizam*) of the madrasas," Mufti Jamil Ahmad Thanawi (d. 1995), the leading jurisconsult at the Jami'a Ashrafiyya, a prominent Deobandi madrasa of Lahore, had listed thirty "useful" purposes madrasas fulfill in society. To him, as also to Ludhianawi, useful knowledge for the madrasa is only religious knowledge, and anything less, or more, is detrimental to the madrasa's raison d'être: the maintenance of religion in society.[99]

Ideas such as those of Ludhianawi and Jamil Thanawi resonate in the writings of many others on the question of reform. There are, however, many shades of opinion among the 'ulama in this matter.[100] Mawlana Muhammad Yusuf Banuri, the founder of the Jami'at al-'Ulum al-Islamiyya of Karachi, conceded, for instance, that many of the texts studied in madrasas are sometimes "barely intelligible" without extensive commentaries and glosses. He held such texts to be "obscure" because they were written and introduced into madrasas during a period of Muslim intellectual decline in the later Middle Ages. For someone not merely reared on but actively contributing to the long tradition of studying and writing commentaries, as we saw in the previous chapter, this is a striking observation. Yet Banuri's purpose in this remark was not to subvert the madrasa's learning but ultimately to salvage it. Some of the texts conventionally used in madrasas ought to be replaced, he wrote, by *earlier* ones, which are simpler, clearer, and more authoritative. "We do not want to do away with the traditional sciences, but seek only to create greater competence in them through the introduction of better books. We do not want 'modernism' (*tajaddud*) but rather to reach further back (*taqadum*)."[101] Banuri recognizes the need for the introduction of new subjects (for example, modern philosophy, a "new scholastic theology," economics) in the madrasa too,[102] but only in tandem with the strengthening and deepening of the religious sphere.

Muhammad Taqi 'Uthmani, the vice-president of the Dar al-'Ulum madrasa of Karachi, tends to a similar conclusion, though one based on a more nuanced view of the history of madrasa education. He observes that the precolonial curriculum of the madrasa in South Asia was wide-ranging:

> This system of education encompassed Arabic linguistics, exegesis, hadith, law, theology, logic and philosophy, arithmetic, medicine, and engineering. Given that the Dars-i Nizami comprised all religious and nonreligious [literally: worldly] sciences, the Muslim students graduating from this system of education were capable of fulfilling their responsibilities in all fields of practical life. Consequently, whichever field of life one chose in accordance with one's own taste and abilities, one had all the opportunities to advance in it. . . . The basic purpose of this system of education was to enable a person to develop a mastery of his religion, to strengthen his beliefs and base his practical life on religious foundations, to be fully acquainted with demonstrative proofs for the rectitude of his belief and practice, so that foreign ideas would not deceive him. . . . Once he had completed this education, a student could fearlessly take up medicine and science, logic and philosophy, or exegesis, hadith, and law; in no case was there any fear that he would lose the right path.[103]

Taqi 'Uthmani claims that so long as the "true spirit" and ideals of the Dars-i Nizami, as outlined here, were secure, there was a willingness to adapt to change; indeed, if Western science and philosophy had come to the notice of Muslim scholars *under Muslim rule*, rather than at a time when they were confronted with the challenge of British colonialism, they would have incorporated much from these new disciplines. However, when the 'ulama perceived British colonialism as intent upon destroying their religion, they had no choice but to conserve their intellectual resources by rejecting any further changes in them.[104] Yet despite his historically informed view of the madrasa's intellectual evolution, Taqi 'Uthmani continues to speak of the madrasa as a "purely religious" institution and of the need to preserve it as such now.[105] Having become the guarantee of the preservation of religion in society, the style and substance of this education—notwithstanding even medieval doubts about the place of 'foreign' and ancillary sciences in the madrasa—ought to continue without substantial change until such time as the mainstream institutions of education are themselves "completely transformed, through revolutionary changes, into purely Islamic ones." Only then, he says, can one contemplate integrating the madrasa into the mainstream.[106]

Yet modern subjects have in fact come to be tolerated, provided the integrity of the madrasa's "purely religious" education can be preserved. Taqi 'Uthmani's own career illustrates some of the distance between the madrasa's rhetoric and its reality, though both the stridency of the rhetoric and the reality vary from one madrasa to another. Though he received all his religious education at the Dar al-'Ulum, a madrasa established in 1951 by his father, Mufti Muhammad Shafi', he also has degrees of *mawlawi fadil*—an advanced degree in Oriental studies instituted by the British in the late nineteenth century—from the Punjab University, Lahore,[107] bachelor's degrees in arts and in law from the University of Karachi, and a master's degree in Arabic from the Punjab University.[108] While the extent of his exposure to non-madrasa education is exceptional among his peers, a growing proportion of the 'ulama have in fact had some form of education in the modern schools.[109] At the level of primary school education, major madrasas now include courses from the government school system as part of their curriculum—a measure, no doubt, of the influence exerted by government reform committees;[110] and some madrasas, including Taqi 'Uthmani's Dar al-'Ulum, have modern schools, providing education along lines similar to the government schools, attached to them.[111] Even so, in contemporary Pakistani madrasas, subjects from the government school system are typically treated as a separate segment of education which students are expected to deal with as a prelude to their real vocation, the Dars-i Nizami.[112] However they are understood, "purely religious studies" occupy an exclusive space even within the madrasa. Rather than mitigating this sense of exclusivity, the presence of new elements from the government school system serves, ironically, to reinforce it.

The 'Ulama's Religious Sphere

In the epilogue to his history of the Calcutta Madrasa published in 1959, Mawlana 'Abd al-Sattar, a lecturer at the madrasa, vigorously emphasizes the importance of this institution in the preservation of Islamic learning and in the Islamization of society. But with equal vigor he also laments the declining fortunes of the madrasa, and, more generally, of religious education in all its forms. He cites several reasons for this decline, noting in particular the hostility towards madrasas on the part of those who are reared in the English system of education. It is odd, he says, that while specialization is valued in all fields of modern knowledge, madrasas are criticized—and deemed harmful for "national interests"—precisely because they train their students to specialize in the Islamic sciences. "What this means is that . . . though the preservation and welfare of our society requires farmers, blacksmiths, tailors, and clerks, it needs no religious ʿulama [*sic*]." "Times have changed," he says. "Religion (*madhhab*) no longer has any importance for the nation (*qawm*). Religion has become the pastime of the idle. In such circumstances, what use can the nation have for those who occupy themselves with the religious sciences?"[113]

At issue for ʿAbd al-Sattar is evidently not simply the madrasa and the usefulness of its learning, but the broader question of the place of religion in society. Others among the ʿulama who have written on the question of madrasa reform have likewise insisted that the debate on the madrasa is a debate on the status and future of Islam itself, for the madrasa is both the bastion of Islam and its guardian. This equation between Islam and the madrasa is not just a polemical and, doubtlessly to some, persuasive argument against reform; it is also an argument for differentiating religion from other areas of life and thereby for asserting its autonomy in society. The issue here is not the separation of religion and state, or of society and state—which, some have argued, had come about in Muslim societies from the first centuries of Islam[114]—but rather a recognition by the ʿulama themselves of greater differentiation *within* society, with religion occupying a distinct, inviolable, autonomous sphere. Inasmuch as the functional differentiation of the religious from other spheres is at the heart of secularization in modern societies,[115] the ʿulama might be said to have accepted this facet of secularization. Yet the recognition of this functional differentiation does not derive from any commitment to the idea of secularization itself, but is intended rather to serve as a means of resisting or limiting the encroachments of the modern state.

Though the ʿulama themselves have come to insist on this differentiation, none are more conscious of what it entails in terms of a certain diminution of their influence than they are. In his criticism of the *Report* of 1979, Mawlana Yusuf Ludhianawi bitterly complains, as have many others before and since, that those schooled in the English system of education—and under their influence almost everyone else—did not even count graduates of the madrasa among the educated. Ludhianawi recalled an incident when a bus conductor snubbed a madrasa student's request for a reduced bus fare but accepted a reduced fare from students of an English school, for the latter, he said, were "really students" and therefore entitled to that special concession.[116] The point of this seemingly trivial anecdote is to draw attention to the decline in the ʿulama's social standing and, from the ʿulama's perspective, in the deference accorded to religion in society.

Laments on an inexorable decline are a familiar topos in Muslim litera-ture.[117] However, as Jonathan Berkey and Michael Chamberlain have shown for medieval Cairo and Damascus, respectively, the social status of the 'ulama and the prestige accorded to religious learning were apparently quite different in medieval times from what they are in many modern Muslim societies.[118] Berkey shows, for instance, that in medieval Cairo no firm barriers existed between education and religious devotion—and between scholars and nonscholars—so far as people's interest in hadith and the religious sciences was concerned; he shows too how various (oth-erwise external) segments of society—the Mamluk military aristocracy, women, and ordinary people—could all come together to participate in sessions where hadith was heard and transmitted.[119] Though some 'ulama even then had reservations about sharing religious knowledge with all and sundry,[120] popular participation in hadith sessions was nevertheless a mark of reverence for such knowledge, and for the 'ulama, who were devoted to it. In many Muslim societies, much of the intellectual life con-tinued to be dominated by the 'ulama until the early decades of the twenti-eth century.[121] With mass higher education, the rise of new secular and religious intellectuals, and, of course, the overarching claims of the mod-ern nation-state, the situation has obviously changed for the 'ulama. It is in this new context that they seek to define religion as a distinct sphere. For all the novelty, at least for the 'ulama, of this view of Islam and its place in society, it does claim for the 'ulama the prerogative to define—if often in terms patently borrowed from colonial and postcolonial bureau-cratic analyses—not merely what constitutes 'religious' education or the usefulness of such education, but Islam itself. Underlying this claim is the 'ulama's view of themselves as "religious experts"—a significantly novel formulation on which more is said in chapter 4.

Yet if we ought to heed the 'ulama's laments about their decline, we cannot also be oblivious to the fact that the decline in question has proved less severe than they would have us believe. The total number of madrasas has grown, not diminished, in Pakistan; and despite the emergence of the new religious intellectuals, it is the 'ulama and their madrasas that primar-ily sustain the structure of religious life (for example, in supplying prayer leaders and preachers to mosques, offering religious guidance to ordinary believers, and fulfilling the Qur'anic imperative of "commanding right and forbidding wrong";[122] they also provide education to many who never make it to government schools, or drop out from them).[123] Unlike, say, in Morocco, as described by Dale Eickelman, the ranks of the madrasa-educated scholars are anything but being diminished in Pakistan.[124] And the situation may be similar in other Muslim countries as well. For in-stance, predictions about the decline of al-Azhar of Egypt[125] have proved premature. According to Malika Zeghal, the primary and secondary institutes run by the Azhar had "89,744 students at the beginning of the 1970s and more than 300,000 at the beginning of the 1980s. . . . Nearly a million students between the ages of 5 and 19 were under the charge of the Azhar at the beginning of the 1990s."[126] Such growth predates, but no doubt contributes to, the public and political roles the ʿulama came to play in many societies in the last quarter of the twentieth century.

In Egypt, the contemporary prominence of the Azhar in the public sphere is intimately, if unexpectedly, related to changes in the curriculum since the early 1960s.[127] A similar connection between madrasa reform and religiopolitical activism has, so far, been lacking in the case of Pakistan. Yet the madrasas there, too, are hardly as impervious to change as the rhetoric of many ʿulama, on the one hand, and government reform committees, on the other, seems to suggest. Whether or not those associated with the madrasas realize or admit it, the very effort to preserve Islam "unchanged" in a rapidly changing world involves considerable redefinition of what Islam means, where to locate it in society, and how best to serve its interests. For the Pakistani ʿulama, as we have seen, one way to serve such interests is to define Islam as occupying a distinct sphere in society and to equate the autonomy of this sphere and their own authority and identity with a textually embodied religious tradition. This way of conceiving Islam leads, however, to considerable tension between the claims of the religious sphere and those of another ideal also frequently invoked in the ʿulama's discourses: the Islamic state.

IV

Conceptions of the Islamic State

I N HIS 1997 WELCOMING address to the students of the Dar al-'Ulum of Karachi, Mufti Muhammad Rafi' Uthmani, the president of the madrasa, characterized this institution as a safe haven from the corruption and anarchy of the larger society, a miniature model of an Islamic society and state: "This is a secure fortress. There might be curfew imposed outside, there might be strikes and riots out there. But one doesn't even get to know about it here in the Dar al-'Ulum, until one reads in the next day's papers that there was a riot next door. God has created a small world for us here." He goes on to instruct the freshmen: "Practice living according to the sunna here and you will know the pleasure of life. . . . Everyone will have peace and comfort here, and such pleasure and happiness as the rest of the world does not know. We will then be confidently able to show everyone what an Islamic government is like. We can tell them to come and see our little model, our example of an Islamic society. So begin the new academic year with the resolve that we will establish the rule of the sunna in the Dar al-'Ulum."[1]

Even as they celebrate and defend their distinct religious sphere, many among the 'ulama of Pakistan (including Rafi' 'Uthmani) have also appealed, repeatedly and often forcefully, to the ideal of an Islamic state. Yet if this is a state that supposedly upholds and implements Islamic norms *everywhere*, then the 'ulama's distinct religious sphere must necessarily cease to exist as soon as such a state comes about. Indeed, the 'ulama often speak of their religious sphere in terms that suggest its interim character, viz., as a necessary space that must be preserved *until* the state itself becomes "truly" Islamic. To allow the state to encroach on the madrasa, the symbol of this distinct sphere, any sooner would be to allow the destruction of the only space where Islamic ideals are still preserved.[2] Such formulations barely conceal a deeper, unresolved tension, however, between the aspirations of a modern state—any modern state, including an Islamic one—and the 'ulama's emphasis on the necessity of maintaining their own authority and autonomy in it. This chapter seeks to analyze certain facets of this tension to understand what the 'ulama mean when they speak, as they often do, of an Islamic state: How do they define their own position in such a state? And how does their political thought compare with other contemporary and competing visions of the state?

The Ambiguities of the Islamic State

That relations between the ʿulama and the modernizing elite, some facets of which we have seen in chapter 3, have typically remained tense is not for any lack of the latter's professions of commitment to Islam. As intellectuals and as the ruling elite, the modernists have often continued to regard Islam as an important, even fundamental part, of their identity. Indeed, they have sometimes outdone each other in acknowledging the principle that Islam ought to play a prominent role in public life. For instance, in 1949, the modernist-dominated Constituent Assembly of Pakistan adopted with much fanfare the so-called Objectives Resolution which provided, *inter alia*, that "sovereignty over the entire universe belongs to God Almighty alone, and the authority which He has delegated to the State of Pakistan through its people for being exercised within the limits prescribed by Him is a sacred trust." The Resolution further promised that the Muslim citizens of the state "shall be enabled to order their lives in the individual and collective spheres in accord with the teaching and requirements of Islam as set out in the Holy Quran and the Sunna."[3] These are strong claims, indeed, and neither the ʿulama nor the Islamists have allowed them to be forgotten. The modernists may have intended them as little more than symbolic affirmation of the new state's Islamic identity, however, as indicated by the designation of the Ojectives Resolution as only a preamble to all three of Pakistan's successive Constitutions (1956, 1962, and 1973), not as an integral and enforceable part. As the chief justice of the Supreme Court stated in 1973, "[I]t will serve the same purpose as any other preamble serves, namely that in the case of any doubt as to the intent of the lawmaker, it may be looked at to ascertain the true intent, but it cannot control the substantive provisions [of the Constitution]."[4]

The so-called repugnancy clause in Pakistan's successive constitutions offers another instance of the strong Islamic claims of the modernist state even as it illustrates some of the ambiguities of such claims. Pakistani constitutions have provided that no law would be enacted that is "repugnant" to the Qur'an and the sunna, and that the existing laws would be brought into conformity with these foundational sources.[5] There has been less discussion on the provision itself, however, than on who ought to be entrusted with it. Echoing a provision in the Iranian Constitution of 1906, whereby a board of five leading religious scholars was to be empowered to decide whether any proposed legislation was in conformity with the shariʿa,[6] the Pakistani ʿulama had proposed a similar function for themselves in the 1950s; but the idea evoked much opposition and was soon dropped.[7] There also was considerable discussion about entrusting this function to the Supreme Court. Eventually, however, the responsibility was assigned to the Council of Islamic Ideology, a body created to guide the executive and the legislature on matters Islamic. Yet the Council was given no more than an advisory function, and even then its 'ulama members continued to be carefully counterbalanced by others who came from largely secular backgrounds.[8]

The Islamic claims of the state were set on a new footing under General Muhammad Zia al-Haqq, whose military regime (1977–88) derived legitimacy from the assertion that it existed to promote and implement a thoroughgoing program of "Islamization." The *zakat* tax was enforced; certain aspects of Islamic criminal law were put into effect; the number of 'ulama on the Council of Islamic Ideology was increased; a Federal Shari'at Court was created with appellate jurisdiction over certain cases of Islamic criminal law and the authority to hear petitions on whether particular laws were, in fact, repugnant to the Qur'an and the sunna; and, not least, the Objectives Resolution was upgraded for the first time from a preamble to an integral part of the Constitution.[9] Towards the end of his reign, Zia al-Haqq promulgated the Enforcement of Shari'ah Ordinance, 1988, which laid down that the shari'a would be "the supreme source of law in Pakistan and the Grundnorm for guidance of policy-making by the state." Questions about the repugnancy of particular laws to the shari'a were to be referred by the courts to the Federal Shari'at Court. Yet these measures served, perhaps more than anything else, to highlight where the real locus of authority lay—even in determining the contours and scope of the Islamization project—and to underscore the ambiguities and constraints of the public rhetoric on Islam. Most strikingly, perhaps, the very ordinance that professed to make the shari'a the "supreme law of Pakistan" also expressly removed large and important areas of the law from the jurisdiction of the Shari'at Court: "[I]f the question relates to Muslim personal law, any fiscal law or any law relating to the levy and collection of taxes and fees or banking or insurance practice and procedure, the Court shall refer the question to the High Court which shall decide the question within sixty days."[10] The final authority to determine questions of repugnance to the shari'a was thus vested not in the Shari'at Court, which was itself dominated by Western-trained modernist judges, but in the high courts, which were even more distant from the 'ulama. Constitutional and legal developments in the 1990s illustrate further some of the ambiguities of the state's Islamic rhetoric; I review these briefly here before examining the 'ulama's conception of an Islamic state.

General Zia al-Haqq was killed in a plane crash in August 1988. The government of Benazir Bhutto, which succeeded him, had little taste for his Islamization policies. Its keenness to distance itself from those policies, while striving not to confirm the prime minister's popular image as highly

Westernized and unfavorably disposed to any significant role for Islam in public life, required a difficult balancing act that in the end was performed less than adroitly. The new government allowed Zia al-Haqq's Shari'ah Ordinance to lapse before it could be passed into law by the popularly elected and more powerful lower house of parliament, the National Assembly. But the upper house, the Senate, was controlled at this time by the opposition Islamic Democratic Alliance (Islami Jumhuri Ittihad), and, in an effort to embarrass the government, it passed, in May 1990, a "shari'a bill" of its own. But before this bill, which was broadly similar to Zia al-Haqq's lapsed ordinance, could be debated in the National Assembly, the government itself was dismissed by the president on charges of widespread corruption. The next government was headed by Nawaz Sharif, a protégé of Zia al-Haqq and the leader of the Pakistan Muslim League, which, in alliance with other parties comprising the Islami Jumhuri Ittihad, had defeated Benazir Bhutto in the elections. Though far from being dominated by the 'ulama, this alliance did have the support of many 'ulama organizations, and it had campaigned against Bhutto's People's Party for, among other things, the latter's alleged lack of Islamic commitment. Another shari'a bill was promptly introduced in the lower house to signal that commitment, and after a rapid passage through both houses the Enforcement of Shari'ah Act was put into effect in May 1991. Yet, as Charles Kennedy observes, for all the rhetoric about this act being "one of the most important events in Islamic history," it was intended more for political effect than to bring about any real change in the political or legal system of the country. Tellingly, the jurisdiction of the Federal Shari'at Court was neither expanded nor clarified in relation to that of the higher courts; it was the latter, not the 'ulama, who would still interpret issues of conformity or repugnance to the shari'a, and they were expected to do so in ways not different from earlier practice.[11]

Nawaz Sharif's first government was dismissed by the president in 1993, and was followed by another government under Benazir Bhutto, which in turn was dismissed by the president in 1996. During his second term in office (1997–99) Nawaz Sharif returned to the promise of implementing the shari'a more forcefully than before. The Enforcement of Shari'ah Act of 1991 may, in the view of his supporters, have been an event of historic proportions, but even that was not enough. The government, which enjoyed the largest majority in Pakistan's checkered parliamentary history, now proposed a constitutional amendment (the fifteenth amendment) to the Constitution of 1973. As introduced in the lower house of parliament in August 1998, this proposed amendment reaffirmed the sovereignty of God, the function of the state to "enable" its Muslim citizens to live according to the principles of the Qur'an and the sunna, and the Islamic injunction of establishing "a social order based on Islamic values." It went on to propose adding the following article—2B—to the Constitution:

2B . . . [1] The Holy Quran and Sunnah of the Holy Prophet (peace be upon him) shall be the supreme law of Pakistan. . . .

[2] The Federal Government shall be under an obligation to take steps to enforce the Shariah, to establish salat [ritual prayer],[12] to administer zakat [alms tax], to promote amr bil ma'roof and nahi anil munkar (to prescribe what is right and to forbid what is wrong), to eradicate corruption at all levels and to provide substantial socio-economic justice, in accordance with the principles of Islam, as laid down in the Holy Quran and Sunnah.

[3] The Federal Government may issue directives for the implementation of the provisions set out in clauses [1] and [2] and may take the necessary action against any state functionary for non-compliance of the said directives.

[5] The provisions of this Article shall have effect notwithstanding anything contained in the Constitution, any law or judgement of any Court.

According to article 239 of the 1973 constitution, any proposed amendment had to be approved by a two-thirds majority in both houses of parliament. The amendment proposed by the Nawaz Sharif government sought to also change that procedure. It was now proposed (article 239, 3A-D) that "for the removal of any impediment in the enforcement of any matter relating to the Shariah and the implementation of the injunctions of Islam" future constitutional amendments only needed a simple majority in both houses or, failing that, a simple majority of the members voting in a joint session of the parliament.[13] The proposed amendment to the procedure for bringing about future amendments was bitterly contested by opposition parties, indeed by many within the ruling party itself, and the revised bill did not contain this provision. This revised bill was passed by the lower house in October 1998.[14] The government did not, however, have the necessary two-thirds majority in the upper house. The prime minister campaigned vigorously for the passage of the bill and called upon the 'ulama, among others, to help silence all its opponents. But the Senate never voted on it, and Nawaz Sharif's second government ended—again prematurely—with a military coup in October 1999.

The Islamizing initiatives of Zia al-Haqq and Nawaz Sharif gave unprecedented salience to the position of Islam in public life and in the national discourse. Yet these governments were no less dominated by the modernizing, Western-educated elite than any other regimes in Pakistani history. Unlike other governments, they strove hard to cultivate the 'ulama's favor. But ultimately the state remained suspicious of the 'ulama, as indeed did they of it. Whether it was the Council of Islamic Ideology or the Federal Shari'at Court or the collection and disbursement of zakat or decisions about which Islamic laws would be given effect and how, it was the modernists, not the 'ulama, who controlled the instruments of Islamization. And they made little secret of what they thought of the 'ulama with whom they were supposed to be working. For instance, here is how the former chief justice of the Federal Shariat Court, the hallmark of Zia al-Haqq's Islamization, characterized the 'ulama's view of the world:

> [T]he bipolarity between religion and the rational sciences is the creation of those who conform to *taqlid* and consequently hate progress, advancement, modernism. . . . In this there is a selfish strain too. [They believe that] what they do not know and do not understand ought to be reproved and censured, because they crave for nothing but to establish their own superiority over all others and to reign supreme over them. Their supremacy cult and the insatiable lust for power for which, like all the priestly class [*sic*] in history, they have been accused [*sic*] for centuries, is compulsive enough for condemning and sometimes subjecting to Fatwas of heresy, men who are proficient in other fields of learning.[15]

Nawaz Sharif's aborted fifteenth amendment had sought to strengthen the power of the executive branch of the federal government, against the provinces and against the judiciary, much more than it had sought to strengthen the power of the 'ulama. The original draft of the amendment, as cited earlier, had proposed enabling the government to carry through constitutional amendments like any other law, with a simple majority, as long as it could be shown that the interest of the shari'a was being served. Likewise, the government could "take the necessary action against any state functionary" for failure to comply with its directives in matters relating to the shari'a. Both proposals were dropped in the revised text of the proposed amendment, but not before critics had vociferously opposed the attempted centralization of power in the hands of the federal government, and especially in the person of the prime minister. It was not the courts, let alone the 'ulama, but the executive branch itself that was to be the final arbiter of what the shari'a required and how to serve its interests. Besides enhancing its own power, the government was suspected of trying, through the renewed focus on the implementation of the shari'a, to draw attention away from a faltering economy, on which international economic sanctions after Pakistan's nuclear tests in May 1998 had put severe strains. The government was also under pressure to sign the international nuclear nonproliferation treaty to renounce future tests, but the religious parties opposed this treaty as a constraint on Pakistan's sovereignty, just as they opposed increasing pressure from the International Monetary Fund to reform the economy according to its dictates. Finally, the U.S.

missile strikes against terrorist training camps in neighboring Afghanistan in August 1998 had led to loud accusations that the Pakistani government had been aware of and complicit in this attack. This, then, was the broad context in which the fifteenth amendment was proposed. There were strong grounds for suspicion of the government's motives in proposing the amendment, and despite Nawaz Sharif's efforts to muster 'ulama support, many even among the latter remained highly suspicious of the proposal.[16]

Indeed, professions of an Islamic commitment on the part of the modernizing ruling elite have, paradoxically, *increased* the 'ulama's ambivalence towards the state. This was already evident in the opposition to an Islamizing regime's proposed reform of the madrasa, as we saw earlier, and we will examine this ambivalence further in this chapter. But before we do so, let us briefly consider some of the 'ulama's own ideas on what is undoubtedly the most critical function of an Islamic state—the implementation of Islamic law.

Implementing Islamic Law

One of the most influential if vaguely formulated statements of what the Pakistani 'ulama mean by an Islamic state was articulated by a congregation of leading religious scholars in 1951. The twenty-two-point declaration then adopted stated, *inter alia*, that the real ruler and lawgiver is Allah, the law of the land is to be based on the Qur'an and the sunna, and no law is to be allowed that contravenes either of these foundational sources. The state is to be based not on considerations of geography, race, or language, but "on those principles and goals which are founded on the code of life presented by Islam." The state is to be responsible for fulfilling the Qur'anic injunction of "commanding right and forbidding wrong," it is to uphold Islamic practices and rituals, and it is to make provisions for Islamic education in accordance with the requirements of the different "recognized" Islamic sects.[17] Irrespective of differences of religion or race, the state is to provide for the basic needs of the people, including food, clothing, housing, medical care, and education, and ensure to its citizens all those rights that the shari'a has given to them, including the rights to life, honor, religion, freedom of expression, and earning a living. The "recognized" Islamic sects are to enjoy religious freedom within the limits of the law, and matters pertaining to laws of personal status are to be decided according to their respective schools of law. The non-Muslim inhabitants of the state are to have religious freedom and the right to their own religious education and the preservation of their culture, within the limits of the law. The propagation of views that contravene the basic principles of the Islamic state are to be prohibited, however; and finally, no interpretation of the Constitution that is opposed to the Qur'an and the sunna is to be valid.[18]

Again and again the 'ulama have invoked this declaration in elaborating on their conception of an Islamic state, and the principles enunciated here have been reiterated in various formulations.[19] That these principles are all quite vague is not a fatal objection from their viewpoint, for as Mawlana Taqi 'Uthmani writes:

> When we say that Islam has provided us with directions for all spheres of life, we do not mean to suggest that the Qur'an, or the sunna, or Islamic law has a ruling on every single particular of life. We mean, rather, that, in all spheres of life, Islam has provided basic principles in whose light all the particulars can be determined. The same is true of the Constitution. Islam has provided us with some basic directives in this regard. No human being has the right to alter these directives; even if the whole nation agrees on something that contravenes these directives, it cannot contravene them. However, once these directives are followed, other subsidiary matters can be settled according to the Muslim community's collective consultation.[20]

The 'ulama's rhetoric takes it as self-evident that the *only* reason the Muslims of South Asia wanted a separate homeland was to have an 'Islamic state;' there simply is no other rationale for this state. An Islamic state is not one in which Muslims are simply a numerical majority, as they are in Pakistan, but one in which the law of God is implemented. The question of *whether* this law, the shari'a, ought to be implemented can hardly arise, for a Muslim, by definition, cannot want it any other way; nor can a state be Islamic except in this way.[21] What merits consideration, then is not whether but *how* to implement the shari'a. This way of formulating the question is not a small measure of the extent to which the 'ulama have been able to hold the modernists accountable for the ambiguities of their own rhetoric.

In what follows I focus primarily on the work of Mawlana Taqi 'Uthmani, whom I have already mentioned in earlier chapters, to illustrate how the question of implementing Islamic law has been treated by the contemporary 'ulama. He has served as a judge of the Federal Shari'at Court, established as part of Zia al-Haqq's Islamization campaign, and he is the vice-president of the Dar al-'Ulum madrasa of Karachi.[22] His father, Mufti Muhammad Shafi', who founded this madrasa, had for many years been the chief jurisconsult at the parent seminary in Deoband. The family moved to Pakistan in 1949, and Shafi', one of the most ardent of the Deobandi 'ulama supporting the demand for Pakistan, played an active role in the debates over an Islamic constitution for the new state.[23] Taqi 'Uthmani has continued that work, combining extensive writings on classical works of hadith and varied aspects of the Islamic legal tradition with regular commentary on current constitutional and legal issues and, in particular, on the implementation of Islamic law in Pakistan.[24]

According to Taqi 'Uthmani, there are two options for a state as it contemplates the mode of implementing Islamic law. The first is simply to declare the shari'a as the law and require the courts to henceforth rule according to it. The burden of discovering what the shari'a actually prescribes on any given matter would then rest on the courts. The other option is to codify the shari'a.[25] Both options, Taqi 'Uthmani notes, have several advantages as well as dangers. The advantage of the first approach is that "one would not have to wait even for a single day for the shari'a to be implemented." It is in this manner that law has been interpreted and applied for centuries by premodern Muslim judges, and the courts in present-day Saudi Arabia adhere to the same approach.[26] The major problem with this option is, however, the lack of judges well-acquainted with the Islamic legal tradition. For judges trained in the British legal system, even the language—Arabic—of the Islamic legal texts is unfamiliar, let alone the content of most of those works. Nor is language the only problem, for even among the 'ulama not all are competent to deal with the niceties of fiqh or substantive law. The major texts and manuals of Islamic law are, moreover, from a different day and age, and to determine how to apply their rules and underlying principles to modern problems would be an extremely difficult task. There would be, finally, considerable variation in the courts' interpretation of the shari'a, not to mention the capriciousness of interpretation should the judge be less than upright.[27]

Many of the problems just mentioned can be minimized through codification of the law—by which Taqi 'Uthmani means the thoroughgoing process of turning various facets of the shari'a into systematic and comprehensive legal codes akin to those that are the basis of the continental legal systems.[28] But codification in this sense comes with its own set of difficulties. The principal problem is that to wait until the shari'a has been fully codified would be to postpone its actual implementation almost indefinitely. Conversely, to implement various shari'a-based codes as they become available would be tantamount to accepting, at least for some time, serious contradictions in the legal system, with some aspects of this system governed by the shari'a (as it is being codified) and the rest by the law and legal norms inherited from British colonial rule. Furthermore, if an *uncodified* shari'a can lead to arbitrary legal practice, a codified shari'a might have the opposite effect, viz., a rigidity entailing judgments that might contravene some of the basic principles underlying the shari'a.[29] Despite such problems, Taqi 'Uthmani's preference is clearly for a codified shari'a, *without* waiting until the shari'a has been fully codified. Rather, he suggests proceeding with the implementation of the law in its present,

uncodified form even as the process of codification continues apace. Whatever difficulties this poses must be faced, he says. We are dealing with the
law of God, after all, and no cost is too high in implementing it.[30]

Precisely how codification is to proceed admits, Taqi 'Uthmani notes,
of two further options. The first is to amend the existing laws in a way to
bring them into conformity with the shari'a. This, of course, is the directive laid down in the successive constitutions of Pakistan with the intention of making it an Islamic state, and it is precisely for the implementation of this directive that the Council of Islamic Ideology exists. The other
option is for the shari'a to be codified afresh. It is not necessary, Taqi
'Uthmani argues, to submit the entire legal system uniformly to one option or the other. "The majority of the existing laws of the country are of
an administrative nature, and the question of permissible and forbidden
[according to the shari'a] seldom arises in their regard. Examples of such
laws include the Railways Act, the Factories Act, the Press and Publications Ordinance, etc." It would suffice to make amendments to such laws
to ensure that nothing in them contradicts the shari'a.[31] On the other
hand, there are certain kinds of law that require to be codified anew, for
the principles on which they are presently based are in fundamental conflict with the shari'a's teachings as well as with the shari'a's principles of
interpretation. The conceptual bases of these laws are different in English
common law and in the shari'a, he says, and "even if, hypothetically,
everything that is explicitly in conflict with the Qur'an and the sunna is
excised from English law, that law can still not be characterized as Islamic
law. For the former is the product of an entirely different context, and its
guiding concepts cannot be separated from the framework in which it has
evolved."[32]

Taqi 'Uthmani's approach to the implementation of the shari'a is not
that of a gradualist, for he would like to see it enforced even while the
task of codification (and of bringing various laws into conformity with
the shari'a) continues apace. It nevertheless is an approach that envisages
a *gradual* transformation of the country's legal system. Certain other
'ulama, while also professing to accommodate many existing laws into
the shari'a, have called for a much more radical transformation of the
political and legal system;[33] and the admiration that many of them have
expressed for the Taliban's rough and ready execution of the hudud[34] and
other punishments suggests, at least, that they are not enamored of the
meticulous work involved in the codification of the shari'a.[35]

Most 'ulama do not, however, oppose the *principle* of codification, in
Pakistan and in other contemporary Muslim societies. Indeed, it is safe
to say that when they speak of an Islamic state in the context of the modern world, they typically mean a state based on a *codified* shari'a law.
This is a point worth stressing because the concept of codification is rela-

tively new in the history of the shari'a and thus its acknowledgement is, in some important ways, a considerable departure from the earlier practices of the 'ulama. Medieval rulers did, no doubt, exercise their "secular" legal authority to supplement and sometimes to override the shari'a; and there are precedents, especially in Ottoman history, of the judges being bound to rule according to the restrictions laid on them by the sultans.[36] Nevertheless, for much of Islamic history, the shari'a is better understood not as a code in the modern sense of the term but, as Nathan Brown and others have argued, as an ongoing discursive tradition articulated in and through practices associated with educational and judicial institutions.[37] In certain contemporary Muslim societies there continues to be much resistance to the codification of the shari'a. For instance, in Saudi Arabia, many 'ulama see codification as a threat to the authority of the judge to decide individual cases in the light of his reasoned judgment as guided directly by the foundational scriptural texts (ijtihad) or, where appropriate, by the work of earlier legal masters. Given that Saudi 'ulama enjoy an influence in the state and an autonomy in the execution of the law unparalleled in any other Sunni state, codification is also seen as potentially strengthening the state over against the 'ulama, and for threatening to make the latter subservient to the former—and is opposed for these reasons.[38] So rather than taking the idea of codification for granted, we need to ask: Why do the Pakistani 'ulama, as well as those in most contemporary Muslim societies, appear to concede so easily the need for codification of the law? Further, what role do they assign to themselves in this project?

Besides the obvious fact that the Pakistani 'ulama do not enjoy the sort of authority in the state that the Saudi 'ulama do, three considerations help answer the first question. First, while all major schools of Sunni law have, over the centuries, continued to adapt themselves to changing circumstances, there are considerable differences in the degree to which 'ulama of different schools have insisted on their ability or authority to depart from the existing legal tradition. The Hanbalis, for instance, who comprise the predominant legal school in Saudi Arabia, have allowed vast latitude in ijtihad, whereas the Hanafi school, to which most Pakistani and Indian 'ulama belong, has been much more insistent that the adherents of this school conform to the opinions recognized as authoritative in it. This insistence became more stringent in colonial times, as we saw in chapter 1. Modern initiatives towards codification, then, can be thought of as continuing the already well-established practice of adhering to the texts and doctrines recognized as authoritative in one's school of law (taqlid).[39]

Second, in most Muslim societies the law—including areas of shari'a law and especially in matters of personal status—has existed in a codified form since colonial times.[40] This allows the proponents of the shari'a's implementation to demand that such codification be now extended to other areas as well. What makes such demands possible is, again, a changed conception of the shari'a: not an ongoing discursive process, which works (as it did for centuries) through particular institutions and practices, but a set of discrete laws, which can be codified and implemented—that is, the shari'a as content rather than process.[41]

Third, codification is also a pragmatic way of implementing Islamic law. On the one hand, as we have already noted, it can be argued that much of the law that already exists in a codified form will remain unaffected insofar as it is not repugnant to the shari'a, so the legal system would not have to be dismantled and built afresh. On the other hand, 'ulama have also argued that the judges educated in the modern secular legal tradition can be retrained to implement shari'a law in its codified form. The modernist judges need not fear, then, that they would necessarily be replaced once the shari'a becomes the law of the land.[42]

The latter argument is patently meant to assuage modernist fears. But it is accompanied by the insistence that, so far as the actual project of codification is concerned, the 'ulama alone must be in charge of it; for only they have the "expertise" in the Islamic legal tradition equal to the task of now codifying it. The same, indeed, is true of all legislation in matters Islamic. In a view that has not given much comfort to those who would reconcile Islam and democracy, the 'ulama have insisted that even when it is the popularly elected representatives of the people who formally pass all legislation into law, it is the 'ulama alone whose guiding hand must effectively shape all Islamic laws. As Mufti Muhammad Shafi' of the Dar al-'Ulum of Karachi wrote, "If a board of highly skilled medical doctors is constituted to resolve the *economic* problems of the country, or economists are gathered from all over to conduct research into a *medical* problem, the result would only be failure and a waste of time. Likewise, if laws are to be made for the country on the basis of the Qur'an and the sunna, then the people needed for the task are those who have deep insight and rich experience with the fields of knowledge pertaining to these."[43]

The codification of the shari'a need not close all doors to the shari'a's further elaboration, any more than taqlid itself need do so. Unlike Saudi Arabia's Hanbali 'ulama, latter-day Hanafi 'ulama have often been reticent in claiming the abilities for ijtihad, as already noted. But many of the Hanafis do clearly recognize that ijtihad within the limits of their legal school remains a necessary and ongoing venture. This is a point worth emphasizing in view of the perception widely shared among many ordinary Muslims, Muslim modernists, and Islamists, as well as Western scholars of Islam, that the 'ulama are so mired in "blind imitation" of earlier authorities as to be altogether averse to any change. In a book entitled *The Legal Status of Taqlid*, Taqi 'Uthmani argues, for instance, that while the "common people"—that is, those who do not possess any formal training in religion—as well as many among the 'ulama themselves must firmly adhere to the established legal positions of their school of law, it is possible for those who are highly versed in the Islamic juristic tradition to not only expound on that tradition or choose among variant positions within their own school of law, but also to continue working out rulings on matters that are not dealt with in the standard texts of their school.[44] Even though these scholars are not competent to exercise such constructive legal thinking (ijtihad) on all matters, it is possible for them to practice ijtihad in what might be described as an itemized fashion, that is, with respect to certain particular matters that need attention.[45] For the 'ulama there are definite perimeters—divinely mandated perimeters— beyond which no legislation and no change in the existing tradition can be contemplated. By the same token, areas not regulated by the existing Islamic tradition are the space in which new initiatives are to take place.[46] Taqi 'Uthmani's formulations here do not go much beyond doctrines widely accepted in medieval legal theory; nor, indeed, does he intend them to. But what he says suffices to show that the 'ulama are scarcely opposed to change in the corpus of their legal tradition.

Elements of Ambivalence

Neither codification of the law nor a continuing ijtihad is, in itself, seen by many among the 'ulama as a threat to their authority. But just as things would go dangerously awry in any area of life unless the 'experts' in the relevant field handled it, so too is codification flawed and ijtihad perilous, in their view, unless performed by the experts. The modern 'ulama's characterization of themselves as experts in religion who ought to be recognized, as experts and specialists are in other areas of life, is commonly encountered in their writings and statements.[47] But as with so many of the terms and concepts that punctuate their discourses, we need to recognize the novelty of such characterizations. Distinctions between those who possess the knowledge that is religiously and culturally valued and those who are lacking in it—the 'alim and the jahil, or "ignorant"—were central to the premodern 'ulama's worldview, of course; and ways of ranking those who had some claims to knowledge, of distinguishing who had less or more expertise in given matters, have likewise long remained part of the 'ulama's culture.[48] What is new is not the 'ulama's claiming expertise in this or that area—say, Arabic grammar or hadith or law or theology—but a view of the world in which religion comes to constitute a specialization, with its own indispensable experts who are to be viewed as at least on par with experts in any other "field."[49]

In part, this way of looking at themselves is a response to a changed world in which the 'ulama, their institutions of learning, and the epistemological assumptions on which their discourses have long been based have come to hold little appeal or meaning to those increasingly drawn to modern, secular institutions. To many of the latter, the 'ulama's way of doing things is simply not "useful," sometimes not even intelligible. This is strikingly exemplified in the fact that the 'ulama—literally, the "possessors of knowledge (*'ilm*)"—have sometimes been characterized as uneducated by those schooled in the modern college and university system.[50] The 'ulama's insistence on their own expertise is also a response to the fragmentation of their authority, with new challengers—among them the modernists and the Islamists—claiming that the interpretation of the foundational texts is not the privilege of the 'ulama alone and that, in any case, their interpretations are out of tune with the needs of the modern world.[51]

But more is at stake for the 'ulama than a desire for recognition as experts in a modern society. Their insistence also betrays a certain ambivalence on their part towards the state itself. Such ambivalence has deep roots.[52] As Baber Johansen has shown with reference to the Hanafi school, the most widespread of the Sunni schools of Islamic law, premodern Hanafi jurists were keen to limit the sphere in which the Muslim government could exercise unrestrained, or "absolute," authority. These jurists distinguished between, on the one hand, the "claims of men" (*huquq al-'ibad*), which could be settled privately between individuals, and, on the other, the "claims of God" (*huquq Allah*) or the "claims of the law" (*huquq al-shar'*), which were to be upheld by the state. Concerned that in upholding the claims of God which, unlike the claims of men, were not negotiable, the state could assume authoritarian styles and infringe upon the rights of the individual, the jurists took it upon themselves to define the claims of God in highly restricted terms, covering only "the collection of a few taxes, the protection of Islamic worship and the enforcement of a penal law equipped with—considering the middle ages—many safeguards for the individual."[53] The jurists argued, in effect, that an all-powerful God suffers no loss even if the claims of God are given less than their due.[54] In the words of the early-nineteenth-century Damascene jurist Ibn 'Abidin, "This is not so because we are treating the claims of the law lightly, but because the human being is in need and the law is not."[55]

The modern 'ulama take a more expansive view of the powers of the state: the state must not merely let people live an Islamic life but should actively uphold and implement Islamic law; it must *enable* people to live according to such law, and it must allow nothing that contravenes it. Yet they also share with their medieval precursors an ambivalence towards the state. And as the power of the state has grown to encompass all facets of the life of its citizens, so too have the 'ulama's suspicions of it. But the

ambivalence is not just that of the 'ulama. The power of the modern nation-state to intrude into and regulate all aspects of the life of its citizens
means that religion occupies an uneasy place in *any* modern state. As
Talal Asad observes with reference to the contradictory claims of the modern secular state, the nation-state "requires clearly demarcated spaces that
it can classify and regulate: religion, education, health, leisure, work, in-
come, justice, war"; yet the "space that religion may properly occupy in
society has to be continually redefined by the law because the reproduc-
tion of secular life within and beyond the nation-state continually affects
the clarity of that space."[56] This is true not just of states that profess to
be secular but also of those, like Pakistan, that do not. For all its self-
characterization as an Islamic Republic, Pakistan's institutions and system of governance are, after all, far more indebted to the categories and
structures of British colonial rule than they are subservient to "the sovereignty of God." At the same time, however, because of the ideological
claims that the state does make, the positions of Islam and of the 'ulama
in the state become even more fraught with ambiguity. The modernist
elite acknowledge the public role of Islam but seem shocked when confronted with the implications of their own extravagant rhetoric. The
'ulama, for their part, call for a "truly" Islamic state, but they also have
misgivings about the power and intrusive reach of the state. This intru-
siveness can, ironically, become more, not less, menacing under the mantle
of Islam. For instance, modernist judges of the higher courts have sometimes justified what the 'ulama see as nothing but capricious and misguided tampering with Islamic law as *their own* legitimate ijtihad in an
Islamic state.[57] As the judges of the Lahore High Court stated in 1959:
"If we be clear as to what the meaning of a verse in the Qur'an is, it will
be our duty to give effect to that interpretation *irrespective of what has
been stated by [the medieval] jurists.*"[58] Furthermore, as Jamal Malik has
observed, state-sponsored initiatives of Islamization are not merely efforts
to appease Islamic sentiment or secure legitimacy for a ruling elite often
sorely lacking in it; in Pakistan, Islamization has also served to strengthen
the state's control of society, to extend and deepen its reach into new
areas, including facets of religious life.[59] Islamization has also served as
the instrument for enhancing the government's own authority, as we have
seen with reference to the constitutional amendment proposed by the government of Prime Minister Nawaz Sharif in 1999.

It is in the context of this ambivalence towards the state, towards
even—and perhaps especially—an Islamizing state, that we can make
sense of the 'ulama's view of themselves as religious "experts," comparable to experts in any other area of life. This view expresses their efforts
not only to define their role in a modern society and state and to shape
both according to their prescriptions, but also to ward off the encroach-

ments of the state on what they see as *their* own distinct sphere, *their* area of competence. The two projects do not sit comfortably with each other, but ambiguities about the place of Islam in public life afford them ample room to be conducted simultaneously. Another manifestation of the same ambivalence is, of course, the insistence that the madrasa represents a distinct religious sphere that must be protected against the encroachment of the state.

I have limited my discussion so far to the 'ulama in relation to the modernists. But the ambivalence that we have noted in the 'ulama's attitudes towards the state can perhaps be brought out more clearly when we view them in relation to, on the one hand, the Sunni Islamists—viz., the "lay" ideologues and activists who seek to make the state Islamic through public implementation of scriptural norms—and, on the other, the 'ulama of Shi'i Iran's Islamic Republic. I do this in the following section by focusing on Sayyid Abu'l-A'la Mawdudi (d. 1979) of Pakistan and on Ayatollah Khumayni (d. 1989) of Iran.

Competing Conceptions of the State

Sayyid Abu'l-A'la Mawdudi, one of the most influential Islamist thinkers of the twentieth century, had a long career as a journalist, Qur'an exegete, and political activist in pre-independence India and in Pakistan. Between 1924 and 1927, he was the editor of *al-Jami'a*, the journal of the Deobandi political organization, the Jam'iyyat al-'Ulama'-i Hind. Later, however, he engaged in a bitter polemic against Mawlana Husayn Ahmad Madani, the leader of the Jam'iyya, in opposing Madani's position on united nationalism (see chapter 1). But Mawdudi was equally opposed to the Muslim League's demand for Pakistan, for he believed nationalism to be incompatible with Islam and, in any case, considered the Western-educated leadership of this party unfit to lead the demand for an Islamic state. He created his own organization, the Jama'at-i Islami, in 1941, to train a community of "righteous people" who alone, he believed, could truly guarantee real and long-lasting political change. For all his initial opposition to the demand for Pakistan, he moved to the new state and played an active role in shaping the public discourse on the Islamic state. His numerous writings, of which the most significant is his six-volume Urdu commentary on the Qur'an, have continued to be highly influential in Islamist circles throughout the Muslim world.[60]

Mawdudi's relations with the 'ulama were complex and contradictory.[61] He was more willing than many other Islamists have been to acknowledge the value and relevance of the premodern Islamic juristic and exegetical tradition to the understanding and interpretation of Islam in the modern world.[62] In an unmistakably tactical gesture of friendship to-wards the 'ulama, he also acknowledged the importance of certain com-mentaries on hadith by them and included these works prominently alongside others that he thought ought to be the basis for training students in Islamic law.[63] Mawdudi worked closely with the leading 'ulama in artic-ulating the demands of the religious parties for an Islamic constitution in the early years of Pakistan's independence; and at critical junctures in Pakistani history his party acted in concert with the 'ulama. Indeed, his own career and that of his party, the Jama'at-i Islami, represent one of the earliest instances of collaboration between the Islamists and the 'ulama anywhere in the Muslim world—a phenomenon that would be observed later in Egypt and elsewhere.

Yet Mawdudi also remained harshly critical of the 'ulama. "The old-fashioned schools," he noted with reference to the madrasas, "are steeped in conservatism to such an extent that they have lost touch with the mod-ern world. Their education has lost all contact with the practical problems of life and has become barren and lifeless. It cannot, therefore, produce people who might be able to serve, for instance, as judges and magistrates of a progressive modern state."[64] Needless to say, the 'ulama responded in kind, arguing that Mawdudi's lack of formal religious education made him unqualified to speak authoritatively on Islam and objecting, often with considerable polemical zeal, to his interpretations of the Qur'an.

But the differences between them ran deeper. Mawdudi's ideology rested heavily on the idea of preparing a new community of righteous individuals, well-schooled in what he took to be fundamental Islamic norms and ready to lead the rest of society on the path of an Islamic "revolution." Though he spoke frequently about the need for revolution-ary change, it has been persuasively argued that Mawdudi—unlike, say, Sayyid Qutb of Egypt, who was in many ways deeply influenced by Maw-dudi's thought—did not envisage recourse to violent means. His 'revolu-tion' was to be brought about by his righteous individuals—people, espe-cially in positions of leadership, whose training and extended Islamic socialization would be the surest means not only of bringing about effec-tive change but also of serving as a bulwark against any temptations to deviate from the straight path once they had been set on it.[65] This idealistic vision was compromised in the early years of Pakistan, when Mawdudi's Jama'at-i Islami decided to participate in electoral politics even before his righteous individuals were at hand. And Mawdudi's followers have continued to struggle with this tension between "education as cultural engineering"[66] and active political participation in what they regard as an inherently flawed political system.[67] Decision-making in Mawdudi's state would be the prerogative of the *amir*, the head of the polity, and though the amir would be expected to act in consultation with others, Mawdudi's political writings made it clear that he did not envisage a role for the 'ulama in guiding the Islamic state. The sort of individuals Mawdudi wanted to train in bringing about the desired social and political transformation would replace *both* the Westernized modernists and the 'ulama, for he regarded both as impediments to the Islamic state. To the 'ulama, on the other hand, an Islamic state without a central role for those drawn from within their own ranks would be inconceivable; indeed, it is a contradiction in terms. Mawdudi, however, saw no such contradiction, and here lies the source of much friction between him and the 'ulama.

But there is an even more fundamental disagreement between Mawdudi and the 'ulama, which returns us to the 'ulama's aforementioned ambivalence towards the state. For Mawdudi, Islam and the Islamic state are ultimately synonymous: to promote an Islamic way of life, the authority of the state and the active intervention of its resources are essential, so that striving for the establishment an Islamic state itself becomes a Muslim's ultimate calling. "[T]he struggle for obtaining control over the organs of the state, when motivated by the urge to establish the din [religion] and the Islamic Shari'ah and to enforce the Islamic injunctions, is not only permissible but is positively desirable and as such obligatory."[68] As he put it elsewhere: "Acknowledging that someone is your ruler to whom you must submit means that you have accepted his Din. He now becomes your sovereign and you become his subjects. . . . *Din, therefore, actually means the same thing as state and government*; Shari'ah is the law of that state and government; and '*Ibadah* [worship] amounts to following and complying with that law."[69]

The state, for Mawdudi, is not just a means to an end, viz., to live according to norms and in pursuit of goals intended by God; it becomes an end in itself.[70] For their part, even as they have sought to *use* the state as an instrument of Islamization and to assert their own specialized role in it, the 'ulama have typically been unwilling to grant such sweeping powers to the state or even to make everything else subservient to the goal of establishing an Islamic state. As Taqi 'Uthmani writes in his critique of Islamist positions such as Mawdudi's, it is as though even the fundamental rituals of religion come to be conceived of by them not as practices Muslims must undertake because they are an irreducible part of being a believer, but rather because they are socially useful in inculcating the habits and the discipline that assist in the project of striving for an Islamic state.[71] The implications of such a position are plainly grave, he says; for if the liturgical rituals are seen merely as a means to an end, then it follows that these could be substituted with some other means if such means would bring one closer to the desired ends.[72] Secularism is a form of unbelief, says Taqi 'Uthmani, for it goes to the extreme of maintaining that religion is limited only to certain rituals and to one's private life, and that it has nothing to say on matters of "material life," which is recognized to have "its own god[s]."[73] But Islamists such as Mawdudi go to the other extreme: "[I]n their zeal to counter secularism, and in their focus on the political dimension of the shari'a, they have made all of Islam a political religion, instead of making politics a part of religion."[74]

The ambivalence of the Sunni 'ulama towards the potentially all-encompassing authority of the state is brought out more fully when seen in relation to Ayatollah Khumayni's evolving doctrine of "the authority of the [preeminent] jurist" (*wilayat al-faqih*), which became the basis of the post-1979 Islamic Republic of Iran. In lectures delivered in Najaf in Iraq, nearly a decade before his triumphant return from exile in 1979, Khumayni had offered a major reinterpretation of the scope of juristic authority in Shi'i Islam.[75] He had argued that it was wrong to suppose, as leading Shi'i scholars had, that the jurists were the "deputies" of the hidden imam in matters of faith and practice but not in politics, which remained the preserve of the imam himself. Building on the position of the *marja' al-taqlid*—an institution that had emerged in the nineteenth century and signified the recognition of one (or later, of several) top-ranking Shi'i jurists as the "focus of emulation," or preeminent authority, in the Shi'i world of learning—Khumayni argued that the person occupying this position ought to also wield the hidden imam's *political* authority and accordingly ought to establish and guide the Islamic state. If, he argued, an Islamic state is one that is based on the shari'a, then it is the person most knowledgeable in the shari'a who ought to be entrusted with the governance of such a state. And the most eminent of the jurists was, by definition, such a person. This remarkable new doctrine has continued to be opposed by many leading Shi'i scholars in and outside of Iran, during Khumayni's lifetime and after his death. Nevertheless, Khumayni's leadership of the Iranian revolution and his unmatched stature in the post-revolution state ensured that this doctrine would become the foundation of the new Islamic Republic.[76]

Yet Khumayni did not stop with this reformulation of the jurist's authority. Shortly before his death, and in the midst of a constitutional crisis precipitated by questions about the proper separation of powers in the state, Khumayni further expanded the scope of the supreme jurist's authority and, in effect, that of the government guided by him. In a public letter to the Iranian president, 'Ali Khamene'i, Khumayni rebuked him for taking too restricted a view of the power of the government in relation to Islamic law. The scope of an Islamic government's power, he argued, is in fact *not* constrained by the limits of Islamic law. The government's function is not merely the implementation of the law as it already exists. Exercising the "deputyship" of the Prophet and of the hidden imam, the government is the ultimate authority which defines the shari'a, rather than the other way around. "I should state," Khumayni wrote, that the government which is a part of the absolute viceregency of the Prophet of God . . . is one of the primary injunctions of Islam and has priority over all other secondary injunctions, even prayers, fasting and hajj. . . . The ruler can close down mosques if need be, or can even demolish a mosque which is a source of harm. . . . The government is empowered to unilaterally revoke any shari'ah agreements which it has concluded with the people when those agreements are contrary to the interests of the country or of Islam. It can also prevent any devotional or non-devotional affair if it is opposed to the interests of Islam and for so long as it is so. The government can prevent hajj, which is one of the important divine obligations, on a temporary basis, in cases when it is contrary to the interests of the Islamic country.[77]

Khumayni's position here seems to depart radically from the stance he had articulated in 1970. Then, he was arguing for the jurist's political authority on the grounds that the most knowledgeable person in Islamic law ought to govern the state based *on that law*. The law itself seemed to be taken as a given, and it was apparently only a matter of how best to uphold it; and it had to be upheld stringently. "The *fuqaha* [jurists; singular: *faqih*] are the trustees," he had said in a 1970 lecture,

who implement the divine ordinances in levying taxes, guarding the frontiers, and executing the penal provisions of the law. They must not allow the laws of Islam to remain in abeyance, or their operation to be affected by either defect or excess. If a *faqih* wishes to punish an adulterer, he must give him one hundred lashes in the presence of the people, in the exact manner that has been specified. He does not have the right to inflict one additional lash, to curse the offender, to slap him, or to imprison him for a single day. Similarly, when it comes to the levying of taxes, he must act in accordance with the criteria and the laws of Islam. . . . If a *faqih* acts in contradiction to the criteria of Islam (God forbid!), then he will automatically be dismissed from his post, since he will have forfeited his quality of trustee.[78]

Nearly two decades later, he was assigning to the jurist, and to the state under his guardianship, the authority to extensively rework the law or suspend it as the needs of the time demanded. Yet, a closer reading of Khumayni's 1970 lectures suggests considerable wavering even then on whether the goal of an Islamic state was merely to uphold the given law or, conversely, to employ it towards some greater good. As he had stated in one of those lectures: "Islam regards law as a tool, not as an end in itself. Law is a tool and an instrument for the establishment of justice in society, a means for man's intellectual and moral reform and his purification."[79] On the face of it, Khumayni's 1988 statement about the ruler even closing down mosques or revoking shari'a agreements or preventing the *hajj* seems shocking, seems indeed to put him altogether outside the juristic tradition; yet it is prefigured in his earlier statement that the law might merely be a means to an end. More importantly, what the idea as articulated in 1988 ultimately amounts to is that the shari'a is not a closed system but one that can, through ijtihad, be adapted—even radically adapted—to changing circumstances, and that what are discerned to be the "true" interests of Islam at any given point have priority over existing interpretations of the shari'a.

What is far more significant in the 1988 statement than the scope of the jurist's authority is the effective collapsing of the distinction between the authority of the supreme jurist and the authority of the state: one is now the expression of, and coeval with, the other.[80] It is here that the ambivalence of the Sunni 'ulama towards a state that might acquire the potential for making such claims stands in bold relief. The ambivalence does not lie in the idea that leading jurists and religious scholars should guide the Islamic state—that, after all, is the essence of their conviction, as we have seen; it consists, rather, in the fear that in the guise of upholding Islam the state might make it subservient to its own goals and ultimately absorb it within itself.

The 'ulama reflect this ambivalence collectively, though in many guises. It is reflected in wide-ranging debates in contemporary Iran on the scope of the jurist's authority and on issues of religious authority in general.[81] It is echoed in the debate on the codification of the law in present-day Saudi Arabia, with such codification threatening—in this context—not just to make the 'ulama subservient to the state but also to concentrate religious and political authority in the state itself. In Egypt, the 'ulama of the Azhar religious establishment, who occupy a difficult space between the government and the Islamists (the latter with their own many shades), often reflect a similar tension. These Egyptian 'ulama have typically been portrayed by Western scholars as almost unconditionally supportive of the Egyptian regime as it fights the Islamist challengers. But quite apart from the existence of varied political positions within the Azhar 'ulama, as we will see in chapter 6, there is more to the Azhar's opposition to the Islamists than a commitment to the stability of the regime: among other things, there is also the same ambivalence about the larger claims that the Islamists' state would make.

The possibilities that the 'ulama see in the state as the instrument of Islamization, then, are often counterbalanced by the dangers that it represents to a religious tradition that the 'ulama seek to maintain as relatively independent.[82] Two points are worth making in concluding this discussion. First, it is no doubt tempting to characterize the 'ulama's view of an Islamic state as based merely on self-aggrandizement—on the idea that a state is Islamic as long as the 'ulama themselves have an important role in it. This is precisely how the modern 'ulama have often been perceived and portrayed, of course, and not just by their modernist detractors.[83] What such a characterization neglects, however, is that the 'ulama are arguing not only about their own role in the polity (they are, no doubt, doing that) but also about the Islamic tradition as historically elaborated and as handed down over the centuries. The 'ulama of different Muslim societies are often rooted in diverse facets of that tradition, and they differ considerably in their actual acquaintance with it. But, as I have argued earlier, it is in continuity with this tradition that they see themselves; and this, above all else, is what sets them apart from the modernists, the Islamists, and other new religious intellectuals, even as it gives the 'ulama themselves a broadly shared worldview. The argument over their role in the state—or their ambivalence towards the state—is an expression of the continuing debate over how the Islamic tradition ought to inform the life of Muslims in the contemporary world. This debate involves many more people than the 'ulama, of course; but their discourses, all too often neglected, are also a critical and an increasingly significant part of it.

Second, the modern 'ulama's ambivalence towards the state has, ironically, served them rather well. For it has allowed and even forced them to pursue, with considerable flexibility, several options simultaneously: they have continued to press the state on its Islamic promises, but at the same time, they have gradually expanded the scope of their own activities at the grassroots level of society. Some of these activities involve providing basic education and other social services that the state itself is too inefficient to assure to many of its citizens; other activities, in Pakistan, have taken the form of creating new and radicalized sectarian identities, and a new community consciousness based on these identities. New technologies allow the 'ulama to forge effective ties at local levels; but they assist them no less in establishing new links with like-minded individuals, groups, and institutions in the greater Muslim world. New forms of community, local as well as supranational, are not a renunciation of the ideal of an Islamic state; nor do these new or reconfigured communities do much to resolve the elements of ambivalence in that ideal. But they do underscore a new prominence of the 'ulama, a reassertion of their religious authority, and a more vigorous insistence on their own multifaceted relevance to contemporary Muslim society *and* the state.

About the same time that Mufti Rafi' 'Uthmani was speaking of the madrasa as a small replica of an Islamic society and state, as we saw at the beginning of this chapter, he also published a small booklet in which he addressed himself to the 'ulama on the question of their political role. Here he argued not that the 'ulama and their religiopolitical organizations should separate themselves from the rest of society (that was not his point in the welcoming address to his madrasa students either) but, rather, that they should reinvigorate their religious identity and thereby that of the society around them in new ways. He was writing in the context of widespread sectarian riots in the country and the 'ulama's initiatives towards forging an alliance in their ranks to counter them; but he was also writing in the broader context of the repeated failure of the 'ulama and their religiopolitical organizations to achieve any significant success in the electoral politics of Pakistan—either on their own or in alliance with other parties. The 'ulama, in Rafi' 'Uthmani's view, needed to rethink their options. "Secularism" [sic] had made inroads even on the 'ulama's organizations, he said, by which he meant that they had often shown themselves willing to compromise their principles for political advantage. Those working for the religiopolitical organizations were increasingly unfamiliar with the precepts of religion, he observed, and the religious identity of these organizations had become limited to outward appearances, whereas in practice their commitment to the shari'a appeared to have been overtaken by their sense of political expediency.[84] He believed that this problem was costing the 'ulama the trust of the people. The solution was that they should collaborate with other, nonreligious, parties only on their own terms. In cooperating with such parties the 'ulama ought to ensure that none of these alliances relegated them to merely an "insignificant subordinate" (tabi' muhmil). If they were not able to find allies on these terms, then, Rafi' 'Uthmani suggested, a different course ought to be considered:

> Would it not be better if our organizations, or some unified group comprised of them, focused all their attention on individual development, the reform of society, commanding right and forbidding wrong, providing religious education to the common folk and the elite, public service, creating welfare centres in rural and urban areas, and on raising the rate of literacy in the country by imparting the ability to read the Qur'an? Rather than becoming insignificant subordinates to different groups, or functioning as a weak and suspect group in the elections, we should act as an honest broker (thalith): the supremacy of the word of God should be our goal, and the removal—with wisdom and according to the example of the prophets—of everything reprehensible in politics, society, and economy should be our practice. In pursuing these goals, we should address the government, the opposition, and the people. Rather than being a party in the election process, we can send people of character to the assemblies of power, and thus adopt a path through which the Renewer of the Second Millennium[85] had, astonishingly, brought about a peaceful religious revolution in the politics of the Indian subcontinent. This, then, is another way, which after careful consideration, might well lead to the solution of the problems confronting the Muslim world and, in particular, those confronting Pakistan.[86]

This striking statement is misleading in certain ways. For one thing, it can be interpreted to suggest the 'ulama's distancing themselves from active politics, but that, as we will see in chapter 5, is hardly the case. One might also get the impression from Rafi' 'Uthmani that only in the mid-1990s was the option of grassroots activism being recommended or considered. In fact, however, the 'ulama's activism at this level of society was nothing new: Deobandi reformism was, after all, a type of grassroots activism from the very beginning. Conversely, what was new and unprecedented was happening not in the mid 1990s but already for more than a decade by then. Rafi' 'Uthmani's post factum "advice" to the 'ulama is better understood as a rhetorical reaffirmation of this activism rather than a call to initiate it. Presenting it as a new option for the 'ulama was probably also a way of distancing them from the ugly face of militant sectarianism, which had been the most striking expression of this grassroots activism since the early 1980s.

V

Refashioning Identities

OLIVIER ROY has argued that the Islamists' failure to take over the state and shape its institutions according to their own prescriptions has led, since the 1980s, to a growing reorientation of their movements towards grassroots activism in Muslim societies.[1] Roy makes this point with reference to the Islamists rather than the 'ulama, though for the latter as well, religiopolitical activism at local and grassroots levels has become a major expression of their contemporary prominence in several Muslim societies. But the 'ulama's grassroots activism does not signify renunciation of the path to the Islamic state, as Roy suggests it does in case of the Islamists. Rather than thinking in dichotomous terms or stark choices between top-down and grassroots Islamization or, for that matter, between politically activist and quietist positions, it is more accurate to conceive of these as options to which the 'ulama have often been drawn in various combinations simultaneously. In Pakistan grassroots activism is not so much a reaction to the failure to Islamize the state from the top down as it is, in part at least, itself the *effect* of top-down Islamization. At the same time, this activism is also the product of, and is sustained by, a complex configuration of local as well as international factors, social and economic changes, and the possibilities created by modern technology.

To attribute this grassroots activism merely to the bankruptcy of Islamism is not only to take too restricted a view of Islamism itself (and of what constitutes its "failure" in the contemporary Muslim world); it is also to misunderstand the many different expressions of this activism, the complexity of the context in which it has emerged, and, once again, to ignore *the 'ulama* as part of this larger context. This chapter examines the religiopolitical activism of the 'ulama of Pakistan at the grassroots and other levels with reference to what, since the early 1980s, has been its most significant manifestation: the radicalization of Sunni and Shi'i identities and the far-reaching changes in the religious landscape that have accompanied it. Towards the end of this chapter, and more fully in the next, we move beyond Pakistan to consider instances of the 'ulama's activism in a number of other societies and to assess its relationship with facets of contemporary Islamism.

Aspects of a Sectarian Discourse

The history of conflict between the Sunnis and the Shi'a extends over more than a millennium. At issue between the two communities historically has been a dispute over questions of legitimate authority. According to the Shi'a, most of the Companions of the Prophet, the *sahaba*, conspired after the Prophet's death to dispossess 'Ali (his nephew and son-in-law), and after him his descendants, the imams, of their divinely ordained right to the Muslim community's leadership. In the Shi'i view of history, the Companions and their successors were hypocrites and usurpers who never ceased to subvert Islam for their own interests. Conversely, the Sunnis revere the sahaba, and especially the *khulafa' al-rashidun*, the four immediate "rightly guided" successors of the Prophet (of whom 'Ali was the last), as second only to the Prophet in religious authority.[2]

Relations between the Sunnis and the Shi'a have not always been tense. But when they have been such, the form, expression, and intensity of conflict have varied considerably in accordance with the peculiarities of context. In South Asia, the Sunnis and even many Hindus often participated with vigor in the rituals of Muharram, when the Shi'a commemorate the martyrdom of their third imam, Husayn.[3] However, as Juan Cole has argued, with the increasing influence of the Shi'i 'ulama in the Shi'i princely state of Awadh in the first half of the nineteenth century, the ruling elite began to adopt policies that clearly favored the Shi'a over against the Sunnis and the Hindus.[4] The changing relations between the Shi'a and others were reflected in the Muharram rituals. Insisting on the ritual cursing of the first caliphs of Islam, the Shi'i 'ulama of Awadh argued that while the Shi'a might hide their true opinions (*taqiyya*) when living in a hostile environment, there was no justification for such dissimulation in a Shi'i-ruled state. Where all had once participated together in the same processions of Muharram, Sunnis now began to organize their own Muharram processions, which sometimes came into violent conflict with the Shi'i processions.[5] It is significant, however, that commemorating the martyrdom of Husayn was still too important for many Sunnis to abandon it altogether in favor of an alternative, *Sunni* ritual; and many continued to participate in the Shi'a's processions. Yet in response to the Shi'i vilification of the Rashidun caliphs, many Sunnis took to reciting the praises of their heroes from among the Companions of the Prophet. This ritualized commemoration of the sahaba, like the Shi'i execration of them, did not fail to exacerbate sectarian tension in early-twentieth-century Lucknow.[6] But it expressed more than how the Lucknow Sunnis felt about the sahaba. As Sandria Freitag has argued, this assertiveness was also the product and the expression of a new Sunni upward mobility in late-colonial Lucknow.[7] As these examples illustrate, forms of ritual commemoration and expressions of sectarian tension have long remained receptive to their particular contexts. Conflict between the Shi'a and the Sunnis in Pakistan since the 1980s is unprecedented in the scale of its violence, but it is no different from earlier expressions of hostility between these communities in being the product of its own peculiar configuration of varied pressures and circumstances.

Yet even as tensions between these communities are defined by the peculiarities of context, certain symbolic issues have continued to be prominent in the long history of these tensions. Of these issues, the single most important one is the question of how Islam's earliest history is viewed and, more specifically, the Shi'i attitude towards the Companions of the Prophet Muhammad. It is on this issue that the Sunnis and the Shi'a have clashed most often, not just in South Asian but also in Islamic history.[8]

The Muslims of Pakistan are predominantly Sunni, and most belong to the Hanafi school of Sunni law. But Pakistani censuses do not provide the sectarian affiliation of the country's Muslim inhabitants, which makes it hard to know the precise proportion of those who are not Sunnis. Estimates about the size of the Shi'i population range from as much as a quarter to less than 2 percent of the total population, though the more accurate figure seems closer to about 15 percent.[9]

Issues of sectarian significance were not prominent in the course of the movement for the establishment of Pakistan. But it was not long after the creation of the state that they forcefully surfaced. Of the factors that directly bear on issues of sectarian identity in Pakistan, the following may be singled out here. First, in the "sectarian upbringing"[10] of several leaders of radical Sunnism in Pakistan, the Ahmadi controversy has played a considerable role. Anathematized by most Muslims for their belief that Mirza Ghulam Ahmad (d. 1908), the founder of the Ahmadi community, was a prophet, the Ahmadis have been the target of several campaigns of religious violence as well as of government persecution.[11] There were extended disturbances in the Punjab in 1953 to force the government to formally designate the Ahmadis as "non-Muslims" and to have Muhammad Zafrullah Khan, the Ahmadi foreign minister of Pakistan, removed from his position. Both of these demands, supported by prominent 'ulama from various sectarian persuasions, were unsuccessful, even though the disturbances led to the dismissal of the Punjab government and the imposition of martial law in the province.[12] But in 1974, the government of Zulfiqar 'Ali Bhutto did capitulate to the pressure of the religious parties and, through a constitutional amendment, declared the Ahmadis a non-Muslim minority in the state.[13] Religious leaders have continued to agitate for further restrictions on the Ahmadis, some of which were imposed by the Zia al-Haqq regime in 1984.[14] The Ahmadi controversy has a twofold bearing on sectarian, Shi'i-Sunni conflict in Pakistan. On the one hand, though certain prominent leaders of the Pakistani Shi'a are known to have supported the persecution of the Ahmadis, the history of violence against the latter has supplied the *anti-Shi'a* front with some of its most vigorous leadership. Many of the leading activists of the Sipah-i Sahaba Pakistan, the militant Sunni organization that I describe later in this chapter, began their political careers agitating against the Ahmadis.[15] On the other hand, the constitutional definition of a Muslim so as to exclude the Ahmadis has led to demands, spearheaded by the Sipah-i Sahaba, to further define Islam so as to exclude the Shi'a, too. In a state that professes to be guided by the fundamental principles of Islam, the Ahmadi controversy has contributed to sectarian discourse by forcefully raising, and keeping alive, such questions as who a Muslim "really" is (irrespective of one's own claims in that regard) and what position a Muslim (and those who are not Muslim, or are not recognized as such) has in that state.

A second and more immediate catalyst in the radicalization of sectarian identities was the wide-ranging program of Islamization initiated in early 1979 by the military regime of General Zia al-Haqq. Among the highlights of this program, some of which we have observed in earlier chapters, was the imposition of zakat, an Islamic tax, which, the government decreed, would be automatically collected from people's bank accounts. But Shi'i and Sunni schools of law differ quite markedly in their stipulations on zakat, as they also do in many other areas of law.[16] The government's decision to impose this tax according to the prescriptions of the Hanafi school of Sunni law thus created intense resentment among the Shi'a and proved a powerful stimulus towards their political mobilization in Pakistan. Efforts to mobilize the Shi'a had taken place in earlier years as well: on various occasions Shi'i groups had voiced demands for the unfettered practice of their Muharram rituals, the protection of their pious endowments, and separate religious education in government schools.[17] But the Shi'a saw the Islamization program of the late 1970s as an especially grave threat to their community interests. And the fact that this perceived threat coincided with the spectacular success of the Shi'i revolution in Iran no doubt accounts for much of the self-confidence with which they responded to it.

Radicalized Identities: The Shi'a

In July 1980, the Shi'a from all over the country converged in Islamabad, the capital, and marched on the government ministries to express their grievances; this show of strength was unprecedented and was deemed sufficiently threatening to extract, even from a military regime, promises that the protestors' demands would be met. These demonstrations were led by a new but highly organized "movement," the Tahrik-i Nifaz-i Fiqh-i Ja'fariyya (Movement for the implementation of the Ja'fari law [hereafter TNFJ]).[18] As articulated by the TNFJ, the principal demand of the Shi'a was that zakat not be imposed on them by the state or according to the stipulations of Sunni (Hanafi) law. The Shi'a were to be left alone to regulate their religious life through their own leaders and in accordance with their own doctrines. The TNFJ also demanded "effective" representation for the Shi'a at the highest levels of the state, including representation in bodies advising the government on matters of Islamization itself.[19] Though the TNFJ was able to have the Shi'a exempted from zakat, it soon came to represent a much more ambitious vision than the principal demand that had brought it into existence suggests (on the manifesto of the TNFJ, see below).[20] As its very name proclaimed, this was a movement for the *implementation* of Shi'i law. Opponents alleged that the TNFJ sought to have Shi'i law enforced on Sunnis too and that this goal was only an extension of Iran's commitment to "export" its Shi'i revolution. The TNFJ has always denied this,[21] though the allegation was damaging enough to eventually force a change of the organization's name to the more politic "Tahrik-i Ja'fariyya Pakistan" (Movement of the Ja'fari-Shi'a of Pakistan).[22]

The TNFJ was founded by Mufti Ja'far Husayn (1916–83), one of the more prominent Shi'i religious scholars of Pakistan. Born in Gujranwala in the Punjab in a noted Shi'i family, Ja'far Husayn studied in a local *Sunni* madrasa before proceeding to Lucknow and later to Najaf, in southern Iraq, for further studies.[23] Besides teaching at Shi'i madrasas in his native Gujranwala for most of his lifetime, he actively represented the Shi'a in public life. He served on government committees involved in proposing Islamic provisions for Pakistan's first constitution (1956) and on the Council of Islamic Ideology in the time of General Ayub Khan and also of General Zia ul-Haqq. Alarmed by the latter's Islamization project, he resigned his membership of the Council in 1979 and was in the same year chosen as the Qa'id-i Millat-i Ja'fariyya (leader of the Ja'fari [Shi'a] community). The TNFJ came into being the following year and was led by Mufti Ja'far Husayn until his death in 1983.[24]

His successor, 'Allama 'Arif Husayn al-Husayni (1946–88), was a young cleric from Parachinar in the tribal areas of the North-West Frontier Province. While Mufti Ja'far Husayn's career until the late 1970s was not especially noted for confrontational politics,[25] al-Husayni came of age in a markedly different social milieu. Najaf in the 1960s was much more than a major center of Shi'i learning, as it had been for Mufti Ja'far Husayn. By the time al-Husayni went to study at the madrasas of Najaf in 1967, a new generation of Shi'i scholars was well-advanced along the path of drastically redefining their role as one of active social and political engagement, a role that was a conscious departure from the accommodationist stance of the elder Shi'i mujtahids.[26] Al-Husayni stayed in Najaf for six years, and came into contact there with, among others, Khumayni.[27] That he was influenced by some of the implications of what Chibli Mallat has characterized as the "Renaissance" of the 1960s[28] is best attested perhaps by his being expelled from Najaf by the Iraqi authorities for political involvements (of which no details are known, however).[29] Al-Husayni later went to Iran and spent another four years in Qumm, which, like Najaf, was a major center not only of learning but also of Shi'i political opposition.[30] He returned to Pakistan in 1978, on the eve of the revolution in Iran. Involved in the political mobilization of the Shi'a from the start, and with such impeccable credentials as studying at the premier institutions of Najaf and Qumm and, not least, counting Khumayni as a mentor, he was soon prominent enough to succeed Ja'far Husayn as the leader of the TNFJ in 1983. He led the Shi'a through 1988, in which year he was assassinated.[31]

The manifesto of the TNFJ, formally issued in 1987, is a document of considerable interest and deserves brief consideration here.[32] It prescribes the Qur'an and the sunna as the fundamental sources of Pakistan's Constitution and of all laws, but lays down that each "recognized" Islamic school of thought or sect is to be governed by its own interpretation of what the Qur'an and the sunna mean.[33] All sects are to be given "effective" representation on the Council of Islamic Ideology, a body charged by the Constitution of Pakistan with the function of advising the government on all matters pertaining to Islam in public life.[34] The demand for religious freedom figures prominently, and it is stated to include the right to the unhindered observance of Muharram as well as the right to proselytize for one's faith.[35] There is no dearth of rhetoric on the need for a complete overhauling of Pakistan's economic, social, and political systems; and the lack of true commitment to Islam on the part of the ruling elite and the state's subservience to the "imperialist powers" are among the factors the manifesto emphasizes as the causes of Pakistan's problems. Finally, a significant aspect of the TNFJ's proposed mechanism for change is to create a "Popular Islamic Army": based on compulsory military training for all able-bodied males, this army is seen as helping to reduce the distance between the military and the people (the military regime of General Zia ul-Haqq was still in power in 1987) and as reviving the spirit of holy war.[36]

The emergence of a noisy Shi'i organization in Pakistan in the wake of the Iranian revolution caused considerable consternation to many Sunnis. Though the manifesto of the TNFJ was not explicitly sectarian, it is not difficult to visualize how many a wary Sunni interpreted it. That Islam and its fundamental sources are to mean different things to different people was disquieting, for instance: while the 'ulama were willing to acknowledge that matters of personal status might be decided according to the laws recognized by each sect, any further concessions threatened to take away the Sunni majority's ability to prescribe what the religious law of the land would be and, perhaps even more grievously, it suggested that Islam can, and should, have several competing yet equally valid—because officially recognized—forms. The proposal concerning a "Popular Islamic Army" could scarcely fail to raise suspicions about the militant ambitions of the Shi'a; and though Sunni religious parties usually also compete with each other in denouncing the "imperialist powers," the TNFJ's condemnation of them was strongly reminiscent of Iran's revolutionary rhetoric and, to many Sunnis, yet another confirmation of the Shi'i party's ideological indebtedness to Iran.

Freedom of religious observance meant, to those hostile to the Shi'a, the freedom to vilify the Companions of the Prophet and hence to attack the Sunni view of Islam itself. The Shi'a were known, after all, to vent their hostility towards many of the Prophet's Companions in the course of the Muharram observances, and it is during these that sectarian tensions have most often turned into rioting. On the other hand, the right to propagate one's faith was liable to be understood as the right to preach *Shi'ism* in what is a predominantly Sunni country. There is in fact considerable evidence of Shi'i preaching, especially in rural and small-town Punjab.[37] Such proselytism is, however, as likely to be directed against rival Shi'is as it is against the Sunnis. The former include, in particular, the "Shaykhiyya," who are regarded by many among the mainstream Twelver Shi'a as venerating the imams with unacceptably exaggerated beliefs, and whose strong mystical orientation is seen as likewise suspect.[38] That Shi'i preachers have internal rivals to contend with is not the only reason why it is hard to know with any certainty who might be the object of their energies. Sunnism itself has long remained a rather amorphous entity, as Sunni sectarians themselves acknowledge. Indeed, it is precisely this amorphousness, this lack of a self-conscious identity, that they see as the most potent threat facing their community. And the TNFJ came to typify this threat for them.

An aggressive, confrontational style of politics was characteristic of the TNFJ under the leadership of al-Husayni. His assassination in August 1988 was a major setback to the party, and since then it has progressively moved towards a more moderate stance. The aforementioned change of its name to Tahrik-i Ja'fariyya Pakistan (TJP) was part of this development. But the TNFJ/TJP is not all there is to Shi'i political activism. As the Tahrik-i Ja'fariyya increasingly cultivated an image of moderation, there were dissensions within its ranks and splinter groups developed.[39] The most militant of these is the Sipah-i Muhammad Pakistan.[40]

Though not a "youth wing" of the TJP, the Sipah-i Muhammad—which itself was later fragmented into several extremist groups[41]—is very much a young men's organization. A rural or small-town background; some education in the government school system; religious studies at madrasas in the Punjab or elsewhere in Pakistan and, not infrequently, in Iran;[42] and participation in the war in Afghanistan against the Soviet occupation of that country (1979–89) are fairly typical of the leadership of the Sipah-i Muhammad. 'Allama Sayyid Ghulam Riza Naqvi (b. 1960), who played a prominent role in the Sipah-i Muhammad's early career, illustrates this as well as anyone else. Born in Khanewal district in the Punjab, Naqvi attended college in Jhang, studied at madrasas in Multan and Lahore, and then went to Iran for further religious education. He also fought in Afghanistan during the Soviet occupation, an experience to which he, like many other Shi'i and Sunni militants, owed much of his military training. Naqvi later established a madrasa in Jhang and was involved in sectarian conflict there before coming, in 1993, to live, preach, and lead his organization in Thokar Niaz Baig, a traditionally Shi'i stronghold in the suburbs of Lahore.[43]

Since its inception in 1991, the Sipah-i Muhammad has frequently been linked to much anti-Sunni violence in the Punjab, in Karachi, and elsewhere in the country. The organization was critical of the TJP for what it saw as the latter's failure to protect the Shi'a from Sunni militancy.[44] For its part, the TJP has tended to maintain a discreet distance from the Sipah-i Muhammad, though without explicitly condemning its militancy. To Sunni radicals, the difference between the TJP and the Sipah-i Muhammad is only one of strategy, however, and both are taken to stand for undermining Sunnism in Pakistan. Few Sunni or Shi'i militants would agree, however, that their own rival sectarian organizations in fact exhibit considerable similarities with each other. In its recourse to violence, the Sipah-i Muhammad's methods match those of the Sipah-i Sahaba, as does the social background of many of its leaders. Networks of mosques and especially of madrasas are crucial means for both Shi'i and Sunni radical groups to exert and extend their influence, and both have profusely used the medium of print to disseminate their creed. And each has adduced the violent activities of the other as the reason for its own existence.

Radicalized Identities: The Sunnis

The Sipah-i Sahaba is an offshoot of the Jam'iyyat al-'Ulama'-i Islam, the Deobandi organization that was formed in 1945 when some 'ulama had separated from Husayn Ahmad Madani and the other "nationalists" of the Jam'iyyat al-'Ulama'-i Hind (see chapters 1 and 2). The Jam'iyyat al-'Ulama'-i Islam has played a considerable role in Pakistani electoral as well as agitational politics: it participated in the anti-Ahmadi agitations in 1953 and again in 1974; it led a coalition government in the Northwest Frontier Province between 1971 and 1973; and in 1977, it was part of the Tahrik-i Nizam-i Mustafa, a multiparty electoral alliance against the government of Zulfiqar 'Ali Bhutto and the Pakistan Peoples Party. The elections of 1977 were widely perceived to have been rigged in favor of the incumbent Bhutto, to which the Nizam-i Mustafa alliance responded by launching a massive, country-wide agitation that crippled the Bhutto government and led to the imposition of martial law by General Zia al-Haqq.[45]

The Sipah-i Sahaba was established, under the Zia al-Haqq regime, in September 1985. It was founded in Jhang, a middle-sized city in the district of the same name in the Punjab,[46] by Mawlana Haqq Nawaz Jhangawi (1952–90). Born in a poor rural household of Jhang, he had attended a government school for some time but soon after had settled for a madrasa education. In 1973, he began his career as a preacher (*khatib*) and prayer-leader (imam) in a Deobandi mosque in urban Jhang—roles in which he was to continue till his assassination in 1990. That mosque is now known by his name, as is the town quarter (*mahalla*) in which he lived. The Sipah-i Sahaba was founded in the same mosque.[47]

Like many of those who were later to play a leading role in the Sipah-i Sahaba, Haqq Nawaz had participated in the agitation which led, in 1974, to the Ahmadis being declared non-Muslims in Pakistan. Many Sunnis had all along regarded the Shi'a, too, as non-Muslims, and the precedent set by the constitutional excommunication of the Ahmadis was not lost on them. Nor did Shi'i political activism in Pakistan in the wake of the Iranian revolution, as well as Zia ul-Haq's Islamization, contribute to sectarian harmony. Militant confrontations between the Shi'a and the Sunnis began from the early 1980s. Sectarian violence was not confined to Jhang, though it is not fortuitous (at least according to radical Sunnis) that the Sipah-i Sahaba emerged there. The following account comes from a biography of Mawlana Haqq Nawaz by one of his close associates. It is simplistic and tendentious, yet not without some factual validity; and in any case, it is revealing of this Sunni organization's own worldview:

Jhang was a backward district dominated by feudal lords (*jagirdars*). . . . They found license in Shi'ism for the life of pleasure and libertinism they desired, and so the rural gentry had become Shi'i. Under their influence, the peasants and other members of the lower castes also went over to Shi'ism. But even those who didn't had remained neither Shi'i nor Sunni, and had no sense of shame at being devoid of religious identity. Sunk in ignorance, they retained some of their traditional customs in the name of Sunnism (*sunniy-yat*), while in other respects they had become assimilated with the Shi'a. They knew nothing of their beliefs, nor of their religious orientation (*maslak*); they did not practice their faith, nor were they bothered about not practicing it. All they had were certain rites of ignorance (*rusum-i jahiliyyat*) and nothing else. In all matters of happiness and grief in life, they were as one. . . . If anyone tried to reform this situation and to indicate to them the differences between the Shi'a and the Sunnis, he was accused of fomenting discord, of being a sectarian; he would be deemed undesirable, and would no longer be allowed in the area. . . . Mawlana Haqq Nawaz, after he became convinced of what the truth was, began preaching; and he was defiant in the face of all opposition.[48]

The ignorance of "true" Islam in the countryside remained a major theme of much reformist literature in the nineteenth and twentieth centuries, and not just in Deobandi discourse.[49] The above account is of interest, however, for explicitly linking such ignorance to the influence of Shi'-ism. Jhang is indeed dominated by rural magnates who profess Shi'ism, and the latter do wield considerable social and (as *pirs* associated with local shrines) religious influence on the lower classes, as the account suggests. In the Sipah-i Sahaba's view of things, this landed gentry not only exploits the peasantry in social and economic terms,[50] but has also led them astray even in matters of the faith. The above description, and much else in the Sipah-i Sahaba's rhetoric, also seems to evoke the image, tendentious yet powerful, of an "original" Sunnism: the people of the area were once committed to Islam and should, by being rescued from the influence of Shi'ism, be brought back to it. Religious reform in this context must mean making people aware of a sectarian identity ("the differences between the Shi'a and the Sunnis") they are presumed to have lost. They must, in short, be made (or remade) Sunnis. Conversely, as noted earlier, there is evidence of Shi'i proselytizing in the countryside, too, in Jhang as elsewhere in the Punjab, and it is not just Sunni madrasas but also Shi'i ones whose numbers have grown dramatically in recent decades.[51] For all the difficulties in interpreting such evidence, it is tempting to see the allusion in the above account to people coming under the influence of Shi'ism as recognition of inroads Shi'i preachers may have made in the countryside.

Though the Sipah-i Sahaba's rhetoric necessarily equates local forms of religious belief and customary practice with the influence of Shi'ism (even as it equates Sunnism with a text-based, urban Islam), there seems little reason to believe that the rural audience to which radical sectarian organizations address themselves have had any but the most perfunctory prior acquaintance with the urban Islamic tradition. Imparting a sectarian identity is therefore less a case of "converting" rural peasants to Sunnism from Shi'ism (or the reverse) and much more of confronting local practices with the Islam of the urban religious scholars and institutions. It is this local Islam, combining Shi'i, Sunni, and Sufi elements, that the Sipah-i Sahaba sees as "Shi'ism" and that it seeks to combat. This struggle is of course also a way of resisting the influence of pirs, many of whom in the Punjab are not only rural magnates but also adherents of Shi'ism.[52] But there is another side to this sectarian struggle—and one which goes beyond the Shi'a. Inasmuch as many of these shrine-based pirs are associated with the Barelawi sectarian orientation rather than expressly with Shi'ism, the Sipah-i Sahaba's sectarian radicalism also represents a struggle *within* the ranks of the Sunnis. A consequence of the Deobandi Sipah-i Sahaba's spearheading of the struggle against the Shi'a has, in fact, been the gradual rise of the Deobandis to prominence as against other Sunni groups, and most notably at the expense of the Barelawis.[53] Among the Shi'a, for their part, the rise of militant sectarian organizations has likewise contributed to the marginalization of the mystically oriented Shaykhi Shi'a in the countryside.

The Sipah-i Sahaba's formal goals are easily defined: to combat the Shi'a at all levels, to strive to have them declared a non-Muslim minority in Pakistan, to proscribe Muharram processions (which it regards as a major cause of sectarian riots), and to make Sunni Islam the official religion of the state. The ideal polity is taken to be that of the "rightly-guided (Rashidun) caliphs" of early Islam, and it is that model that the organization pledges to emulate in Pakistan.[54] But it is not enough to draw inspiration from that golden age. As a mark of affirming symbolic commitment to it, the Sipah-i Sahaba would have the death anniversaries of the Rashidun caliphs (as well as of several other prominent Companions of the Prophet) instituted as days of national commemoration, and would have the highest honors of the state designated by the names of these caliphs.[55] These are among the signs of a Sunni, and hence truly Islamic, state, a state whose commitment to Sunnism ought to be as visible as it is profound. And it is for the 'ulama to deepen and strengthen this commitment, to launch and lead the people on the path to this Islamic state. "The enemies of Islam have fostered the idea that the men of religion ought to have nothing to do with politics," Mawlana Haqq Nawaz said in a speech in 1989. But to abandon the political sphere is to leave it to the corrupt and the ungodly.[56] "If the system of governance of the rightly guided caliphs were in place in the country, it would not matter if you [the 'ulama] were to engage yourselves in ascetic practices in the wilderness. But today is not the time for such behavior."[57]

Even as an unmitigated hostility towards the Shi'a defines the stance of the Sipah-i Sahaba, its own symbolism shows unmistakable signs of Shi'i influence. Zealous adoration of the Companions of the Prophet has manifest similarities with the Shi'i veneration of the imams. One may even detect a conscious effort here to claim for Sunnism its share of charismatic leaders, other than the Prophet, who would be the object of intense personal devotion—a tendency "orthodox" Sunnism has traditionally resisted against both the Shiʿa and the Sufis.[58] Devotion to the Companions is inscribed, literally, on the Sipah-i Sahaba's multicolored flag, which features a hadith of the Prophet ("My companions are like stars; you will find guidance in whomsoever [of them] you follow") with a crescent and five stars.[59] More generally, the Sipah-i Sahaba's symbolism is also interpretable as a response to the ceremonials of Muharram. In the past, and occasionally even now, local Sunnis would join in such processions and ceremonies, both because they too revere the memory of Husayn and because these processions have often provided colorful entertainment to the people. The Sipah-i Sahaba aspires to substitute a new set of commemorative occasions for the Shiʿi ones. The counterceremonies are intended not so much to attract the Shiʿa as to prevent Sunnis from being attracted to Shiʿi gatherings, as well as, more generally, to demonstrate that the Sunni tradition has no dearth of occasions to commemorate. *Cultural* Shiʿism is in fact more of a challenge than Shiʿi militancy, for many (putative) Sunnis are unsuspecting victims of it or are exposed to its lure. In the Sipah-i Sahaba's worldview nothing is more urgent, therefore, than to make people "rediscover" their Sunni identity and to define for them, in terms that are both negative ("Muharram processions are un-Islamic") and positive ("The sahaba must be rescued from Shiʿi vilification, their honor guarded, their memory revived and revered"), what this identity consists in.

The Sipah-i Sahaba's call for a self-consciously Sunni ritual is an example of what Catherine Bell has characterized as the "invention of ritual." Arguing against those who hold that if ritual is to have any efficacy, the fact of its having been invented by someone must remain concealed from those who practice it, Bell notes that even patently invented rituals can function as all rituals do. Recently invented rituals are no different from the supposedly timeless ones in providing "modes of communal socialization"; and, as in the case of many state-sponsored rites in the former Soviet Union, many recently minted rituals might continue to appeal to older traditions and customs and be adopted by the people as much for that as for any other reason.[60] In the case of the Sipah-i Sahaba's call that the death anniversaries of the Companions be marked as national holidays, likewise, no effort is made to hide the novelty of this proposed practice. For the operative consideration here is that the people whose memory is thereby to be celebrated, and the reverence for that memory, do indeed go back to Islam's first generations. The novelty of the ritual is thus counterbalanced by the traditional roots of what the ritual seeks to celebrate. What distinguishes the Sipah-i Sahaba's ritual symbolism from earlier celebrations of the Companions' memory, however, is its effort to appropriate the modern nation-state to the cause of Sunnism. It is crucial, yet not sufficient, to make people conscious of their Sunni identity. Sunnism must suffuse the institutions of the state, and Sunni celebrations must become part of state ceremonial. The inspiration for this sectarian vision of an Islamic state seems, ironically, to be indebted above all to post-1979 Iran, where Shi'i Islam enjoys a central position as the legitimating ideology and official religion of the state.

Indeed, no event has created among radical Sunnis a greater sense of urgency to combat Shi'ism than the Iranian revolution. Though the revolutionary regime was keen to forge ties with the Sunni Muslim world and to win the support of Sunni Islamists, its profoundly Shi'i character disillusioned and alarmed many Sunnis.[61] At the same time, the success of the revolution encouraged the Shi'a outside Iran to assert a more active, even aggressive, presence in their local communities. A major expression of this assertion was the massive production and dissemination of pro-Iranian and specifically Shi'i literature, in Urdu in the case of Pakistan. Iranian cultural centers had some involvement in this activity,[62] but more frequently Shi'i scholars, preachers, and madrasas of Pakistan took the initiative in their own hands. In doing so, they have produced works that—depending on the writer's taste, the audience, and the level of the writer's education—have ranged from the scholarly to the most rabidly anti-Sunni and specifically anti-sahaba.

While such works had, of course, been written and read in the past, their proliferation—not to mention the suspicion that the resources of a revolutionary Shi'i state were behind them—antagonized many Sunnis in Pakistan. To have such writings proscribed has remained a major concern of the Sipah-i Sahaba.[63] To mobilize Sunni opinion and to bring home the horrors of the Shi'i threat, it has also ensured that lurid accounts of sacrilegious Shi'i writings on the Companions reach wide audiences,[64] and not just in Pakistan.[65] In 1994, Mawlana Zia al-Rahman Faruqi (d. 1997), the then head of the Sipah-i Sahaba and owner of the publishing house where most of the organization's literature has been produced, announced plans to bring out a massive compendium of (selections from?) no less than one hundred and sixty-five Shi'i books. "This will be something new in Pakistan, and indeed in the history of Islam," Faruqi asserted, probably with some justice. "We will take this document to jurisconsults (muftis) of fifty-eight [Muslim] states, and obtain, on the basis of it, the fatwa that the Shi'a are infidels. Obviously, when so many books characterizing the sahaba as unbelievers and apostates are brought to the attention of the 'ulama of every [Muslim] country, no mufti would any longer be able to consider the Shi'a to be Muslims."[66]

The publications of the Sipah-i Sahaba, especially its monthly journal, aptly called the *Khilafat-i Rashida*, have sought to forge a sectarian bond by informing their readers about not only what the Shi'a, or Iran, might be doing against them, but also what the Sunnis are, at last, doing for themselves. The *Khilafat-i Rashida* has made efforts to keep its readers informed of the Sipah-i Sahaba's activities, often in minute detail: its combating the Shi'a and their influence in different parts of the country; its catering to the social and economic needs of the indigent Sunnis and, especially, the families of Sunnis killed, disabled, or imprisoned due to sectarian violence; and the uninterrupted extension, in Pakistan but also abroad, of its organizational network.[67] All this, together with the effects of much other sectarian literature, have helped create an "imagined community" of sectarian Sunnism in Pakistan,[68] a community united in devotion to the Companions but brought together by much more than the symbolism of the Sipah-i Sahaba.

Social and Economic Bases

Much of the support for sectarian organizations comes from the middle classes. Sectarianism is largely an urban phenomenon, though, as noted, it is part of the Sipah-i Sahaba's purpose to combat agrarian magnates (who are all too often also influential in the adjoining urban centers) and to bring an aggressive Sunni identity to the countryside. In Jhang, where the Sipah-i Sahaba was founded, much of the support for this organization comes from urban Sunni businessmen who are believed to handle a large part (nearly 80 percent according to some estimates) of the commercial activity in the district.[69] This Sunni bourgeoisie includes a substantial number of migrants from India, who settled in urban Jhang at the time of the partition of the subcontinent in 1947.[70] Jhang's predominantly agricultural economy is dominated by a landed elite who are believed to control nearly 65 percent of all land in the district.[71] Though the Shi'i rural magnates are "native" to the region, sectarian affiliations are not clearly drawn along urban/rural or native/settler lines: there are urban Shi'a (often with considerable stakes in business) and rural Sunnis too; and Mawlana Haqq Nawaz, the founder of the Sipah-i Sahaba, was himself a "native."[72] Nevertheless, a commercial (and, to a lesser extent, industrial) bourgeoisie[73] is clearly the most important source of support upon which the Sipah-i Sahaba draws in Jhang and in other urban areas. Associations of local traders (*anjuman-i tajiran*) have been known to actively respond to the Sipah-i Sahaba's calls for general strikes and protest marches, and the latter have often originated in the main bazaars.[74]

Though urban Jhang is dominated by a Sunni bourgeoisie, the Shiʻa are also part of the bourgeoisie in Jhang, as indeed elsewhere. In fact, the Shiʻa probably comprise a greater proportion of the urban middle class than they do of the Pakistani population as a whole. Some of the very prominent business families, especially of Karachi, are Shiʻi.[75] Many urban middle class Shiʻa profess to be "secular," which is often interpreted as their response to the perception that Islamization in an overwhelmingly Sunni country must mean the privileging of Sunni institutions over Shiʻi.[76] Yet the proportion of "secular" Sunnis is surely no smaller than that of the Shiʻa, and much of the support for the Shiʻi sectarian organizations comes from the middle class too.[77]

While it is in places like urban Jhang, as well as in numerous small towns (qasbas) of the Punjab, that sectarian conflict has tended to take place most often, it is noteworthy that many urban supporters of sectarian organizations have a not-too-distant rural background. Many urban migrants bring with them memories of the high-handedness of the rural magnates, and it is not difficult to visualize them being attracted to calls for combating the latter's feudal oppressiveness and to the ideological legitimation offered for it. In an urban milieu where administrative and judicial authorities are inefficient and corrupt, and are widely held to act in concert with the landed elite, the Sipah-i Sahaba's appeal to the interests of the "common man" and its challenge to established but corrupt authority—rural magnates, pirs, urban administrators—also carries force. Mawlana Haqq Nawaz, himself a man of humble origin, had a reputation for being much concerned with the welfare of the poor and the helpless, and he was known to regularly spend time at government courts helping out poor illiterate litigants. As the Sipah-i Sahaba began to gain increasing prominence and come into frequent conflict with the local administrators and the Shiʻi gentry, the organization's heroic image steadily grew, together with that of its leader.

Olivier Roy has remarked in another context on the role of the Shiʻi clergy in resocializing Shiʻi migrants from a tribal-rural milieu into an urban setting.[78] In Pakistan such a function is not confined to the Shiʻa. Sunni ʻulama, madrasas, and especially an organization such as the Sipah-i Sahaba have played a similar role. But it is not only to marginalized urban migrants that the Sipah-i Sahaba and, no doubt, Shiʻi madrasas and sectarian organizations offer support and anchorage. They appeal as well to the upwardly mobile middle class and especially to the commercial bourgeoisie or those aspiring (often without success) to join their ranks. It is such people, often themselves of a rural background, who have been among the principal supporters of the sectarian organizations both of the Sunnis and the Shiʻa.

TABLE 1
Growth of Madrasas in the Punjab, 1975–2001

Division	1975	1980	1985	1990	1994	2001
Bahawalpur	278	417	598	795	883	971
D. G. Khan	153	217	297	363	411	397
Multan	45	102	179	212	325	363
Lahore	75	120	170	219	323	356
Rawalpindi	58	85	119	157	169	186
Sargodha	75	98	130	148	149	164
Gujranwala	52	66	96	131	140	154
Faisalabad	?	?	?	?	112	124
Total					2512	2715

Sources: Zindagi, February 17, 1995; *The News* (March 7, 1995); ibid., May 26, 1997; *Dawn*, January 22, 2002. (Figures for Faisalabad division were not available prior to 1994.)

The numbers as well as the resources of those who saw themselves as the middle class, especially in the Punjab, grew tremendously from the mid-1970s through the mid-1980s. One of the principal reasons for this was the outflow of Pakistani labor overseas during these years. This remarkable movement of labor, the dramatic changes in status and expectations it entailed, and not least, the social and economic dislocations many labor migrants suffered on their return, are also part of the context in which radical sectarianism has emerged in Pakistan. According to one estimate, "[a]pproximately 10 million people or 11 per cent of the total population (a figure which includes dependants) have benefited directly from the exodus to the Middle East. The vast majority of the beneficiaries come from low-income households. On average, their salaries increased between 600 and 800 per cent."[79] Most of the labor migrants came from a rural background,[80] though a majority of them returned to settle in urban areas.[81] Such migrants, of whom the Punjab contributed about 70 percent,[82] typically worked abroad for only four or five years, however; and by the mid-1980s, migration abroad was in decline and the number of returnees was at its peak.[83]

That the emergence of sectarian organizations dates to the same time as the return, in increasing numbers, of the labor migrants is not fortuitous. These sectarian organizations responded to the search of many people—including but not only labor migrants returning from abroad—for an urban religious identity that would accompany, and perhaps facilitate, their quest a middle class status. A shared sectarian identity not only cemented other bonds—common business interests, rural or kinship ties, a shared experience of working in the Middle East and similar problems of assimilation into a new urban milieu on return—but helped also in forging the sense of belonging to a new and distinct community. The bonds of this community are constantly reiterated: praying in the same mosques behind a prayer leader who may also be one of the leaders of the sectarian organization one supports;[84] jointly bearing the financial burdens involved in the maintenance and growth of mosques[85] and madrasas (see table 1), as well as in supporting families of those who have fallen victim to sectarian violence; subscribing to the publications of madrasas and sectarian organizations, and, in case of businessmen, advertising in them too;[86] and being constantly made aware, through these publications but also through the mosque preacher, of how members of this sectarian community elsewhere are engaged in activities similar to their own.[87]

The career of Mawlana Isar al-Qasimi (1964–91), a leader of the Sipah-i Sahaba, illustrates some of the socioeconomic context of sectarian commitments. Isar al-Qasimi's family had migrated from Ambala in eastern Punjab to settle in a village in rural Lyallpur (now Faisalabad) at the time of the partition of India. His father spent many years in the Middle East, as have many activists and supporters of the Sipah-i Sahaba. After completing his education, which involved studies at three different madrasas in Lahore, Isar al-Qasimi tried to set up his own business but failed. In 1985, he began preaching in a mosque in Okara in the Punjab besides teaching in a madrasa he had established there. After the Sipah-i Sahaba was founded, Isar al-Qasimi came to Jhang, on the bidding of Mawlana Haqq Nawaz, to preach in one of the market towns of the district. A fiery orator, Isar al-Qasimi soon came into conflict with Shi'i magnates of the area, denouncing them for their high-handed dealings with their peasants, especially Sunni peasants, and mobilizing Sunni opposition against them. Many of those who rallied to the Sipah-i Sahaba's cause as represented by him were small peasants who doubtlessly felt empowered by the aggressive Sunni identity he helped them acquire.[88] But his supporters also included successful shopkeepers and businessmen. It was no accident that, in what became a familiar pattern, the Shi'i agrarian magnates of the area responded to his challenge by having shops owned by Sunnis attacked and burned.[89]

After the assassination of Mawlana Haqq Nawaz in February 1990, Mawlana Isar al-Qasimi became the deputy leader of the Sipah-i Sahaba and, as the symbolic mark of his succession, also the prayer leader and preacher at Haqq Nawaz's mosque in Jhang (Mawlana Zia al-Rahman Faruqi, the aforementioned publisher from Faisalabad, was chosen to head the organization.)[90] The same year, Isar al-Qasimi contested elections to both the National and Punjab assemblies; he won both seats, defeating for the National Assembly seat a powerful Shi'i rural magnate of the Sial family of Jhang[91] and becoming the very first member of the

TABLE 2
Sectarian Riots in the Punjab 1989-94, 1997–98

Year	Incidents	Persons Injured	Persons Killed
1989	67	102	10
1990	274	528	32
1991	180	263	47
1992	136	240	44
1993	90	247	38
1994	115	249	37
1997	97	175	200
1998	36	80	78

Sources: The Nation, September 1, 1994; *Dawn*, January 1, 1998; *Dawn*, December 28, 1998.

Note: The figures for 1994 include incidents up to but not later than August 17, 1994. Note that these are official and thus probably rather conservative estimates; the actual number of casualties may have been much higher.

Sipah-i Sahaba to enter parliament. (Haqq Nawaz Jhangawi had contested elections to the National Assembly in 1988, but had lost to one of the most influential landlords of the area.)[92] It was not long, however, before sectarian tensions took their toll, as they had for many other leaders of radical sectarianism, and in January 1991, Isar al-Qasimi was assassinated in Jhang.[93]

As is typical of radical religious movements, the fact that the leaders frequently fall victim to violence does nothing to dampen either the zeal of their followers or the attractions of the resort to violence. For the Sipah-i Sahaba, as indeed for the Shi'i organizations, violence from sectarian opponents only reinforces their perception of threat from the "other," and hence their raison d'être of "safeguarding," often through violent retaliation, their sectarian kin from that threat (see table 2). Like mosques, madrasas, print, a shared social background, and common economic interests, religiously sanctioned violence and growing lists of martyrs[94] also contribute to the sense of community. Such sacrifices of blood seldom fail to reinforce and sanctify the shared sectarian identity or to give it an added, unrelenting dynamic.

Sectarian violence has clearly exacted a heavy toll in the Punjab, but, as table 3 illustrates, it is not limited to this province. Though it is in the Punjab that the principal sectarian organizations (the Sipah-i Sahaba, the Tahrik-i Ja'fariyya, and the Sipah-i Muhammad and their splinter groups) are based, their activities also extend to other parts of the country.[95] In a comparative study of incidents of ethnic conflict in contemporary South Asia, anthropologist Stanley Tambiah identifies "focalization" and

TABLE 3

Notable Incidences of Sectarian Violence in Pakistan, 1997–2001

January 1997	Twenty-six people, including Zia al-Rahman Faruqi, the head of the Sipah-i Sahaba, killed in a bomb explosion in Lahore (Punjab).[1]
February 1997	Seven people, including the director of the Iranian cultural center, killed in Multan (Punjab);[2] five people killed in Lahore.[3]
April 1997	Nine people killed near Bahawalpur (Punjab).[4]
August 1997	Eight people killed in Shorkot; four in Jhang; eight in Sheikhupura; four in Multan; six in Khangarh (all in the Punjab).[5]
September 1997	Five Iranian military cadets killed in Rawalpindi (Punjab).[6]
October 1997	Four Sunni madrasa students killed in Multan.[7]
November 1997	Habib Allah Mukhtar, the president of the Jami'at al-'Ulum al-Islamiyya madrasa of Karachi (Sindh) assassinated.[8]
January 1998	Twenty-two Shi'is killed and over fifty injured near Lahore.[9]
October 1998	A leading Sunni mosque preacher killed in Islamabad (the federal capital).[10]
January 1999	Four Shi'is killed in an attack on an *imambargah* in Multan[11]; five including the Shi'i custodian of a shrine, killed in Multan.[12]
April 1999	Four Shi'is killed in Dera Ismail Khan (the North-West Frontier Province).[13]
October 1999	Nineteen people killed in sectarian violence in Karachi.[14]
December 1999	Twelve Sunnis killed in Haripur (the North-West Frontier Province) in dispute with the local Shi'a over the building of an imambargah.[15]
April 2000	Nineteen Shi'is killed in various incidents, including an attack on an imambargah in Attock (Punjab).[16]
May 2000	Muhammad Yusuf Ludhianawi of the Jami'at al-'Ulum al-Islamiyya madrasa assassinated in Karachi.[17]
January 2001	Five people belonging to the Jami'a Faruqiyya of Karachi, including two professors of hadith and a mufti, assassinated.[18]
March 2001	Nine people killed in Lahore in a pro-Sipah-i Sahaba mosque;[19] seventeen people killed in sectarian riots in Hangu (the North-West Frontier Province).[20]
May 2001	Mawlana Salim Qadri, leader of the Barelawi Sunni Tahrik, assassinated in Karachi along with five others.[21]
October 2001	Six Shi'a killed in shooting in a Karachi imambargah;[22] four killed in shootings at two Sunni madrasas of Karachi.[23] Seventeen Christians killed in a church shooting in Bahawalpur (Punjab).[24]

TABLE 3 *cont.*

Notable Incidences of Sectarian Violence in Pakistan, 1997–2001

Note: This table is based on reports in Pakistani newspapers. Also see Nasr, "Rise of Sunni Militancy," 141, table 1: "The Worst Instances of Sectarian Violence, 1988–97."

[1] *The News*, January 24, 1997. For a list of incidents of sectarian violence in the Punjab during 1997, see Azmat Abbas, "Punjab's Worst Year of Sectarian Violence," *Dawn*, January 1, 1998. Of those killed in 1997, 118 were Shi'a and 77 were Sunnis (*Dawn*, January 19, 1999).

[2] *The News*, February 21, 1997.

[3] Ibid., February 28, 1997.

[4] Ibid., April 25, 1997.

[5] *Dawn*, January 1, 1998.

[6] Ibid.

[7] Ibid., October 21, 1997.

[8] For news reports on this incident and the ensuing strike called by the leading 'ulama to protest this killing, see *Dawn*, November 3–8, 1997.

[9] *Dawn*, January 12, 1998; *The Nation*, January 12, 1998.

[10] *Dawn*, December 12, 1998.

[11] Ibid., January 5, 1999.

[12] *The News*, January 24, 1999.

[13] Ibid., April 27, 1999.

[14] Ibid., October 2–3, 1999.

[15] Ibid., December 28, 1999.

[16] Ibid., April 8, April 13, April 27, 2000.

[17] Ibid., May 19, 2000. For the protests and violence following this incident, ibid., May 19–20, 2000.

[18] *Al-Faruq*, 16/12 (March 2001): 7–12.

[19] *Dawn*, March 13, 2001.

[20] Ibid., March 19, 2001.

[21] *Newsline* (June 2001): 22, 39–41.

[22] *Dawn*, October 5, 2001.

[23] Ibid., October 7, 2001.

[24] *The News*, October 29, 2001; *Dawn*, October 29, 2001. No group claimed responsibility for this action, but Deobandi militants were widely suspected. This terrorist act was highly unusual, however, in that much of the sectarian violence in Pakistan had hitherto targeted members of rival *Muslim* sects (although sectarian rivals don't consider each other to be "really" Muslim) but not people belonging to other religious communities.

"transvaluation" as two processes that extend the scope of such conflict to include ever larger numbers of people: focalization, he suggests, consists in the "process of progressive denudation of local incidents and disputes of their particulars of contexts and their aggregation. *Transvaluation* refers to the parallel process of assimilating particulars to a larger, collective, more enduring, and therefore less context-bound cause or interest."[96] Similar processes are at work in extending the scope of sectarian causes to ever larger numbers of people, and to areas where these may not have been immediately felt before or where the social and economic contexts in which sectarian (or other) conflict takes place is different. The network of mosques and madrasas, and the proliferation of sectarian publications and of party cells, all ensure that a supralocal sectarian community now exists whose members can relate, and react, to the tribulations of their sectarian kin anywhere, irrespective of local context.

This network also provides members of the community with remarkable mobility. The career of Mawlana Muhammad A'zam Tariq (b. 1961), who formerly represented the Sipah-i Sahaba in the lower house of the Pakistani parliament, spans both the Punjab and Sind, for instance, and thanks in part to him, so does the influence of his organization. He was born in the Sahiwal district of the Punjab but studied at a madrasa in Karachi and later established a mosque for himself in that city. After the founding of the Sipah-i Sahaba, this mosque became its principal organizational unit. Beginning with his position as the prayer leader and preacher of this mosque, A'zam Tariq rose to lead the Sipah-i Sahaba first in Karachi, then in the province of Sind as a whole, and finally, at the national level as the deputy leader of the organization. On the assassination of Mawlana Isar al-Qasimi, he was elected from a constituency in Jhang to fill Isar al-Qasimi's position in parliament.[97] The sectarian community is supralocal even as it is constantly reinforced by local conditions and grievances.

Types of Religious Leadership

Unlike the 'ulama discussed in chapter 2, the Sunni 'ulama whose careers we have briefly noted in this chapter did not usually have much claim to intellectual distinction. They are "peripheral 'ulama," to borrow and adapt political scientist Malika Zeghal's characterization of the increasingly activist 'ulama on the "periphery" of al-Azhar in contemporary Egypt.[98] As in Egypt, however, there are important ties that join the higher-ranking 'ulama with the peripheral ones. If Mawlana Haqq Nawaz's "sectarian upbringing" came in the struggle against the Ahmadis, it is worth noting that some of the more distinguished 'ulama had also honed their polemical skills against the Ahmadis, the Barelawis, the modernists, and others before turning their attention more fully to the Shi'a. One of the most influential of these was the Indian scholar Mawlana Manzur Nu'mani (d. 1996), who was mentioned earlier as the author of a commentary on hadith as well as a popular primer on Islam. Besides being the founder and long-time editor of a monthly religious magazine, Nu'mani's claims to distinction included membership on the advisory board of the Deoband madrasa and, together with his close friend Abu'l-Hasan 'Ali Nadwi, a long-time membership in the Saudi-sponsored Rabitat al-'alam al-Islami. Like Nadwi, again, he was actively involved in the work of the Tablighi Jama'at.[99] Early in his career Nu'mani had engaged in public disputations with the Barelawis as well as with Hindus of the Arya Samaj.[100] But he is best known for a book entitled *The Iranian Revolution, Imam Khumayni, and Shi'ism*, which he wrote late in life and which became a best-seller not just in South Asia but also in many other parts of the Muslim world. In 1987, he wrote another, shorter treatise on Khumayni and Shi'ism in the form of a request for a fatwa (*istifta'*). Initially published in his monthly magazine, *al-Furqan*, this treatise was sent to leading 'ulama and madrasas in India and Pakistan to solicit their juristic opinion on the Shi'a's unbelief. These responses were then published serially in *al-Furqan* and, later, in the form of a book.[101]

Nu'mani believed that many Muslims had mistaken the political triumph of the Shi'i revolutionary movement in Iran for a reassertion of Islam itself, without being aware that Shi'ism was not part of "Islam" at all. In their ignorance of its blasphemous beliefs, many a youthful Muslim had even been converting to Shi'ism.[102] He wanted to set the record straight, he said, and he urged other 'ulama (and, indeed, anyone reading his work[103]) to do the same. He appealed to the religious scholars to "do whatever they can" to make ordinary Muslims aware of the dangers of Shi'ism, a threat to Islam that was being promoted with nothing less than "the resources of a powerful state."[104]

Manzur Nu'mani was but one among several prominent religious scholars to urge on the sectarian foot soldiers and to lend his moral and polemical support to the peripheral 'ulama leading the charge. Others included Mufti Wali Hasan (d. 1995) of the Jami'a Banuriyya of Karachi, who issued a fatwa in response to Nu'mani's query, which was then circulated among and endorsed by many other Pakistani 'ulama;[105] Mawlana Sami' al-Haqq of the Dar al-'Ulum Haqqaniyya in the North-West Frontier Province;[106] and Mawlana Yusuf Ludhianawi of the Jami'at al-'Ulum al-Islamiyya in Karachi. As we saw in chapter 3, Ludhianawi had been one of the severest critics of government efforts towards reforming madrasas. But he also had an influential career as a sectarian polemicist, which involved a lifelong association with the struggle against the Ahmadis and intense hostility towards the Shi'a. He was assassinated, presumably by the latter, in May 2000, to become one of the most highly visible casualties of sectarian terrorism.[107]

The leading religious scholars do not say that the Shi'is should be killed, only that they are infidels in light of their vilification of certain early Islamic figures as well as some of their other beliefs. But enough justification is thereby provided to the peripheral 'ulama and their operatives—who are often little more than mercenary terrorists on both sides—to wage an ongoing war against their sectarian opponents. The leading 'ulama have often tried to stay at the level only of an intellectual and moral struggle against the Shi'a. But sectarian violence has an important "performative" dimension to it. And the fact that they too have been targeted—Ludhianawi, for instance—as the trophies of such violence shows that, in view of their opponents, there are no firm boundaries between the militants on the ground and those seen as urging them on from a distance.[108]

The 'ulama we have discussed in the foregoing—the high-ranking ones and the peripheral—are all Deobandi. But are there further distinctions to be made within the ranks of the Deobandi 'ulama themselves, so far as sectarian radicalism is concerned? In an important recent study, Seyyed Vali Reza Nasr has argued that sectarianism in contemporary Pakistan is the outcome and expression of the effort by one group of Deobandi 'ulama to dominate the religious and political landscape of the country. Some of the followers of Husayn Ahmad Madani, who, it will be recalled, had opposed the demand for a separate Muslim state, lived in the regions that became part of Pakistan. These 'ulama (whom Nasr calls the Madani Group) were viewed with suspicion in the new state because of their earlier stance, which had set them apart from the followers of such pro-Pakistan 'ulama as Ashraf 'Ali Thanawi and Shabbir Ahmad 'Uthmani (characterized by Nasr as the Thanawi Group). The 'ulama of the Madani Group, Nasr argues, tried to rehabilitate themselves in the new polity by focusing on an easy target: the position of the minorities in this self-professed Islamic state. This led them to play an active role first in the religio-political agitation against the Ahmadis and later against the Shi'a. In both cases, they were asserting their own role in politics, reinstituting themselves as legitimate religious and political leaders, and reconnecting with Madani's *political* legacy, even as the 'ulama of the Thanawi group were, and have remained, largely content to stay out of active political involvements.[109]

This is an ingenious argument, but it is too schematic to be persuasive. As Nasr is aware, it was Shabbir Ahmad 'Uthmani and the 'ulama of what he calls the Thanawi Group who had founded the Jam'iyyat al-'Ulama'-i Islam as a political party to muster support for the demand for Pakistan;

and Shabbir Ahmad 'Uthmani had himself played an influential role in the early debates on an Islamic constitution for the new state. Another leading pro-Pakistan figure was Zafar Ahmad 'Uthmani, the son-in-law of Ashraf 'Ali Thanawi and the author of the hadith commentary *I'la al-sunan*, which we examined at some length in chapter 2. 'Uthmani had been active in East Bengal in his support of the Pakistan movement, and later he served as the national leader of the Jam'iyyat al-'Ulama'-i Islam. 'Ulama' like Taqi 'Uthmani of the Dar al-'Ulum of Karachi—whom Nasr would implicitly put in the Thanawi Group of largely apolitical 'ulama[110]—are especially devoted to the memory of Ashraf 'Ali Thanawi. But in view of Taqi 'Uthmani's extensive discussion of how the state ought to implement Islamic law, it is hard to consider his work largely apolitical.[111] There is considerable ambivalence in his writings towards the large claims that the state can and does make on the religious sphere, and this is what sets the 'ulama apart from the Islamists, as we saw; but there is little to suggest that politics itself is seen as suspect by such 'ulama. Taqi 'Uthmani's elder brother, Mufti Rafi' 'Uthmani, the president of the Dar al-'Ulum, is an even more striking illustration of the difficulty of neat categorizations between the political and the apolitical 'ulama. His pronouncements on the madrasa as a miniature Islamic society and state, his misgivings about electoral politics, and his argument that the 'ulama must devote themselves with greater energy to Islamization from below (see chapter 4) might suggest an apolitical vision. But misgivings about electoral politics do not necessarily signify an apolitical stance; and the grassroots activism that Rafi' 'Uthmani recommends is itself a means towards gradually gaining enough leverage for the 'ulama to act as a force in national politics. Also worth noting is Rafi' 'Uthmani's active support of the Afghan struggle against Soviet occupation. Students from his madrasa participated, and some were killed, in this war; and Rafi' 'Uthmani himself visited the war front, later writing a detailed account of this war to celebrate the memory of its many martyrs.[112]

It is not my contention here that we should dissolve all distinctions among the 'ulama. There no doubt are politically quiescent 'ulama just as there are more radically inclined ones; and some have devoted themselves primarily to academic pursuits while others wage sectarian battles on the street. The activities and attitudes of the contemporary 'ulama are more accurately ranged along a broad spectrum of options and possibilities, however, than they are fixed in mutually exclusive or dichotomous groupings. For instance, grassroots activism can and often does continue along with efforts to press the government in power to implement Islamic measures from the top down. The 'ulama's intellectual productivity often continues unhampered by their political involvements; indeed, the prestige gained from the former is an important part of the influence they are able to exert in the latter. And as Zafar Ahmad 'Uthmani's refutation of united nationalism as part of his *I'la al-sunan*, and Taqi 'Uthmani's considerable attention to issues pertaining to the implementation of Islamic law, illustrate, many of their intellectual involvements are eminently "political." In *this* respect, there is much in common between Manzur Nu'mani and Taqi 'Uthmani, or between the vehemently pro-Taliban Sami' al-Haqq (on whom more later[113]) and Rafi' 'Uthmani, or between Yusuf Ludhianawi and Haqq Nawaz. That the 'ulama have been drawn to potentially radical options is a relatively new phenomenon, as is the radicalization of sectarian identities in Pakistan. Nasr is doubtlessly correct in arguing that this sectarian radicalism represents the increasing domination of the Deobandi 'ulama over 'ulama of other sectarian persuasions, for instance the Barelawi.[114] For, as noted earlier, the Sipah-i Sahaba's attack on the rural magnates militates not only against the Shi'a but also against the Barelawis, who, like the Shi'a, are often also closely associated with rural Sufi shrines. But, pace Nasr, this radicalism is not limited to one distinct segment of the Deobandi 'ulama; nor, for that matter, is it at all clear that the roots of this radicalism lie in the position of the nationalist 'ulama of late-colonial India.

Expanding Horizons—In and Outside Pakistan

Before the severe Sunni backlash against them dimmed their hopes and restricted the scope of their activities, Shi'i activists and scholars were often eager to win adherents in the countryside, viewing their potential converts not only as wayward Shi'is but also as rural Sunnis. Activists of the Sipah-i Sahaba, for their part, continue to define their goals in proselytism as rescuing people from the influence of Shi'ism, to which they have been subjected by ignorance or by virtue of subservience to Shi'i rural magnates. The veneer of either Shi'i or Sunni Islam has remained extremely thin in the countryside, however, and as noted earlier, both are usually components of a broader mix of locally accepted practices. Part of the significance of sectarianism lies, then, in bringing an urban, text-based tradition to the countryside in the form of an aggressive and self-consciously Sunni or Shi'i Islam, even as urban audiences themselves are educated, or reeducated, in this "true" Islam. The Sipah-i Sahaba's effort to bring a Sunni identity to the people means introducing them to a very different form of Islam than they are familiar with. The nerve centers of this new Islam are not Sufi shrines but madrasas and sectarian organizations; and the feudal pirs are no longer the guardians of rural Islam but, in this worldview, the enemies of the true faith. Shi'i religious scholars and preachers have likewise attempted to acquaint rural or recently urbanized people, professing some devotion to certain Shi'i ceremonies and rituals, to an Iranianized form of Shi'ism[115] sustained by madrasas, sectarian organizations, and Shi'i literature.[116]

As an agent of religious change sectarianism has assisted the 'ulama in asserting their influence and in extending it to areas where previously such influence was minimal. But this influence is not just that of those we have called the peripheral 'ulama in the context of Pakistani sectarianism—those who have been in the trenches, so to speak, in this struggle. Just as the work of the leading 'ulama offers justifications for the radical Sunnis to wage their struggle against the Shi'a, so too does that struggle expand the influence of the 'ulama in general, not only that of the peripheral ones or those associated directly with the Sipah-i Sahaba. When leaders of the Sipah-i Sahaba instruct their followers to concentrate on reading religious literature as a way of deepening their newfound identities, they have in mind more than the literature produced by the organization itself.[117] Such exhortations serve equally to expand the audiences, the sphere of influence, of the 'ulama as a whole.

That financial support for sectarian organizations comes from the middle class, as we saw earlier in this chapter, means that sectarianism creates opportunities for the 'ulama not only to extend their reach in society through such support but to expand and deepen it within this class itself. With this expanding influence, acquired in the course of the struggle against the Shi'a (and before them, the Ahmadis), the Deobandi 'ulama have also come to eclipse Barelawi forms of shrine-based religiosity *within* Sunnism. What is more, they have begun to "dominate the Islamist discourse at the cost of such lay Islamist parties as the Jama'at-i Islami,"[118] which has also traditionally drawn its support from the urban middle classes.

The significance, then, of sectarianism in Pakistan is manifold. It is an agent of Islamization from below, and it is a mechanism for the expansion of Deobandi reformism. Though it comes at the expense of the Barelawis and the Shi'a, it is, overall, also an expression of *the 'ulama's* growing influence. The latter is, indeed, a phenomenon much broader than sectarianism itself and one that is to be witnessed in many other contemporary Muslim societies as well (see chapter 6). So far as Pakistan's Deobandi 'ulama are concerned, the past quarter century has seen an expansion of their influence not only within the country but also outside it. If sectarianism is the most important expression of the former, the strange career of the Taliban in neighboring Afghanistan is surely the most striking illustration of the latter.

The Taliban emerged in response to the massive dislocations caused in Afghan society during and after the Soviet invasion of 1979.[119] During the course of the Soviet occupation and the Afghan resistance against it, more than three million Afghans came to reside in Pakistan as refugees.[120] Large numbers of young refugees found their way into Pakistani madrasas, and numerous new madrasas (and other schools) were created to cater to their needs.[121] They provided food and lodging to the refugees, and a religious education.[122] Afghan students were encouraged to return to their homeland to participate in the ongoing war, and others—Pakistani nationals and those who had come to study in these madrasas from other countries—often felt motivated to go as well. Mawlana Sami' al-Haqq's Deobandi madrasa, the Dar al-'Ulum Haqqaniyya, in Akora Khattak near Peshawar in the North-West Frontier Province, played an especially important role in the war. Afghans had always formed part of the student body of this madrasa, and some of these students were to become prominent in the Afghan resistance.[123] During the Soviet occupation, Afghan students at this madrasa—"400 out of 680 (about 60 per cent)" in 1985[124]—were exempt from the normal boarding restrictions imposed on other students; and *al-Haqq*, the monthly magazine of this madrasa, served as an important vehicle for propagating the cause of *jihad* in Afghanistan, and indeed, as a veritable "war reporting magazine."[125]

The Soviet occupation of Afghanistan ended in 1989, but that did not bring peace to this troubled land. The factions that had led the struggle against the Soviet forces now fought bitterly against one another. As the Pakistani journalist Ahmed Rashid has put it, "The country was divided into warlord fiefdoms and all the warlords . . . fought, switched sides and fought again in a bewildering array of alliances, betrayals and bloodshed."[126] It was in this context that a new movement arose, towards the end of 1994, to challenge these warlords, to bring an end to their continued conflict, and to restore Islamic norms that the erstwhile *mujahidin* were seen to have betrayed. Though led by Afghans of the Pashtun ethnicity—the numerically dominant of the country's numerous ethnic groups—this movement had strong ties with Pakistan and was, in fact, rooted in the Deobandi madrasas, especially of Pakistan's North-West Frontier and Balochistan provinces. It was in these madrasas that numerous young Afghans had come of age during the years of the Soviet occupation. By 1996, these Taliban (literally: students) had taken the capital, Kabul, and were soon in control of much of the country—a control they were to maintain for the next five years.

Along with Saudi Arabia and the United States, Pakistan had been actively involved in supporting the anti-Soviet Afghan struggle. And the rise of the Taliban can itself be traced to Pakistani efforts to continue to influence the course of Afghan politics in pursuit of its own geostrategic goals. In particular, it has been argued, the Taliban were conceived as a means of pacifying Afghanistan so as to use it as a safe conduit of Central Asian oil from Turkmenistan through Pakistan to the Arabian Sea. This abortive aspiration involved not only strategic planners in Pakistan but also the U.S. conglomerate Unocal, which was part of the consortium committed to building an oil pipeline through Afghanistan.[127] It also involved the Deobandi political organization, the Jam'iyyat al-'Ulama'-i Islam. The latter had been at the forefront of the effort to establish new madrasas to accommodate Afghan refugees during the Soviet occupation; and its leaders—Mawlana Fazlur Rahman and the aforementioned Mawlana Sami' al-Haqq—were, for several years, key players in maintaining contact between the Taliban and the Pakistani government.[128]

Unocal withdrew from the pipeline project as a result of the outcry in the United States at the Taliban's grim human rights record and especially their treatment of Afghan women.[129] Successive Pakistani governments, however, continued their support of the Taliban, despite the highly questionable success they (and Pakistan's often quasi-independent military intelligence) may have had in exerting their influence on the Taliban, let alone in furthering their own goals. But even Pakistan was forced to dramatically change course in the wake of the terrorist attacks on the World Trade Center and the Pentagon on September 11, 2001, in which several thousand people were killed. The United States linked these attacks to the Saudi radical Islamist, Usama bin Laden, who since 1996 had been living in Afghanistan under the protection of the Taliban. Under intense American pressure, Pakistan's military government agreed to cooperate in the U.S.-led effort to capture or kill Bin Laden, destroy the terrorist camps in Afghanistan, and remove the Taliban from power for their refusal to hand over Bin Laden to the United States. For all the protestations of the Pakistani president, General Pervez Musharraf, that Pakistan had no choice but to side with the United States in this war, that the country would receive desperately needed economic assistance from the United States, and that most of the Pakistani people—the "silent majority"—supported his decision to become part of the U.S.-led coalition, this crisis put unprecedented strains on the fabric of Pakistani society.[130] It also put new strains on the relations of the 'ulama with the state.

Staunch Deobandis, the Taliban had continued after their rise to power to maintain close ties with Pakistani 'ulama, and especially with the Dar al-'Ulum Haqqaniyya. "In 1999 at least eight Taliban cabinet ministers in Kabul were graduates [of this madrasa] . . . and dozens more graduates served as Taliban governors in the provinces, military commanders, judges and bureaucrats."[131] Not surprisingly, the monthly magazine of this madrasa had hailed the Taliban as "the architects of the renaissance of Islam, the standard bearers of the system (*nizam*) of the Khilafat-i Rashida in the twenty-first century."[132] And Mawlana Sami' al-Haqq, the president of this madrasa, had hoped, not long after the Taliban capture of Kabul, that movements similar to theirs would arise in Pakistan "so that the people of Pakistan too can enjoy the fruits of an Islamic system."[133] Such sentiments had won considerable notoriety for Sami' al-Haqq, in Pakistan as well as on the international scene, even before the September 2001 terrorist attacks created considerable media interest in his madrasa. (Already in June 2000, *The New York Times Magazine* had devoted a cover story to this madrasa.)[134]

"The fruits of an Islamic system" have a sectarian taste, however, and on this the Taliban and Sami' al-Haqq concur with the Sipah-i Sahaba as well as with many other Deobandis. Thousands of Shi'a from the rival Hazara ethnicity had been massacred when the Taliban captured Mazar-i Sharif in northern Afghanistan in August 1998.[135] Also killed on this occasion were eleven Iranian diplomats—an incident that very nearly brought Iran and Afghanistan to war with each other. Members of the Sipah-i Sahaba, together with members of various Muslim groups fighting against Indian control of the disputed territory of Kashmir, are known to have trained in Afghan military camps.[136] At a time when there seemed to be a strong possibility of war between Iran and Afghanistan, Mawlana A'zam Tariq of the Sipah-i Sahaba was quoted as being "ready to send 20,000 militants [*sic*] to fight alongside the Taliban if Iran tried to impose a war on Afghanistan."[137] Along with the Jam'iyyat al-'Ulama'-i Islam and the Jama'at-i Islami, the Sipah-i Sahaba was at the forefront of anti-American protests when U.S. military operations were launched against the Taliban in October 2001.[138] There was active recruitment for jihad in Afghanistan, and thousands of Pashtun tribesmen, Islamists, and Deobandi volunteers crossed into Afghanistan to fight alongside the Taliban against the United States and the troops of the anti-Taliban Northern Alliance.[139] In the following weeks, as the Taliban rule crumbled before massive American airstrikes, many of those captured and killed by the forces of the Northern Alliance were said to be from Pakistan.[140]

The Deobandi 'ulama were never unanimously euphoric about the Taliban, however. In a letter to the leaders of the Taliban shortly after the latter's capture of Kabul, a number of leading Deobandi 'ulama of Karachi had congratulated them on their victories but had also expressed the hope that the "Taliban would do everything possible to ensure that Afghanistan commences its journey on the path of culture and civilization and [thereby] establishes a luminous example for other countries." Without referring explicitly to the Taliban's extremely controversial closing of schools for girls, this letter also emphasized the expectation that everyone—man and woman—would receive "basic education" under the Taliban.[141] In June 1997, an editorial entitled "The Government of the Taliban: Better Expectations" in *al-Balagh*, the monthly journal of the Dar al-'Ulum of Karachi, had again expressed hope not only that the Taliban would attend to the educational needs of the people but that "in addition to considering the requirements of Islam, the system of education would also take account of the needs of the time."[142] Couched in the language of advice and expectations, these mildly worded criticisms pointed to a certain discomfort among some of the 'ulama regarding the policies of the Taliban. 'Ulama' like Taqi 'Uthmani, whose madrasa took the lead in voicing these criticisms, travel extensively in the Muslim world and make frequent visits to Europe and the United States, where they address Muslim as well as non-Muslim audiences.[143] In terms of intellectual activity, too, there is a great gulf between the Deobandi Taliban and Deobandi scholars like Taqi 'Uthmani. The latter has published extensively on law and hadith and, as we saw in chapter 5, he is an active contributor to debates on the implementation of Islamic law. The Taliban, on the other hand, never showed much inclination for any religious scholarship or intellectual engagement whatsoever. Not all, nor even most, of those who count themselves or are reckoned to be among the 'ulama—in Pakistan or elsewhere—are necessarily "scholars" in any conventional sense; but in case of the Taliban, the very designation as "students" underscored not only how this movement emerged but also the modesty of its intellectual claims.

Yet if the narrow world of the Taliban remained very different from the broader horizons of 'ulama like Taqi 'Uthmani, the former, for all their checkered career, did nonetheless represent an extension of Deobandi influence outside South Asia. Leading Deobandi 'ulama—among them Mufti Rafi' 'Uthmani of the Dar al-'Ulum, the elder brother of Taqi 'Uthmani—were invited as state guests to Afghanistan as if to put on display not just the new Islamic state but also the Deobandi influence on it.[144] If regular visits to Western countries have, in recent years, become a means for 'ulama like Taqi 'Uthmani to reach new audiences among immigrant Muslim communities, the Taliban, too, have been a facet—albeit a very different one—of that expanding Deobandi influence. Given, moreover, that the Taliban were only erstwhile "students," they could be seen, while still in power, not only as the instrument of Deobandi influence but also as the necessary *object* of such influence. In giving its advice to the Taliban leadership, the aforementioned letter from Karachi's Deobandi 'ulama had stated as much: "There is no lack of highly accomplished scholars of religion and of technical experts in the Islamic world. We hope that, in making Afghanistan an Islamic welfare state, no delay would be allowed in utilizing the insight and experience of these sincere and erudite 'ulama and technical experts."[145]

Far more important, however, than the short-lived opportunity to provide this "expert" guidance to the Taliban's Islamic state is what the Taliban's career in Afghanistan has meant for the Deobandi 'ulama in Pakistan. As the former "students" of these Pakistani 'ulama, the Taliban have helped enhance the latter's profile, their religiopolitical capital, *within* Pakistan—and this even the fall of the Taliban is unlikely to dissipate. A striking illustration of this enlarged profile was offered in April 2001, when the Jam'iyyat al-'Ulama'-i Islam organized a large international conference near Peshawar, in the North-West Frontier Province, to celebrate the achievements of Deoband as a reformist movement. Participants came from throughout Pakistan, from India (including the head of the Jam'iyyat al-'Ulama'-i Hind and the Deoband madrasa's own top-ranking professor of hadith), Afghanistan, and from other places. And among those whose messages were read out to the more than half a million people or so who had gathered for this three-day conference were the Taliban leader, Mullah Muhammad 'Umar, and even Usama bin Laden.[146] This was a peaceful show of force, of Deoband's international standing, even—somewhat awkwardly—of Islamic universalism and sectarian amity.[147] But its scale was unusual, and the conference would have been inconceivable without the symbolic significance of the rise of the Deobandi Taliban in neighboring Afghanistan.

On other occasions the rhetoric has been more strident. The specter of "Pakistani Taliban" taking over the state has often been raised in Pakistani and international media, and never more so than after Pakistan joined the American war effort against the Taliban. Though the Pakistani ruling elite have vehemently and repeatedly denied that possibility,[148] it is worth noting that certain Deobandi 'ulama have sometimes adopted precisely such rhetoric to threaten the government. Following the assassination of Habib Allah Mukhtar, the president of the Jami'at al-'Ulum al-Islamiyya of Karachi and one of the signatories to the aforementioned November 1996 letter of advice to the Taliban, some 'ulama were reported to have "warned the government against adopting an indifferent attitude [towards the assassination] and threatened that 'Pakistani Taliban' will march towards Islamabad . . . if it continued to remain unmoved."[149] As the closest Pakistani ally of the Taliban, the Jam'iyyat al-'Ulama'-i Islam displayed considerable, though carefully calibrated, belligerence in the wake of Pakistan's decision to side with the United States against the Taliban. Before impassioned gatherings of protestors, leaders of the organization branded president Pervez Musharraf as a "traitor,"[150] threatened the removal of his government through mass agitations,[151] and affirmed, with the Taliban leadership, that jihad against the United States had become incumbent on Muslims everywhere.[152]

Such challenges have come, *inter alia*, from Mawlana Sami' al-Haqq and Mawlana Fazlur Rahman of the Jam'iyyat al-'Ulama'-i Islam, the Sipah-i Sahaba, and from leaders of the Jama'at-i Islami.[153] Once again, some of the Deobandi 'ulama have been rather more ambivalent. After the United States gave an ultimatum to the Taliban to turn over Usama bin Laden, thirty-three scholars of Karachi's Dar al-'Ulum—including Mawlana Rafi' 'Uthmani and Mawlana Taqi 'Uthmani—issued a written appeal to the Taliban to be mindful of the interests of Pakistan and Afghanistan in this crisis and to try to resolve it with "an open mind." They recognized, the 'ulama said, the difficult choices confronting the Pakistani government in this crisis, and they approved of its cooperation with others in combating terrorism. At the same time, however, these 'ulama also criticized the American stance as "unjust" because, to them, Bin Laden's culpability for the terrorist attacks had yet to be established and to go to war without doing so meant "giving official sanction to terrorism with the backing of state power."[154] After military operations against the Taliban began in October 2001, the 'Uthmani brothers joined a larger group of 'ulama to reiterate some of these views, in terms that were notably harsher but clearly stopped short of declaring jihad against the United States or making violent threats against the Pakistani government.[155] Others were not so reticent, as we have seen. Yet even when they come only from some of their more radicalized fellow travelers, the strident rhetoric and the militant activism both serve to enhance the political capital of the Deobandi 'ulama in general—and of this none of them are likely to be entirely unaware.

Given the ties between the Pakistani Deobandis and the Taliban, and the symbolic importance of the latter as a mark of Deobandi influence abroad, the dislodging of the Taliban with Pakistani help has exacerbated tensions between many of the 'ulama and the Islamists, on the one hand, and the ruling elite, on the other. The ban imposed by General Musharraf's government on a number of sectarian organizations, including the Sipah-i Sahaba and the Tahrik-i Ja'fariyya, but also on organizations primarily active in Indian-controlled Kashmir, has contributed to tensions between the government and Islamist groups, and perhaps within the military establishment itself. The militant organizations active in Indian Kashmir have long been seen in Pakistan as contributing to the Kashmiri people's struggle for freedom from Indian control, after all, and they have maintained close ties with the Pakistani military; indeed, it was only under the immediate threat of war with India that the government of General Musharraf seems to have been forced, in early 2002, to sever its ties with such groups. So far as the 'ulama are concerned, ongoing governmental efforts to regulate the affairs of the madrasas are, likewise, a cause of considerable misgivings towards the government. This is not only because 'ulama regard their madrasas as the custodians of a beleaguered Islam (see chapter 3), but also because they have tended to see the government's current initiative to enhance its oversight of madrasas as a response to American pressure to do so. The state's effort to redefine the religious sphere as represented by the madrasa has always been anathema to the

Pakistani 'ulama, but the perception that this initiative has now become part of the U.S.-led global War on Terrorism greatly raises the stakes for them as they champion the madrasa's autonomy.

The 'ulama are still far from the centers of power; indeed, they seem even more so in the aftermath of the events of September 11, 2001. Yet the tensions in Pakistani society, the ambiguities about the place of Islam in public life, and the range of activities in which the 'ulama can or do participate all ensure a considerable, and continuing, influence for them. The past quarter century has witnessed new and growing expressions of religiopolitical activism, and other, newer modes of action are likely to continue emerging—at the grassroots and at other levels. The banning of sectarian organizations does not suffice, by itself, to erode the bases of radical activism, any more than renewed governmental efforts to regulate madrasas—even when such efforts are less riddled with contradictons than they have been in the past—necessarily divest the 'ulama of their varied roles.

There seems little reason to doubt, then, that the 'ulama's engagement with society and the state will continue to assume forms that are not only varied but also malleable and overlapping, and that often reinforce one another as they evolve in tandem with other trends and tensions within and outside Pakistan. But as the short-lived career of the Taliban, for all its peculiarities and failures, reminds us, the Pakistani 'ulama are not unique in their new prominence. The Shi'i religious establishment of revolutionary Iran is, of course, the preeminent instance of what Martin Riesebrodt has called "radicalized traditionalism."[156] But in a number of predominantly Sunni societies, as well, the 'ulama have acquired a new prominence in recent decades.

VI

Religiopolitical Activism and the ʿUlama: Comparative Perspectives

THERE IS NO parallel in the Sunni Muslim world to the authority the highest-ranking Shiʿi religious scholars have wielded since the emergence of the position of the marjaʿ al-taqlid in the second half of the nineteenth century, a position which, in turn, became the basis for Khumayni's reformulation of the doctrine of wilayat al-faqih in 1970 and for the rise to power of the Shiʿi religious establishment with the Iranian revolution of 1979. Insofar as the actual assumption of political power by the ʿulama is concerned, perhaps the closest contemporary parallel to the Shiʿi ʿulama of Iran was represented by the strongly anti-Shiʿa Sunni Taliban of Afghanistan. But in several other Muslim societies, too, the ʿulama have come to play new and highly significant religiopolitical roles. This chapter examines the context in which these roles have emerged in a number of contemporary societies, both where Muslims comprise a numerical majority and where they are a minority. While comparative perspectives have frequently informed our discussion of the Pakistani ʿulama in the previous chapters, the discussion here foregrounds the comparative dimension in order to understand what underlies the ʿulama's contemporary activism. Why have the ʿulama's activist roles emerged when they have, in particular since the last quarter of the twentieth century? How do the ʿulama relate to the Islamists in their societies? And what do facets of this religiopolitical activism have in common across Muslim societies? These are among the questions I focus on in the following.

The ʿUlama and the State in Egypt

The Egyptian ruling elite, like those in other Muslim societies, have long depended on the ʿulama for religious legitimacy. But, as elsewhere, they have often also made efforts to restrict the power of the ʿulama—an effort that, in modern times, has typically taken the form of "reforming" and regulating the ʿulama's educational institutions. In examining the debate on madrasa reform in British India and Pakistan, we have seen how it provided the context in which new conceptions of religion began to emerge; these conceptions are, in turn, closely related to the ʿulama's view of themselves as religious specialists in a modern society and polity. Governmental initiatives towards reform manifested differently in different Muslim societies, and they varied not only in their thoroughness but also in their effects. As the case of Egypt and the reform of the Azhar—arguably the most prestigious center of learning in the Sunni Muslim world—illustrates, those effects sometimes diverged from anything the government policy makers could have anticipated.

The most thoroughgoing reform of the Azhar, effected under President Nasser in 1961, was intended to integrate the 'ulama, once and for all, into the educational mainstream.[1] Nasser was remarkably successful in this goal, at least in the short term. The Azhar was placed under the supervision of the Ministry of Endowments to facilitate its more effective regulation, and the regulation of religious life through it. At the same time, a new kind of Azhar graduate was envisaged, one who would be at home in both religious learning and the modern secular sciences. Yet the very effectiveness with which this restructuring was imposed on the Azhar had consequences that can only be described as paradoxical. As Malika Zeghal has argued, it was precisely this success that helped pave the way for the 'ulama's increasing involvement in Egyptian politics in the 1980s. The Azhar's structural reform in 1961 and the consequent incorporation of the modern secular sciences into its educational concerns meant that it was not long before its graduates began speaking in new ways not just to the conservative segments of society but also to the modern-educated ones. The "modernization of knowledge . . . blurr[ed] the frontiers drawn not only by public opinion, but also social scientists, between the Islamists and the ulema." With exposure to new forms of education, the 'ulama and the university-educated Islamists were able to comprehend and interact with each other much more effectively than they had ever done before. This has especially been the case with those Zeghal characterizes as the "peripheral" 'ulama, the Azhar-trained scholars and preachers who do not occupy important positions within the Azhar establishment but who are often influential outside it, thanks in part to their affinity with Islamist trends.[2]

If trying to immerse the Azhar into the educational mainstream has had unforeseen consequences, the same is true of the efforts to enhance the content of religious instruction in mainstream, government-sponsored education. This effort began in the nineteenth century and is traceable to the conviction of colonial officials—and later, of postcolonial ones—that values of political submissiveness could be effectively cultivated among the people through the teaching of religion. But, as Gregory Starrett has shown, the objectified conceptions of Islam that Egyptian children have been fed in government schools have had the once again unintended consequence of nourishing what he calls the Islamic Trend, or what others have characterized as Islamist movements.[3] The work of Starrett and the work of Zeghal converge in showing how the policies of successive governments have contributed both to the salience of objectified understandings of Islam in the public sphere and to reducing the distance between the Islamists and the 'ulama.

Even as the Egyptian political elite have striven to regulate and reform the Azhar, they have also sought to legitimize themselves and their policies with the help of the leading 'ulama associated with that institution. The services of the Azhar were used to help legitimize Arab nationalism and socialism under Nasser (1952–70), and then, under Sadat (1970–81), to *delegitimize* the socialists and the Nasserists. Later, during Sadat's presidency and then under Mubarak (1981–), the Azhar's energies were mobilized as a counterweight against Islamist radicals. That the Azhar has sometimes been called upon to dim the very hopes the government had itself created is illustrated by the case of Arab socialism, but it is especially in evidence in the often uncomfortable public debates on the implementation of the shari'a.

As part of the effort to seek the favor of Islamist groups and the 'ulama and to mobilize them against the regime's Nasserist and socialist opponents, Sadat's new Constitution of 1971 had declared that the principles of the shari'a were to be "a principal source of legislation" in the state. A constitutional amendment in 1980 went further, recognizing the shari'a as "*the* principal source" of legislation. Even before this amendment, legal codes were being prepared in the parliament to demonstrate the government's commitment to the implementation of Islamic law. The parliamentary committee entrusted with this task was required to follow the Azhar's expert guidance in this project;[4] and 'Abd al-Halim Mahmud, the Shaykh al-Azhar (1973–78) during much of Sadat's rule, was among the most ardent proponents of the immediate implementation of the shari'a.[5] Towards what proved to be the end of his rule, Sadat realized, however, that his regime's affirmations of the salience of Islam in the state had greatly emboldened its Islamist critics without doing very much to solidify the regime's legitimist credentials. As Sadat began to backtrack on the implementation of the shari'a (his successor, Mubarak, followed suit more vigorously) the Azhar establishment once again came to the regime's aid. Contrary to 'Abd al-Halim Mahmud's earlier calls for the *immediate* implementation of the shari'a, the Azhar now counseled, against the Islamists, a gradualist approach to the implementation of the shari'a and the Islamization of the laws.[6]

Yet even as the Azhar establishment has continued to stand by the regime and its initiatives, which have not always been consistent or coherent, younger, peripheral 'ulama associated with the Azhar have adopted a much more aggressive attitude on the question of the shari'a's implementation, as well as on a broad range of other issues concerning the position of Islam in public life. As noted earlier, the changes brought about by reforms in the Azhar itself have led to considerable affinity between the worldview of these peripheral 'ulama and the very Islamists whom the Azhar establishment strives to combat on the government's behalf.

But even the support of the Azhar establishment comes at a price. For the dependence of the Egyptian state on the Azhar has enabled the latter to insist, with considerable effectiveness, on its own prerogative to authoritatively define the perimeters of all that would be Islamically acceptable. Insofar as this effort is directed against the Islamists, it suits the purposes of, and has been aided by, the state. Indeed, as the Islamist threat seemed to intensify in the early 1990s, so did both the government's dependence on the Azhar and its willingness to see the scope of the institution's activities expand.[7] Yet by the same token, the government is forced to accommodate the Azhar even where the Azhar's "official" discourses diverge from the government's preferred policies. The Azhar has sought, in recent years, to enhance its own voice in the public sphere, not least by striving to muffle other voices.[8] For instance, it has been active in overseeing censorship of materials deemed religiously objectionable and in its attack on secular intellectuals. It is probably not fortuitous that the secular intellectual Faraj Fuda, who was assassinated in 1992, had shortly before been denounced as an apostate by a group of 'ulama.[9] Shaykh Muhammad al-Ghazali, a member of the Islamic Research Council of the Azhar, later justified this act by arguing that should the government fail in its obligation to punish apostates, others could not be blamed for undertaking it.[10] The same year, an "'Ulama Front" was revived, after many decades, with the blessings of Jad al-Haqq, the Shaykh al-Azhar (1982–96), to counteract what were perceived to be activities contrary to Islam. This organization played an important role in opposing the United Nations International Conference on Population and Development (ICPD), which was held in Cairo in September 1994, for its positions on abortion and premarital sexual relations. The Azhar's vocal opposition to the conference was a major embarrassment to the Egyptian government, which was hosting it.[11] The 'Ulama Front was also active in the campaign against Nasr Hamid Abu Zayd, a Cairo University professor who was accused of apostasy.[12] Mubarak's current regime strives to project a liberal face internationally, as demonstrated in its hosting the Cairo conference; yet it has also continued to not just acknowledge but strengthen the Azhar's ability to set the terms of religious debate in the public sphere. In 1994, the Majlis al-Dawla, a court that rules on issues of jurisdiction, acknowledged the overarching authority of the Azhar over censorship and made the Ministry of Culture subservient to it in this respect.[13] While the delegation of such powers might, of course, be justified in the government's view as a means of combating the Islamists with greater effectiveness through a more powerful, more "autonomous," and thus more credible al-Azhar, it has remained unclear precisely how effectively—and at what cost to its own religious legitimacy—the regime itself can regulate the course that the Azhar adopts on particular issues.[14]

The Azhar 'ulama thus exert their influence at several levels of the Egyptian society and state. Their most familiar, and derided (by many Islamists as well as the peripheral 'ulama), role is that of legitimizing the policies of the state. But that very function enables the Azhar to progressively enhance its influence, to extend the range of matters on which it can authoritatively speak. At the same time, the Azhar's own peripheral 'ulama have affinities with the Islamists—with their demands for the implementation of the shari'a, and with their forms of radical activism.

The 'ulama's ties with the Islamists are articulated at more than one level. Radical Islamist groups have long sought religious guidance from 'ulama on the periphery of the Azhar: 'Umar 'Abd al-Rahman (b. 1938), later convicted in the 1993 bombing of the World Trade Center in New York, had acted as the mufti of the Jama'a Islamiyya and the Jihad groups and was said to have authorized the latter's assassination of President Sadat.[15] At the same time, peripheral Azhar 'ulama and Islamists have acted in concert in opposing secular intellectuals and the ICPD, and in calling for the implementation of the shari'a. The Azhar establishment's own stance on the ICPD was in almost complete consonance with that of the moderate Islamists of the Muslim Brotherhood, so it is no surprise that the latter praised the Azhar in no uncertain terms on this matter.[16]

New forms of Islamist activism have also helped enhance the 'ulama's influence. Carrie Rosefsky Wickham and other scholars have argued that since the 1980s, Egypt has seen the emergence of an urban Islamic community at the grassroots level—a community sustained by ties between the lower-middle-class (sha'bi) neighborhoods and the university graduates, as well as by private mosques, private voluntary organizations, independent preachers, and the wide dissemination of Islamic literature.[17] Those who comprise this loosely organized "parallel Islamic sector," as Wickham calls it, maintain close connections with business and other economic interests and with the state bureaucracy. As in Pakistan, where the remittances of expatriate labor from the Gulf states dramatically expanded the ranks of the middle class and made new and unprecedented resources available for the support of sectarian organizations, the rise of the parallel Islamic sector in Egypt was made possible by large-scale remittances sent home from other Arab states. The number of Egyptian workers in Libya and the Gulf states "grew from about 10,000 in 1968 to 1.2 million in 1985. All told, an estimated 2.7 million Egyptian migrants worked outside the country in the twelve years from 1973 to 1985. . . . [O]fficial Egyptian worker remittances averaged over $3 billion in the early 1980s."[18]

Those associated with the institutions of the parallel Islamic sector often emphasize their exclusively "religious" concerns. Rather than engage in overt political activism, they seek to foster a self-conscious Islamic identity at the grassroots of society. Yet, as Wickham observes, the significance of this parallel sector goes far beyond its being a mechanism of religious change at the grassroots: its institutions provide financial support to Islamist groups, and those associated with this sector or influenced by its range of activities constitute recruiting grounds for these groups.[19] And the informality of the networks that constitute this parallel sector help elude governmental regulation, even as its insistence on *religious* concerns increases the political costs of governmental repression.[20]

As often highly popular and influential preachers in some of the private mosques,[21] as muftis associated with Islamic investment companies to legitimize their operations,[22] and as members of local neighborhood communities, the peripheral 'ulama, too, are part of the parallel Islamic sector.[23] What is perhaps more significant—though this has not been examined by students of contemporary Islam in Egypt—is that the parallel Islamic sector represents new opportunities for the expansion of the 'ulama's influence. Even though most of those associated with this sector are lay people—for example, university graduates—rather than 'ulama, and the most popular preachers in contemporary Egypt are not associated with the Azhar or with government-controlled mosques,[24] the effort to deepen and enhance people's religious commitments at the grass roots may arguably extend, at least potentially, the reach of the 'ulama's discourses. As a worker at an Islamic bookstore in Cairo stated in 1991, underlining the religious nature of the parallel Islamic sector's appeal: "A few young people but not many are interested in social and political affairs; most people are interested in 'fiqh' and explanations of the Quran. They aren't that interested in books on politics or the reform of society or, at least, that's not what most people come here to buy."[25] Such literature may "reflect the reformist agenda of the Muslim Brotherhood,"[26] as Wickham notes; but quite apart from affinities between that agenda and the Azhar's own concerns, demand for works on fiqh and the Qur'an may be taken equally to create larger audiences for the *'ulama's* discourses in these and other genres.[27]

If at least some of the Azhar 'ulama are part of this parallel sector and partake of a shared religious and political outlook, it is hardly surprising that they have opposed governmental moves to better regulate this sector. In the 1990s, the Azhar became increasingly involved in overseeing, censoring, and licensing the production of "Islamic" materials, as already noted. Yet in 1996, some of the Azhar's own 'ulama expressed strong disapproval of a government initiative to require the licensing of all preachers by the Ministry of Religious Affairs.[28] This indicates, once again, contestation within the ranks of the Azhar ʿulama on how closely to toe the government line; but it also reveals that the ʿulama seek to maintain their ties with the parallel Islamic sector even as the Azhar jealously guards its own role as the guardian of religious life.

How does the multifaceted expansion of the roles that the Egyptian ʿulama play in society compare with the activism of the Pakistani ʿulama? In briefly considering this question, we should note first that the character of the madrasas in Pakistan is quite different from that of the Azhar. Though certain madrasas of Pakistan (and India) enjoy great prestige, and not just in the Indian subcontinent, there is no single institution comparable to the Azhar of Egypt (nor, for that matter, is there a position like that of the Grand Mufti). Thus, while the Azhar was a natural target of government efforts to regulate the ʿulama and their institutions, with the reasonable expectation that once the Azhar was brought under control the affairs of the Egyptian ʿulama *as a whole* could be regulated, no single institution in South Asia offers such prospects.

The madrasa of Deoband in Uttar Pradesh, India, comes closest to the stature of the Azhar (it is often compared to the Azhar by the Deobandi ʿulama), but the ʿulama associated with Deoband represent only one of many sectarian orientations among the modern South Asian ʿulama; moreover, despite the prestige of the madrasa at Deoband, other madrasas of the same orientation are only loosely (if at all) connected with the parent institution. The connection of the Deobandi madrasas of Pakistan with the parent madrasa in Deoband is largely due (and is really confined) to the fact that many of the founders of these Pakistani madrasas were graduates of the madrasa at Deoband. It has, therefore, been extremely difficult for the modernizing elite in Pakistan to effectively exert their influence over these madrasas, many of which do not have, and do not seek, any "official" recognition. The loose organization of the Pakistani madrasas has stood them well in resisting government regulation. It has also helped the madrasas in forging ties of their own with other groups within and outside the country. Given the decentralization and relatively loose organizational ties among the madrasas of Pakistan, it might, in fact, be more appropriate to compare them not with the Azhar at all, but rather with the "parallel Islamic sector" of contemporary Egypt, which is far less amenable to state control than the Azhar has been.

Pakistani madrasas' greater success at resisting government regulation has meant that, though many Pakistani ʿulama have been exposed to some form of modern Western education, their exposure is not comparable in scope to that of the ʿulama of the Azhar.[29] In Egypt, as demonstrated by

Zeghal, the 'ulama's new political roles are the paradoxical result of the government's very success in trying to reform, modernize, and regulate the Azhar. In Pakistan, on the other hand, the 'ulama's religiopolitical activism can be partly attributed to the limitations on the government's ability to regulate the 'ulama. Incidentally, these two opposite paths to political activism, and their different relationships with attempted governmental regulation, may suggest a modification of Zeghal's argument, in that we have to look beyond the role of regulation in trying to explain this activism.

Yet irrespective of the role and effects of government efforts at reforming or regulating the affairs of the 'ulama, the paths to the 'ulama's activism in Egypt and Pakistan may not be all that different. An important common factor in both cases is the effort of the government to utilize the energies of the 'ulama for its own goals. In Egypt, as already noted, it is the concessions that the government was forced to give to the Azhar in exchange for the 'ulama's support that, in part, underlie the 'ulama's renewed vigor in politics. In Pakistan, especially during and after the eleven-year reign of General Zia al-Haqq, many 'ulama were crucial to the government's effort to influence the outcome of the war—against the Soviet occupation, and then the ensuing civil war—in Afghanistan, and 'ulama of the Deobandi persuasion have played a critical role in facilitating the government's relations with the Taliban. The Pakistani 'ulama were made use of in this way without any concomitant success in the regulation of their activities; whereas in Egypt, it is within a framework of governmental regulation that the 'ulama are often called upon to promote the government's various political projects. In both cases, however, governmental effort to employ the services of the 'ulama has led, in varying measures, to new forms of religiopolitical activism on the part of the latter.

In both Pakistan and Egypt, ambiguities about the place of Islam in the polity have also contributed to strengthening the 'ulama's public roles. Both states acknowledge a conspicuous public position for Islam, and yet both regularly fail to live up to the logic of their own promises. The rhetoric of such promises has been more extravagant in Pakistan than in Egypt, but in each case at least some of the expansion of religious discourse, and the 'ulama's public prominence, is attributable to the policies of the ruling elite. Yet we should also be wary of the temptation to reduce the 'ulama's activism to either the failed manipulation of the governing elite or to the ambiguities of the latter's ample rhetoric. We need to give more credit, as it were, to the 'ulama themselves, to their efforts in the cause of what they take to be the imperatives of the Islamic tradition and what they regard as their own proper role in upholding those imperatives. The same, *mutatis mutandis*, is true of other contemporary Muslim societies.

The Saudi 'Ulama

The influence of the 'ulama in the Kingdom of Saudi Arabia is founded on the alliance, in the eighteenth century, between Muhammad al-Sa'ud (r. 1745–65), a tribal chief from Najd, and Muhammad b. 'Abd al-Wahhab (d. 1791), the puritanical reformer after whom the 'Wahhabi' movement is named.[30] The rule of the Saudi family has been through many vicissitudes since that alliance was forged, but the 'ulama have continued to be central to its conceptions of political legitimacy.

Most Saudis belong to the Hanbali school of Sunni law, which as reinterpreted according to the teachings of Ibn 'Abd al-Wahhab, is the basis of the Saudi legal system. The scope of the Saudi 'ulama's authority derives from Hanbali and Wahhabi affirmations of the principle of ijtihad—reasoned reflection on the basis of the foundational texts to arrive at solutions to the problems at hand. As we saw in chapter 4, the Hanafis require that in matters already "settled" in their school of law, one ought to follow the earlier teachings (taqlid), though as we also saw, this does not preclude the necessity of "limited" forms of ijtihad for them. The Hanbalis of modern Saudi Arabia, for their part, often follow the lead of the more eminent contemporary scholars as well as the teachings of the masters of their school of law. But the scope of a Saudi qadi's independence in reaching a decision on the basis of his own ijtihad nevertheless remains very considerable. It has also been jealously guarded by the 'ulama.

Medieval legal theorists recognized that the ruler, too, was a legitimate locus of legal authority, and that this authority could be exercised within the bounds of the shari'a. Characterized as "shari'a politics" (siyasa shar'iyya), the ruler's legal authority complemented that of the jurists, and in the Ottoman legal system, the ruler often also laid down the limits within which the jurists and their discourses (fiqh) would be allowed to operate. Premodern 'ulama and rulers have typically competed with each other as to how this relationship of fiqh and siyasa would be defined, how each would affect the scope of the other. As Frank Vogel has argued, the ruler was the dominant partner in the Ottoman legal system; in the modern Saudi one, on the other hand, it is the 'ulama who have the defining role.[31] A corollary of this dominance of the jurists' fiqh over the ruler's siyasa is the Saudi 'ulama's assertion of their right to decide cases brought to them according to their ijtihad rather than in accordance with legal principles or laws enunciated by the state. This "microcosmic" vision, as Vogel characterizes it,[32] of how the shari'a ought to be practiced translates into the opposition of many Saudi 'ulama to the codification of the shari'a—which, as we saw earlier, is something 'ulama in most other Muslim societies have come to embrace. While the state has continued to issue laws in the form of royal decrees (nizam) to supplement the shari'a law and to foster greater uniformity in how the law is implemented, the microcosmic vision has led many judges in contemporary Saudi Arabia to set aside even these royal decrees in their own judicial practice.[33]

Uniformity of judicial practice has been sought not only through the "secular" decrees of the king, however, but also, and more effectively perhaps, through the edicts of the leading establishment 'ulama. Since 1971, the latter have constituted the influential Board of Senior 'Ulama';[34] and, in a further effort to make the 'ulama subject to greater centralized regulation, the head of this Board has, since 1993, held the official position of Grand Mufti of the state. Yet given the influence and independence that the 'ulama have historically enjoyed in society, the government's efforts to curtail that autonomy have, at best, been hesitant. The ideological underpinnings of the 'ulama's autonomy also put governmental efforts to restrict it at a decided disadvantage. After all, the Saudi state itself acknowledges the authority of the 'ulama to interpret the shari'a. By contrast, in Pakistan for instance, this is a matter of contention between the 'ulama and the modernist judges of the higher courts; and, even in Egypt, it is the Supreme Constitutional Court, not the Azhar, that rules on the question of whether particular laws are in conformity with the shari'a.[35] What is more, as Vogel has shown, the Saudi state also acknowledges the principle that a qadi can, if he so wishes, rule according to his own ijtihad rather than what the state or even the senior 'ulama might tell him to do. With such acknowledgement, it is hard to also insist that the qadis conform to royal decrees or even to a particular, state-sanctioned interpretation of sacred law.

Given the importance placed on ijtihad, the shari'a law as interpreted and applied in contemporary Saudi Arabia is hardly static. It continues to evolve and change, but it has tended to do so on terms defined by the 'ulama rather than by the state. Significantly, some of these changes have served to further enhance the scope of the 'ulama's authority in the judicial system at the expense of the ruler's. As Vogel demonstrates, matters that the Islamic legal tradition has long regarded as falling in the purview of the ruler's "discretionary" punishments (ta'zir) have increasingly come to be entrusted to the shari'a courts headed by the 'ulama. This has partly been in response to international criticism of Saudi justice, to demonstrate that it is not the ruler's capricious judgment but the courts' due process that is followed in all matters. But since it is the 'ulama who staff these courts, the result of this development has been further expansion of the sphere of their judicial authority. Yet oddly enough, as Vogel notes, "the king himself has done little or nothing to resist this trend. Although fundamental changes were being made in the division of jurisdiction to favor the 'ulama over the king, both King Khalid and King Fahd seemed to collude with the 'ulama in bringing them about. This represents the sudden surrender without a fight of territory that for centuries has been the ruler's."[36]

Why have the Saudi ruling elite not been able to resist the 'ulama's claims to autonomy or the expansion of their authority? In part it is because the 'ulama's authority is based on the doctrine of ijtihad and a religious scholar's or judge's *independent* right to undertake it. More generally, it is hard for a state that professes to have the shari'a as its basic law and which recognizes the 'ulama as the interpreters of the shari'a to dispute that expansion in the reach of the law can mean anything but an expansion in the shari'a's regulation of state affairs—in a word, in the authority of the 'ulama. The Saudi state has, moreover, depended heavily on the legitimation it derives from the leading 'ulama. Yet this way of legitimizing its rule also continually exposes it to calls not just for *greater* implementation of the shari'a but also, what is the other side of the same coin, to allegations that it has fallen short in its professed religious aspirations. The state's response to such attacks has been to reaffirm and extend its dependence on the 'ulama while also striving to curb the more radical dissidents.

When in 1979 a band of Wahhabi zealots, dissatisfied with the performance of the Saudi state in living up to its puritanical ideology, briefly took control of the Ka'ba in Mecca, the Board of Senior 'Ulama' came to the regime's rescue by sanctioning the use of force and the resulting shedding of blood in a sacred space (*haram*) where both are expressly prohibited.[37] Much more significant—for the legitimacy of the regime, the credibility of the religious establishment, as well as the emergence of new, radicalized voices within the ranks of the 'ulama—was the sequence of events leading up to the Gulf War of 1991. After Iraq occupied neighboring Kuwait and threatened to invade Saudi Arabia, the latter decided to seek the assistance of the United States and other Western countries in meeting the Iraqi threat, allowing Western troops to be stationed within its territories and to conduct military operations against Iraq from there. This decision did more than expose the military weakness of the Saudi state and its dependence on the United States. It also meant that non-Muslim troops were to be stationed in Islam's holiest land, from where they were to conduct military operations against a fellow Muslim state.

Notwithstanding their competition with the ruling elite over matters of legal jurisdiction (a competition in which the elite have continued to cede ground), the interests of the leading 'ulama have, since the alliance in the eighteenth century, remained intimately tied to those of the Saudi state. Unsurprisingly, therefore, the Board of the Senior 'Ulama' supported the regime's conduct during the Gulf War. But many other 'ulama were not impressed by the state's decision any more than they were by the religious establishment's willingness to go along with it. In the aftermath of the

Gulf War, they individually and collectively offered "advice" (*nasiha*) to the Saudi regime to undertake extensive reforms and spoke out against the state's dependence on the West. Demands for reform came from both the liberal critics of the regime[38] and those dissatisfied with it on religious grounds. The 'ulama were prominent among the latter, but also present in this group were Islamist dissidents of various shades and backgrounds.[39] In May 1991, a Memorandum of Advice, signed by more than one hundred 'ulama and Islamists, was sent to Shaykh 'Abd al-'Aziz Bin Baz (d. 1999), the head of the Board of Senior 'Ulama' (and later the grand mufti of the state), to be passed on to the king. "This advice," stated the letter to Bin Baz that prefaced this document,

> is the result of the tireless efforts of your sons, students of Islam, preachers and university professors. . . . Our purpose is to follow the teachings of Islam that request advice and consultation. We would like you to read it and add what is missing and improve on it. . . . Whatever is good in this advice is a gift from God and whatever is wrong is our responsibility and we stand corrected. Finally we would like you to endorse it and submit it to the Custodian of the Two Holy Mosques [the king].[40]

In essence, the Memorandum of Advice called for a *greater* role for the 'ulama in the supervision of religious life in the Saudi society and state, bringing all laws and judicial administration into conformity with the shari'a, ensuring fundamental rights and social welfare, administrative and economic reform, the development of a strong military, and a reorientation of Saudi foreign policy along Islamic lines.[41]

The 'ulama who were signatories to this document or who voiced their criticism of the Saudi regime during and after the Gulf War represent the Saudi version of the 'ulama's new radicalism and therefore deserve some consideration here. I examine their position with reference to one of the most well-known among them, Shaykh Safar al-Hawali.

We might characterize these dissident 'ulama as "peripheral" in the sense that they were not part of the official religious establishment, which was represented by the Board of Senior 'Ulama' with Shaykh Bin Baz at its head. They were the products of the Islamic universities in Saudi Arabia, which are the functional equivalents of the larger Pakistani madrasas or of the Azhar and its related institutes. (Islamic universities have also been established with Saudi funding in Islamabad, Pakistan, and in Kuala Lumpur, Malaysia.) In terms of their overall administrative structure, these universities are patterned largely on the American university system, but they are devoted primarily to the study of Islam and they train their students to become qadis, preachers, and religious specialists working in sundry other areas.

That the 'ulama and the Islamists could come together in signing the Memorandum of Advice to the king was not only because they had shared grievances but also because these Islamic universities had helped bridge the gulf between them. The Islamist ideologue Abu'l-A'la Mawdudi of Pakistan had participated in the discussions on the structure of the Islamic university at a time that such a university was being planned in Medina.[42] Members of the Muslim Brotherhood have taught in Saudi universities: the distinguished Syrian scholar 'Abd al-Fattah Abu Ghudda is a notable example;[43] and Muhammad Qutb, the brother of Sayyid Qutb, whom Nasser had executed in 1966, was the dissertation advisor for Safar al-Hawali at the Umm al-Qura Islamic University of Mecca.[44] The radical Egyptian *shaykh* 'Umar 'Abd al-Rahman had himself taught in Saudi Arabia, though not in an Islamic university, for three years ending shortly before the assassination of President Sadat.[45] Students from different Muslim countries interacted in these universities: the Islamic University of Medina, whose graduates numbered more than 10,000 by the end of 1997, allocates 85 percent of its seats to Muslims from outside Saudi Arabia.[46] And many Saudi graduates of these universities are known to have taken some part in the Afghan struggle against the Soviet occupation. All of this provided a climate in which many of the younger 'ulama were socialized in these universities.

Safar al-Hawali had studied at the Islamic University of Medina, and he completed his master's degree and Ph.D. at the Umm al-Qura University in Mecca. His master's thesis was titled "Secularism (*al-'almaniyya*): Its Origins, Development, and Manifestations in Muslim Life." And to give us some sense of his intellectual formation before he had embarked on his oppositional career, his Ph.D. dissertation focused on the Murji'a, a theological and religiopolitical movement in the first centuries of Islam. This movement had contributed significantly to the early development of Sunni Islam, though it had come to be seen by the later Sunni orthodoxy as permitting moral laxity by emphasizing "faith" over "works." Many of the Murji'a were also political quietists, who regarded rebellion against constituted political authority as wrong.[47]

In his dissertation, which was later published as a book, al-Hawali says that he is concerned with the Murji'a not as an "historical sect" but as an ongoing "intellectual phenomenon." To study it as the former would be merely an "academic" exercise (he uses the word "academic" in Arabic transliteration); but to study this trend as a continuing phenomenon means that one can trace its manifestations throughout Islamic history.[48] Al-Hawali seeks to show how the separation of reformist activism from faith distorts the true meaning of Islam, even as it makes activist reformists such as the Wahhabis susceptible to being branded as extremists.[49] At the time it was written, the dissertation was clearly meant to support the official Saudi ideology of Wahhabism. That ideology, of course, is never put in question even later; only the record of the Saudi state in living up to it is challenged. Yet in view of al-Hawali's subsequent role as one of the leading dissident 'ulama, his underlining of the integral relationship of faith and action prefigures here an intellectual justification, if one was needed, for religious activism. (The critique of a movement also associated with political quietism is, of course, no less of a prefiguring of his later stance, though he does not dwell on this aspect of the Murji'a.) That being religious is merely a matter of holding the right beliefs—the view that is characteristic of Murji'ism as an "intellectual phenomenon"—has become influential among the Muslim youth, according to al-Hawali. This view has exposed the Muslim world to the insidious inroads of secularism and to Western influences. The separation of religion from life and of faith from practice are, al-Hawali says, expressions of the same basic problem: a distorted understanding of religion. And it is this distortion, so often neglected by the 'ulama themselves—that is, by the very people who ought to concern themselves the most with it—that he seeks to rectify.[50]

For preachers like al-Hawali, the dire consequences of a false understanding of Islam, of the Muslim world's subservience to the West, of the Saudi state's failure to live up to its Wahhabi ideals, and of the 'ulama's own negligence in guiding the people all culminate in the crisis of the Gulf War of 1991. In his writings and speeches al-Hawali was one of the most vocal critics of the Saudi dependence on Western military forces and of the leading 'ulama's support of this measure.[51] A useful introduction to his position is his treatise entitled *Facts Regarding the Gulf Crisis*, written shortly before the war itself and addressed to the Board of Senior 'Ulama' and its head, "the father" Bin Baz.[52] Here al-Hawali elaborates at length on his conviction that the advent of Western troops in the region was not only an expression of Muslim subservience to the West but also the culmination of long-standing Western designs to establish a military presence in the region and to directly control the Arab world's economic resources. The treatise is meant as a "working paper" (*waraqat 'amal*)[53] to lay bare the "facts" behind the crisis and propose ways of dealing with it. In the context of the latter, he recommends the establishment of committees of "experts" to examine, *inter alia*, the causes of the state's military weakness and strategies towards strengthening its defenses; to consider options in case the Western powers were contemplating the division of the state or changes in its political and social structure; to study the impact of the crisis on the economic future and stability of the state; and so forth.[54] Ultimately, however, the causes of this crisis are religious, and so, in the final analysis, should be the solution. It is the duty of the religious scholars to explain to all the real cause of this calamity . . . [viz.]: our departure from the shariʿa of God, our openly committing things forbidden by Him; our friendship with the enemies of God; our slackness in fulfilling the rights of God and in calling [people] to them. The rulers and the ruled, the scholar and the layman (*al-ʿalim waʾl-jahil*), the young and the old, the man and the woman are, in varying degrees, all culpable for this failing—except those to whom God has been merciful in enabling them to stand up with the truth in confronting this calamity.[55]

The ʿulama must realize their duty in providing "advice" (*yansuh*) to the people in this crisis. "Some people assert that this is not the business of the ʿulama. . . . But whose business is it then?" he asks rhetorically:

Should we leave [such guidance] . . . to the sycophants among the poets and to the secularists who lack all discernment? Should we leave the matter to those who blacken the pages everyday and fill the air with their speeches and their solutions while you [the leading ʿulama] either support them or are silent! All—even commercial artists—are speaking about the crisis. The only ones who are silent, or have been silenced, are the scholars and preachers, except those who simply support the status quo without reference either to the mistakes of the past or the demands of the future. *You* must strive to set this community (*umma*) straight—may God enable you to do so! Strive to redeem your honor and the credibility of [your] calls to [belief in] God's unity, which has been grievously hurt everywhere because of this stance [of yours]. Do not despise yourself by desisting from an action with which God would raise you in this world and in the next. For you are the ʿulama, the best of all communities, and you [are supposed to] walk on the path of the forbears.[56]

It is hard to concur with political scientist Mamoun Fandy's view of this book as being "little . . . concerned with theology or Islam," or with his suggestion that "[f]rom this book alone it is very difficult for anyone to detect that Hawali is a religious activist."[57] Fandy makes these assertions to argue that this book is, in fact, essentially a study of "the geostrategic implications of the Gulf War."[58] But while one can broadly agree with this characterization, it is unnecessary and misleading to do so by denying the profoundly *religious* basis of al-Hawli's critique, as the passages quoted above should amply demonstrate. We cannot understand the criticism of preachers like al-Hawali—criticism that landed him in prison, as it did some of the other ʿulama—without recognizing that the appeal to religion is not a mere justification for this criticism but its very basis. The appeal to the senior ʿulama is, likewise, no mere rhetoric; it is central to the preacher's view of what has gone wrong and how to remedy it.

Al-Hawali, on whom I have focused here, offers us an illustration of what was in fact a broad trend of religious criticism that emerged in the Saudi kingdom in the wake of the Gulf War.[59] Certain reforms of some significance were instituted in response to such criticism, including a Basic Regulation (1992) and the first-ever consultative assembly in the Saudi state.[60] The opposition to the Saudi state has continued, though mostly from dissidents outside the kingdom; and it has spawned everything from the use of print and information technology in protesting against Saudi policies to the resort to terrorism in seeking to undermine the state.[61] We need not concern ourselves with this opposition here, though two concluding points are worth making.

First, as in the cases of Egypt and Pakistan, the Islamic claims and concessions of the Saudi state are critical to the context in which the 'ulama's own demands are articulated. It might seem surprising that the dissident 'ulama should have demanded *greater* implementation of the shari'a in a state whose liberal critics were, not without reason, already complaining about the degree to which the shari'a, and the 'ulama, already permeated public life. But such a demand for the "true" implementation of the shari'a only underscores the power of the 'ulama to set—and continually *re*set—the terms of religious and political discourse in states that draw all or most of their legitimacy from public appeals to Islam.[62]

Second, though there is no parallel to the thoroughgoing reforms of the Azhar in case of the Saudi 'ulama, they, like the peripheral Egyptian 'ulama, were often exposed to considerable outside influences. The Islamic universities may have played an important role in enabling the Saudi 'ulama to act in concert with the Islamists, as we have seen. Their exposure was not only to Islamist trends, however. The information media and modern means of communication also enabled 'ulama like al-Hawali to closely follow and react to trends in international politics, to perceive what incessant globalization might entail, and even to take a sustained interest in developments in domestic American politics and society.[63] These 'ulama are not "antimodern." If, in part, they strive to build on the state's own acknowledgment of the public role of Islam, they are also, as Fandy argues, products of a globalizing modernity whose perceived effects on Islam and Saudi society spur them into activism.[64] In this, as in many other respects, they are in accord with the Islamists.[65]

In the next section I turn to the 'ulama of India, a state in which Muslims are a numerical minority and which, unlike Pakistan, Egypt, and Saudi Arabia, professes to be a secular state. We do not see here the sort of new religiopolitical roles that we observe in Pakistan, Egypt, and Saudi Arabia, or in Afghanistan and Iran. But the ways in which the 'ulama have sought to provide guidance and leadership, including political leadership, to the

Muslim community, and some of the tensions that are evident in the choices they have made as leaders of the community, add an important dimension to our comparative view of the contemporary 'ulama.

The Indian 'Ulama

As we saw in chapter 1, a number of prominent Deobandi 'ulama, led by Husayn Ahmad Madani and the Jam'iyyat al-'Ulama'-i Hind, had opposed the establishment of a separate state for the Muslims of India. After partition, these "nationalist" 'ulama decided to focus their energies on providing leadership to the Muslim community of an independent India primarily in the religious and cultural arena. In the context of a secular Indian state, the only power available to them was in the realm of education and moral persuasion, and it was through these instruments—rather than the state, which was dominated by non-Muslims—that they hoped to preserve the individual and religious identity of the Muslim people.[66] But they also expected the secular nation-state, for its part, to leave Islamic law and culture to them, and to desist from interfering with the Muslim community's religious and cultural life.[67]

The secular state did, indeed, recognize its Muslim citizens as comprising a distinct cultural and religious community,[68] and as Yohanan Friedmann has observed, it "attempted to place the 'ulama and Muslims who were, or became[,] closely associated with them in a role of leadership in the Muslim community."[69] Since independence, the 'ulama have continued to energetically expand the reach of their educational institutions. Of the 576 madrasas surveyed in a recent report on institutions of Islamic education in India, 99 were established between 1901 and 1950, and 449 between 1951 and 1994.[70] Two of South Asia's most prestigious institutions of Islamic learning—the Dar al-'Ulum of Deoband and the Dar al-'Ulum of Nadwat al-'Ulama, Lucknow, both located in Uttar Pradesh—have seen remarkable growth in recent decades. According to the aforementioned report, Deoband had 1160 studens in 1945–46, 1005 in 1970–71, and 3044 in 1993–94. The growth of the Nadwat al-'Ulama' is far more remarkable. The number of students in its Dar al-'Ulum in 1945–46 was merely 69; in 1970–71, it had 273 students, and in 1993–94, it had outstripped Deoband with its 4064 students.[71]

Yet even as the state has demarcated a cultural and religious sphere for Muslims, as it does for its other communities, it has also continued to threaten—as all modern nation-states do—the very boundaries it constructs or acknowledges. While they have never altogether eschewed politics,[72] many among the 'ulama have increasingly come to emphasize the need for greater political involvement in the face of the challenges that the modern state appears to pose to the Muslim community. As the Nad-wat al-'Ulama's Sayyid Abu'l-Hasan 'Ali Nadwi (d. 1999), the most prominent Indian religious scholar of his generation and one of the lead-ing Sunni 'ulama on the international scene, wrote in explaining his own growing involvement in Indian politics since the 1960s:

[This is] an age when the sphere of governmental operations is no longer confined to collecting taxes, administering the state, and defending the na-tion. [The government] can interfere in all spheres of life and can make new laws to regulate all its aspects; it can create a uniform civil code for the entire country; it can create a new curriculum for the intellectual and moral forma-tion of the youth and thereby influence even their accepted religious beliefs and sever their link with their past, their culture and their civilization; it can change the language, or alter the script in which the language is written. . . . In a country where there is no other means for protecting oneself against danger than through the right to express one's opinion [in the general elec-tions], and through political influence and practical wisdom, it is inconceiv-able for the [Muslim] community to abstain from democratically exerting its influence on national politics. [To so abstain would be especially inconceiv-able] given that this community's concept and sphere of religion encompasses the entirety of life. . . . [Those who believe that Muslims should stay away from politics, or that they ought to concentrate] merely on establishing wel-fare and charitable institutions or only on strengthening their economic posi-tion or the standards of their education, are, in fact, recommending a path of collective suicide. For [in abstaining from politics] Muslims would not be able to defend their collective identity, nor their rituals and family law; they would not be able to preserve their doctrinal or cultural integrity; and quite apart from leading others and proselytizing to them—which is the proper role of this community—they would not even be able to live a free and re-spectable life.[73]

Nadwi's long intellectual and political career offers a fascinating glimpse both into efforts to preserve Muslim identity in the framework of a secular nation-state as well as into the often conflicting bases of the 'ulama's leadership of the community. Nadwi is not typical of the Indian 'ulama, but as a highly distinguished scholar and, arguably, as one of the most influential leaders of the Muslims of India in the 1980s, his career deserves some consideration.

As we noted in chapter 3, the Nadwat al-'Ulama' was founded in the late nineteenth century to reform religious education. This meant, *inter alia*, an unusually high emphasis on inculcating among its students the ability to speak and write in modern Arabic. Over the course of its history, the Nadwat al-'Ulama' has moved almost entirely in the direction of Deo-band, but the emphasis on the Arabic language and a self-conscious orientation towards the Arab world have continued to be hallmarks of this institution. Nadwi[74] himself has written extensively not only in Urdu but also in Arabic, and some of his writings have been addressed primarily to an Arab audience.

Undoubtedly the best known of his numerous writings is a book written at a time when Nasser's appeal to pan-Arabism and Arab socialism had made deep inroads into the Arab world. This book, entitled *What Has the World Lost with the Decline of the Muslims?* (*Madha khasira'l-'alam bi'l-inhitat al-muslimin?*), published in its later editions with a foreword by the Egyptian Islamist Sayyid Qutb, is at once an extended indictment of Western "materialism" and a fervent appeal to the Muslims—but above all to the Arabs—to renew their commitment to Islam.[75] Only Islam, Nadwi says, assures that ideal balance between the spiritual and the material, the other-worldly and the mundane, in which all human perfection lies.[76] Through Islam alone can Muslims regain their universal leadership, and the world recover what it has lost with their decline; and it is the Arabs—with their special, divinely ordained relationship with the Prophet and Islam, and as the inhabitants of lands that are not only the cradle of Islamic civilization but now also the repository of great material wealth—who must lead the way.[77] But the Arabs of the twentieth century, far from leading the way to an Islamic revival, have found a new religion in nationalism.[78] Though in part a reaction to Arab grievances against Ottoman rule, nationalism for Nadwi is ultimately a Western plot to divide the Muslims and to blunt the force of their "Islamic consciousness" (*al-shu'ur al-Islami*). Whatever the Arab nationalists might think, this consciousness is the only real basis of Arab identity, the sole guarantee of their future.[79]

The Arabs' lack of commitment to Islam, of which Arab nationalism is the most dangerous and destructive form, amounts, for Nadwi, to a modern-day *jahiliyya*, a highly charged concept in the Islamic religious tradition that Nadwi has helped to make part of the Islamist lexicon.[80] Jahiliyya is the Islamic theological characterization for the world before Islam; it connotes not merely the worship of deities other than the one, true God, but, like Islam, and in competition with it, a complete way of life and conduct, even a "civilization."[81] But it is a way of life defined by the absence or distortion of all standards of moral valuation:

> [Before Islam] everything in the jahili man's ways of thinking was in disarray. . . . Absolute and certain knowledge had become doubtful to him, and matters of doubt absolute certainty. . . . People were entirely preoccupied with the material and this-worldly, and everything was in the wrong shape or at the wrong place. . . . Criminals were happy and fortunate in that society,

and the virtuous miserable. There was no greater foolishness than to be virtuous in that society, and nothing was more admired than the lack of all manners and morals.[82]

Islam and jahiliyya are mirror images, and Nadwi's reified rendering of the two squarely defines the one in terms of what the other is not. The yardstick of the right and the wrong, of the right and wrong shape or place of things, of certainty and doubt, and of sin and virtue here is a reified, utopian Islam, which is taken to be the very essence of a moral order. Any deviation from this moral order is for Muslims a slippage back into the jahiliyya, which is the more reprehensible for signifying not just ignorance of Islam but its renunciation.[83]

Nadwi's polemic against Arab nationalism accorded well with the opposition to nationalism by Islamist groups in the Middle East and especially by Saudi Arabia. The latter in particular was threatened by the Nasserist ideology of social revolution and by Egypt's challenge for the leadership of the Arabs. The emotional ties of ancestral origin (Nadwi's ancestor had come to India from Arabia) and of creed (his family's affinity with the Wahhabis) were reinforced by a common opposition to Nasserist nationalism.[84] Nadwi was associated with the Rabitat al-'alam al-Islami—the Muslim World League, a pan-Islamic organization sponsored by Saudi Arabia to counteract Nasserism[85]—from its inception, and his ties with the Saudi religious and political elite also seem to have earned much financial assistance for the Nadwat al-'Ulama.[86]

Though his thought has undoubtedly tended to support some of the concerns of Saudi foreign policy, Nadwi's opposition to Arab nationalism—his appeal for a revival of Islamic zeal among the Arabs—is rooted in a strong sense of Muslim identity in India. For if a new jahiliyya, complete with its false gods, has all but overwhelmed the Arabs, then the consequences are not limited to the Arabs alone. Repeatedly in his writings Nadwi has dwelt on the theme that the faltering of the Arabs' commitment to Islam means their betrayal of Muslims everywhere. That the Arabs had begun to look for what united them as a nation, to the exclusion of all other peoples, meant a weakening of ties between Arab and non-Arab Muslims even as it strengthened those between Muslim and non-Muslim Arabs. But as people like Nadwi have insisted, the Arab cultural heritage is not only meaningless without, and really inseparable from, Islam, it is also the shared heritage of all Muslims. The Muslims of India have contributed no less than any other people, no less than the Arabs, to the growth and richness of Islamic civilization. Yet only those Arabs who are aware of their Islamic roots can really appreciate the role and significance of India in the history of Islam. A secular Arab nationalism threatens not only to sever the links between Muslim India and the Arab world but also to rob India of recognition for its contribution to Islamic civilization. It is an abiding concern of Nadwi's work to acquaint both the Arabs and the Indian Muslims with that contribution. He is also concerned to bring out the Muslim contribution to India itself. The concern with highlighting this contribution is at once an invitation to the Arabs to renew their Islamic commitments—which Muslim India is shown to have preserved all along—and an affirmation of Islamic identity and its Middle Eastern roots in India.

If Indian Muslims look up to the Arabs for leadership and identity *because* they have traditionally thought of them as the first bearers of Islam, then the Arabs' forsaking an Islamic for an Arab national identity cannot but be profoundly disquieting. In addressing the Arabs against the backdrop of the nationalistic fervor of the 1950s, and in drawing attention to the predicament of the Indian Muslims in a secular, Hindu-dominated India, Nadwi skillfully juxtaposes three varieties of jahiliyya: the pre-Islamic, the modern Arab nationalistic; and, in India, the jahiliyya of Hindu polytheism and idolatry as well as of attachment to locality and local customs, against which, Nadwi says, the Muslims have continued to struggle till the present. Arab nationalism is a reversion to jahiliyya not only because the nation rather than Islam becomes the object of devotion, but also, and by the same token, because the pre-Islamic Arab past, the historical jahiliyya that Islam ought to have completely obliterated, becomes sacrosanct in competition with Islam itself. Even more grievously, so far as Indian Muslims are concerned, the modern Arab jahiliyya also gives justification to attacks on Muslim efforts to preserve a distinct identity in India. For if the Arabs can return to their non-Islamic past, why must the Muslims of India not do the same?[87] Further (though this remains implicit in the present context), if the Arabs can contemplate subsuming their religious identity into a secular and nationalist ethos, why should the Muslims of India not do the same? Such questions pose a greater challenge to Muslim identity in India, Nadwi says, than have many a conspiracy against Islam in the past; and ironically, it is the conduct of the Arabs that provides the inspiration for this challenge.[88]

This sense of betrayal by the Arabs is accompanied by a stern and vigorous declaration of the continuing Indian Muslim commitment to Islam:

> If the entire world were to abandon Islam, our determination would not be weakened. Even if the Turks returned to their 'Turani' nationhood (*qawmiyya*) and to the customs, beliefs, and glories of their first jahiliyya; the Iranians to their Sasanian nationhood, seeking honor in their ancestors Rustam and Suhrab; Egypt to its Pharaonicism (*firʿawniyyatiha*); and the people of Arabia—may God not will this—to their jahiliyya and its heroes: [let it be

known that] we have not bound our future to any community or nation. We have associated our future and its course with the will of God and His religion. That the entire mankind becomes infidel can be no excuse for us to do the same. . . . We have pledged to God that we will persevere in His religion and continue to cling to it. And God has vouched for the permanence of His religion and for the continued existence of a group in the community that will hold on to it.[89]

A similar sentiment was voiced by Nadwi in his inaugural address at the eighty-fifth anniversary of the founding of the Nadwat al-'Ulama', celebrated with great enthusiasm (and with a large number of delegates from the Arab world) in 1975:[90]

By the grace of God, the Muslims of India are to a large extent autonomous as regards Islam. They draw guidance from the earliest and most authoritative sources of Islam—the Qur'an and the sunna and from the lives of Islam's earliest representatives. . . . Their faith and their life are tied to the radiance of Islam, not to the ephemeral glimmerings of Muslim nations or Arab states.[91]

That Indian Islam is autonomous is a remarkable statement. It is meant not to deny that Muslims of India are part of the Muslim world, or that they are affected by developments elsewhere, but to assert that their religious commitment does not presuppose or depend on that of Muslims elsewhere. This assertion may have been intended as a statement of fact, but it also has a clearly rhetorical motive: If Muslims of India can hold onto Islam even in the face of a non-Muslim majority that threatens to obscure their religious identity, why cannot Muslims elsewhere, and especially the Arabs, do at least that much? The Arabs are doubly culpable for their loss of faith: it has led to their own decline in the world, and though others will continue to persevere in their devotion to Islam, the Arabs have nevertheless let them down.

Yet for all the autonomy of Islam in India, the Arabs do matter, and it is significant that this autonomy is invoked precisely in addressing them. But it is only the ideologically committed Arabs who matter, as Nadwi makes clear in stirring rhetoric calculated to strike a receptive emotional chord among those dissatisfied with nationalist or secularist panaceas in the Arab world:

If you want, O Arabs, to help us in any way or to wish any success to us, know that it is not any material or monetary assistance that we need. We only ask one thing of you: that you be an example of steadfastness in faith and act as you did in the past—as the bearers of the eternal message of God, driving away all those who adhere to anyone but Allah or to any religion but Islam. If you did this, you would have given us all the help [we need].[92]

Islam in India, then is anything but immune to how Islam fares else-where, especially, but not only, among the Arabs.[93] Nadwi's ambivalence in defining Indian Islam's autonomy is brought out most clearly when he sets out to elucidate Islam, and Islamic culture in India, not for the Arabs or even for Indian Muslims, but for his Hindu compatriots. Nadwi has written introductory books on Islam and Muslim culture for a non-Muslim, primarily Hindu, audience to remove misunderstanding and mini-mize the communal conflict endemic in India.[94] As historian Partha Chatterjee has argued in a study of Hindu nationalist constructions of Indian history, "Islam here is either the history of foreign conquest or a domesti-cated element of everyday popular life. The classical heritage of Islam remains external to Indian history."[95] It is such constructions of Islam that Nadwi seeks to counteract, describing what Muslims have historically contributed to society and culture in India and, in more recent times, to the struggle for India's freedom from colonial rule. Nadwi also proposes to show in these writings that Muslims are as much a part of, and loyal to, India as are the Hindus:

> Their culture, which has taken centuries to evolve, is a combination of both Islamic and Indian influences. This two-fold aspect has, on the one hand, endowed it with a beauty and a richness which is characteristically its own and, on the other, it holds forth the assurance that this culture will operate here not like an alien or a traveller but as a natural, permanent citizen who has built his home in the light of his peculiar needs and circumstances.[96]

Yet when it comes to actually describing what is *Indian* about Islam in India, Nadwi adopts a tone that seems laden with strikingly negative overtones: "Indian Muslims have adopted numerous rites and customs of the soil that are not found among Muslims elsewhere."[97] These include rites of marriage, public fairs and festivities, social distinctions based on caste and profession—all of which he regards as unfortunate borrowings from the Hindus. Ironically, then, even as Nadwi writes to foster mutual understanding between Hindus and Muslims, what is "Indian" about Muslim culture turns out for the most part not to be "Islamic" at all. The "Indian influences" on this culture are acknowledged—largely, perhaps, for the sake of Nadwi's putative Hindu audience—but when not derided, they remain unexplored. Acknowledgment of their existence does serve, however, to sharpen the sense of an immutable Islamic essence, which the Muslims have preserved and cultivated and which ultimately remains pure and distinct from any such influences.[98] At the same time, Nadwi is also at pains to emphasize the loyalty and devotion of India's Muslims to the nation-state, despite all his strictures against *Arab* nationalism or his discomfort with the Muslim communalism that led to the creation of Pa-kistan. And he insists on the need for communal harmony between Muslims and Hindus.[99] In these respects he is akin to Husayn Ahmad Madani and the nationalist 'ulama of the years preceding and immediately following partition. Yet as in the case of Madani, his conceptions of communal harmony and, more broadly, of a secular nation-state, are predicated not on similarities between the two communities, still less on religious and cultural symbiosis; they are based rather on recognition of distinct, immutable identities.[100] And there is no question that, for Muslims, the sources of this identity lie not in the historical experience of Islam in India but in being part of the greater Muslim world and awareness of being such.

This awareness has other functions too. As Nadwi states in his autobiography, the fact that a large number of dignitaries from the Arab world (including the Shaykh al-Azhar) attended the elaborate celebrations marking the eighty-fifth anniversary of the Nadwat al-'Ulama' in 1975 demonstrated to the government of India as well as to the majority (Hindu) community that Muslims constitute an international community and that Muslim leaders of India are respected in the Muslim world.[101] The same message would have been conveyed when, in 1980, Nadwi was awarded the Faisal Award—named after King Faisal of Saudi Arabia (d. 1975)—by the government of Saudi Arabia for distinguished service to Islam. The first recipient of this award, the previous year, had been the Islamist thinker Sayyid Abu'l-A'la Mawdudi of Pakistan. Nadwi and Muhammad Natsir, a former prime minister of Indonesia, were both recipients of this award in 1980.[102]

Though Nadwi was less than candid on this account, recognition in the Arab and Muslim world was, arguably, a critical and increasingly important basis of his position *in India*. Events in the 1980s showed that besides being a preeminent religious scholar, he had also become one of the most influential leaders of the Muslim community in India. In 1983, he was chosen as the president of the All India Muslim Personal Law Board, which was to play a major role in Muslim politics in the coming years. This Board had been established in 1973 to defend the right of the Muslim community to be governed by its own laws of personal status and to resist any government initiatives towards the creation of a uniform civil code for citizens of India, as the Constitution required.[103] The challenge came in April 1985, when the Supreme Court of India gave its judgment on a case involving an indigent divorced Muslim woman, Shah Bano, who had filed for continuing financial support from her former husband.

The husband had argued that under Islamic law, he owed no payment to his former wife after the end of her "waiting period" following the divorce. The High Court of the state of Madhya Pradesh, however, had ruled in favor of Shah Bano. The Supreme Court upheld this verdict, asserting that the relevant provisions of India's Code of Criminal Procedure—which provided that divorced women could claim maintenance for the duration of their life from their former husbands—were not in conflict with the teachings of the Qur'an, when rightly understood, on the matter of provision for divorced women.[104] In reaching this decision the Supreme Court had, for all intents and purposes, assumed the authority to interpret the Qur'an.[105] This was extraordinary not only because it was non-Muslim judges who did so, but also because the Court thereby departed from the avowed refusal of earlier courts to do just that. As we saw in chapter 1, the Privy Council had much earlier laid down the view that "it would be wrong for the court . . . to put their own construction on the Koran in opposition to the express ruling of commentators of . . . great antiquity and high authority."[106] The higher courts in Pakistan have frequently sought to discern the true intent of the Qur'an and/or the sunna in reaching their decisions, irrespective of what the medieval exegetical or juristic tradition holds on the matter in question; and this has been a matter of considerable contention between the 'ulama and the modernists. But for the Hindu Chief Justice of the Supreme Court[107] of a Hindu-dominated state to rule on what the Qur'an "really" means and how this interpretation should regulate the Muslim minority's matters of personal status was seen by the 'ulama as a severe assault on their community's identity.

Muslim modernists in India applauded the decision of the Supreme Court as helping to protect and ameliorate the rights of Muslim women, and they endorsed the Court's call for the uniform civil code that the Constitution had long promised.[108] But the 'ulama of almost all sectarian persuasions were united in their opposition to this verdict.[109] Large segments of the Muslim population were galvanized into action by the Muslim Personal Law Board, and many prominent Muslim politicians also supported the Board's demand that the Supreme Court's decision be overturned through parliamentary legislation. It was to the opponents of the decision, not its supporters, that the Congress-led government of Prime Minister Rajiv Gandhi was most receptive. He met repeatedly with Nadwi and other members of the Muslim Personal Law Board.[110] And in February 1986, the Muslim Women (Protection of Rights on Divorce) Bill was passed by the parliament in what was seen by its opponents as a major blow to the rights of Muslim women as well as to prospects of a uniform civil code. The legislation overturned the Supreme Court's decision and essentially reiterated the 'ulama's position—viz., that a divorced woman was entitled to financial support from her former husband only during her "waiting period" rather than for the duration of her life; after that, she was to be supported by her own relatives or, failing that, by the Muslim charitable endowments (waqf).[111]

Nadwi was not the only leader of this successful struggle against the Supreme Court verdict, nor were the 'ulama alone in this agitation.[112] The issue was seen as threatening Muslim identity in a state where they were a beleaguered minority, and framed as such, it had broad resonance in the Muslim community. A stringently defined legal tradition had taken precedence over the interests of women earlier, as we saw in the case of what had preceded the Dissolution of Marriages Act of 1939; and the defense of the shari'a was again seen, by the 'ulama and those supporting them, as a greater good—indeed, a necessity—that had to override any other considerations in the Shah Bano controversy. The fact that the government already recognized the 'ulama as legitimate, indeed authoritative, representatives of Muslim popular opinion enabled them to play a leading role in this controversy, and this recognition, in turn, strengthened their leadership.

Yet Nadwi's leadership role in the Shah Bano controversy also points to a remarkable paradox. His position in the community and among the 'ulama of India owed not a little, as I have argued, to the perception of his distinguished position in the Muslim world. His ability to represent the Muslim case to the government likewise owed something to that same perception. And as Nadwi acknowledges in his autobiography, he did not desist from reminding the prime minister of his stature abroad. Fearing that Rajiv Gandhi would be persuaded by the argument that if many Muslim countries had modified their laws of personal status, India could follow them in doing so, Nadwi emphasized to him that Islam in India was not subservient to any other Muslim country and that Muslims elsewhere recognized the authority of the leading *Indian* 'ulama.[113] The paradox, however, is this: If this recognition in the greater Muslim world enabled him to make his case authoritatively to the government and the public, his appeals to his authority abroad and his very career as an ardent advocate of Indian Islam's ties with the greater Muslim world could not but fuel Hindu nationalist denunciations of the "foreignness" of Islam in India.

I do not intend to suggest any direct correlation between the rise of Hindu nationalism since the 1980s and discourses such as Nadwi's, even though the latter do seem to lend some credence to the former's rhetoric. Representatives of Muslim "secular modernists" have argued that under the 'ulama's leadership, the community's refusal to accept the terms of life in a modern secular nation-state, for instance, by accommodating itself to a uniform civil code, has fueled the rise of Hindu nationalism. The destruction in December 1992 of the Baburi Masjid, a mosque in Ayodhya in Uttar Pradesh dating to the Mughal era and located at the site believed by some to be the birthplace of the Hindu god Rama, is seen, on this interpretation, as the price of the "victory" in the controversy over Muslim personal law.[114] It has also been argued that the open support of Rajiv Gandhi's government for the demands of the Muslim Personal Law Board and, later, its tacit support of the Hindu nationalists laying claim to the site of the Baburi Masjid were two parts of the same cynical strategy to keep a fragile Congress party in power: by garnering conservative Muslim support in the first instance and conservative Hindu support in the second.[115]

The rise of Hindu nationalism—the discussion of which falls outside the scope of this work—is too complex a phenomenon to be reduced either to Muslim insistence on communal identity or to governmental manipulation, however.[116] There doubtlessly is more to the influence of the 'ulama than either the gullibility of their Muslim audience or the governing elite's "pandering" to them.[117] As in other, Muslim societies, their influence rests, ultimately, on their appeal to the preservation of the Islamic religious tradition. The perception of Nadwi's stature in the Arab and Muslim world strengthened his bargaining power at home, as we have seen. But that perception itself rested on the notion that recognition abroad, especially in the Arab world, signified greater "authenticity," a superior and more authoritative claim to represent the interests of the community and those of the faith. Yet if the 'ulama's influence is not to be reduced to government manipulation, the role of the state as providing a context in which the 'ulama have been able to articulate their roles and their increasing prominence in public life is, nevertheless, scarcely to be denied. And this is as true of India as it is of Pakistan, Egypt, or Saudi Arabia.

Interpreting 'Ulama Activism

The religiopolitical activism of the 'ulama, facets of which we have examined in the foregoing, can only be understood in the specific contexts in which it has been articulated. Yet it is equally crucial that we also consider what it shares across Muslim societies. The latter perspective not only helps us understand the overall context of this activism better, it also accounts for its more or less contemporaneous emergence, especially since the last quarter of the twentieth century, in a number of Muslim societies. In broad terms, we can try to understand the Sunni 'ulama's contemporary activism with reference to three sets of factors: the ties with the Islamists; international patronage; and, more speculatively, the impact of the Iranian revolution on the 'ulama. We have already encountered these factors earlier and in various guises, but they now merit a closer, comparative look.

The Islamists and the 'Ulama

The relations between the 'ulama and the Islamists vary not only from one society to another but also, in some cases, from one group of Islamists, or 'ulama, to another. But almost everywhere there is considerable interaction between the two. For instance, in both Egypt and Saudi Arabia the leading 'ulama have remained closely tied to the state, but the "peripheral" 'ulama have fostered often close links with the Islamists. In the case of Pakistan, the Deobandi 'ulama have remained much more ambivalent towards Islamists, as seen in their difficult relations with Mawdudi and his Jama'at-i Islami. Yet Mawdudi and the 'ulama were also able to collaborate in formulating the demands for an Islamic constitution, as well as on other issues relating to debates on Islam in Pakistan. And in their participation in the jihad in Afghanistan, in the continuing Muslim insurgency in Indian Kashmir, in sectarian radicalism in Pakistan, and in protesting against the American-led military operations in Afghanistan in the wake of the September 2001 terrorist attacks, those with a madrasa background have participated side by side with others of a more Islamist profile. Nor is it only a matter of madrasa graduates and college graduates working alongside one another; as we saw in the case of many a sectarian activist in Pakistan, exposure to modern, "secular" institutions *and* a madrasa training are often combined in the same person. Such shared background does not break all distinction between the Islamists and the 'ulama, but it does often facilitate an exchange and cross-fertilization of ideas between them; and it can become the basis of shared participation in activist causes.

Nor should the peripheral 'ulama be too rigidly separated from the more distinguished or better recognized scholars, or even from those comprising the official religious establishment. As we saw in the discussion of sectarian radicalism in Pakistan in chapter 5, there is considerable affinity between the leading 'ulama and those lesser lights who are actually fighting the sectarian battles. Further, influential scholars like Abu'l-Hasan 'Ali Nadwi maintained ties both with Islamists of the Muslim Brotherhood as well as with leading 'ulama everywhere. Such multiple ties were, in turn, assisted by the Saudi state's patronage of Islamists like Mawdudi and the Muslim Brothers *as well as* of the 'ulama; or by General Zia al-Haqq's efforts to associate both with his Islamizing regime. In Egypt, state-sponsored reforms and other changes served to make the 'ulama more receptive to influences from the outside world, enabling them, as Zeghal has shown, to interact as never before with the Islamists. The Islamic universities in Saudi Arabia likewise helped bring together people from many different backgrounds.

More fundamentally, however, and apart from the crucial roles of state patronage (on which more will be said later) and of exposure to modern education, some of the challenges to which the 'ulama and the Islamists have responded are similar. We should not, therefore, be surprised to see expressions of some affinity between them, or to see the 'ulama themselves become increasingly activist. It is not only the Islamists but also the 'ulama who have reacted to the failed promises of liberal, nationalist, and socialist ideologies; or who reject what they perceive to be the all-encompassing claims and prescriptions of Western, secular rationalism in favor of efforts to anchor authority, identity, and community in transcendent religious norms;[118] or who strive to resist the encroachments of the modernizing state on all spheres of life, including the religious.

Analyzing the thought of Sayyid Qutb, Roxanne Euben has argued that Qutb's challenge goes beyond pointing to the inadequacies and the false promises of the Egyptian state. His is a critique of post-Enlightenment secular rationalism itself, a rationalism that "regards human comprehension as the determinant not only of how we come to know the world, but also what constitutes legitimate knowledge."[119] Such epistemological assumptions obviously leave little room for conceptions rooted in the authority of religion. By virtue of his critique of such assumptions, and for all the other differences, Euben finds Qutb in the company of many Western critics—Hannah Arendt, Alasdair MacIntyre, Charles Taylor, among others—of what are taken to be unrelenting claims of secular modernity.[120] As she points out: "[A]n argument for the authority of knowledge that is by definition beyond human reason . . . is neither pathological nor unfamiliar to the West but . . . one part of a larger effort to 'reenchant' the world defined by disenchantment, one attempt among many to seek an overarching moral unity as an antidote to what is seen as the subjectivism, atomism, and fragmentation of contemporary life."[121]

Though the 'ulama are not part of Euben's account (except for a brief comparison of Qutb and Khumayni), much the same can in fact be said of many of the Sunni 'ulama. Mawlana Taqi 'Uthmani of Pakistan has argued, for instance, that while there is much scope for the use of human reason, it can only operate within the limits set by divine revelation. Those limits themselves are neither deducible from, nor subject to, reason. There is scope for ijtihad, he argues, but only in areas not explicitly ruled on by revelation. The disagreement over the scope of human rationality is, for him, the decisive difference between an Islamic and a secular view of the world.[122] And on this the Islamists and the 'ulama are in complete agreement. The title of the essay in which Taqi 'Uthmani makes this argument—"Fundamentalism (bunyad-parasti) Has Become a Curse Word"—is itself telling: for all his differences with the Islamists, he recognizes himself to be at one with them when it comes to a critique of modern rationalism.

Yet if the 'ulama draw on and respond to some of the same issues as do the Islamists, the former often have advantages that the latter do not. For one thing, the ruling elite have sometimes enhanced the scope of the 'ulama's authority as a counterweight to the Islamist challenge to their regimes. But this has enabled the 'ulama not only to challenge the Islamists on behalf of the state, but also to challenge the state itself on behalf of Islam. At the same time, as we have noted, the peripheral 'ulama are able to maintain ties both with the establishment 'ulama who are defending the state as well as with the Islamists challenging it. This is true not only of Egypt but, as Mamoun Fandy has noted, of Saudi Arabia as well, where the peripheral 'ulama might be seen as "part of the conservative trend that the establishment ulama use whenever they feel that their position in government has become weaker in relation to the secular trend."[123]

Further, in the case of the 'ulama who are close to Islamist positions, the political cost of government repression might be higher than it is in the case of the lay Islamists. As Malika Zeghal has observed, part of the reason why Shaykh 'Umar 'Abd al-Rahman, who was implicated in the assassination of Sadat, was treated relatively leniently and later released from prison was because of his status as one of the 'ulama, with ties to the Azhar: "To accuse the shaykh 'Abd al-Rahman was, in a sense, also to accuse the 'ulama—who had always known how finally to reconcile with the regime."[124] The 'ulama of the southern Philippines (on whom more is said in the next subsection) offer another example of the relatively freer hand that 'ulama have enjoyed in society as opposed to other political activists. Muslim rebels have carried on a separatist struggle against the Christian-majority state since the early 1970s, and many 'ulama have been part of this underground movement. As Thomas McKenna has shown, many "above ground" 'ulama, even when not formally associated with the rebels, have often remained "connected to their underground ulama colleagues by kinship links, cohort ties, and shared convictions."[125] Significantly, these "above-ground" 'ulama were critical in disseminating the ideology of the separatists among the people, even under martial law. Yet because of their recognized position as *religious* scholars, even a martial law regime allowed them to continue relatively unfettered: "*[R]eligious speech* remained one of the few forms of public discourse permissible under martial law," with the result that "members of the aboveground ulama quickly became important spokespersons for the Muslim opposition."[126]

The 'ulama's ties with the Islamists, their ability to appeal to some of the same audiences as the Islamists, the opportunities created by their "religious" vocation to elude the heavy hand of governmental regulation, and not least, the space opened for them by government repression of radical Islamists are, in various combinations, part of what underlies their religiopolitical roles in a number of contemporary Muslim societies.

International Patronage

If, as we have seen, the 'ulama skillfully drew on the opportunities created by the state's recognition of Islam and/or of themselves to articulate their religiopolitical roles, such roles have benefited no less from international patronage from beyond the national borders. Saudi Arabia has been the source of much of such patronage, and that is my primary focus here. But other instances can also be cited. I should like, in fact, to begin with one that concerns the impact of the Azhar on the Muslims of the southern Philippines. Unlike many other Muslim societies where the 'ulama have existed for centuries, in the Philippines the 'ulama are a relatively recent phenomenon.[127] A local nobility, the *datu*s, had crystallized during the American colonial period to function as community leaders, ritual specialists, and local representatives of the central government—functions they continued in independent Philippines. From the 1950s, however, the Philippine Muslims were increasingly also exposed to influences from the greater Muslim world. In particular, the Egyptian government under Nasser began to sponsor substantial numbers to study at the Azhar.[128] Thanks to this Egyptian, and later Saudi, patronage, a new, highly visible, and activist group of 'ulama had emerged in the southern Philippines by the early 1980s.[129]

The 'ulama—or "*ustadzes*," as they were often called to distinguish them from local religious leaders, the datus—represented a new form of authority. Though madrasas had been established since the 1950s by foreign Muslim missionaries, the ustadzes established new ones where knowledge of the Arabic language was emphasized and provisions were made for extensive training in the Qur'an, hadith, and history.[130] The ustadzes were critical of local customs and rituals, especially those attending upon marriage and death; and in opposition to the ideology of "sanctified inequality" on which the position of the datu nobility rested, theirs was a more egalitarian Islam. As in the case of the sectarian Sunni radicalism in the Punjab province of Pakistan, the ustadzes' religious reform also meant an attack on entrenched social and economic privilege. And again as in Pakistan, the activism of the new Philippines 'ulama was aided, in part at least, by their ties with local businessmen and urban professionals.[131] The new 'ulama were a challenge not only to the datus, however, but also to the state, with which the datus were closely allied. This was particularly true with those among the ustadzes who also maintained close ties with, or became part of, the separatist Muslim struggle. Since the early 1970s, this struggle had been led by the Moro National Liberation Front, but in 1984 a splinter group was established as the Moro *Islamic* Liberation Front. The latter represented a new salience of Islam and of the 'ulama in this struggle, a greater emphasis on Islamic rather than nationalist identity, and a renewed stress on ties with the Muslim world. (Indeed, for a time, its headquarters were located in Lahore, Pakistan).[132]

Though Egypt and Saudi Arabia competed in the 1960s for leadership in the Arab and Islamic world, the prestige of the Azhar was no match for the oil resources of the Saudis. Indeed, the Azhar itself has been the beneficiary of Saudi patronage. In the Philippines, though it was the Azhar that initially played a leading role in the 'ulama's emergence in the Muslim south, Saudi patronage has probably contributed much more over the years in sustaining the 'ulama, their reformist endeavors, and their religio-political activism.[133] But the Philippines is only one of the numerous instances of Saudi patronage worldwide (among other things, Saudi Arabia finances, wholly or partially, more than 1500 mosques and 200 "Islamic centers" throughout the world).[134] My purpose here is not to document these instances, however, but only to indicate briefly how this patronage relates to the 'ulama, with reference to South Asian examples.

As we have seen, Saudi patronage is amply reflected in the career of Abu'l-Hasan 'Ali Nadwi, and the rise of the Nadwat al-'Ulama' as one of the largest institutions of Islamic learning in South Asia surely also owes something to the same. Among other ventures, Saudi support for the educational enterprises of the Ahl-i Hadith of India and Pakistan, whose religious orientation comes closest to that of the Saudi Wahhabis, is especially noteworthy. Faisalabad's Jami'a Salafiyya (established in 1955), the premier educational institution of the Ahl-i Hadith in Pakistan, is affiliated with the Islamic University of Medina, the Imam Muhammad ibn Sa'ud Islamic University of Riyadh, and Umm al-Qura University of Mecca. Students from this madrasa are regularly sent for higher studies to Saudi Arabia, and many return to teach in this and other Ahl-i Hadith madrasas.[135] A similar madrasa, also called Jami'a Salafiyya, has also been established in Islamabad on a vast plot of land allocated for the purpose by the government of Pakistan.[136] The Jami'a Salafiyya of Banaras, India, a large educational complex that houses 500 students, was inaugurated in 1966 by the Saudi ambassador and was financed in part by Saudi Arabia, Kuwait, and the United Arab Emirates.[137]

Deobandi madrasas, too, have often sought to attract Saudi assistance. A madrasa in Kohat, a remote town in the North-West Frontier Province of Pakistan, claims, for instance, to have formulated its goals in accordance not only with those of other Deobandi madrasas in Pakistan and the parent madrasa of Deoband in India, but also with those of the Islamic University in Medina and the Islamic Institute in Doha, Qatar.[138] The Jami'a Faruqiyya of Karachi, a Deobandi madrasa that was established in 1967 and, in 1991, had 1775 students, is among the more successful Pakistani madrasas in terms of Saudi as well as other foreign support. One of the departments of this madrasa is the Institute of Arabic Language and Islamic Studies (Ma'had al-lugha al-'arabiyya wa'l-'ulum al-islamiyya), which caters especially to the needs of advanced students from abroad. The curriculum of this department is said to be a mix of styles found in South Asia and the Arab Middle East. Most of the students here are from the Fiji Islands, the Philippines, Indonesia, and Malaysia, and the institute itself is run by graduates of the Islamic University of Medina.[139] The Jami'a Faruqiyya also received financial assistance from Iraq, at a time when Iraq and Saudi Arabia were allied against post-revolution Iran. On the completion, in 1984, of one of the madrasa's construction projects, which had been funded by the Iraqi government, Iraq's minister of endowments (*awqaf*) was among the participants in the ceremony marking the occasion; funds for the construction had also been received from elsewhere in the Middle East, including Saudi Arabia.[140] Such sources of material support have enabled the Jami'a Faruqiyya to become one of the first madrasas in the Indian subcontinent to adopt computer technology.[141] The madrasa is also an active publisher of "Islamic" materials and publishes its monthly journal simultaneously in Urdu, English, Arabic, and a regional language, Sindhi—a feat that surpasses even the Saudi-supported Islamic University of Islamabad.[142]

It is, finally, worth noting that Saudi financial support was crucial to the establishment of numerous madrasas for Afghan refugees in Pakistan. The Taliban would later emerge from many of these madrasas, and Saudi Arabia was one of only three countries—the other two were Pakistan and the United Arab Emirates—to immediately recognize the Taliban as constituting the legitimate government of Afghanistan.

What has been labeled "Saudi patronage" in the present discussion comes not only from the state but also from Saudi-sponsored international associations like the aforementioned Rabitat al-'alam al-Islami or from wealthy private individuals. Such patronage has not only helped extend Saudi influence in the Muslim world, it has also directly promoted certain Saudi national interests. For instance, the Saudis saw Nasser's influence in the Arab world with alarm, and Nadwi's polemic against Nasserism and pan-Arabism was directly in accord with Saudi policy. Later, Saudi patronage helped muster the support of many Sunni 'ulama against the Iranian revolution, which the Saudis again saw as a threat to the stability of their regime. We have already mentioned the Jami'a Faruqiyya of Karachi in this regard. It is also worth recalling that Mawlana Manzur Nu'mani, the Indian scholar who wrote the polemic against Khumayni and Shi'ism, was a close friend of Nadwi as well as a member of the Rabitat al-'alam al-Islami;[143] Nadwi not only wrote the preface to this work but later also authored a polemical work on Shi'ism himself.[144]

With the exception of the Taliban, however, there does not seem to be any *direct* correlation between Saudi patronage and the 'ulama's activism; and even in that case, international patronage was only one of the many factors that underlay the emergence of the Taliban. Sectarian conflict in Pakistan has its own complex roots and dynamics, as seen in chapter 5, and we should be wary of any simplistic equation between Sunni militancy and Saudi support, or, for that matter, between Shi'i reassertion in

Pakistan and Iranian patronage. Likewise, there is more to Nadwi's career than his support for certain causes important to the Saudis. The religiopolitical activism of the 'ulama in the various cases we have considered springs from a variety of factors, and to try to reduce it to any single or overarching cause is to misunderstand its depth. Saudi patronage must be reckoned as one of these factors, but only as one among many others. What the 'ulama made of Saudi patronage depended, more often than not, on how successfully they were able to utilize it in combination with the variety of other factors that defined the particular contexts in which their activist or other roles were framed.

The Impact of Iran?

The impact of the Iranian revolution is not enough to explain the radicalization of sectarian identities in Pakistan, and yet neither the reassertion of the Shi'a nor the Sunni reaction it provoked is conceivable without this revolution. Middle Eastern Arab regimes, too, felt much threatened by the revolutionary rhetoric of the Iranian regime and by its professed (or perceived) desire to "export" the revolution; and at least some of their patronage of the Sunni 'ulama seems to have been motivated by the effort to garner the latter's support against Shi'i Iran.[145] 'Ulama' like Manzur Nu'mani and Abu'l-Hasan 'Ali Nadwi felt, moreover, that the appeal of a politically resurgent Islam was attracting the Sunni youth to Khumayni's message and that this threatened to expose these Muslims to the influence of Shi'ism as well. They and other 'ulama consequently wrote not just against Khumayni, but specifically against Shi'ism, to reveal its "real" face and demonstrate that to be a Shi'i was not to be a Muslim at all. The struggle against Shi'ism and Khumayni's perceived appeal called, in short, not just for greater vigilance but also for more active involvement in public and political life on the part of the *Sunni* 'ulama.

But is there more to the impact of the Iranian revolution on the latter? For all the ambivalence of the Sunni 'ulama towards Khumayni's conception of an Islamic government, it is tempting to speculate that the example of those associated with the latter continues to invite the Sunni 'ulama to assert their own political leadership. That they have often been virulently anti-Shi'i or anti-Khumayni[146] does not, of course, mean that they have remained untouched by the Iranian revolution. Notably, while the politically activist 'ulama have themselves been reticent in acknowledging any possible influence from Iran, such influence is precisely what the opponents of these 'ulama have sometime alleged to be at work. In the southern Philippines, for instance, a representative of the datu nobility opposing the election of an 'ulama-supported candidate for governor expressed his opposition as follows:

It is a Shi'a principle that the ulama participate directly in government. . . . This is a Shi'a policy. In Iran, the ulama want to be political leaders. I am not suggesting that in Islam the ulama cannot participate in politics. However, if the ulama comprise the political leadership, there will be no one to preach. The ustadzes have no need to be elected. They already have positions. They are already persons of authority because they have much knowledge. . . . We do not want to create ayatollahs and mullahs here in the Philippines. If we did, we would be diverting from the Sunna . . . related by Imam Shafii [the founder of the school of Sunni law predominant throughout Southeast Asia]. We must follow the straight path.[147]

Polemical statements such as this are not decisive proof of just how indebted the Sunni 'ulama are to the Iranian example. Yet the fact that the politically activist roles of the former have, in many cases, emerged *after* that revolution does leave open for consideration the possibility of Iranian influence. Given, moreover, that the Sunni 'ulama have themselves acknowledged the impact of the revolution on "the Sunni youth," and that sectarian Sunni organizations like the Sipah-i Sahaba of Pakistan have even sought to devise Sunni rituals to compete with Shi'i ones, it is scarcely far-fetched to suppose that the impact of the Iranian revolution on the 'ulama has not been without significance.

Rethinking Muslim Politics (with the 'Ulama in It)

The sort of activism that we have examined in this and the previous chapters contributes to our understanding of Muslim politics in several important ways. Leaving aside the question of what Muslim politics *in specific instances* would look like when we take the 'ulama as seriously as we do any other actors in the public sphere, at least three broad facets of their relevance to the study of contemporary politics can easily be singled out. Their contemporary activism reminds us, first, of the variegated composition of the Muslim public sphere; second, it draws our attention to the complexity of the 'ulama's own position in contemporary societies; and finally, to return to a continuing theme of this book, it suggests the relevance of the Islamic religious tradition to contemporary Muslim politics.

Dale Eickelman and Jon Anderson have drawn attention to an emerging "religious public sphere" in Muslim societies, arguing that it is emerging "less from associations [that are] more strictly the domain of civil society, than from ways of dealing confidently with others in an expanding social universe of shared communication."[148] Eickelman and Anderson emphasize the role of new media in the articulation of religious discourses, the emergence of new religious intellectuals, and "new understandings of the role of religion in society."[149] Islamists and the new religious intellectuals often define themselves against the 'ulama, compete for authority with them, and sometimes dismiss them either as stooges of the government or as utterly mired in an anachronistic tradition. This chapter has attempted to provide some glimpses of the 'ulama's religiopolitical activism in a few contemporary societies, not an overview of the competing religious and political discourses in these societies. Yet the illustrations offered here should suffice to show that the 'ulama are often important players in the public and political arena, that they not only compete but also interact with Islamists, and that, in some cases, they may have strategic advantages that the Islamists do not. There can be little doubt about either the fragmentation of religious authority in contemporary Islam or the significance of the new religious intellectuals. But it is not enough for an understanding of contemporary Muslim societies to focus only on the latter. The emerging Muslim public sphere is also the arena of the 'ulama's activism, and any serious understanding of that sphere is hard to achieve without adequate attention to the 'ulama.

The bases and expressions of the 'ulama's position in the public sphere are complex, multifaceted, and often contradictory. As we saw, the Egyptian 'ulama have been able to advance their position both by siding with the government against the Islamists and by siding with the Islamists against the government. In the Philippines the underground 'ulama and other rebels have waged a separatist struggle against the state while other 'ulama have remained "above ground" and stood apart from the guerrilla struggle; yet it is the latter's "religious" discourses that have served as a major means for disseminating the separatist ideology among the people. In Pakistan, as we saw in chapter 5, it is the lower-ranking 'ulama who wage the actual battles against their sectarian rivals, but leading religious figures continue to provide important intellectual support. In Saudi Arabia, though the senior 'ulama have defended the state against the peripheral 'ulama, they all agree on the centrality of the 'ulama's role. In Muslim societies like Egypt and Pakistan the 'ulama have been associated with top-down Islamization through the implementation of the shari'a, but they are equally part of ventures in grassroots Islamization—ventures that, in Pakistan in particular, have enhanced and deepened their influence in society. My point is not that it is the *same* 'ulama who undertake these different activities; in some societies, notably in Egypt, 'ulama of different standpoints are often pitted against each other, with the peripheral 'ulama often highly critical of the leading establishment figures. Yet while it obviously makes a lot of difference on which side the 'ulama are playing, so to speak, the fact that they can play on more than one side suggests, at the very least, that any notion of the 'ulama as utterly tied to the interests of the ruling elite, or as unable to adapt their interests to changing needs and circumstances, must be laid to rest. It also suggests an enlargement in their role, *qua* 'ulama, in society as a whole. And the fact that establishment 'ulama and oppositional 'ulama often have shared interests—a common vision of the place of Islam in society and of their own role with reference to it—suggests that we should not draw the lines between and among the 'ulama too stringently. Nor should we be surprised by the flexibility (some would say opportunism) with which they can sometimes define their positions and roles in the public arena.

The activism of the 'ulama points to the political resonance of the Islamic religious tradition. The more astute among students of contemporary Islamist trends have often cautioned against temptations to reduce these trends to a sum of social, economic, and political grievances in dysfunctional authoritarian states. They have rightly reminded us to not lose sight of the intellectual and religious bases of the Islamist movements, to take seriously the meaning and significance of their appeal to the "superior" claims of foundational texts and transcendent ideals against those of "man-made" ideologies and institutions. As Roxanne Euben has argued with reference to the thought of the Egyptian ideologue Sayyid Qutb, "there is a moral power to fundamentalist ideas that cannot be explained only by variables outside of the ideas."[150] The 'ulama invite us to take a step further, however. If the appeal of many Islamists and new religious intellectuals is often predicated on their claims to a *new* reading of Islam, often in the light of their modern learning and by showing how such rereading makes better sense both of Islam and of the modern world, the appeal of the 'ulama is, by contrast, grounded in their guardianship of the religious tradition as a continuous, lived heritage that connects the past and the present. The Islamists, too, invoke earlier authorities and other facets of the tradition that to them represent "true" Islam; and the 'ulama's tradition has, all along, continued to be updated and variously reconfigured. Yet in an age when identity, cultural authenticity, and religious authority resonate widely with many people—and not just in Muslim societies—we can scarcely discount the appeal of the 'ulama's identification with the religious tradition as a critical basis of their position. The 'ulama's strong identification with this tradition has often been deemed to marginalize them in a rapidly changing society. And under the impact of modernization and rapid social change, it has no doubt done so in many ways. Yet in the context of the new salience of religion in public life in the last decades of the twentieth century, it is precisely their claims to authoritatively represent an "authentic" Islamic tradition in its richness, depth, and continuity that may have become the most significant basis of their new prominence in the public sphere.[151]

Epilogue

The 'Ulama in the Twenty-First Century

I N A PAPER titled "The Leadership Role of the 'Ulama," presented in March 1992 at a seminar in Lucknow and later published, an Indian religious scholar Mawlana Wahid al-din Khan (b. 1925) offered a bold and broad-ranging critique of the intellectual and political concerns of both the 'ulama and the Islamists. He noted that the "criterion of power" has changed in the modern world: power is now measured in intellectual and technological terms, and this is the real basis on which Western societies have risen to and maintained their position of dominance in the world.[1] The 'ulama, however, have tended to conceive of this dominance in exclusively political terms, without understanding the profound changes of which it is the result.[2] They have remained so immured in a political view of the world that the significance of other changes, or of the need to adapt themselves and their followers to those changes, has continued to escape them. To Wahid al-din, one of the most serious consequences of this emphasis on the political dimension of Muslim decline is that the 'ulama see everywhere only "injustice, conspiracy, and affliction" but not the new opportunities that are equally the product of the transformations of modernity.[3] The Qur'anic verses (94.5–6) in which God promises that "hardship" is accompanied by "ease," or "relief," have, according to Wahid al-din, been misinterpreted by modern exegetes like Mawdudi to mean that relief is to come *after* hardship. But, Wahid al-din notes, the verse in question actually speaks of ease *together with* hardship, which means that adverse circumstances might themselves point to new openings.[4] Thus, even such undesirable circumstances as colonial rule and Western domination have resulted in new opportunities for the 'ulama. For instance, the modern age rests on guarantees of "freedom of thought" and security from religious persecution, which together with modern means of communication, have opened new avenues for the spread of Islam.[5] Yet the 'ulama have not merely failed to take advantage of the opportunities that have become available to them; they also remain oblivious to the challenges of this new age. In a world that owes its creativity to freedom of belief and expression, the notion of departing from the paths charted out earlier has remained unacceptable to the 'ulama, as has the very idea that it might be legitimate to take a critical view of their forbears.[6]

Elsewhere Wahid al-din Khan has argued passionately for the need to continuously undertake ijtihad to "respond to the intellectual and practical problems of the modern age in a way that one can take full account of the spirit of Islam while addressing the new needs [of the time]." This is what he characterizes as the "reconstruction of Islamic thought," a task urgently required of Muslims.[7] It is often argued, he notes, that there is no longer any scope for "absolute ijtihad" (*ijtihad-i mutlaq*), that is, for formulating new legal rulings in light of the foundational texts; the only kind of ijtihad that is often acknowledged still to be possible is a "limited" one, viz., the effort to expand the boundaries of one's school of law in accordance with the agreed-upon principles of the school and only by analogy with existing rulings.[8] Yet, Wahid al-din notes, scholars have always existed who have, in fact, undertaken ijtihad of the former sort, and there is no reason why this should not continue to be so now.[9] The problem, he says, is not that people have come to lack the ability for ijtihad, but that the tolerance for criticism, which is a precondition for intellectual endeavors such as ijtihad, has declined: "It would be more correct to say that, in later centuries, it was not the gate of ijtihad but that of criticism and disagreement that came to be closed. Henceforth, the agreed-upon principle was that only that ijtihad was acceptable that did not affect [the authority of] someone [from the past], but any ijtihad that did so was ruled out."[10]

Wahid al-din acknowledges that ijtihad is an onerous undertaking. But, he asks, how does one determine whether a particular individual has the requisite qualities for it? One might describe the qualities that are theoretically needed, but the claim that someone does, in fact, possess those qualities is a different matter. Ijtihad requires that one be not just sufficiently learned but also "God fearing." Yet the latter is not a demonstrable quality, and it can be judged only by God. "The fact is," he writes, that

> ijtihad is . . . something done as the result of an inner calling; it is not done through formal appointment. . . . There is obviously the danger that some people would perform ijtihad though they are incompetent to do so. But it is not possible to check [*sic*] such people through some writ or regulation. Such incompetent mujtahids have existed at all times and will continue to exist. The only safeguard against such people is the law of God that truth alone thrives in this world and falsehood soon perishes by itself.[11]

The fear of ijtihad, in Wahid al-din Khan's analysis, is related to a larger fear of change on the part of the 'ulama. Change, to the latter, is the result not of legitimate, evolving historical processes, which must be understood and faced, but of "conspiracies," which have to be uncovered and resisted. As a result, great ingenuity has been used in uncovering such conspiracies but very little in understanding processes of change or adapting

Islam to them.[12] And yet it is the latter project on which the well-being of Islam and the Muslims really rests.

The intellectual heritage of Islam is a product, Wahid al-din says, of a time when Muslims were politically dominant. It reflects the needs of those earlier times, and cannot, for that same reason, provide solutions for Muslims in a changed world. As an example, he adduces the juristic rulings regarding a person accused of slandering the Prophet Muhammad, for which the prescribed punishment has usually been death. He lists a number of works on this subject, and notes that they were all written at a time when Muslims were in a position of political strength in the world.[13] The precedents from the life of the Prophet that the jurists draw on in affirming the capital sentence for the slanderer are from the Medinan phase of his life, when he had established a polity, and not from the Meccan phase, when he was a struggling prophet and when incidents of "slander" had in fact occurred but had been ignored. The modern muftis do not realize, he says, the implications of the fact that the political circumstances today are very different. Those who are politically dominant in the world are people for whom unlimited freedom of expression is the "foremost sacred principle." Consequently (in what is an obvious reference to the controversy over Salman Rushdie's *Satanic Verses*), as soon as a mufti declares anyone a slanderer, the latter "becomes an instant hero [*sic*] to the leading nations," and this serves only to confirm the international media in their image of Islam as a "barbaric religion."[14]

Medieval exegetical writings, likewise, characterize the many Qur'anic injunctions that counsel patience in the face of oppression as "abrogated" by other verses that recommend the path of fighting the unbelievers.[15] And yet patience, he says, is "the most important of Islam's commands."[16] In short, the medieval juristic and exegetical works "do not encompass the circumstances of later times. Consequently, for all their virtues, such works have become irrelevant to the modern age. This, more or less, is true of the entire corpus of writings which today is called the 'Islamic library.'"[17]

The path that Wahid al-din Khan himself recommends is that of focusing exclusively on a patient, apolitical proselytism. This, he believes, is the surest guarantee of the ultimate success of Islam.[18] Even in the face of such severe challenges to India's Muslims as the destruction of the Baburi Masjid in 1992 by Hindu nationalists, and the communal frenzy that followed this episode, he has counseled patience and moderation. Indeed, he has argued that any demands that the mosque be rebuilt are only likely to exacerbate the hostility against the Muslims and so prove counterproductive. The shari'a requires Muslims to protect the sanctity of the mosque, he writes, but the shari'a lays far greater emphasis on the protection of life and on safeguarding the greater interests of the Muslim community. These interests would be served by moving beyond the Baburi Masjid. Instead of striving to rebuild it (that is, even if it were possible to do so), the effort should be on securing guarantees from the government for the protection of *other* historical Muslim sites.[19] And in general, Muslims should avoid all issues that can cause or heighten discord between themselves and the Hindus.[20]

This position on the Baburi Masjid has led critics to see Wahid al-din Khan as a "BJP Maulana," a scholar who by advising patience in the face of Hindu nationalist aggression is doing little more than serving the interests of the Hindu right-wing Bharatiya Janata Party (BJP).[21] But while his stance on the disputed mosque no doubt appeals to the BJP, not all of his views would be equally welcome. His is an emphasis on peaceful proselytism, as we have seen, but inasmuch as it is the non-Muslims—including the Hindus—who are the object of this effort, those seeking to *reaffirm* a Hindu identity could scarcely be pleased with it.[22] Further, while he has argued that the Indian Muslims should move beyond their single-minded devotion to the protection of the Urdu language—long the symbol of their cultural identity—to learn India's regional languages, he recommends that path only as a means of "self-development," not as a prelude to the loss of their identity. And, to him, this self-development is "a primary condition for the propagation of Islamic teachings in this country."[23] He has, moreover, argued fervently against a uniform civil code for the people of India—an issue which, it would be recalled, was at the heart of the Shah Bano controversy.[24]

Wahid al-din Khan's insistence on proselytism (*tabligh*) obviously suggests his affinity with the Tablighi Jama'at, which originated in India in the early decades of the twentieth century and maintains an important presence there. Indeed, in a short tract written in the 1960s, he lavishes much praise on the leaders and adherents of this movement for their selfless devotion to the goal of revitalizing Islam through a patient, person-to-person dissemination of its message.[25] Some observers of the Tablighi Jama'at have discerned a conscious avoidance of political involvements on the part of its members, though other scholars have disputed this conclusion.[26] This is a large movement, however, with operations in many countries and involving thousands of people, which means that any broad generalizations about an apolitical stance, or the lack of one, must remain suspect. There are those among its supporters who insist on calling people to a revitalized religious commitment to the exclusion of all other concerns, but for others proselytism seems not to preclude political goals. Wahid al-din Khan does, in any case, argue that political aspirations are best avoided. That this is itself a political stance of some significance in the context of a state that, in recent decades, has seen an anti-Muslim Hindu nationalist movement rise to power goes uncommented in his writings.

If there is some affinity between Wahid al-din Khan and the Tablighi Jama'at on the crucial issue of proselytism, however, there is much that also sets them apart. While lauding the latter's efforts in "reviving the essence of religion," he observes that there are several different ways of furthering the interests of Islam, that the course one adopts must be responsive to changing times and circumstances,[27] and that "the need to work in *different arenas* is . . . acute."[28] Implicit here is his criticism of the Tablighi Jama'at for its lack of intellectual engagement with the challenges facing Muslims. As he notes with some derision, the entire movement of the Tablighi Jama'at is being run on the basis of a single work—Muhammad Zakariyya's *Fada'il-i a'mal*[29] For Wahid al-din, on the other hand, a sustained effort to come to grips with and respond to modern intellectual challenges is precisely what Muslims most need, and he finds no recognition of this in the Tablighi Jama'at.

What also sets Wahid al-din apart from the Tablighi Jama'at is his attitude towards the Islamic religious tradition as represented by the 'ulama. While he himself has a madrasa education and was, for many years, editor of the Jam'iyyat al-'Ulama-i Hind's weekly journal,[30] he remains highly critical of the 'ulama—not of those belonging to this or that sectarian orientation, but of the 'ulama as a whole. More grievously from the viewpoint of the latter, he is skeptical of the value or relevance of the religious tradition they stand for. The Tablighi Jama'at, on the other hand, is a movement largely comprised of 'lay' preachers, but it has always maintained close ties with Deobandi 'ulama. And even when it is only the *Fada'il-i a'mal* of Muhammad Zakariyya (himself a Deobandi scholar) that shapes their vision of Islam, they maintain a deep reverence for the Islamic religious tradition as mediated by the Deobandi 'ulama.

Precisely because of his background, Wahid al-din Khan's critique of the 'ulama remains, in many ways, an internal critique, and it is here that much of its significance may be said to lie. Such internal critiques are, of course, not unique to him. As we noted in chapter 3, Shibli Nu'mani, who was actively associated with the founding of the Nadwat al-'Ulama' at the end of the nineteenth century, was highly critical of the existing madrasas even as he professed to be "a strong supporter of traditional education." Muhammad 'Abduh, a figure associated more closely than anyone else with the reform of madrasa education in Egypt and with the larger project of revitalizing Islam in a changed world, is, of course, the preeminent example of a critic from within the 'ulama's ranks. Following his lead, Azhar scholars and administrators like Muhammad Mustafa al-Maraghi and Mahmud Shaltut later sought to reform the Azhar from within.[31] Though their vision of reform may often have differed from that of the Egyptian ruling elite,[32] an internal sentiment for reform no doubt gave the government considerable leverage—unlike, say, in Pakistan, where such sentiment has remained notably clouded by the 'ulama's suspicions of the government—to carry through its own initiatives even when they were more drastic than those proposed internally.

Important voices calling for a radical rethinking of the religious tradition have also emerged within the Shi'i religious establishment of contemporary Iran. As early as in the 1960s, a respected young religious scholar, Murtada Mutahhari, along with some of his associates, had given serious attention to a major overhauling of the Shi'i madrasa system.[33] After the revolution of 1979, and especially after Khumayni's death a decade later, bold and novel formulations which have implications for all aspects of the Islamic tradition, for issues of religious authority, for the position of women, and for the relationship between Islam and politics, have been put forth. Such formulations have come from new religious intellectuals like 'Abdolkarim Sorush, but importantly, others emanate from madrasa-educated 'ulama like Hujjat al-Islam Sayyid Muhsin Sa'idzadeh.[34] Like Sorush, Sa'idzadeh has argued that interpretations of religion ought to be distinguished from religion itself,[35] and that religious authority should not be vested exclusively in a particular institution or group.[36] Sa'idzadeh has also called for a drastic reevaluation of issues of gender in Islam, suggesting that the lack of women's equality with men is merely a product of the ways the religion has tended to be interpreted in history—ways that, in themselves, hold no particular sanctity and should therefore be amenable to change. Sa'idzadeh's ideas have not been well received by the more conservative members of the religious establishment, any more than have been those of, say, 'Abduh or of Wahid al-din Khan. Nevertheless, the fact that such ideas have come from within is worth underlining, not only because they represent some recognition of the need for drastic change among the 'ulama but also because, being from within, they are likely to have a greater resonance for other 'ulama than similar critiques from Western-educated modernists.

Most of the 'ulama whose work we have considered in this book eschew a radical reform or rethinking of their tradition, however. A wholehearted recognition that the tradition requires major changes and that the 'ulama ought to set themselves on the path of bringing those about has been rare. Yet the lack of such an acknowledgment (which itself represents a reasoned position and ought to be seen as such) has not precluded changes of varying significance. New ways of conceptualizing the shari'a, efforts to reach new audiences, new conceptions of religion and of the 'ulama's position in society and polity, and new roles of religious and political activism are, as we have seen in the preceding chapters, some of the many facets of change that continue to sweep through the world of the 'ulama. Such changes are not the product of some grand blueprint for bringing them about; nor are they necessarily recognized as "changes." Many, indeed, are the paradoxical product of the 'ulama's very effort to conserve their tradition in a changing world. Whether or not they acknowledge this, such an effort necessarily entails continuous redefinition of themselves, their stances, and their intellectual resources.

Yet we should not focus only on what, despite the 'ulama's professions to the contrary, is new in their modern careers, for elements of novelty often exist side by side with other, older, and themselves varied elements in their discourse. As we observed in chapters 1 and 4, the shari'a has often been viewed as a rigid, codelike structure in modern Muslim societies, and, as Nathan Brown has pointed out, it is this view that is the basis of contemporary demands for the implementation of the shari'a in order to make the state "truly" Islamic. Yet older conceptions of the shari'a's flexibility have also continued to exist and to be put to use in political argument, as we saw with reference to nationalist 'ulama like Husayn Ahmad Madani. In various contexts the 'ulama have invoked the unchangeability and the flexibility of the shari'a to assert their own distinctive authority as its interpreters and guardians, and they have done so both by drawing on the earlier juristic tradition and by striving to adapt themselves to the changes around them. Their ambivalence towards the state itself expresses aspects of earlier misgivings towards the rulers, but it also reflects new uncertainties: for example, a sense of both the new possibilities *and* the dangers that a modern nation-state represents for them.

We can view such ambivalence as illustrating differences within the ranks of the 'ulama and also as suggestive of how a long-standing scholarly culture finds itself at a loss in an alien world. But while both of these explanatory options no doubt illuminate some of the contradictions of the modern 'ulama, it is also crucial that we not mistake the flexibility of their discourses for incoherence. Multiple discourses have long existed side by side in the world of the 'ulama; and, in this respect again, the modern 'ulama are often not altogether different from their precursors.

Forms of ijtihad, for instance, can and do continue to exist within the overall framework of taqlid. We have observed this with reference to the modern South Asian 'ulama, but the same is often true of 'ulama elsewhere. To take an example from a Muslim country we have not studied in this work, consider the case of Indonesia's Nahdlatul Ulama, a major organization created in the early twentieth century in the face of challenges to the 'ulama's authority from modernist reformers. The organization now includes not just 'ulama but has a broad-based membership in rural and urban areas as well as urban politicians and intellectuals. And it has played an important role in Indonesian politics. This culminated in

October 1999 with the election of Abdurrahman Wahid, the leader of the Nahdlatul Ulama, as the president of Indonesia—albeit a controversial and short-lived presidency.[37] The Nahdlatul Ulama lays particular stress on conforming to the authority of its Shafi'i school of law (taqlid) and on adherence to certain ritual practices that other reformers see as not "truly" Islamic. Yet as anthropologist Martin van Bruinessen reminds us, "Taqlid is not necessarily rigid. Ironically, in the late 20th century, traditionalist *ulama* [of the Nahdlatul Ulama] often appear more flexible than the [modernist] spokesmen for reformist Islam, many of whom have not evolved beyond the positions taken at the beginning of this [i.e., the Twentieth] century."[38]

In politics, as we have seen with reference to Pakistan, efforts to Islamize society from the top down, through the implementation of Islamic law, exist alongside activism at the grassroots level. Discussions of how the law ought to be implemented in the context of a modern state engage the 'ulama no less than do politically activist efforts to promote such implementation. Among the 'ulama's writings, moreover, highly specialized works have continued to be produced alongside works for popular audiences. These specialized works exist not as a mere relic of the past, but because they serve to articulate religious authority in the present, just as more popular, or populist, works do in their own way.

Writing for different audiences, in different modes, and—literally and figuratively—in different languages, is not new for the 'ulama. That they have often continued to do so should alert us to the different ways in which they have articulated their discourses to meet the exigencies or constraints of a particular situation. Anthropologist Ziba Mir-Hosseini has written of her shock and dismay at discovering that Hujjat al-Islam Sa'idzadeh, whose work she admired for its bold calls for gender equality on the basis of a reconstituted Islamic jurisprudence, wrote not only in defense of Islamic feminism in *Zanan*, a feminist, women-run journal of Tehran, but also published anonymous critiques of feminism in *Payam-e zan*, a clerical and conservative male-run journal from Qom:

> I was stunned by the inconsistency: I could not understand how [Sa'idzadeh]
> . . . could simultaneously defend and attack a single position. I saw the article
> [in critique of feminism] as a betrayal of *Zanan*, and kept asking how he
> could contribute to two journals with such divergent political orientations
> and gender views. But he saw no contradiction in this, and repeated, mantra-
> like: "you must separate ideas from actions."[39]

Mir-Hosseini goes on:

> As our collaboration continued, and I learned more about the intellectual
> trajectories of clerics, the politics of gender, and of women's journals in Iran,
> I came to understand that the inconsistency was an illusion. I also came to

understand what Sa'idzadeh meant by his mantra, and that his critique of "cultural invasion" and feminism in the *Payam-e Zan* article was in effect a necessary step in the evolution of his thinking. His contributions to *Zanan* did not mean that he endorsed or identified with *Zanan*'s political views; rather, it was the only forum in which he could express his own views without disguising them in the complex circular style prevalent in Houzeh [madrasa] writing.[40]

The multiplicity of the actions and discourses of the 'ulama that we have studied in this book suggests a far more flexible understanding of the world, and of Islam, than is often acknowledged—and not just by observers or critics of the 'ulama but often also by themselves. They have continued to accommodate changes, both small and large, and, in this respect, the 'ulama of the twentieth or the twenty-first century are not very different from those of the earlier centuries. This flexibility means that the new and the old can subsist together in the religious tradition, even as the old is reconfigured in often novel ways. It also means that, far from having been marginalized in the face of challenges to their author-ity—challenges from the modern nation-state or from Islamist activists and the new religious intellectuals, for instance—the 'ulama have often continued to be, or have become, active and important players in many contemporary Muslim societies.

Yet what 'ulama like Sa'idzadeh in Iran and Wahid al-din Khan in India seek, or what Muslim modernists like Sorush and Muhammad Shahrur and Fazlur Rahman have called for, is change or flexibility of a very differ-ent order than what most 'ulama have been willing to accept. This change is premised on the recognition that the foundational texts must be inter-preted afresh; the religious tradition reevaluated, critiqued, and radically rethought, and only *then* parts of it appropriated for their present "use-fulness." However significant the particular adjustments and transforma-tions of the 'ulama might be—and as this book has argued, these transfor-mations are both wide-ranging and often highly significant—it is on this issue that, with some exceptions, the 'ulama remain unrelenting. This is no mere intransigence. Rather, it is the central basis of all their claims to religious authority and of their identity as 'ulama. Irrespective of the de-gree to which the 'ulama have actually accommodated changes in partic-ular societies and states, it is on the claim to guard, represent, and inter-pret the Islamic tradition that their status as "religious experts" is predi-cated. And as I have argued in chapter 6, the 'ulama's insistence on main-taining a continuous link with this tradition is also the basis of their religious and political roles in contemporary Islam. To put this last point differently, many among the 'ulama actively engage in varied intellectual pursuits, but these, in themselves, are not necessarily the basis of the 'ula-ma's standing; nor are their writings necessarily of interest for their intellectual sophistication. The interest of these writings lies rather, as does that of the 'ulama's activities in general, in the continuing link with the Islamic religious tradition they claim and constantly reaffirm. This claim continues to be a powerful one, even when the tradition itself is constantly undergoing often-unacknowledged modifications. But to embark on a venture of systematically reshaping that tradition in, say, the realm of law, as Sa'idzadeh in Iran or Wahid al-din Khan in India urges the 'ulama to do, would undermine the very ground on which their position and their conception of Islam rests.

Unlike the modernists but like the Islamists, the 'ulama do not usually believe that Islam needs to be phrased in the idiom of the modern age (that it is, in fact, so phrased by them is a different matter, however). Yet unlike most Sunni Islamists, they typically do not believe that "true" Islam is different from what has emerged out of a centuries-old tradition of discourse. At issue, then, is the well-worn question of how the interests of Islam are best served: Are they served better by trying to interpret the foundational religious texts in a way that modern exigencies and values seem to require? Or should a long-standing religious tradition as histori- cally articulated guide the position one adopts in facing these exigencies and in evaluating modern norms? Such questions are not peculiar to Islam, of course, let alone to the 'ulama. Contemporary Christian theolo- gians like Lutheran George Lindbeck have expressed serious reservations, for instance, about the attempts by liberal theologians to "translate" reli- gion into the idiom of the time, to present it in terms of shared founda- tions and universal principles, in order to make it not just more intelligible but also more appealing. This mode of presentation, he believes, distorts the peculiarities of a religious tradition, undermines its internal coher- ence, and despite the promise of immediate gain, does a disservice to the vitality and appeal of the tradition in the long term.[41] For his part, Lind- beck proposes a method that "resembles ancient catechesis more than modern translation. Instead of redescribing the faith in new concepts, it seeks to teach the language and practices of the religion to potential adherents. This has been the primary way of transmitting the faith and winning converts for most religions down through the centuries."[42] Lind- beck acknowledges that this "cultural-linguistic" approach is unlikely to appeal to many liberal theologians, who, with good reason, would fail to see in it a way of successfully maintaining or enlarging the ranks of their audience.[43] But he believes that, paradoxical as it is, "[r]eligious communi- ties are likely to be practically relevant in the long run to the degree that they do not first ask what is either practical or relevant, but instead con- centrate on their own intratextual outlooks and forms of life."[44]

Something similar could be said by the Pakistani 'ulama in explaining why madrasas should not be integrated into the nation's educational mainstream, or what is wrong with modernist interpretations of Islam. Yet even as they strive to demarcate and defend their own religious sphere, to resist molding themselves according to what might be thought of as the changing needs of the time, the 'ulama also continue to enlarge their audiences, to shape debates on the meaning and place of Islam in public life, to lead activist movements in pursuit of their ideals. For them, there is no single way of defending their ideals or of making them practical or relevant in the world. There are different paths to adopt. Yet this is a multiplicity that is guided by a broadly shared way of looking at the world, at themselves and, above all, at the Islamic tradition of which they profess to be both the custodians and the authoritative interpreters.

Notes

INTRODUCTION

1. Non-English words used frequently in this study will usually be italicized only at their first occurrence.

2. For this characterization and those to whom it refers, see Dale F. Eickelman and James Piscatori, *Muslim Politics* (Princeton: Princeton University Press, 1996), 43–44, 77, and passim; also cf. Dale F. Eickelman and Jon W. Anderson, eds., *New Media in the Muslim World: The Emerging Public Sphere* (Bloomington: Indiana University Press, 1999).

3. There is extensive scholarly literature on the 'ulama and their institutions of learning in premodern Muslim societies. See, among others, A.K.S. Lambton, *State and Government in Medieval Islam* (Oxford: Oxford University Press, 1981); Muhammad Qasim Zaman, *Religion and Politics under the Early 'Abbasids* (Leiden: Brill, 1997); George Makdisi, *The Rise of Colleges: Institutions of Learning in Islam and the West* (Edinburgh: Edinburgh University Press, 1981); Richard Bulliet, *The Patricians of Nishapur* (Cambridge: Harvard University Press, 1972); Jonathan P. Berkey, *The Transmission of Knowledge in Medieval Cairo: A Social History of Islamic Education* (Princeton: Princeton University Press, 1992); Michael Chamberlain, *Knowledge and Social Practice in Medieval Damascus, 1190–1350* (Cambridge: Cambridge University Press, 1994); Nicole Grandin and Marc Gaborieau, eds., *Madrasa: La transmission du savoir dans le monde musulman* (Paris: Editions Arguments, 1997); R. C. Repp, *The Mufti of Istanbul: A Study in the Development of the Ottoman Learned Hierarchy* (London: Ithaca Press, 1986); Haim Gerber, *Islamic Law and Culture, 1600–1840* (Leiden: Brill, 1999); Ishtiaq Husain Qureshi, *Ulema in Politics: A Study Relating to the Political Activities of the Ulema in the South Asian Subcontinent from 1556 to 1947* (Karachi: Maaref, 1972). For a broad overview and further bibliography, see *The Encyclopaedia of Islam*, 2d ed. (Leiden: E. J. Brill, 1960–), 10: 801–10, s.v. " 'Ulama" (by C. Gilliot et al.).

4. On the impact of print, electronic, and information technologies on religious change and the resultant "fragmentation" of authority, see *inter alia*, Eickelman and Anderson, *New Media in the Muslim World* (for other references, see chapter 2 in the present volume). On the similar impact of mass education, see Dale F. Eickelman, "Mass Higher Education and the Religious Imagination in Contemporary Arab Societies," *American Ethnologist* 19/4 (1992): 1–13; Eickelman and Piscatori, *Muslim Politics*, 37ff.; Gregory Starrett, *Putting Islam to Work: Education, Politics, and Religious Transformation in Egypt* (Berkeley: University of California Press, 1998). The most ambitious sociological examination of the global consequences of information technology attempted so far is Manuel Castells, *The Information Age: Economy, Society and Culture*, 3 vols. (Oxford: Blackwell Publishers, 1996–98); see especially vol. 2, *The Power of Identity*.

5. On the "reflexivity" of modernity and its implications for systems of knowledge and social relations in general, see Anthony Giddens, *The Consequences of Modernity* (Stanford: Stanford University Press, 1990).

6. Olivier Roy, *The Failure of Political Islam* (Cambridge: Harvard University Press, 1994), 20. In an otherwise sophisticated comparative study of fundamentalism, Martin Riesebrodt defines it as "radicalized traditionalism," "a traditionalism that has become reflexive." See *Pious Passion: The Emergence of Modern Fundamentalism in the United States and Iran* (Berkeley: University of California Press, 1993), 16, 23, and passim. Though he is concerned only with American Protestant fundamentalism in the early twentieth century and with Iranian Shiʿism before the revolution of 1979, his notion of *radicalized* traditionalism leaves little doubt that—like many others who use the term—he sees "traditionalism" itself as largely static and politically passive. The merit of Riesebrodt's definition of fundamentalism is its effort to see this phenomenon as a modern and in many ways novel one, even when its adherents appeal to a mythical past; but his assumption that "traditionalism" itself is a largely monolithic phenomenon remains problematic.

7. Cf. Roy, *Failure of Political Islam*, 90–93; on the ʿulama's discourses as a closed system, cf. 90; on the "lumpen-intelligentsia," 84ff.

8. Even when scholars bring very different assumptions to their analysis of modern Islamic movements and trends, they often agree in their view of the ʿulama. Compare, for instance, Roy's view of the ʿulama with that of John Esposito and John Voll, both prominent and influential contributors to the literature on contemporary Islam: John L. Esposito and John O. Voll, *Makers of Contemporary Islam* (New York: Oxford University Press, 2001), 14–17 (on the "decline of the ulama").

9. Figures based on Nadhr Ahmad, *Jaʾiza-i madaris-i ʿarabiyya-i Maghribi Pakistan* (Lahore: Muslim Academy, 1972), 695; *Report qawmi committee baraʾi dini madaris-i Pakistan* (Islamabad: Ministry of Religious Affairs, 1979), 198; *Zindagi* (February 17, 1995), 39; *Dawn*, January 22, 2002. Also see table 1 in chapter 5 of the present work.

10. Jeffrey Stout, "Commitments and Traditions in the Study of Religious Ethics," *Journal of Religious Ethics* 25/3 (1998): 23–56: quotation is from 49. Emphasis in original.

11. There is a growing body of literature on tradition, the invention of tradition, and its redefinitions. The collection of essays in Eric Hobsbawm and Terence Ranger, eds., *The Invention of Tradition* (Cambridge: Cambridge University Press, 1983) is now a minor classic in this genre. For a more recent example, see Lata Mani, *Contentious Traditions: The Debate on Sati in Colonial India* (Berkeley: University of California Press, 1998), which demonstrates the "modernity of [the] discourse on tradition" (77) with reference to the debate on the widow burning (*sati*) in colonial India. On the malleability of "tradition" in contemporary Muslim politics, see Eickelman and Piscatori, *Muslim Politics*, 22–45; also see Marilyn Robinson Waldman, "Tradition as a Modality of Change: Islamic Examples," *History of Religions* 25 (1986): 318–40. For a postmodernist critique of theological appeals to the Christian tradition, see Kathryn Tanner, *Theories of Culture: A New Agenda for Theology* (Minneapolis: Fortress Press, 1997), 128–38.

12. For an influential example of such works, cf. Daniel Lerner, *The Passing of Traditional Society: Modernizing the Middle East* (Glencoe: The Free Press, 1958).

13. William A. Graham, "Traditionalism in Islam: An Essay in Interpretation," *Journal of Interdisciplinary History* 23/3 (1993): 495–522; quotation is from 522.

14. Ibid., passim.

15. For some reflections, see ibid., 496f.

16. For his concept of tradition, see Alasdair MacIntyre, *After Virtue*, 2d ed. (Notre Dame: University of Notre Dame Press, 1984), 204–25; idem, *Whose Justice? Which Rationality?* (Notre Dame: University of Notre Dame Press, 1988); idem, *Three Rival Versions of Moral Enquiry: Encyclopaedia, Genealogy, and Tradition* (Notre Dame: University of Notre Dame Press, 1990). For critiques of MacIntyre, see, *inter alia*, John Horton and Susan Mendus, eds., *After MacIntyre: Critical Perspectives on the Work of Alasdair MacIntyre* (Notre Dame: Notre Dame University Press, 1994); Jeffrey Stout, *Ethics after Babel: The Languages of Morals and their Discontents*, 2d ed. (Princeton: Princeton University Press, 2001); idem, "Commitments and Traditions"; Stephen Holmes, *The Anatomy of Antiliberalism* (Cambridge: Harvard University Press, 1993); Jennifer A. Herdt, "Alasdair MacIntyre's 'Rationality of Traditions' and Tradition-Transcendental Standards of Justification," *Journal of Religion* 78/4 (1998): 524–46.

17. MacIntyre, *Whose Justice?* 12.

18. Ibid., 393.

19. Ibid., 346, 350. On the "incommensurability" of traditions, see ibid., 370–88; for some critiques of this idea, see Paul Kelly, "MacIntyre's Critique of Utilitarianism," in *After MacIntyre*, ed. Horton and Mendus, 136ff; Andrew Mason, "MacIntyre on Liberalism and Its Critics: Tradition, Incommensurability and Disagreement," in *After MacIntyre*, ed. Horton and Mendus, 225–44.

20. MacIntyre, *Whose Justice?* 370–88; quotation is from 387. Also cf. George A. Lindbeck, *The Nature of Doctrine: Religion and Theology in a Postliberal Age* (Philadelphia: The Westminster Press, 1984), 128ff. for a "postliberal" critique of theological liberalism's foundationalism and the penchant for translating religion into the idiom of the day. To Lindbeck, "[a]s modern culture moves ever farther away from its religious roots, these translations become more strained, complex, and obscure to the uninitiated. Relativism increases and foundational appeals to universal structures of thought, experience, or *Existenz* lose their persuasiveness" (130).

21. Critics of MacIntyre, such as Stephen Holmes, consider this critique of liberal decontextualization to be the essence of his position (cf. Holmes, *Anatomy of Antiliberalism*, 103). But they also note the serious inconsistencies in this position. To Holmes, "There seem to be two MacIntyres: one says that moral obligations derive from concrete social contexts and traditions; the other claims that they are imposed directly by God on the individual soul. This fundamental tension racks and vitiates his thought" (103). What MacIntyre finds really troubling about liberalism is, according to Holmes (96f.) not so much its decontextualizing tendencies as its secularism.

22. MacIntyre, *Whose Justice?* 392; also see 326–48 and 370–85.

23. Cf. Kelly, "MacIntyre's Critique of Utilitarianism," 137.

24. Ibid., 137.

25. Mason, "MacIntyre on Liberalism and its Critics," 226ff.

26. Martha Nussbaum, "Recoiling from Reason," *New York Review of Books* (December 7, 1989): 36–41; quotation is from 40; quoted in Jean Porter, "Openness and Constraint: Moral Reflection as Tradition-Guided Inquiry in Alasdair MacIntyre's Recent Works," *Journal of Religion* 73/4 (1993): 514–36, at 522. Porter offers a general defense of MacIntyre's view of tradition-guided modes of inquiry, and defends him against a reading of his work in terms of its authoritarian implications. (I owe this reference to John P. Reeder Jr.)

27. See MacIntyre, *Three Rival Versions of Moral Enquiry.*

28. MacIntyre, *Whose Justice?* 364; cf. 370–88. Also see MacIntyre's rejoinder in his "A Partial Response to My Critics," in *After MacIntyre*, ed. Horton and Mendus, especially 290–98; idem, "Incommensurability, Truth, and the Conversation between Confucians and Aristotelians about the Virtues," in *Culture and Modernity: East-West Philosophic Perspectives*, ed. Eliot Deutsch (Honolulu: University of Hawaii Press, 1991), 104–22. (I owe this reference to John P. Reeder Jr.)

29. Talal Asad, *The Idea of an Anthropology of Islam* (Washington, D.C.: Center for Contemporary Arab Studies, Georgetown University, 1986), 14. Asad explicitly acknowledges his debt to MacIntyre's conception of tradition (21 n. 26) but does not, here or elsewhere, examine the differences between the latter's formulation and his own. One difference between them seems to lie in Asad's greater attentiveness to *institutions* as constitutive of tradition, in addition to ideas and arguments "extended through time." Yet MacIntyre's conception of tradition does not necessarily preclude attention to institutions. Following Asad, I will therefore leave aside the question of the possible differences between his and MacIntyre's notions of tradition, or the implications of such differences.

30. Ibid., passim; cf. Starrett, *Putting Islam to Work*, 7f. Asad's criticism is directed primarily at fellow anthropologists of Islam, and in particular at the writings of Ernest Gellner and Clifford Geertz. For a more extended critique of Geertz, see Talal Asad, "The Construction of Religion as an Anthropological Category," in *Genealogies of Religion: Discipline and Reasons of Power in Christianity and Islam* (Baltimore: Johns Hopkins University Press, 1993), 27–54. For the formulation "foundational texts," I am indebted to Bernard Weiss. *The Spirit of Islamic Law* (Athens: University of Georgia Press, 1998), 116 and passim.

31. On the shari'a as a "total discourse" comprised of, and encompassing, large areas of Muslim life and thought in premodern Muslim societies, see Brinkley Messick, *The Calligraphic State: Textual Domination and History in a Muslim Society* (Berkeley: University of California Press, 1993), 3 and passim. For other works on Islamic legal thought and practice, and for a discussion of Islamic law, see chapter 1.

32. MacIntyre, *After Virtue*, 222.

33. On the broad consensus of medieval Islamic historians on the origins of Islam, a consensus within which important disagreements are, however, preserved, see, for example, Fred M. Donner, *Narratives of Islamic Origins: The Beginnings of Islamic Historical Writing* (Princeton: Darwin Press, 1998), 26f., 286ff. On the possible role of the governing elite in fostering a consensus among early historians and jurists, cf. Tarif Khalidi, *Arabic Historical Thought in the Classical Period* (Cambridge: Cambridge University Press, 1994), 45f. Also cf. Michael Cooperson, *Classical Arabic Biography: The Heirs of the Prophets in*

the Age of al-Ma'mun (Cambridge: Cambridge University Press, 2000), 192, on intertextuality as the "quintessential literary achievement of pre-modern Arabic prose. The single most important consideration when seeking to understand both the documentary and literary effects of a report is . . . the presence of other reports that substantiate, contradict, or complement it, and by virtue of these relationships set up a necessary interpretive and critical chain of associations in the reader's mind."

34. Marshall G. S. Hodgson, *The Venture of Islam* (Chicago: University of Chicago Press, 1974), 3: 419; also 428.

35. See MacIntyre, *Whose Justice?* 385–86.

36. Another important intellectual and political trend is, of course, secularism. Though guiding state ideology and the ruling elite in many instances, of which the most notable example is Turkey, this trend has, however, been generally rather less influential in terms of adherents and intellectual discourse than has either the modernist or the Islamist.

37. Modernist Islamic thought has been extensively studied by Western scholars of Islam. For a broad orientation to the varied and evolving facets of modernist thought, see, *inter alia*: Albert Hourani, *Arabic Thought in the Liberal Age, 1798–1939* (Oxford: Oxford University Press, 1983); Aziz Ahmad, *Islamic Modernism in India and Pakistan, 1857–1964* (London: Oxford University Press, 1967); Christian W. Troll, *Sayyid Ahmad Khan: A Reinterpretation of Muslim Theology* (Delhi: Vikas Publishing House, 1978); Fazlur Rahman, *Islam and Modernity: Transformation of an Intellectual Tradition* (Chicago: University of Chicago Press, 1982); Daniel Brown, *Rethinking Tradition in Modern Islamic Thought* (Cambridge: Cambridge University Press, 1996); Adeeb Khalid, *The Politics of Muslim Cultural Reform: Jadidism in Central Asia* (Berkeley: University of California Press, 1998); Wael B. Hallaq, *A History of Islamic Legal Theories: An Introduction to Sunni Usul al-fiqh* (Cambridge: Cambridge University Press, 1997), 207–54; Robert W. Hefner, *Civil Islam: Muslims and Democratization in Indonesia* (Princeton: Princeton University Press, 2000).

38. Bruce B. Lawrence, *Defenders of God: The Fundamentalist Revolt against the Modern Age*, 2d ed. (Columbia: University of South Carolina Press, 1995). The scholarly literature on Islamist movements is vast. Some notable studies include: Hamid Enayat, *Modern Islamic Political Thought* (Austin: University of Texas Press, 1982); Gilles Kepel, *Muslim Extremism in Egypt: The Prophet and the Pharaoh*, tr. John Rothschild (Berkeley: University of California Press, 1985); idem, *Jihad: Expansion et declin de l'Islamisme* (Paris: Gallimard, 2000); S.V.R. Nasr, *The Vanguard of the Islamic Revolution: The Jama'at-i Islami of Pakistan* (Berkeley: University of California Press, 1994); idem, *Mawdudi and the Making of Islamic Revivalism* (New York: Oxford University Press, 1996); Roy, *Failure of Political Islam*; Riesebrodt, *Pious Passion*; Roxanne L. Euben, *Enemy in the Mirror: Islamic Fundamentalism and the Limits of Modern Rationalism* (Princeton: Princeton University Press, 1999).

39. Cf. Euben, *Enemy in the Mirror.*

40. Cf., for instance, Mamoun Fandy, *Saudi Arabia and the Politics of Dissent* (New York: St. Martin's Press, 1999); idem, "CyberResistance: Saudi Opposition

between Globalization and Localization," *Comparative Studies in Society and History* 41 (1999): 124–47.

41. Shahrough Akhavi, "The Dialectic in Contemporary Egyptian Social Thought: The Scripturalist and Modernist Discourses of Sayyid Qutb and Hasan Hanafi," *International Journal of Middle East Studies* 29 (1997): 377–401, especially 383ff.

42. Euben, *Enemy in the Mirror*, 84f.

43. On Hanafi, see Akhavi, "The Dialectic," 387ff.; Issa J. Boullata, *Trends and Issues in Contemporary Arab Thought* (Albany: State University of New York Press, 1990), 40–45; on al-Jabiri, see ibid., 45–55. For a brief introduction to al-Jabiri's thought in English, see his *Arab-Islamic Philosophy: A Contemporary Critique*, translated from the French by Aziz Abbassi (Austin: University of Texas Press, 1999).

44. Shahrur has written several books but the best introduction to his thought and method is his *al-Kitab wa'l-Qur'an* (Cairo: Sina li'l-nashr, 1992). For a discussion of his thought, see Hallaq, *Islamic Legal Theories*, 245–54; Dale F. Eickelman, "Islamic Religious Commentary and Lesson Circles: Is There a Copernican Revolution?" in *Commentaries—Kommentare*, ed. Glenn W. Most (Gottingen: Vandenhoeck & Ruprecht, 1999): 121–46; idem, "Islam and the Languages of Modernity," *Daedalus* 129/1 (2000): 119–35.

45. Rahman, *Islam and Modernity*, 145ff.; quotation is from 146.

46. Kepel, *Muslim Extremism in Egypt*, 79. On Mustafa's group and ideology, see ibid., 70–102. In 1977, members of this group kidnapped and murdered a religious scholar of al-Azhar who had formerly served as the minister of pious endowments, an act which expressed the group's hostility as much for the official religious establishment as for the government with which it was allied. But this act of radical confrontation with the Egyptian government also brought about the demise of the "Society of Muslims" and the execution of its leader.

47. Sayyid Qutb, *Social Justice in Islam*, translated by William E. Shepard as *Sayyid Qutb and Islamic Activism: A Translation and Critical Analysis of* Social Justice in Islam (Leiden: Brill, 1996), 22. On Qutb and his work, see Shepard's introduction, ix–lix; Kepel, *Muslim Extremism*, especially 36–69; Euben, *Enemy in the Mirror*.

48. Qutb, *Social Justice*, 12f.; also cf. 15 n. 70.

49. Sayyid Abu'l-A'la Mawdudi, *Islamic Law and Constitution*, tr. and ed. Khurshid Ahmad (Lahore: Islamic Publications, 1967), 111. On Mawdudi and his relations with the 'ulama, see chapter 4 of the present study.

50. As Akhavi notes with reference to Hasan Hanafi, for instance: "For Hanafi, the 'heritage' by itself has no inherent value. Its worth is measured by being the source for generating a scientific theory of action that can be put to use for the individual's benefit" ("The Dialectic," 391). Boullata makes a similar point in *Trends and Issues*, 40.

51. Cf. Eickelman, "Islamic Religious Commentary," 121–46.

52. Shahrur, *al-Kitab*, 44 (emphasis added). Also partially cited in Eickelman, "Islamic Religious Commentary," 126. Shahrur is not suggesting that earlier commentaries should be altogether jettisoned. They are a record of the "historical interaction with the Book and are, as such, part of the Arabic Islamic heritage" (Shahrur, *al-Kitab*, 44). But to acknowledge that they are earlier records of the

struggles to understand the mind of God is quite different from saying that they ought to enter in one's own deliberations as one embarks on deciphering the mind of God, or that one's own effort must be part of the cumulative tradition they represent. (For the term "cumulative tradition," I am indebted to Wilfred Cantwell Smith, *The Meaning and End of Religion* [San Francisco: Harper & Row, 1978], 154–69.)

53. Cf. Eickelman, "Islamic Religious Commentary," 146: "The form of religious commentary and discussion circles may suggest continuing strong links with the past, but their practice now conveys significantly different ideas of person, authority, and responsibility."

54. On 'Abduh and his influence, see Hourani, *Arabic Thought*; Malcolm Kerr, *Islamic Reform: The Political and Legal Theories of Muhammad Abduh and Rashid Rida* (Berkeley: University of California Press, 1966); on Shaltut, see Kate Zebiri, *Mahmud Shaltut and Islamic Modernism* (Oxford: Clarendon Press, 1993). On 'ulama in relation to the Islamists, see Malika Zeghal, *Gardiens de l'Islam: Les ulama d'al-Azhar dans l'Egypte contemporaine* (Paris: Presses de la fondation nationale des sciences politiques, 1995); idem, "Religion and Politics in Egypt: The Ulema of al-Azhar, Radical Islam, and the State (1952–94)," *International Journal of Middle East Studies* 31/3 (1999): 401–27. For further discussion, see chapter 6 of the present study.

55. Cf. Asad, "The Limits of Religious Criticism in the Middle East: Notes on Islamic Public Argument," in *Genealogies of Religion*, 200–236, especially 236.

56. On Deoband, see Barbara D. Metcalf, *Islamic Revival in British India: Deoband 1860–1900* (Princeton: Princeton University Press, 1982). Also see Ziya-ul-Hasan Faruqi, *The Deoband School and the Demand for Pakistan* (Bombay: Asia Publishing House, 1963); Rashid Ahmad Jallundhari, *Bartanawi hind main musulmanon ka nizam-i ta'lim: Aik naqidana ja'iza*, vol. 1, *Dar al-'ulum Deoband* (Islamabad: National Book Foundation, 1989). On the Barelawis, see Usha Sanyal, *Devotional Islam and Politics in British India: Ahmad Riza Khan Barelwi and His Movement, 1870–1920* (Delhi: Oxford University Press, 1996); idem, "Generational Changes in the Leadership of the Ahl-e Sunnat Movement in North India during the Twentieth Century," *Modern Asian Studies* 32 (1998): 635–56; Metcalf, *Islamic Revival*, 296–314. There still is no standard work on the Ahl-i Hadith, but for a brief overview, see ibid., 268–96; on the leading figures of this movement, see Abu Yahya Imam Khan Nawshahrawi, *Tarajim-i 'ulama-yi Ahl-i Hadith-i Hind* (Lahore: Riyad Brothers, n.d.).

57. On the Ahmadis, see Yohanan Friedmann, *Prophecy Continuous: Aspects of Ahmadi Religious Thought and its Medieval Background* (Berkeley: University of California Press, 1989).

58. Metcalf, *Islamic Revival*, 351f.

59. One important exception to this is Metcalf's partial translation of and commentary on a highly popular reformist work for Muslim women, which was written by the eminent Deobandi scholar Ashraf 'Ali Thanawi early in the twentieth century. See Barbara D. Metcalf, *Perfecting Women: Maulana Ashraf 'Ali Thanawi's* Bihishti Zewar (Berkeley: University of California Press, 1990). On Thanawi, see chapter 1 of the present study.

60. Notable work concerned in various ways with Sunni 'ulama in modern Muslim societies includes: Dale F. Eickelman, *Knowledge and Power in Morocco:*

The Education of a Twentieth-Century Notable (Princeton: Princeton University Press, 1985); Zeghal, *Gardiens de l'Islam*; Frank E. Vogel, *Islamic Law and Legal System: Studies of Saudi Arabia* (Leiden: Brill, 2000); Zamakhsyari Dhofier, *The Pesantren Tradition: The Role of the Kyai in the Maintenance of Traditional Islam in Java*, Program for Southeast Asian Studies Monograph Series (Tempe: Arizona State University, 1999). On the Pakistani 'ulama, Leonard Binder's *Religion and Politics in Pakistan* (Berkeley: University of California Press, 1961) examines their participation in constitutional debates during the first decade of the country's history; and Jamal Malik's *Colonialization of Islam: Dissolution of Traditional Institutions in Pakistan* (Delhi: Manohar, 1996) looks at the 'ulama in the context of the Islamization policies of General Zia al-Haqq (1977–88). Neither work deals exclusively with the 'ulama.

CHAPTER 1. ISLAMIC LAW AND THE 'ULAMA IN COLONIAL INDIA

1. The most influential formulations of this position are Joseph Schacht, *Introduction to Islamic Law* (Oxford: Clarendon Press, 1964); N. J. Coulson, *A History of Islamic Law* (Edinburgh: Edinburgh University Press, 1964). For a brief review of the history of Islamic legal studies in the West, on which I draw here, see Judith Tucker, *In the House of the Law: Gender and Islamic Law in Ottoman Syria and Palestine* (Berkeley: University of California Press, 1998), 11ff.; for a more detailed account, see Baber Johnson, *Contingency in a Sacred Law: Legal and Ethical Norms in the Muslim Fiqh* (Leiden: Brill, 1999), 42ff.

2. See, for instance, Johansen, *Contingency*; Wael B. Hallaq, *Law and Legal Theory in Classical and Medieval Islam* (London: Variorum, 1995); idem, *History of Islamic Legal Theories*; idem, *Authority, Continuity, and Change in Islamic Law* (Cambridge: Cambridge University Press, 2001); Messick, *The Calligraphic State*.

3. See, for instance, R. C. Jennings, "Kadi, Court, and Legal Procedure in Seventeenth-Century Ottoman Kayseri," *Studia Islamica* 48 (1978): 136–62; idem, "Limitations on the Judicial Powers of the Kadi in Seventeenth-Century Ottoman Kayseri," *Studia Islamica* 50 (1979): 151–84; Galal El-Nahal, *The Judicial Administration of Egypt in the Seventeenth Century* (Minneapolis: Bibliotheca Islamica, 1979); Wael B. Hallaq, "From Fatwas to Furu': Growth and Change in Islamic Substantive Law," *Islamic Law and Society* 1 (1994): 17–56; Johansen, *Contingency*, 61 and passim.

4. Wael B. Hallaq, "Was the Gate of Ijtihad Closed?" *International Journal of Middle East Studies* 16 (1984): 3–41.

5. Sherman A. Jackson, *Islamic Law and the State: The Constitutional Jurisprudence of Shihab al-Din al-Qarafi* (Leiden: E. J. Brill, 1996).

6. Recent revisionist work on the rhetoric, complexities, and functions of taqlid includes: Jackson, *Islamic Law and the State*; Hallaq, *Authority, Continuity, and Change*, 86–120, 236–41, and passim. Also see Vogel, *Islamic Law*, passim; and chapter 4 of the present work.

7. Tucker, *In the House of the Law*.

8. Ibn 'Abidin, *Sharh al-manzuma al-musammat bi-'uqud rasm al-mufti* (Damascus: Matba'at al-ma'arif, 1301 A.H. [printed with independent pagination in Ibn 'Abidin, *Rasa'il* {n.d., n.p.}]), 1–59; quotation is from 51. On Ibn 'Abidin, see Gerber, *Islamic Law and Culture* passim. For Ibn 'Abidin's views on the importance of taking customary practices into account, see ibid.,104–15; Hallaq, *Authority, Continuity, and Change*, 219–35. On the notion of *qarina* (plural: *qara'in*), see Wael B. Hallaq, "Notes on the Term Qarina in Islamic Legal Discourse," *Journal of the American Oriental Society* 108 (1988): 475–80.

9. Ibn 'Abidin, *Nashr al-'urf fi bina ba'd al-ahkam 'ala'l-'urf*, in *Rasa'il* (Damascus: Matba'at al-ma'arif, 1301 A.H.), 17; cited and discussed in Gerber, *Islamic Law and Culture*, 110ff.; also see Hallaq, *Authority, Continuity, and Change*, 231f.

10. There are exceptions, however. See, for instance, J. S. Grewal, *In the By-Lanes of History: Some Persian Documents from a Punjab Town* (Simla: Indian Institute of Advanced Study, 1975).

11. On judicial administration under the Mughals, see Muhammad Bashir Ahmad, *The Administration of Justice in Medieval India* (Karachi: The Manager of Publications, 1951); Jadunath Sarkar, *Mughal Administration* (Calcutta: M. C. Sarkar & Sons, 1952), 91–118; P. Saran, *The Provincial Government of the Mughals, 1526–1658* (1941; Lahore: Faran Academy, 1976), 336–408; Zameeruddin Siddiqi, "The Institution of the Qazi under the Mughals," in *Medieval India: A Miscellany* (Bombay: Asia Publishing House, 1969), 1:240–59; Bhatia, *Administrative History of Medieval India*; Radhika Singha, *A Despotism of Law: Crime and Justice in Early Colonial India* (Delhi: Oxford University Press, 1998), 4ff.

12. Singha, *A Despotism of Law*, 7.

13. As Muzaffar Alam has demonstrated, moreover, the "shari'a" itself could signify quite different things in the writings of medieval Indian political theorists. See Alam "Shari'a and Governance in the Indo-Islamic Context," in *Beyond Turk and Hindu: Rethinking Religious Identities in Islamicate South Asia*, ed. David Gilmartin and Bruce B. Lawrence (Gainesville: University Press of Florida, 2000), 216–45.

14. See J. S. Grewal, "The Qazi in the Pargana," in *Studies in Local and Regional History*, ed. J. S. Grewal (Amritsar: Guru Nanak University, 1974), 1–36; idem, *In the By-Lanes of History*, introduction and passim; Siddiqi, "The Institution of the Qazi," especially 253ff. Also cf. Muzaffar Alam, *The Crisis of Empire in Mughal North India: Awadh and the Punjab, 1707–48* (Delhi: Oxford University Press, 1986), 114: "The *zawabit* (state laws) and secular considerations regulated the policies and the functions of the state in medieval India, but the *sharia* remained the point of reference in daily civil and penal matters and the *ulama* almost exclusively staffed the legal departments."

15. *Al-Fatawa al-Hindiyya fi madhhab al-imam al-a'zam Abi Hanifa al-Nu'man*, 6 vols. (Beirut: Dar al-ma'rifa, 1393 A.H.; repr. of the Bulaq edn.: al-Matba'a al-amiriyya, 1310 A.H.), 1: 2–3 (hereafter *'Alamgiriyya*). There has been no scholarly study yet of this important work. For an introduction to its contents and compilers see, however, Muhammad Ishaq Bhatti, *Barr-i saghir Pak wa Hind main 'ilm-i fiqh* (Lahore: Idara-i thaqafat-i Islamiyya, 1973), 257–364.

16. *'Alamgiriyya*, 1: 2. Also cf. Saqi Musta'ad Khan, *Maasir-i-'Alamgiri*, tr. Jadunath Sarkar (Calcutta: Royal Asiatic Society of Bengal, 1947), 315f.

17. Cf. Gregory C. Kozlowski, *Muslim Endowments and Society in British India* (Cambridge: Cambridge University Press, 1985), 105; Bhatia, *Administrative History*, 159. As Radhika Singha has suggested, the emperor may also have been trying to assert state authority through this compilation, an effort that "would be taken up again in the Anglo-Muhammedan law as it evolved in the [East India] Company's criminal courts." Singha, *A Despotism of Law*, 16.

18. Cf. Weiss, *The Spirit of Islamic Law*, 116ff.

19. See, for instance, "Kitab adab al-qadi," in *'Alamgiriyya*, 3: 306–450, passim. See also 3: 362, on the possibility for a Hanafi judge to have a Shafi'i judge decide certain matters that the former's school would not allow.

20. Ibid., 3: 312.

21. The *'Alamgiriyya*'s compilers had claimed that "for the most part, they have confined themselves to the *zahir al-riwaya*, and have only rarely turned to the *nawadir* and the *dirayat*; [having recourse to the latter] only when they did not find the answer to the problem in the *zahir al-riwaya*, or when they had found the *nawadir* characterized as 'the opinion according to which the fatwas are given' " (*'Alamgiriyya*, 1:3). These claims, however, were less than accurate. Cf. Wael B. Hallaq, "Model Shurut Works and the Dialectic of Doctrine and Practice," *Islamic Law and Society* 2/2 (1995): 122. Also cf. Hallaq, *Authority, Continuity, and Change*, 120, 234.

22. See, for instance, Kozlowski, *Muslim Endowments*; idem, "When the 'Way' Becomes the 'Law': Modern States and the Transformation of *Halakhah* and *Shari'a*," in *Studies in Islamic and Judaic Traditions*, ed. William M. Brinner and Stephen D. Ricks (Atlanta: Scholars Press, 1989), 2:97–112; David S. Powers, "Orientalism, Colonialism, and Legal History: The Attack on Muslim Family Endowments in Algeria and India," *Comparative Studies in Society and History*, 31/3 (1989): 535–71; Scott Alan Kugle, "Framed, Blamed and Renamed: The Recasting of Islamic Jurisprudence in Colonial South Asia," *Modern Asian Studies* 35 (2001): 257–313. For more general studies of colonial law, see J.D.M. Derrett, *Religion, Law and the State in India* (New York: The Free Press, 1968), ch. 15 and passim; Bernard S. Cohn, "Law and the Colonial State in India," in *Colonialism and Its Forms of Knowledge: The British in India* (Princeton: Princeton University Press, 1996), 57–75; Laura Benton, "Colonial Law and Cultural Difference: Jurisdictional Politics and the Formation of the Colonial State," *Comparative Studies in Society and History* 41/3 (1999): 563–88.

23. On the creation of British courts and the administration of civil and criminal justice under the East India Company, see B. B. Misra, *The Central Administration of the East India Company, 1773–1834* (Manchester: Manchester University Press, 1959), 220–377.

24. Quoted in Asaf A. A. Fyzee, *Outlines of Muhammadan Law* (London: Oxford University Press, 1955), 37. Cf. Derrett, *Religion, Law and the State*, 225ff.

25. Garland Cannon, ed., *The Letters of Sir William Jones* (Oxford: Clarendon Press, 1970), 2:720f. For the insistence of early colonial officials that their judicial

decisions be based on explicit scriptural prooftexts, cf. Mani, *Contentious Traditions*, 32ff. and passim.

26. Cannon, *Letters of Sir William Jones*, 2:683f.

27. Ibid., 2:795; cf. Cohn, *Colonialism*, 69, 70.

28. Cannon, *Letters of Sir William Jones*, 2: 720 (italics in the original).

29. Cf. ibid., 2: 721f.; Derrett, *Religion, Law and the State*, 225–73, especially 237–50; Cohn, *Colonialism*, 69ff.

30. Cf. Cohn, *Colonialism*, 70; Cannon, *Letters of Sir William Jones*, 2: 928 n. 2.

31. On al-Marghinani, see *The Encyclopaedia of Islam*, 6: 557–58, s.v. (W. Heffening); Carl Brockelmann, *Geschichte der arabischen Literatur*, 2d ed. (Leiden: E. J. Brill, 1943–49), 1: 376–78.

32. Brockelmann, *Geschichte*, 1: 378f.

33. On al-Haskafi, see Muhammad 'Abd al-Hayy al-Laknawi, *al-Fawa'id al-bahiyya fi tarajim al-Hanafiyya* (Beirut: Shirkat Dar al-Arqam, 1998), 564–66 (no. 383).

34. William H. Morley, *The Administration of Justice in British India: Its Past History and Present State* (London: Williams and Norgate, 1858), 257–323.

35. Singha, *A Despotism of Law*, 27ff.

36. Thomas Babington Macaulay, *Complete Works of Thomas Babington Macaulay* (London: Longmans, Green and Co., 1898), 11: 579; quoted in David Skuy, "Macaulay and the Indian Penal Code of 1862: The Myth of the Inherent Superiority and Modernity of the English Legal System Compared to India's Legal System in the Nineteenth Century," *Modern Asian Studies* 32 (1998): 517. For legal developments in the decades preceding the Penal Code of 1862, see Singha, *A Despotism of Law*.

37. See David Gilmartin, "Customary Law and *Shari'at* in British Punjab," in *Shari'at and Ambiguity in South Asian Islam*, ed. Katherine P. Ewing (Berkeley: University of California Press, 1988), 43–62.

38. Cf. Ayesha Jalal, *Self and Sovereignty: Individual and Community in South Asian Islam since 1850* (London: Routledge, 2000), 139ff., and esp. 142.

39. *Aga Mahomed v. Koolsom Bee Bee* (1897), quoted in Fyzee, *Outlines*, 65.

40. Cf. Kugle, "Framed, Blamed, and Renamed," 280–300, especially 299f. for a similar argument, though without reference to the 'ulama.

41. Cf. the decisive role of British colonial conceptions of an invariant, scripturally grounded tradition in shaping the views of tradition of the *bhadralok*, the Bengali middle class as traced in Mani, *Contentious Traditions*. As Mani argues, "The import of [the colonial] discourse on tradition was not that it contained *bhadralok* perception of *sati* which . . . [in fact] varied between uncritical acceptance and elaborate defense or critique. It was, rather, in the way that a classical notion of tradition, one decidedly conceptual and divorced from the material density of the *bhadralok*'s immediate environment, was to seize their imagination, constitute their field of vision, and generate their maps of the future" (78).

42. Cf. Michael R. Anderson, "Classifications and Coercions: Themes in South Asian Legal Studies in the 1980s," *South Asia Research* 10/2 (1990): 166f.: "In British India a growing feature of the institutionalisation of power was the more systematic management of the knowledges required for governance. . . . A thriv-

ing industry of legal scholarship collected and systematised materials on personal laws so that the 'native law officers' whose opinions had formed the basis of many judicial decisions were no longer employed after 1864." Also cf. D. A. Washbrook, "Law, State and Agrarian Society in Colonial India," *Modern Asian Studies* 15/3 (1981): 673. A judge in British India might still, on rare occasions, ask a plaintiff to have a matter clarified, or do so himself, from a mufti. Cf. Muhammad Khalid Masud, "Apostasy and Judicial Separation in British India," in *Islamic Legal Interpretation*, ed. Masud, Messick, and Powers, 193–203, especially 193, 195, 197; also cf. Muhammad Nadhir Husayn, *Fatawa-i Nadhiriyya* (1913; Lahore: Ahl-i Hadith Academy, 1971), 2: 449; for contemporary India, see Kozlowski, "Loyalty, Locality, and Authority in Several Opinions (fatawa) Delivered by the Mufti of the Jami'ah Nizamiyyah Mâdrasah, Hyderabad, India," *Modern Asian Studies* 29 (1995): 921.

43. Cf. Masud, "Apostasy and Judicial Separation," 197f., 202; Metcalf, *Islamic Revival*, 140–47.

44. David S. Powers, "Kadijustiz or Qadi-Justice? A Paternity Dispute from Fourteenth-Century Morocco," *Islamic Law and Society* 1/3 (1994): 332–66; idem, "Fatwas as Sources for Legal and Social History: A Dispute over Endowment Revenues from Fourteenth-Century Fez," *al-Qantara* 11/2 (1990): 295–341.

45. Tucker, *In the House of the Law*, 20–22.

46. On faskh, see ibid., 81–87.

47. "Al-Shami" ("the Syrian") is a common way in which Indian 'ulama referred to Ibn 'Abidin. Unless otherwise specified, the work they had in mind when so referring to Ibn 'Abidin was his *Hashiyat Radd al-Muhtar*, a gloss on al-Haskafi's *Durr al-mukhtar*. The gloss was, and has continued to be, as influential in South Asia, as al-Haskafi's work itself, if not more..

48. Mufti 'Aziz al-Rahman 'Uthmani, *Fatawa Dar al-'Ulum Deoband*, compiled by Mufti Muhammad Zafir al-din, vol. 8 (Deoband: Dar al-'Ulum, 1972), 160f. No date is given for this issuance of this fatwa.

49. Ashraf 'Ali Thanawi, *Imdad al-fatawa*, ed. Mufti Muhammad Shafi (Deoband: ldarat ta' lifat-i awliya,' [1394 A.H.]). 2: 509f. Also cf. 2: 512: "Question: What is the 'idda of a woman who does not have her regular menstrual cycles because she is nursing her child. . . ? Answer: Her 'idda is three menstrual cycles after divorce; she has to await these cycles however long it takes for her to have them (provided, of course, that she is not too old to have her menstrual cycles)." Abridged in translation.

50. Thanawi, *Imdad al-fatawa*, 2: 377, 381, 383, 385f., 387ff. However, while following the Maliki position on the dissolution of marriage after the husband has been gone for four years, not all muftis insisted on the availability of a Muslim judge to so dissolve the marriage. See, for instance, Muhammad 'Abd al-Hayy Lakhnawi, *Fatawa-i 'Abd al-Hayy*, tr. Khurshid 'Alam (Karachi: Muhammad Sa'id and Sons, 1964), 283. Lakhnawi was a leading 'alim of the Farangi Mahall school of Lucknow.

51. Cf. Thanawi, *Imdad al-fatawa*, 2: 388, 392. On Bhopal and other "princely states," which were not directly subject to colonial rule but were part of (and sometimes important players in) the British colonial system in India, see

Ian Copland, *The Princes of India and the Endgame of Empire, 1917–1947* (Cambridge: Cambridge University Press, 1997).

52. Thanawi, *Imdad al-fatawa*, 2: 487f., 492.

53. Thanawi, *al-Hila al-najiza li'l-halilat al-'ajiza*, Karachi: Qur'an mahall, n.d. [first published in 1931]; also published (with rearranged contents) as *Ahkam-i talaq wa nizam-i shar'i 'adalat, ya'ni al-Hila al-najiza jadid*, ed. Khurshid Hasan Qasimi (Lahore: al-Faysal, 1996 [all references are to the latter edition]), 27; cf. idem, *Imdad al-fatawa*, 2: 381, 488. Demands for the appointment of qadis had often been made by various Muslim groups during the latter half of the nineteenth century: cf. Jalal, *Self and Sovereignty*, 148ff. Note that the 'ulama were willing to countenance a judge who was not versed in the Shari'a but not one who was not a Muslim.

54. Mani, *Contentious Traditions*, 79.

55. Unlike the Hanafis, the Ahl-i Hadith did allow a woman to renounce her marriage *even if* she had been given in marriage by her father or grandfather: see Nadhir Husayn, *Fatawa-i Nadhiriyya*, 2: 396–98.

56. *Fatawa Qadi-khan*, printed on the margins of *al-Fatawa al-Hindiyya fi madhhab al-imam al-a'zam Abi Hanifa al-Nu'man* (Beirut: Dar al-ma'rifa, 1393 A.H.; reprint of the Bulaq edn.: al-Matba'a al-amiriyya, 1310 A.H.), 1:546; *'Alamgiriyya*, I: 339; Ashraf 'Ali Thanawi, *al-Hila al-najiza*, 184ff. Masud, "Apostasy and Judicial Separation," 200. Majid Khadduri, *The Islamic Conception of Justice* (Baltimore: Johns Hopkins University Press, 1984), 152, notes, in discussing legal strategems (*al-hiyal al-shar'iyya*) that "[a] woman seeking divorce but unable to obtain it . . . would be told to apostatize on the grounds that the wedlock between husband and wife would be cancelled if she changed her religion (presumably with the intent of returning to Islam after the divorce.)" But he does not say *who* among the medieval jurists held this view.

57. Muhammad Khalid Masud, *Iqbal's Reconstruction of Ijtihad* (Lahore: Iqbal Academy Pakistan, 1995), 158–60; idem, "Apostasy and Judicial Separation," 193–203. My discussion of Thanawi's initiative and its context is much indebted to Masud's pioneering work.

58. Thanawi, *al-Hila al-najiza*, 190–93; cf. Masud, "Apostasy and Judicial Separation," 193–203.

59. For the text of these Maliki fatwas, see Thanawi, *al-Hila al-najiza*, 197–263.

60. Thanawi, *al-Hila al-najiza*, passim. In justification of these changes Thanawi invokes Ibn 'Abidin's view that important modifications in the law were permissible in the event of extreme necessity (*darura*): Thanawi, *al-Hila al-najiza*, 29f., citing Ibn 'Abidin's treatise, *Sharh al-manzuma al-musammat bi-'uqud rasm al-mufti*.

61. For the text of this Act, see Fyzee, *Outlines*, 145–48; K. N. Ahmed, *The Muslim Law of Divorce* (New Delhi: Kitab Bhavan, 1978), app. 4, 1059–64.

62. Cf. Mushirul Hasan, *Legacy of a Divided Nation: India's Muslims since Independence* (Boulder: Westview Press, 1997), 313f.

63. Cf. Masud, "Apostasy and Judicial Separation," 203. Though Masud does not note this, it is worth observing that Thanawi's aforementioned initiative was indebted not just to the resources provided to him by the Islamic legal tradition,

but probably also to legal discussions in British India. As Gauri Viswanathan has shown in her discussion of British colonial responses to the legal and social problems created by conversion, the Caste Disabilities Removal Act of 1850 saw Hindu converts to Christianity as members of the community they had supposedly left. The rationale for this measure was to ensure to the converts the civil rights (e.g., those of inheritance) that would have been available to them if they had *not* converted. In reality, however, "reaffiliating converts to the religion they had repudiated . . . alienated native converts from both the old and adopted religions." (Gauri Viswanathan, *Outside the Fold: Conversion, Modernity, and Belief* [Princeton: Princeton University Press, 1998], 77–82 and 75–117 passim; quotation is from 81.)

Though Thanawi's fatwas show no direct acquaintance with the Caste Disabilities Removal Act of 1850, there are interesting parallels between his position and the view enshrined in that Act. Membership of the religious community remains assured in both cases, even though that community's religion has been expressly repudiated. In neither case does conversion have any impact on the continuation of the marriage. The 1850 Act served, as Viswanathan shows, to strengthen patriarchal control over young women, and the same was no less true of Thanawi's proposal, or of the Dissolution of Muslim Marriages Act of 1939, which was based on it. It is impossible to ascertain whether or not Thanawi himself was acquainted with the 1850 Act; but it is surely conceivable that the salient idea pertaining to that Act—that one's original community continued to be the basis of all one's claims and rights, even after one had tried to repudiate the religious foundations on which the community was based—was not foreign to him. The similarities between the guiding principles of the Act of 1850 and Thanawi's proposal are too strong to be coincidental. They are also too strong to be attributed only to certain strands of premodern Islamic legal thinking. The 'ulama's world was occupied not only by premodern legal discourses, but also by modern British ones; and it should be no surprise that, to varying degrees, they were responsive to them both.

64. Thanawi, *al-Hila al-najiza*, 63, 73–78.

65. As Barbara Metcalf has noted, early Deobandis had tried, though with only limited success, to establish their own courts in "an attempt to circumvent the British courts with their hybrid Anglo-Muhammedan law." Metcalf, *Islamic Revival*, 145f.; quotation is from 145.

66. Thanawi, *al-Hila al-najiza*, 26f.

67. See Nathan J. Brown, "Shari'a and State in the Modern Middle East," *International Journal of Middle East Studies* 29/3 (1997): 359–76; also see Messick, *The Calligraphic State*.

68. Masud, "Apostasy and Judicial Separation," 202f.

69. On this organization see Yohanan Friedmann, "Jam'iyatul 'Ulama'-i Hind," in *The Oxford Encyclopedia of the Modern Islamic World*, ed. John L. Esposito (New York: Oxford University Press, 1995), 2:362–64; Faruqi, *The Deoband School*, chs. 3–4; M. Naeem Qureshi, *Pan-Islam in British Indian Politics: A Study of the Khilafat Movement, 1918–1924* (Leiden: Brill, 1999), passim. Also see the studies by Peter Hardy and Yohanan Friedmann cited in n. 71, this chapter.

70. Thanawi, *al-Hila al-najiza*, 33f.

71. Peter Hardy, *Partners in Freedom—and True Muslims: The Political Thought of Some Muslim Scholars in British India 1912–1947* (Lund: Scandinavian Institute of Asian Studies, 1971); Yohanan Friedmann, "The Attitude of the Jam'iyyat-i 'Ulama'-i Hind to the Indian National Movement and the Establishment of Pakistan," *Asian and African Studies* 7 (1971): 157–80; idem, "The Jam'iyyat al-'Ulama-i Hind in the Wake of Partition," *Asian and African Studies* 11 (1976): 181–211.

72. See Husayn Ahmad Madani, *Muttahida qawmiyyat awr Islam* ([1938] Delhi: Qawmi ekta trust, [1972]), 8ff., 30ff. for extensive evidence adduced from classical Arabic usage and the Qur'an to distinguish between the connotations of the terms "milla" and "qawm." This work is Madani's most detailed explication of his position on united nationalism. For some of Madani's other major discussions of united nationalism and Indian politics, see *Khutbat-i Madani*, ed. Ahmad Salim (Lahore: Nigarishat, 1990).

73. Madani, *Muttahida qawmiyyat*, 19 and 16ff.

74. Ibid., 25f.

75. Ibid., 42ff.

76. Ibid., 26–28, 42ff. For an analysis of the documents comprising the "Constitution of Medina," see R. B. Serjeant, "The Sunnah Jami'ah Pacts with the Yathrib Jews, and the Tahrim of Yathrib: Analysis and Translation of the Documents Comprised in the So-Called 'Constitution of Medina,' " *Bulletin of the School of Oriental and African Studies*, 41 (1978), 1–42. On the term "umma" as used in these documents, see ibid., 4f., 16, 18.

77. Cf. Friedmann, "The Attitude of the Jam'iyya," 174.

78. Madani, *Muttahida qawmiyyat*, 29ff. and passim.

79. Ibid., 39f.

80. Ibid., 49–51.

81. "Statement on Islam and Nationalism in Reply to a Statement of Maulana Husain Ahmad, published in the *Ehsan* on 9 March 1938," in Mohammad Iqbal, *Speeches, Writings and Statements of Iqbal*, ed. Latif Ahmed Sherwani (Lahore: Iqbal Academy, 1977), 251–63; quotation is from 260.

82. Ibid., 255, 256, 260, and passim.

83. Ibid., 252, 259.

84. Ibid., 263.

85. For Mawdudi's critique of Madani, see Sayyid Abu'l-A'la Mawdudi, "Muttahida qawmiyyat awr Islam," in *Tahrik-i azadi-i Hind awr Musulman* (Lahore: Islamic Publications, 1964), 1: 304–25. Mawdudi's response to Madani was first published in 1939. Madani and the Deobandi 'ulama have, for their part, remained hostile to Mawdudi, his thought and his ideas. See, for instance, Husayn Ahmad Madani, *Mawdudi dastur awr aqa'id ki haqiqat* (Deoband: Maktaba-i diniyya, n.d.) for Madani's attack on Mawdudi's religious beliefs and teachings. For Mawdudi's difficult relations with the 'ulama in general, see Nasr, *Mawdudi and the Making of Islamic Revivalism*, 107–25. Also see chapter 4 of the present work.

86. Mawdudi, *Tahrik-i azadi*, 1: 324f.

87. Ibid., 319–25.

88. See Hardy, *Partners in Freedom*, 38ff.

89. Khaled Abou El Fadl, "Islamic Law and Muslim Minorities: The Juristic Discourse on Muslim Minorities from the Second/Eighth to the Eleventh/Seventeenth Centuries," *Islamic Law and Society* 1/2 (1994): 141–87.

90. Ibid., 153–57.

91. For the specific Hanafi stipulations in this regard, see ibid., 161f.

92. Ibid., 159ff.; quotation is from 159.

93. Cf. Friedmann, "The Attitude of the Jam'iyya," 179f.; Hardy, *Partners in Freedom*, 35, 38.

94. Madani, *Muttahida qawmiyyat*, 39f.

CHAPTER 2. CONSTRUCTIONS OF AUTHORITY

1. Messick, *Calligraphic State*, 30–36.

2. Johansen, "Legal Literature and the Problem of Change: The Case of the Land Rent," in *Contingency*, 446–64; quotation is from 448.

3. See Dimitri Gutas, "Aspects of Literary Form and Genre in Arabic Logical Works," in *Glosses and Commentaries on Aristotelian Logical Texts: The Syriac, Arabic and Medieval Latin Traditions*, ed. Charles Burnett (London: The Warburg Institute, 1993), 28–76. (I owe this reference to Maroun Aouad.)

4. John B. Henderson, *Scripture, Canon, and Commentary: A Comparison of Confucian and Western Exegesis* (Princeton: Princeton University Press, 1991); Daniel K. Gardner, "Confucian Commentary and Chinese Intellectual History," *Journal of Asian Studies* 57/2 (1998): 397–422.

5. Edward Gibbon, *The History of the Decline and Fall of the Roman Empire*, ed. David Womersley (London: Allen Lane, 1994), 1: 84. Also cf. the remarks of James Mill on traditional Islamic education in India: *The History of British India*, 5th ed. (1858; New York: Chelsea House Publishers, 1968) 1: 52ff.

6. Fazlur Rahman, *Islam and Modernity*, 63, 45; also cf. 37f., 70. Also cf. Khalid, *Politics of Muslim Cultural Reform*, 41, where the writing of commentaries in nineteenth-century Central Asia is imputed to a "conservatism of local cultural practices and tastes," which, in turn, is attributed to Central Asia's isolation from the rest of the world.

7. On Mawdudi's commentary, see Charles J. Adams, "Abu'l-A'la Mawdudi's *Tafhim al-Qur'an*," in *Approaches to the History of the Interpretation of the Qur'an*, ed. Andrew Rippin (Oxford: Clarendon Press, 1988), 307–23. On certain aspects of Mawdudi's political thought, see chapter 4 of the present work.

8. Johannes J. G. Jansen, *The Dual Nature of Islamic Fundamentalism* (Ithaca: Cornell University Press, 1997), 51.

9. Shahrur, *al-Kitab wa'l-Qur'an*; Eickelman, "Islamic Religious Commentary."

10. These lectures are translated as "Islamic Government" in Hamid Algar, ed. and trans., *Islam and Revolution: Writings and Declarations of Imam Khomeini* (Berkeley: Mizan Press, 1981). For a discussion of these lectures that is attentive to the exegetical strategies Khumayni deployed in explaining, or explaining away, hadith that had some bearing on his argument, see Michael M. J. Fischer and Mehdi Abedi, *Debating Muslims: Cultural Dialogues in Postmodernity and Tradition* (Madison: University of Wisconsin Press, 1990), 128–46.

11. Metcalf, *Islamic Revival*, 129, 349, and passim.

12. For evocative reminiscences of advanced hadith studies at the Deoband madrasa in the early twentieth century, see Manazir Ahsan Gilani, *Ihata-i dar al-'ulum main bitai huwe din*, ed. I'jaz Ahmad A'zami, (Deoband: Maktaba-i Tayyiba, n.d.), passim. (I am grateful to Professor Z. I. Ansari for drawing my attention to this work.)

13. For a valuable bibliographic survey of the writings on hadith by the 'ulama of India, see 'Abd al-Hayy al-Hasani, *al-Thaqafa al-Islamiyya fi'l-Hind*, 2d ed. (Damascus: Majma' al-lugha al-'Arabiyya bi-Dimashq, 1983), 131–61; see 390–95, for some of the works on hadith published since the early twentieth century. For a comprehensive bibliography of works of (or on) hadith that were translated into Urdu during the nineteenth and twentieth centuries, see Muhammad Nazir Ranjha, *Ahadith key Urdu tarajim* (Islamabad: Muqtadara qawmi zaban, 1995).

14. But other forms of hadith study continue to thrive. Hadith is a major focus of advanced graduate training in Saudi Arabia's Islamic universities, for instance, and critical editions of classical works of hadith and thematic studies pertaining to them account for a large proportion of the theses and doctoral dissertations written at these (and other) universities. For such works, see Muhy al-din 'Atiyya, Salah al-din Hafani, and Muhammad Khayr Ramadan Yusuf, *Dalil mu'allafat al-hadith al-sharif al-matbu'a al-qadima wa'l-haditha* (Beirut: Dar Ibn Hazm, 1995), 1: 42, 65, 72, 112, 114, 117–18, 127, 148, 158, 169, 174–75, 182, 190, 221–22, 224, 230–31, 252–54, 263, 265, 279, 282, 284, 311, **314**, **325**, 334, 337, **348**, 351, **376–78**, 385, 391–93, **400**, 403, 404, **408**, 409, 418, 421, 434–35, **441**, 475, **476–77**, **481**, **483**, 484, 487–88, **492**, 493, 496, 498; 2: (continuous pagination) **502–4**, 506, 508, **511–13**, **519**, 535, 541, 544, 547, 550–57, **561**, 572–75, 590, 606, **612–14**, 616–18, **623**, 626–33, 635–36, 638, **663**, 701–3, 707, 720, **724**, 726. (This bibliographic guide by 'Atiyya, Hafani, and Yusuf is the most exhaustive yet available of published works on hadith as well as of the theses and dissertations on hadith in the Arabic language. The numbers in bold font indicate critical editions of classical texts of hadith or of the writings of prominent premodern scholars of hadith.)

15. For the extensive writings of Ahl-i hadith scholars in the nineteenth and twentieth centuries, on hadith as well as in other areas, see the bibliographic survey of Muhammad Mustaqim Salafi, *Jama'at-i Ahl-i Hadith ki tasnifi khidmat* (Banaras: Idarat al-buhuth al-Islamiyya wa'l-da'wa wa'l-ifta' bi'l-jami'a al-Salafiyya, 1992).

16. On al-Shawkani, see Messick, *Calligraphic State*, 42–45, and index, s.v.; Wali Allah's most famous work is the *Hujjat Allah al-Baligha*: see Shah Wali Allah, *The Conclusive Argument from God*, tr. Marcia K. Hermansen (Leiden: E. J. Brill, 1996).

17. Metcalf, *Islamic Revival*, 278, speaks of the "elite style of the Ahl-i Hadith [as] indicated by the fact that many continued to write in the learned languages of Persian and Arabic rather than in the vernacular of Urdu." She does not note, however, that the scholars of Deoband also often wrote in the Arabic language.

18. On Siddiq Hasan Khan and his writings, see Nawshahrawi, *Tarajim-i 'ulama*, 277–312; Saeedullah, *The Life and Works of Muhammad Siddiq Hasan Khan, Nawwab of Bhopal* (Lahore: Sh. Muhammad Ashraf, 1973); Salafi, *Ja-*

ma'at-i Ahl-i Hadith, 37–40. For his education at the Azhar in Egypt, see Muhammad 'Abd al-Mun'im Khafaji, *al-Azhar fi alf 'am* (Cairo: Maktabat al-kulliyyat al-Azhariyya, 1987), 2: 401.

19. See Ibn Hajar, *Fath al-bari* (Cairo, n.p., [1319–20 A.H.], 1: 2–4, for a history of the printing of this work. The first edition, supported by funds from the nawwab of Bhopal, was published by al-Matba'a al-amiriyya, Bulaq (1: 2). Al-Shawkani's *Nayl al-awtar* is a commentary on *al-Muntaqa min ahadith al-ahkam* of the Hanbali scholar 'Abd al-Salam b. Taymiyya (d. 1254).

20. Nawshahrawi, *Tarajim*, 288–90.

21. Ibid., 292f.

22. On al-Tirmidhi, see Fuat Sezgin, *Geschichte des arabischen Schrifttums* (Leiden: E. J. Brill, 1967), 1:154–59.

23. For a list of his writings, see 'Abd al-Sami' al-Mubarakfuri, "Tarjamat al-mu'allif," appended (with independent pagination) to Muhammad 'Abd al-Rahman al-Mubarakfuri, *Muqaddimat Tuhfat al-ahwadhi* (Beirut: Dar al-kitab al-'Arabi, n. d.), 8–11. The *Tuhfat al-ahwadhi* was first published at Delhi (Idarat al-Hakim [4 vols.]) between 1927 and 1935; the second edition was published at Medina (al-Maktaba al-Salafiyya [10 vols.]) between 1963 qnd 1967, and was reprinted in 1986; another edition was published at Damascus (Dar al-fikr [10 vols.]) in 1979, and yet another at Beirut (Dar al-kitab al-'Arabi) in 1984. Cf. Mustaqim Salafi, *Tasnifi khidmat*, 53; 'Atiyya, Hafani, and Yusuf, *Dalil mu'allafat al-hadith*, 1: 291f. Neither of the latter works provides the complete publication history, however.

24. Zafar Ahmad 'Uthmani, *I'la al-sunan*, 21 vols. (Karachi: Idarat al-Qur'an wa'l-'ulum al-Islamiyya, 1415 A.H.). The publication of this work began in 1923. But it was not until 1982 that the work was published in its entirety. Another edition was published in 1985. For the publication history, see 1: I, 3–4. All references in the following notes are to the 1414 A.H. edition.

25. For the text of the treatise, see ibid., 12: 688–713.

26. For a biography of the author, see 'Abd al-Shakur, *Tadhkirat al-Zafar* (Faisalabad: Matbu'at-i 'ilmi, 1977). Also see Muhammad Taqi 'Uthmani, *Nuqush-i raftagan* (Deoband: Maktaba-i Jawid, 1994), 16–21. Note that " 'Uthmani" is the last part of the name of several 'ulama; when used alone in this and other chapters, it should be understood as referring only to Mawlana Zafar Ahmad 'Uthmani.

27. 'Uthmani, *I'la al-sunan*, 12: 688.

28. Ibid., 12: 688f.

29. For these traditions, see ibid., 12: 688–99.

30. Ibid., 12: 699.

31. Ibn Taymiyya, *Iqtida al-sirat al-mustaqim mukhalifat ashab al-jahim*, ed. Muhammad Hamid al-Fiqi (Lahore: al-Maktaba al-salafiyya, 1978). The work has been translated into English by Muhammad Umar Memon as *Ibn Taimiya's Struggle against Popular Religion* (The Hague: Mouton, 1976).

32. For a concern similar to Ibn Taymiyya's but in the context of a modern Muslim society, see Mohamad Atho Mudzhar, "The Council of Indonesian 'Ulama' on Muslims' Attendance at Christmas Celebrations," in *Islamic Legal Interpretation*, ed. Masud, Messick, and Powers, 230–41.

33. 'Uthmani *I'la al-sunan*, 12: 699f. For a study of this hadith, see M. J. Kister, " 'Do not Assimilate Yourselves . . .' *La tashabbahu*," *Jerusalem Studies in Arabic and Islam*, 12 (1989): 321–71. On other traditions warning against intermingling with unbelievers, as cited by 'Uthmani, see *I'la al-sunan*, 12: 699ff.

34. Ibid., 12:, 700, following (without acknowledgment) Ibn Taymiyya, *Iqtida*, 1.

35. Ibid., 12: 700; Ibn Taymiyya, *Iqtida*, 2.

36. Ibn Taymiyya, *Iqtida*, 1 (Ibn Taymiyya's reason for writing this treatise), 180ff. and passim; Memon, *Ibn Taimiya's Struggle*, 89f., 193ff.

37. On the importance of the Urdu language for the Deobandi 'ulama, see Metcalf, *Islamic Revival*, 198–234 and passim.

38. On language and politics in pre-partition India, see Paul R. Brass, *Language, Religion, and Politics in North India* (Cambridge: Cambridge University Press, 1974).

39. For these traditions, see 'Uthmani, *I'la al-sunan*, 12: 702–11; Ibn Taymiyya, *Iqtida*, 203ff.; Memon, *Ibn Taimiya's Struggle*, 205f.

40. 'Uthmani, *I'la al-sunan*, 12: 702; cf. Ibn Taymiyya, *Iqtida*, 203; Memon, *Ibn Taimiya's Struggle*, 205.

41. 'Uthmani, *I'la al-sunan*, 12: 703f.

42. Ibid., 12: 707f.: "There has arisen in India a great imposter from among the infidels (*dajjal min al-mushrikin*), whom the members of the Congress have taken as their leader, guide, and the head of their troops, and their political activities are in accordance with only his advice and his orders." On Gandhi, see Judith M. Brown, *Gandhi and Civil Disobedience: The Mahatma in Indian Politics, 1928–34* (Cambridge: Cambridge University Press, 1977).

43. 'Uthmani, *I'la al-sunan*, 12: 708ff.

44. Ibid., 12: 708.

45. Ibid., 12: 709.

46. Ibid., 12: 709f.

47. Ibid., 12: 712; the quotation in the single quotes is from the Qur'an: 9.32.

48. "Sufaha" is a multivalent Qur'anic term that was interpreted by early exegetes to mean, *inter alia*, women, children, or anyone not fit to be left in charge of his own affairs. See Ebrahim Moosa, "The Sufaha' in Qur'an Literature: A Problem in Semiosis," *Der Islam* 75 (1998): 1–27.

49. 'Uthmani, *I'la al-sunan*, 12: 712. 'Uthmani goes on: "Herein also is the clearest of demonstrations that the patience of the Prophet in face of the persecution of his [pagan] people, and his forgiveness of them, was not because he was seeking kingship or trying to demolish the power of the enemy [through non-violent struggle], but only to complete the proof [of their infidelity], to preach his message and demonstrate his own position to them; he sought not the goods of the world, but only, and to the extent possible, the reform [of the people]" (ibid.).

50. Ibid., 12: 713. On the importance of dreams as a way of certifying the truth of an idea or statement in the worldview of the modern South Asian 'ulama, see Metcalf, *Islamic Revival*, index, s.v. "dreams."

51. G. W. Leitner, *History of Indigenous Education in the Panjab since Annexation and in 1882* (1883; Patiala: Languages Department Punjab, 1971), vi, vii.

52. Education Commission, *Report by the Panjab Provincial Committee with evidence taken before the committee and memorials addressed to the education commission* (Calcutta: Superintendent of Government Printing, 1884), 4.

53. S. K. Das, *Sahibs and Munshis: An Account of the College of Fort William* (Calcutta: Orion Publications, 1978), 37–40.

54. Farzana Shaikh, *Community and Consensus in Islam: Muslim Representation in Colonial India, 1860–1947* (Cambridge: Cambridge University Press, 1989), 200ff. and passim.

55. A similar justification for the demand for a separate Muslim state—which alone could guarantee that internal divisions were transcended or nullified—was to be central in the 1940s to the rhetoric of the Muslim League, the party that led the movement for Pakistan. See David Gilmartin, "A Magnificent Gift: Muslim Nationalism and the Election Process in Colonial Punjab," *Comparative Studies in Society and History* 40/1 (1998): 415–36. As Gilmartin notes in analyzing the rhetoric of the Muslim League during an election campaign critical to the success of the movement for a separate state, "the existence of internal division gave the rhetorical fear of Hindu domination (and the history of colonialism) its real edge. It was, in fact, the reality of internal divisions among Muslims that gave the demand for Pakistan, a symbol of united moral community, its most powerful resonance" (422).

56. Talal Asad, *The Idea of an Anthropology of Islam*, 15.

57. For 'Uthmani's insinuations about the misguidedness of those who believed in a united nationalism, cf. *I'la al-sunan*, 12: 690.

58. Strange as it may seem, neither Madani nor 'Uthmani go beyond rather general allusions to the shari'a to explicitly invoke the specific Islamic juristic doctrines on which the former's position in support of united nationalism and the latter's in opposition to it are based. But this is by no means unusual in the 'ulama's discourses. In their juristic responsa (fatwas), for instance, the 'ulama often give a particular ruling on the basis of their knowledge of the juristic tradition of their legal school as a whole, without necessarily adducing the precise juristic texts they are following in that particular ruling. Cf. Metcalf, *Islamic Revival*, 143; Messick, *Calligraphic State*, 135ff.

59. On the Hanafi and Maliki positions concerning the status of Muslim minorities in non-Muslim lands, see Abou El Fadl, "Islamic Law and Muslim Minorities," 161–63 and passim.

60. Johansen, *Contingency*, 68; cf. 208f., 233ff.; Abou El Fadl, "Islamic Law and Muslim Minorities," 164ff.

61. It should be noted, however, that Madani and (irrespective of how ordinary Muslims who had stayed in India rather than migrating to Pakistan might have felt) the nationalist 'ulama *did not* expect the new neighboring Muslim state to offer them any protection in India. In fact, in emphasizing their loyalty to the newly independent Indian state, the nationalist 'ulama had urged their followers to sever all ties with Pakistan. Cf. Friedmann, "The Jam'iyyat al-'Ulama'-i Hind in the Wake of Partition," 185, 211.

62. Cf. 'Abd al-Hayy al-Hasani, *al-Thaqafa al-Islamiyya*, 2d. ed. (Damascus: Majma' al-lugha al-'Arabiyya bi-Dimashq, 1983), 142ff.

63. Shabbir Ahmad 'Uthmani, *Fath al-mulhim bi-sharh Sahih al-imam Muslim* (Karachi: Maktaba-i Dar al-'Ulum, 1989), 1: 1.

64. Muhammad Taqi 'Uthmani, *Takmilat fath al-mulhim*, 3 vols. (Karachi: Maktaba-i Dar al-'Ulum, 1407 A.H. [1986–87]).

65. There are long treatments of hudud and of the judiciary in volume 2 of Taqi 'Uthmani's *Takmila*.

66. Rashid Ahmad Gangohi, *Lami' al-darari 'ala jami' al-Bukhari*, 2 vols. (Saharanpur: al-Maktaba al-Yahyawiyya, Mazahir al-'ulum, Saharanpur, 1959); another edition, in 10 vols: Mecca: al-Maktaba al-Imdadiyya, 1395–98). On Gangohi, see Metcalf, *Islamic Revival*, 78, 82, 88, 107f., 141ff., and passim.

67. Another commentary by Gangohi, based on his lectures and compiled by Muhammad Yahya is the *Kawkab al-durri 'ala Jami' al-Tirmidhi*, compiled by Muhammad Yahya Kandahlawi; with glosses by Muhammad Zakariyya Kandahlawi (1st ed.: 2 vols., Saharanpur: al-Maktaba al-Yahyawiyya, 1933–35; 2d ed.: (with an introduction by Abu'l-Hasan 'Ali Nadwi) 3 vols., Karachi: Idarat al-Qur'an wa'l-'ulum al-Islamiyya, 1987). The writing down of the master's lectures is, of course, a long-standing tradition in and outside of the madrasa. For this aspect of medieval Islamic higher learning, see Makdisi, *The Rise of Colleges*, 111–28; also see Messick, *Calligraphic State*, ch. 1, especially 30–36. Note, however, that the form and function of the lecture notes differed from one discipline to another, as indeed one would expect. Yet, *pace* Makdisi, "the atmosphere of a classroom on hadith" need not have "differed dramatically from that of a classroom on law" (ibid., 115). For the former was concerned not solely with the dictation of hadith, as Makdisi suggests, but also with discussions on the contents of hadith and the juristic and theological problems raised by these. In such circumstances, indeed, the distinction between a discussion on hadith and one on law might tend to blur. And many students might well be expected to write not just the Prophetical traditions dictated to them by the master, but also, especially in the milieu of the madrasa, some of the master's discussion of hadith.

68. Cf. Brown, *Rethinking Tradition in Modern Islamic Thought*, 5: "In choosing my sources [i.e., modern writings on the sunna of the Prophet] . . . I have gauged the importance of a work in proportion to the level of controversy it has elicited." See my review of this work in *Islamic Law and Society* 5/2 (1998): 266–69.

69. Cf. Metcalf, *Islamic Revival*, 210.

70. Timothy Mitchell, *Colonising Egypt* (Berkeley: University of California Press, 1991), 150–54; Francis Robinson, "Technology and Religious Change: Islam and the Impact of Print," *Modern Asian Studies* 27 (1993), 229–51; quotation is from 242.

71. On *ijaza*, see Messick, *Calligraphic State*, 92–94.

72. For Thanawi's biographical notice, see 'Uthmani, *I'la al-sunan*, 1: 9–23; for 'Uthmani's notice, ibid., 24–27.

73. Ibid., 1: 3–7.

74. Cf. *Bayyinat* (Karachi: Jami'at al-'ulum al-Islamiyya, January-February, 1978 [special issue dedicated to the memory of Muhammad Yusuf Banuri]), 26f. On Anwarshah Kashmiri, see Anzar Shah Mas'udi, *Naqsh-i dawam* ([1398 A.H.]; Deoband: Shah Book Depot, n.d.); Gilani, *Ihata-i dar al-'ulum*, 78–141; 'Abd al-

Fattah Abu Ghudda, *Tarajim sitta min fuqaha al-ʿalam al-islami fiʾl-qarn al-rabiʿ* *ʿashar wa atharuhum al-fiqhiyya* (Beirut: Maktab al-matbuʿat al-Islamiyya, 1997), 13–81.

75. Cf. Shabbir Ahmad ʿUthmani, "Kalima li-muhaqqiq al-ʿasr al-ustadh al-muhaddith al-shaykh Shabbir Ahmad al-ʿUthmani," appended to Banuri's "Muqaddima," in *Fayd al-bari ʿala Sahih al-Bukhari*, by Anwar Shah Kashmiri (Lahore: al-Matbaʿa al-Islamiyya al-Saʿudiyya, 1978), 1: 80.

76. For different aspects of his career, see the special issue of *Bayyinat* (January-February 1978). *Bayyinat* is the monthly journal of Jamiʿat al-ʿUlum al-Islamiyya, the madrasa Banuri had founded.

77. "Muqaddima," in Kashmiri, *Fayd al-bari*, 1: 12–78.

78. Ibid., 16.

79. John Voll, "Muhammad Hayya al-Sindi and Muhammad ibn ʿAbd al-Wahhab: An Analysis of an Intellectual Group in Eighteenth-Century Madina," *Bulletin of the School of Oriental and African Studies*, 38/1 (1975): 32–39; idem, "Hadith Scholars and Tariqahs: An Ulama Group in the Eighteenth Century Haramayn and their Impact in the Islamic World," *Journal of Asian and African Studies*, 15/3–4 (1980): 264–73.

80. Stefan Reichmuth, "Murtada az-Zabidi (d. 1791) in Biographical and Autobiographical Accounts: Glimpses of Islamic Scholarship in the Eighteenth Century," *Die Welt des Islams* 39/1 (1999): 64–102; quotation is from 78.

81. On the impact of print on Muslim societies, see Robinson, "Technology and Religious Change"; idem, "Islam and the Impact of Print in South Asia," in Nigel Crook, ed., *The Transmission of Learning in South Asia*, ed. Nigel Crook, 62–97; Metcalf, *Islamic Revival*, especially 198–234; Eickelman and Piscatori, *Muslim Politics*, 37ff.; Adeeb Khalid, "Printing, Publishing, and Reform in Tsarist Central Asia," *International Journal of Middle East Studies*, 26 (1994): 187–200; idem, *Politics of Muslim Cultural Reform*, ch. 4 and passim; Messick, *The Calligraphic State*.

82. Cf. Metcalf, *Islamic Revival*, passim.

83. Robinson, "Technology and Religious Change," 245; idem, "Islam and the Impact of Print," 75.

84. Eickelman and Piscatori, *Muslim Politics*, 111; also cf. Robinson, "Technology and Religious Change."

85. Cf. Robinson, "Technology and Religious Change," 242; idem, "Islam and the Impact of Print," 72.

86. For Abu Ghudda's biography, and lists of his teachers, students, and writings, see Muhammad ibn ʿAbdallah al-Rashid, *Imdad al-fattah bi-asanid wa marwiyyat al-shaykh ʿAbd al-Fattah* (Riyadh: Maktabat al-imam al-Shafiʿi, 1999).

87. Ibid., 147, 148, 160, 162.

88. See Abu Ghudda's obituary by Muhammad Taqi ʿUthmani in ibid., 63–69, especially 66.

89. For a complete list of Abu Ghuddha's more than sixty works, see ibid., 180–215.

90. Ibid., 180f., 197, 203. On ʿAbd al-Hayy and his numerous writings, see ʿInayat Allah, *ʿUlama-i Firangi mahall* (Lucknow: Nizami Press, 1988), 199–206.

91. Al-Rashid, *Imdad al-fattah*, 181. The work is entitled *Al-tasrih bima tawatar fi nuzul al-masih*.

92. Al-Rashid, *Imdad al-fattah*, 189f.; 'Uthmani, *I'la al-sunan*, I: 3–7.

93. Al-Rashid, *Imdad al-fattah*, 247–67.

94. Ibid., 216–41.

95. Ibid., 266.

96. Eickelman and Anderson, "Redefining Muslim Publics," in Eickelman and Anderson, *New Media in the Muslim World*, 1–18, especially 12ff.

97. Mufti Muhammad Shafi', *Ma'arif al-Qur'an*, 8 vols. (Karachi: Idarat al-ma'arif, 1969–73).

98. Muhammad Manzur Nu'mani, *Ma'arif al-hadith* (Lucknow: Kutub khana-i al-furqan, [1954]), 1:11. Most of the traditions that are the subject of this commentary are drawn from the *Mishkat al-masabih*, a fourteenth-century collection of hadith, though it is noteworthy that Nu'mani has reorganized them according to his own preferences, thus making it a *new* anthology. For more on Manzur Nu'mani, see his autobiography: *Tahdith-i ni'mat*, ed. 'Atiq al-Rahman Sanbhali Nu'mani (Lucknow: al-Furqan Book Depot, 1997).

99. On this collection, see Barbara D. Metcalf, "Living Hadith in the Tablighi Jama'at," *Journal of Asian Studies* 52 (1993), 584–608; Muhammad Khalid Masud, "Ideology and Legitimacy," in *Travellers in Faith: Studies of the Tablighi Jama'at as a Transnational Islamic Movement for Faith Renewal*, ed. Muhammad Khalid Masud (Leiden: Brill, 2000), 81ff. On the Tablighi Jama'at, besides the volume edited by Masud, see Mumtaz Ahmad, "Islamic Fundamentalism in South Asia: The Jamaat-i-Islami and the Tablighi Jamaat of South Asia," *Fundamentalisms Observed*, ed. in Martin E. Marty and R. Scott Appleby (Chicago: University of Chicago Press, 1991), 510–24; and Shail Mayaram, *Resisting Regimes: Myth, Memory and the Shaping of a Muslim Identity* (Delhi: Oxford University Press, 1997). For further references, see the epilogue to the present work.

100. On Nadwi and his writings, see Muhammad Qasim Zaman, "Arabic, the Arab Middle East, and the Definition of Muslim Identity in Twentieth Century India," *Journal of the Royal Asiatic Society*, ser. 3, 8/1 (1998): 59–81. Also see chapter 6 of the present study.

101. Muhammad Manzur Nu'mani, *Islam kiya hai?* (Lahore: Maktaba-yi madaniyya, n.d.), 7–8.

102. Manzur Nu'mani, *Tahdith-i ni'mat*, 109.

103. Manzur Nu'mani, *Islam kiya hai?* 11.

104. Eickelman and Piscatori, *Muslim Politics*, 38. Also cf. Robinson, "Islam and the Impact of Print," 85f.

105. Brinkley Messick, "Media Muftis: Radio Fatwas in Yemen," in *Islamic Legal Interpretation*, eds. Masud, Messick, and Powers, 310–320.

106. Mawlana Muhammad Yusuf Ludhianawi, *Apke masa'il awr unka hall*, 7 vols. (Karachi: Maktaba-i bayyinat, 1989–97).

107. Ibid., 2: 8.

108. Even less tenable are generalizations about the undifferentiated character of the audience for the works published. Consider the following comment from the usually perceptive Marshall Hodgson: "[I]n the West, the writer or artist can always distinguish two audiences, two settings for his work: that provided by

popular culture, where the drive to the lowest common denominator presses hard, can be continuously leavened by the existence of a more restricted audience, the serious elite. The artist may even speak in one setting in earning his bread and butter, while his best hours are reserved for the less certain but yet potentially important rewards of the other setting. In Cairo or Delhi, it is hard to get a book published if it will have a restricted audience. There tends to be a single, 'popular' audience; the most sophisticated novel is likely to be published serially in a mass-circulation newspaper; musical experimenting is likely to take place in the sound-track of popular films—and within the limits imposed by a very unsophisticated box-office." Hodgson, *Venture of Islam*, 3: 424. That Hodgson's examples here do not include a reference to the 'ulama's writings is odd, and this omission does not seem to be because he regarded them as an exception to this generalization.

109. Elizabeth Eisenstein, *The Printing Press as an Agent of Change: Communications and Cultural Transformation in Early-Modern Europe* (Cambridge: Cambridge University Press, 1979), 1: 310 and 303–450; also cited in Catherine Bell, " 'A Precious Raft to Save the World': The Interaction of Scriptural Traditions and Printing in a Chinese Morality Book," *Late Imperial China*, 17/1 (1996): 160. Bell too expresses reservations about the applicability of "the European experience" to other societies and cultures: see 158–200.

110. Metcalf, "Living Hadith," 603.

111. Ahmad, "Islamic Fundamentalism in South Asia," 516; cf. Metcalf, "Living Hadith," 596, 599. This seems to be one of the reasons why Mawlana Wahid al-din Khan of India, who otherwise applauds the Tablighi Jama'at's activities and himself insists on the preaching of Islam rather than political involvements as the proper work of the 'ulama, is critical of this movement. See Wahid al-din Khan, *Diary* (Delhi: al-Risala Books, 1995), 165. On Wahid al-din Khan, see the epilogue.

CHAPTER 3. THE RHETORIC OF REFORM
AND THE RELIGIOUS SPHERE

1. For the history of governmental reforms of the Azhar, see J. Heyworth-Dunne, *An Introduction to the History of Education in Modern Egypt* (London: Luzac, 1938), especially 1–84; A.F.L. al-Sayyid Marsot, "The Beginnings of Modernization among the Rectors of al-Azhar, 1798–1879," in *Beginnings of Modernization in the Middle East*, ed. Polk and Chambers, 267–80; A. Chris Eccel, *Egypt, Islam and Social Change: Al-Azhar in Conflict and Accommodation* (Berlin: Klaus Schwarz Verlag, 1984); Indira Falk Gesink, "Beyond Modernisms: Opposition and Negotiation in the Azhar Reform Debate in Egypt, 1870–1911" (Ph.D. dissertation, Washington University, St. Louis, Missouri, 2000); Zeghal, *Gardiens de l'Islam*; idem, "Religion and Politics in Egypt; Tamir Moustafa, "Conflict and Cooperation between the State and Religious Institutions in Contemporary Egypt," *International Journal of Middle East Studies* 32/1 (2000): 4–9. For issues pertaining to the reform of religious education in other societies, see Shahrough Akhavi, *Religion and Politics in Contemporary Iran: Clergy-State Relations in the Pahlavi Period* (Albany: State University of New York Press, 1980); Eickelman, *Knowledge and Power in Morocco*; Messick, *Calligraphic State*. A broad-ranging

collection of articles on the madrasa in medieval and modern Islam that is also attentive to issues of reform is Grandin and Gaborieau, *Madrasa: La transmission du savoir.*

2. For the provisions of the 1961 reform, see Khafaji, *al-Azhar fi alf 'am*, 2: 188–227.

3. Francois Burgat and William Dowell, *The Islamic Movement in North Africa*, 2d ed. (Austin: Center for Middle Eastern Studies, University of Texas, 1997), 54.

4. Eickelman, *Knowledge and Power*, 161–80, especially 170.

5. Ibid., 164.

6. Ibid., 165.

7. Ibid., 166.

8. Ibid., 179f.

9. Asad, *Genealogies of Religion*, 207 (emphasis in the original). Also cf. Jose Casanova, *Public Religions in the Modern World* (Chicago: University of Chicago Press, 1994), 63ff. On the evolution of the modern notion of "religion," see Peter Harrison, *"Religion" and the Religions in the English Enlightenment* (Cambridge: Cambridge University Press, 1990).

10. Thomas R. Metcalf, *Ideologies of the Raj* (Cambridge: Cambridge University Press, 1994), 4ff., 66–112, and passim.

11. See Kozlowski, *Muslim Endowments*, on the British distinction between "public" and "private" endowments.

12. For a discussion of the debate on this policy, see Gauri Viswanathan, *Masks of Conquest: Literary Study and British Rule in India* (New York: Columbia University Press, 1989).

13. Education Report from the Director of Public Instruction, Panjab, to the Financial Commissioner, Punjab, 25 June, 1858, section 18; extracts in Leitner, *History*, appendix 6, p. 20.

14. See Leitner, *History*, 71–72 and passim; also see Farhan A. Nizami, "Madrasahs, Scholars and Saints: Muslim Response to the British Presence in Delhi and the Upper Doab 1803–1857" (Ph.D. dissertation, University of Oxford, 1983), 42–58.

15. Extracts from Parliamentary Report (1874, C. 1072-II, part III) in Leitner, *History*, vii.

16. Cf. Metcalf, *Ideologies*, 36–37.

17. I do not intend to suggest, of course, that British categories of analysis were the only source of such distinctions in colonial India, but only that they seem to have substantially contributed to them. Factors other than the impact of colonial rule may have played some part, and even the influence of colonialism had many different manifestations.

18. Cf. Berkey, *Transmission*, passim; Chamberlain, *Social Practice*, 69–90.

19. Ibn Khaldun, *The Muqaddimah: An Introduction to History*, tr. F. Rosenthal (New York: Pantheon Books, 1958), 3: 299–300; Hajji Khalifa, *Kashf al-zunun 'an asami al-kutub wa'l-funun*, ed. G. Fluegel (Leipzig: Oriental Translation Fund, 1835), 1: 114–15.

20. James Mill, Revenue Department dispatch, 18 February 1824, Bengal, E/ 4/710, para. 83 (India Office Library and Records, British Museum) quoted in

Lynn Zastoupil, *John Stuart Mill and India* (Stanford: Stanford University Press, 1994), 32–33. Also cf. the despatch of the Court of Directors to the Bengal Government, 24 October 1832, in *The Correspondence of Lord William Cavendish Bentinck*, ed. C. H. Philips (Oxford: Oxford University Press, 1977), 933–34, on some of the content of useful learning.

21. *Report by the Panjab Provincial Committee*, 369.

22. Ibid., 370.

23. On this controversy, see David Kopf, *British Orientalism and the Bengal Renaissance: The Dynamics of Indian Modernization 1773–1835* (Berkeley: University of California Press, 1969), 7–8, 241–52, and passim; Viswanathan, *Masks of Conquest*, 29ff., 101ff., and passim. On "useful knowledge," see also C. A. Bayly, *Empire and Information: Intelligence Gathering and Social Communication in India, 1780–1870* (Cambridge: Cambridge University Press, 1996), 212–46.

24. Bayly, *Empire and Information*, 215.

25. Cf. Messick, *Calligraphic State*, 101 (Yemen); Starrett, *Putting Islam to Work*, 51f. (Egypt).

26. Cf. A. J. Wensinck et al., *Concordances et indices de la tradition musulmane* (Leiden: E. J. Brill, 1936–88), 4:330; Franz Rosenthal, *Knowledge Triumphant: The Concept of Knowledge in Medieval Islam* (Leiden: E. J. Brill, 1970), 243; Hajji Khalifa, *Kashf al-zunun*, 1: 48–52.

27. Abu Nu'aym al-Isfahani (d. 1038–39), *Hilyat al-awliya' wa tabaqat al-asfiya'* (Beirut: Dar al-kutub al-'ilmiyya, 1997), 10: 437 (para 15767). The mystic quoted here is one Abu 'Abdallah Muhammad ibn Yusuf ibn Ma'dan al-Banna. Also cf. the statement of the Kufan ascetic Muhammad b. Sabih b. al-Sammak (d. 799): "There are many things which if they do not benefit do not harm either; but as for knowledge, if it doesn't benefit/prove useful, it becomes harmful." Al-Khatib al-Baghdadi, *Ta'rikh Baghdad* (Beirut: Dar al-kutub al-'ilmiyya, 1997), 2: 446.

28. Chamberlain, *Social Practice*, 111–13.

29. Cf. Javed Majeed, *Ungoverned Imaginings: James Mill's The History of British India and Orientalism* (Oxford: Clarendon Press, 1992), 196ff.

30. Quoted in A. M. Monteath, *Note on the State of Education in India*, 1862, in *Selections from Educational Records of the Government of India*, vol. 1, *Educational Reports, 1859–71* (Delhi: National Archives of India, 1960), 45–46.

31. For the history of this Madrasa, see 'Abd al-Sattar, *Ta'rikh-i madrasa-i 'aliya*, 2 vols. (Dhaka: Research and Publications, Madrasa-i 'Aliya, 1959). On proposed or actual reforms in the Madrasa, see 1: 47ff. and passim.

32. *Selections from Educational Records*, 1: 21.

33. Ibid., 1: 21.

34. 'Abd al-Sattar, *Madrasa-i 'aliya*, 1: 119–20, 129, 134.

35. *Selections from Educational Records*, 1: 23.

36. Cf. the "revised" curriculum introduced in 1871 in 'Abd al-Sattar, *Madrasa-i 'aliya*, 1: 171–72. Most of the texts that comprise the curriculum are the same as those in the *Dars-i Nizami*.

37. For such apprehensions, see for instance 'Abd al-Sattar, *Madrasa-i 'aliya*, 1: 55, 140–41.

38. Cf. Sayyid Amir 'Ali's evidence before the Education Commission of 1882, quoted in *Report of the Muslim Education Advisory Committee*, 1934, in M.S.A. Ibrahimy, *Reports on Islamic Education and Madrasah Education in Bengal (1861–1977)*, 5 vols. (Dhaka: Islamic Foundation Bangladesh, 1987 [hereafter: Ibrahimy, *Reports*]), 3: 141.

39. Quoted in the *Report of the Madrasah Education Committee*, 1941, in Ibrahimy, *Reports*, 3: 335.

40. See, for instance, William Adam, *Reports on the State of Education in Bengal (1835 and 1838)*, ed. A. Basu (Calcutta: University of Calcutta Press, 1941), 2: 153.

41. On the contradictions in this "preservationist ideal," see Metcalf, *Ideologies*, especially 66–92; also cf. Mani, *Contentious Traditions*.

42. For the recommendations of the various madrasa-reform committees in nineteenth- and twentieth-century Bengal, see Ibrahimy, *Reports*, passim.

43. On Mulla Nizam al-din, see Muhammad Rida Ansari, *Bani-i Dars-i Nizami* (Lucknow: Nami Press, 1973); *The Encyclopaedia of Islam*, 8: 68–69, s.v. "Nizam al-din, Mulla" (F. Robinson); on the Farangi Mahall, Francis Robinson, "Problems in the History of the Farangi Mahall Family of Learned and Holy Men," *Oxford University Papers on India*, vol. 1, pt. 2 (Delhi: Oxford University Press, 1987), 1–27; on the *Dars-i Nizami*, see 'Abd al-Hayy al-Hasani, *al-Thaqafa al-Islamiyya*, 9–17; Akhtar Rahi, *Tadhkira-i musannifin-i dars-i nizami* (Lahore: Maktaba-yi Rahmaniyya, 1978); Nizami, "Madrasahs, Scholars and Saints," 24–32, 279–81; Jamal Malik, *Islamische Gelehrtenkultur in Nordindien: Entwicklungsgeschichte und Tendenzen am Beispiel von Lucknow* (Leiden: E. J. Brill, 1997), 151ff., 522ff.

44. Nizami, "Madrasahs, Scholars and Saints," 30–32.

45. Metcalf, *Islamic Revival*, 87–137; quotation is from 93.

46. Compare Jallundhari, *Dar al-'ulum Deoband*, 117–44.

47. On the Nadwat al-'Ulama', see Muhammad Ishaq Nadwi and Shams Tabriz Khan, *Ta'rikh-i nadwat al-'ulama*, 2 vols. (Lucknow: Nizamat nadwat al-'ulama,' 1983–84) [hereafter Ta'rikh-i nadwa]. This work is the "official" history of the Nadwa. Also see Sayyid Muhammad al-Hasani, *Sirat-i Mawlana Sayyid Muhammad 'Ali Mongiri, bani-yi nadwat al-'ulama* (Lucknow: Maktabat Dar al-'Ulum Nadwat al-'Ulama', 1964 [hereafter al-Hasani, *Mongiri*]); Abu'l-Hasan 'Ali Nadwi, *Karwan-i zindagi*, 6 vols. (Karachi: Majlis-i nashriyyat-i Islam; Lucknow: Maktaba-i Islam,1983–97), passim; Metcalf, *Islamic Revival*, 335–47; Jamal Malik, "The Making of a Council: The Nadwat al-'Ulama'," *Zeitschrift der deutschen morgenländischen Gesellschaft* 144 (1994), 60–90; idem, *Islamische Gelehrtenkultur*, passim.

48. For various criticisms of the traditional madrasas, see *Ta'rikh-i nadwa*, 1: 63–79.

49. Ibid., 1: 139–42.

50. For some aspects of the opposition to the Nadwa, see al-Hasani, *Mongiri*, 143–44, 170ff.; Sanyal, *Devotional Islam*, 217–26; Metcalf, *Islamic Revival*, 342ff.

51. *Ta'rikh-i nadwa*, 1: 57; cf. 1: 125, 249.

52. See Shibli's speech on this occasion in Shibli Nu'mani, *Khutbat-i Shibli*, ed. Sayyid Sulayman Nadwi (A'zamgarh: Dar al-Musannifin, 1941), 128.

53. *Ta'rikh-i nadwa*, 1: 59, citing Abu'l-Hasan 'Ali Nadwi, *Hayat-i 'Abd al-Hayy* (Lucknow: Majlis-i tahqiqat wa nashriyyat-i Islam, 1970), 130.

54. Shibli Nu'mani, *Maqalat-i Shibli*, ed. Sayyid Sulayman Nadwi (A'zamgarh: Dar al-musannifin, n.d.; reprinted Lahore: National Book Foundation, 1989), 8: 91; emphasis added.

55. Quoted in al-Hasani, *Mongiri*, 147–48; *Ta'rikh-i nadwa*, 1: 79.

56. See *Ta'rikh-i nadwa*, 2: 32–81 passim; al-Hasani, *Mongiri*, 204ff., 260–90.

57. Cf. Malik, "Making of a Council," especially 87ff., for an interpretation of the differences among the Nadwa's leaders in terms of their different social origins and cultural orientations.

58. Cf. al-Hasani, *Mongiri*, 71, 82, 119, 167, etc.; *Ta'rikh-i nadwa*, 1: 147, 238; 2: 110, 180, 219, 240, 294, 318f. Indeed, as Sayyid Sulayman Nadwi noted in his speech at the annual session of 1915, disquisitions on the "necessity" (*darurat*) and "usefulness" (*fawa'id*) of the Nadwa's Dar al-'Ulum were a constant feature of all its annual sessions (ibid., 2: 110–11).

59. As Shibli put it in his speech at the annual session of the Nadwat al-'Ulama in 1894: see Shibli Nu'mani, *Khutbat-i Shibli*, 19. On the importance of literature in the Nadwa's curriculum, see *Ta'rikh-i nadwa*, 1: 147; also cf. Zaman, "Arabic, the Arab Middle East," 67ff.

60. Cf. *Ta'rikh-i nadwa*, 1: 148, 218.

61. For the goals of the Nadwa as enunciated on various occasions during its early years, see ibid., 1: 55ff., 139ff., and passim.

62. Cf. Adam, *Reports*, 2: 147, 151; *Report by the Panjab Provincial Committee*, 411.

63. Viswanathan, *Masks of Conquest*.

64. On British notions of representation, Shaikh, *Community and Consensus*.

65. Cf. the following (unattributed) verses celebrating the authority of the *Hidaya*, a compendium of Hanafi substantive law which has long been studied in madrasas: "The *Hidaya*, like the Qur'an, has abrogated whatever books had been written on law; so persist in reading it and carefully attend to its recitation, for thereby will your speech become free of waywardness and falsehood." Quoted in Manazir Ahsan Gilani, *Pak wa Hind main musalmanon ka nizam-i ta'lim wa tarbiyyat* (Lahore: Maktaba-i Rahmaniyya, n.d.), 1: 313.

66. Cf. Shibli Nu'mani, *Khutbat-i Shibli*, 57, 88.

67. Cf. ibid., 18; Shibli Nu'mani, *Maqalat-i Shibli*, 3: 127.

68. Abu'l-Hasan 'Ali Nadwi, *Karwan*, 1: 199–226, esp. 200, 225f.

69. Shibli Nu'mani, *Safarnama-i rum wa misr wa sham* (Lucknow: Anwar al-matabi', n.d.), 58. Also quoted (from a different edition and translated slightly differently) by Christian W. Troll, "Muhammad Shibli Nu'mani (1857–1914) and the Reform of Muslim Religious Education," in *Madrasa*, ed. Grandin and Gaborieau, 151.

70. On madrasas in post-independence India, see Kuldip Kaur, *Madrasa Education in India: A Study of Its Past and Present* (Chandigarh: Centre for Research in Rural and Industrial Development, 1990); Qamar al-din Khan et al., *Hindustan ki dini darsgahen: kull Hind survey* (Delhi: Hamdard Education Society, 1996).

For observations on the role that small local madrasas play in the life of one of the most economically disprivileged Muslim communities, see Wahid al-din Khan, *Mewat ka safar* (Delhi: Maktaba-i risala, 1988), passim. On Wahid al-din Khan, see the epilogue in the present volume.

71. 'Abd al-Sattar, *Madrasa-i 'aliya*, 2: 114ff.

72. Ibid., 2: 114.

73. Recommendations for the reform of madrasas in East Pakistan (now Bangladesh) were also made at various times between 1947 and 1971. See Ibrahimy, *Reports*, vols. 4 and 5, passim. I leave these aside here.

74. Besides the September 11, 2001 terrorist attacks in the United States, an attack on the Indian parliament in New Delhi on December 13, 2001 is also part of the context in which government efforts to regulate madrasas have acquired a new urgency. India blamed militant groups active in Indian Kashmir and supported by Pakistan for this attack, and the two countries came closer to an all-out war than they had since their last full-scale war in 1971. Under intense Indian and international pressure, General Musharraf banned several militant organizations and pledged to regulate madrasas as part of a new effort to curtail various forms of radical activism. For General Musharraf's major policy speech laying out these measures, see *Dawn*, January 13, 2002.

75. Though still uncertain in its implications, the latest initiative towards madrasa reform and regulation seems concerned, among other things, with registering all madrasas, restricting the number of non-Pakistanis studying in them, and creating certain government-sponsored "model" madrasas. For news reports about different aspects of this initiative, see *Dawn*, April 14, 2000; ibid., April 18, 2000; *The New York Times*, June 10, 2000: A6; *Dawn*, July 4, 2001; *The News*, November 8, 2001; ibid., December 8, 2001; *Dawn*, December 14, 2001; ibid., January 10, 2002; ibid., January 13, 2002; *The News*, January 16, 2002; *Dawn*, January 17, 2002; ibid., January 22, 2002; *The News*, January 30–31, 2002; *Dawn*, January 31, 2002; ibid., February 5, 2002; ibid., February 13, 2002.

76. For a list of members comprising each committee, see *Report of the Committee Set Up by the Governor of West Pakistan for Recommending Improved Syllabus for the Various Darul Ulooms and Arabic Madrasas in West Pakistan* (Lahore: Superintendent, Government Printing, West Pakistan, 1962), hereafter *Report* (1962), i; *Report qawmi committee bara'i dini madaris-i Pakistan* hereafter *Report* (1979), 3–7. For a pioneering discussion of the two reports and the reactions to them, see Malik, *Colonialization of Islam*, 123–28, 132–39.

77. *Report* (1962), 3.

78. For these phrases, see ibid., 5, 7, 9, 12, 14.

79. Ibid., 11.

80. Cf. Hallaq, *Islamic Legal Theories*, 134ff.

81. *Report* (1962), 22–23.

82. Ibid., 4.

83. Ibid., 19–30 and appendix 4 (pp. 1–51 of the Urdu text).

84. *Report* (1979), 44.

85. Ibid., 50.

86. Ibid., i, 8–9. The terms used are *marbut karna* (literally: to integrate: p. i), *ham-ahang* [*karna*] (to harmonize; scil., "with the general system of education in

the country": 8), and to establish *yaksaniyyat awr yakjahti* (similarity and unifor-mity) "between the curriculum and system of examinations" of the madrasa and general education.

87. *Report* (1962), 7.

88. For Ludhianawi's detailed critique of the *Report* of 1979, see *Bayyinat* 38/2 (January 1981): 2–28; also see *Bayyinat* 47/1 (May 1985): 35–63. The *Report* of 1979 was also rejected by the Wifaq al-madaris, the network of Deobandi madrasas. For the text of the latter's resolutions in this regard, see *Bayyinat* 38/2 (January 1981): 4–5; 47/1 (May 1985): 45. Also see Malik, *Colonialization of Islam*, 136–38.

89. Ludhianawi, "Basa'ir wa 'ibar," in *Bayyinat* 38/2 (January 1981): 12–13; emphasis added.

90. Ibid., 17. The reference to a "mixed" curriculum is meant, of course, to be contemptuous.

91. Ibid., 16. For a very similar argument, see Mufti Jamil Ahmad Thanawi, *Nisab wa nizam-i dini madaris* (Lahore: Nashiran-i Qur'an Limited, n.d.), 59–60.

92. Ludhianawi, "Basa'ir," in *Bayyinat* 38/2 (January 1981): 27. Making gov-ernment servants out of the madrasa-educated does not everywhere carry the stigma it does in the foregoing statement. For instance, many of the scholars call-ing for the reform of the Azhar of Egypt in the late nineteenth and early twentieth century sought the introduction of modern subjects there precisely to enable grad-uates of the Azhar to compete with others in the quest for government jobs. Eccel, *Egypt, Islam and Social Change*, 313–14.

93. Quoted in *Report of the East Bengal Educational System Reconstruction Committee, 1949–52*, in Ibrahimy, *Reports*, 4: 40; emphasis added.

94. Associations such as the "Dini Ta'limi Council" (established in 1959), however, have been active in India not only in promoting the growth of maktabs and madrasas, but also in trying to promote modern education among Muslims; modern education institutions are often established side by side with the ma-drasas. On the other hand, initiatives towards the reform of the madrasa come not just from the government, but equally, and more persistently, from the mod-ernizing Muslim elite. See Kaur, *Madrasa Education in India*, 199ff. and passim.

95. The 'ulama's reluctance to associate with those in power may also have something to do with their resistance to governmental reform of the madrasa, though the implications of such distrust should not be exaggerated. For if some 'ulama have always insisted on maintaining their distance from the ruling authori-ties, there has never been a dearth of those who were willing to be actively involved in the administration.

96. For this argument, see for instance Thanawi, *Dini madaris*, 66–71. Cf. Gilani, *Nizam-i ta'lim*, 1: 252–316 and passim.

97. Quoted in Muhammad Rashid Rida, *Ta'rikh al-ustadh al-imam al-shaykh Muhammad 'Abduh* (Cairo: Matba'at al-Manar, 1931), 1: 504; emphasis added.

98. Cf. Thanawi, *Dini madaris*, 66–68.

99. Ibid., passim. On his madrasa, the Jami'a Ashrafiyya, see Fayyaz Hussain, "An Ethnographic Study of Jamia Ashrafia, a Religious School at Lahore, with

Special Reference on Socio-Practical Relevance of Its Objectives" (M.S. thesis, Quaid-i-Azam University, Islamabad, 1994).

100. See for instance, the proceedings of the seminar on the education system of madrasas, organized in November 1986 by the Institute of Policy Studies, Islamabad: Muslim Sajjad and Salim Mansur, *Dini madaris ka nizam-i ta'lim* (Islamabad: Institute of Policy Studies, 1987; reprint, 1993).

101. See, for instance, Mawlana Muhammad Yusuf Banuri, "Dars-i Nizami: Chand tawajjuh-talab pahlu," *Jaridat al-ashraf* (Journal of the Jami'a Ashrafiyya Sukkur) (March-April 1994): 26–52; the quotation is from 32.

102. Banuri, "Dars-i Nizami," 31.

103. Muhammad Taqi 'Uthmani, "Pakistan main dini ta'lim ka aik sarsari ja'iza" (A brief survey of religious education in Pakistan), in *Hamara ta'limi nizam* (Our system of education) (Karachi: Maktaba-i Dar al-'Ulum, 1415 A.H.), 74f.

104. Ibid., 75ff.

105. Ibid., 77.

106. Ibid., 59.

107. "Mawlawi fadil" was one of the several degrees in "Oriental" studies at the Lahore Oriental College (founded in 1865). This college, which later became part of the Punjab University, was meant to promote Oriental—Hindu, Muslim, and Sikh—learning while also preparing students for government jobs. On this college, and for the curriculum of the Mawlawi fadil and other degrees, see Leitner, *History*, part 2, 102–19.

108. Since the completion of his studies, 'Uthmani has taught hadith and fiqh at the Dar al-'Ulum. For more on him, see chapter 4.

109. See Government of Pakistan, Ministry of Education, *Pakistan ke dini madaris ke 'ulama-i kiram ki directory*, 1986 (Islamabad: Islamic Higher Education Research Cell, [1987]), 476.

110. For instance, see the curriculum issued by the network of Barelawi madrasas: *Nisab-i ta'lim-i tanzim al-madaris (Ahl-i Sunnat) Pakistan* (Lahore: Markazi daftar tanzim al-madaris Pakistan, 1412 A.H.); and cf. Malik, *Colonialization of Islam*, 164–76.

111. On the primary and secondary school that is part of the Dar al-'Ulum of Karachi, see 'Aziz al-Rahman, *Ta'aruf Dar al-'Ulum Karachi* (Karachi: Shu'ba-yi nashr wa isha'at, Dar al-'Ulum, 1417 A.H.), 26, 35.

112. For a wide-ranging critique of such juxtaposition of "religious" and secular subjects in Muslim societies, and not just in the madrasa, cf. Fazlur Rahman, *Islam and Modernity*, 138f., 141 and passim.

113. 'Abd al-Sattar, *Madrasa-i 'aliya*, 2: 146–47. Compare Asad, *Genealogies of Religion*, 207.

114. For example, Ira M. Lapidus, "The Separation of State and Religion in the Development of Early Islamic Society," *International Journal of Middle East Studies* 6 (1975): 363–85. Also see idem, "The Evolution of Muslim Urban Society," *Comparative Studies in Society and History* 15 (1973), 21–50, especially 28ff.; idem, *A History of Islamic Societies* (Cambridge: Cambridge University Press, 1988), especially 120ff. Closer analysis of religious and political trends in early Islam, and especially of early 'Abbasid history—on which Lapidus's findings are primarily based—reveals, however, that there is little evidence to suggest the

"separation of state and religion" that he posits: see Zaman, *Religion and Politics under the Early 'Abbasids.*

115. Casanova, *Public Religions*, 19ff. and passim.

116. Ludhianawi, "Basa'ir," in *Bayyinat* 38/2 (January 1981): 22–23. Cf. Nathan Brown, "Shari'a and State," 369.

117. Cf. Berkey, *Transmission*, 182ff.; idem, "Tradition, Innovation and the Social Construction of Knowledge in the Medieval Islamic Near East," *Past and Present* 146 (1995): 38–65.

118. Berkey, *Transmission*; Chamberlain, *Social Practice.*

119. Berkey, *Transmission*, 128–218.

120. Cf. Berkey, "Tradition, Innovation and the Social Construction of Knowledge."

121. Eickelman, *Knowledge and Power in Morocco*, 5–6. Also see Eickelman, "Islamic Religious Commentary," 121–46. As Eickelman observes with reference to Morocco in the 1920s and 1930s, "the spatial setting of many religious learning circles . . . [still] indicated a lack of sharp separation from the rest of society" (130). The same might be said of many other Muslim societies until the onset of mass higher education.

122. On this Qur'anic injunction and its significance in Islamic thought and practice, see now Michael Cook, *Commanding Right and Forbidding Wrong in Islamic Thought* (Cambridge: Cambridge University Press, 2000).

123. At the level of primary education, the ratio of dropouts among boys was calculated in 1994–95 to be 43 percent in the urban areas of Pakistan and 78 percent in the rural areas. For girls, the ratio was 59 percent and 88 percent, respectively. See *The News* (June 27, 1995): 2. Such dropouts appear to comprise an increasing proportion of those now studying in madrasas, though many still come without any exposure to government schools. Figures naturally vary, and for a variety of possible reasons, from one madrasa to another. An official of the Khayr al-Madaris, a prominent Deobandi madrasa of Multan, in the Punjab province, (with about 2500 students) reported to the present writer in August 1995 that there were "very few" students who were illiterate at the time of their admission to the madrasa (written personal communication). Conversely, the Jami'a Anwar al-'Ulum, a Barelawi madrasa also in Multan (with about 800 students) reported in July 1995 that the proportion of those who were illiterate prior to admission in the madrasa was about 55 percent (written personal communication). Precisely how to account for such differences remains to be studied.

124. Eickelman, *Knowledge and Power in Morocco*, 167–78.

125. Cf., e.g., Daniel Crecelius, "Non-ideological Responses of the Egyptian 'Ulama' to Modernization," in *Scholars, Saints, and Sufis*, ed. Keddie, 167–209.

126. Zeghal, *Gardiens de l'Islam*, 279 (my translation). Also cf. the remarkable increase in the number of mosques in Egypt, "by 100 percent between 1961 and 1979, leaping from 17,000 to 34,000," and to 50,000 by 1984. Patrick D. Gaffney, *The Prophet's Pulpit: Islamic Preaching in Contemporary Egypt* (Berkeley: University of California Press, 1994), 15.

127. See Zeghal, *Gardiens de l'Islam*. For more on this point, see chapter 6 of the present work.

CHAPTER 4. CONCEPTIONS OF THE ISLAMIC STATE

1. Muhammad Rafi' 'Uthmani, "Jami'a Dar al-'Ulum Karachi ke ta'limi sal, 1417–18, ke aghaz par sadr-i jami'a hadrat mawlana mufti Muhammad Rafi' 'Uthmani sahib ka iftitahi khitab," parts 1 and 2, *al-Balagh* (March 1997): 11–18; (May 1997): 17–38; the quotations are from part 2, 22, 24.

2. Cf. al-Rahman, *Ta'aruf-i Dar al-'Ulum Karachi*, 5.

3. On the Objectives Resolution, see Binder, *Religion and Politics*, 116–54; for the text of the Resolution, 142–43.

4. Cited in Charles Kennedy, "Repugnancy to Islam—Who Decides?," *International and Comparative Law Quarterly* 41 (October 1992): 769–88: quotation is from 781.

5. On the "repugnancy clause," see Binder, *Religion and Politics*, 227ff., 270–71, 273–76, 286ff.; Kennedy, "Repugnancy to Islam."

6. On this provision, which was made part of the Iranian constitution of 1906 by Article 2 of the Supplementary Law adopted by the Iranian Majlis in 1907, see Said Amir Arjomand, *The Turban for the Crown: The Islamic Revolution in Iran* (New York: Oxford University Press, 1988), 57.

7. Binder, *Religion and Politics*, 228ff., 320ff.

8. On this body, see Malik, *Colonialization of Islam*, 33–54.

9. On Islamization under General Zia al-Haqq, see Malik, *Colonialization of Islam*; Anita Weiss, ed., *Islamic Reassertion in Pakistan: The Application of Islamic Laws in a Modern State* (Lahore: Vanguard, 1987); Rudolph Peters, "The Islamization of Criminal Law: A Comparative Analysis," *Die Welt des Islams* 34 (1994): 246–74; Kennedy, "Repugnancy to Islam"; Lucy Carroll, "Nizam-i-Islam: Processes and Conflicts in Pakistan's Programme of Islamisation, with Special Reference to the Position of Women," *Journal of Commonwealth and Comparative Politics* 20 (1982): 57–95; idem, "Orphaned Grandchildren in Islamic Law of Succession: Reform and Islamization in Pakistan," *Islamic Law and Society* 5/3 (1998): 409–47.

10. "Enforcement of Shariah Ordinance, 1988, June 15, 1988, in *All Pakistan Legal Decisions*, Central Statutes 29, quoted in Kennedy, "Repugnancy to Islam," 777. All my quotations from the Ordinance are from the passages cited in ibid., 777. Kennedy's study, on which my discussion here is partly based, provides a useful account of the various legislative initiatives towards the implementation of the shari'a in the late 1980s and the early 1990s.

Note that the term "shari'a" is sometimes spelled in several different ways: e.g., as "shari'ah"/"shariah" (as in "Shariah Ordinance") or, reflecting the common Urdu pronunciation, as "shari'at" (as in "Federal Shari'at Court"). When discussing particular governmental enactments or institutions, I have usually retained these "official," if inconsistent, ways of spelling the term.

11. Kennedy, "Repugnancy to Islam," 779f. The quotation about the historical significance of the Shari'a Act is from Ghulam Hyder Wyne, the then chief minister of the Punjab. Quoted in ibid., 779 n. 44 from *The Pakistan Times*, May 29, 1991. On Pakistani politics during the 1990s, see S.V.R. Nasr, *Islamic Leviathan: Islam and the Making of State Power* (New York: Oxford University

Press, 2001). (I am grateful to Professor Nasr for allowing me to see his book prior to its publication.)

12. The square brackets, except when they refer to the number of the particular clause, are mine; the parentheses are in the original.

13. See "Text of the Fifteenth Constitutional Amendment Bill" in *Dawn*, August 29, 1998.

14. For the text of the revised bill, see *Dawn*, October 9, 1998. For its passage in the lower house, ibid., October 10, 1999.

15. Aftab Hussain, *Status of Women in Islam* (Lahore: Law Publishing Company, 1987), 77f. On taqlid as "blind adherence," see 80 and passim.

16. For detailed accounts of the context of, the discussions on, and the opposition to the proposed fifteenth amendment, see *The Herald* (September 1998) 25–44; *Newsline* (September 1998) 14–30. Foremost among the Islamists who rejected the proposed amendment was Qazi Husayn Ahmad, the amir of the Jama'at-i Islami. As he put it, "When the rulers find their ship is sinking, they are reminded of Islam" (quoted in *The Herald* [September 1998]: 27). But the Deobandi 'ulama's organization, the Jam'iyyat al-'Ulama'-i Islam, was also critical: cf. *Newsline* (September 1998): 16. Another group of religious scholars and Sufis, the Ittihad al-masha'ikh-i Pakistan, also opposed the proposal. The president of this forum, Dr. Khalid Raza Zakori, was quoted as saying that "the ulema and mashaikh of Pakistan [are] ready to extend their fullest support to Islamization in its totality but they would not allow any adventurer to use the name of Islam for increasing his power or for cheating the faithful" (*Dawn*, September 14, 1998). Not all religious groups opposed the proposal, however. For expressions of support for it, cf. *The Herald* (September 1998): 27f.

17. The reference to the "recognized" Islamic sects is meant to exclude the Ahmadis, who are not considered Muslims by the other Muslim groups in South Asia.

18. The provisions of the declaration have been paraphrased here from the full text given in Muhammad Taqi 'Uthmani, *Nifaz-i shari'at awr us-ke masa'il* (Karachi: Maktaba-i Dar al-'Ulum, 1413 A.H.), 19–23, and in Mawdudi, *Islamic Law and Constitution*, 355–58.

19. For example, in the "Views" submitted by the Board on the Teachings of Islam to the Constituent Assembly of Pakistan in July 1950. For the text of this document, see Binder, *Religion and Politics*, 383–429; for a discussion, see 155–82. For another formulation of similar views, see Muhammad Taqi 'Uthmani, "Islami dastur ka mafhum" ("The meaning of an Islamic constitution"), in *Nifaz-i shari'at*, 7–17, where he deduces the basic principles of an Islamic constitution from what he takes to be relevant verses of the Qur'an.

20. Taqi 'Uthmani, *Nifaz-i shari'at*, 9.

21. For examples of such rhetoric, cf. ibid., 8; Sami' al-Haqq, *Iqtidar ke iwanon main shari'at bill ka ma'rika* (Akora Khattak: Mu'tamar al-musannifin, 1991), 25ff., 241ff. Also cf. Mawdudi, *Islamic Law and Constitution*, 107: "No reasonable person can deny that Pakistan was demanded and established in the name of Islam and for the sake of the revival of its glory. It is thus potentially an Islamic ideological state. And this being so, it must be recognized as an incontrovertible fact that it is the state which should play a positive role in the establish-

ment of the Islamic system of life." This forms part of a speech delivered at the Law College, Lahore, in February 1948.

22. For a brief biography of Taqi 'Uthmani, see Fuyuz al-Rahman, *Mashahir 'Ulama'* (Lahore: Frontier Publishing Company, n.d.), 2: 698–700.

23. For a biography of Mufti Muhammad Shafi', see Muhammad Rafi' 'Uthmani, *Hayat-i mufti-yi a'zam* (Karachi: Idarat al-ma'arif, 1994).

24. Taqi 'Uthmani is the editor of his madrasa's monthly journal, *al-Balagh*, and it is primarily in this journal that many of his writings were first published. His political and legal writings have been brought together in his *Nifaz-i shari'at*, on which the following discussion is primarily based. For an earlier collection of his political writings, see his *'Asr-i hadir main Islam kaise nafidh ho?* (Karachi: Maktaba-i Dar al-'ulum, 1397 A.H.). He has written not only on questions pertaining to Islamic law and its implementation, but also on the economy, education, and social issues. For these writings, which have also been recently collected and compiled, see Muhammad Taqi 'Uthmani, *Hamara ma'ashi nizam* (Our economic system) (Karachi: Maktaba-i Dar al-'Ulum, 1415 A.H.); idem, *Islah-i mu'ashara* (The reform of society) Karachi: Maktaba-i Dar al-'Ulum, 1415 A.H.); idem, *Hamara ta'limi nizam* (Our educational system) (Karachi: Maktaba-i Dar al-'Ulum, 1415 A.H.); idem, *Islam awr jiddat-pasandi* (Islam and modernism) (Karachi: Maktaba-i Dar al-'Ulum, 1419 A.H.).

25. Taqi 'Uthmani, *Nifaz-i shari'at*, 50f.

26. Ibid., 51. On the Saudi legal system, see Vogel, *Islamic Law*.

27. Taqi 'Uthmani, *Nifaz-i shari'at*, 51f. Cf. Vogel, *Islamic Law*, 83–117, on a certain tension between the judges' well-recognized right of ijtihad and the efforts of the Saudi rulers to curtail that ijtihad in the interest of a greater uniformity of judicial practice. Despite royal efforts at engendering uniformity by decree, in the end, as Vogel notes, "the only practice . . . that seems capable of unifying Saudi judicial practice involves no formal law or procedure at all, but simply the respect of judges for senior 'ulama: fatwas issued by the Board of Senior 'Ulama' that have a near-legislative effect" (117).

28. On this and other meanings of codification, cf. Vogel, *Islamic Law*, 311f.

29. Though he does not explicitly say so, Taqi 'Uthmani appears to have in mind here what the medieval jurists called the "aims," or the fundamental principles of the shari'a (*maqasid al-shari'a*), which include the protection of life, property, reason, religion, and progeny. See, for instance, Hallaq, *Islamic Legal Theories*, 89, 112, 167ff.

30. Taqi 'Uthmani, *Nifaz-i shari'at*, 53–58.

31. Ibid., 60; cf. Sami' al-Haqq, *Iqtidar*, 37f.

32. Taqi 'Uthmani, *Nifaz-i shari'at*, 61. Taqi 'Uthmani gives no examples of how the English and shari'a laws are in basic conceptual conflict with each other in the instances he mentions. He does, however, give one example (62f.) of how apparently similar terms mean quite different things in the two legal systems.

33. Cf. Sami' al-Haqq, *Iqtidar*, 243: "We would need to wage a great war for the system of the shari'a, a bloody war. We would have to rely on our own prowess . . . and decide whether or not we are the party of God. If we are indeed the party of God, then we should have no relations with, and no expectations from, those who are the party of the devil. Alone, and only with our trust in the help of God,

we would have to move forward, struggle, and wage holy war." Sami' al-Haqq, a former member of the Pakistani Senate, is the president of the Dar al-'Ulum Haqqaniyya, a Deobandi madrasa near Peshawar in the Northwest Frontier Province of Pakistan. (On the role of this madrasa in the Afghan war and its ties with the Taliban, see chapter 6, in the present work.) If Sami' al-Haqq has one foot in the radical stream, however, the other is not far out of step with 'ulama like Taqi 'Uthmani. In 1985, Sami' al-Haqq had introduced a "shari'a bill" as a private member's bill in the Senate, and the foregoing extract is part of a speech lamenting the government's opposition to this bill. (This was the bill passed by the Senate in May 1990, five years after its introduction, but ignored in the lower house of the parliament then controlled by the government of Benazir Bhutto. It was later followed by the Enforcement of Shari'ah Act of 1991. See nn. 10 and 11, this chapter). Despite his ominous warnings about a holy war, the proposals made in this bill were, in fact, not very different from Taqi 'Uthmani's views on the implementation of the shari'a.

34. The *hudud* refer to the punishments (for drinking, theft, adultery, and false accusation of adultery) that are expressly sanctioned by the Qur'an and the Sunna.

35. See, for example, *al-Khayr* (the monthly magazine of the Khayr al-madaris, a leading madrasa of Multan in the Punjab) 14/6 (November 1996): 5f.; also see the special issue of *al-Haqq* (the monthly magazine of Sami' al-Haqq's Dar al-'Ulum Haqqaniyya) devoted to the Taliban: 31/12 (September 1996).

36. Cf. Vogel, *Islamic Law*, 318–25.

37. See Brown, "Shari'a and State."

38. For the debate on codification in Saudi Arabia, see Vogel, *Islamic Law*, 309–62.

39. For the point that the practice of taqlid might be supposed to predispose 'ulama in favor of codification, cf. Vogel, *Islamic Law*, 331f.; on the taqlid of a school of law as a premodern precursor of adherence to codified law, cf. Jackson, *Islamic Law and the State*, xvii, 225.

40. Cf. Fyzee, *Outlines of Muhammadan Law*; David Gilmartin, *Empire and Islam: Punjab and the Making of Pakistan* (Berkeley: University of California Press, 1988), 169ff.; M. Farani, *The Shariat Application Laws (1935–1968)* (Lahore: Pakistan Legal Publications, 1968); Messick, *Calligraphic State*, 54–72; Jakob Skovgaard-Petersen, *Defining Islam for the Egyptian State: Muftis and Fatwas of the Dar al-Ifta* (Leiden: Brill, 1997), 56–65, 199–226.

41. Brown, "Shari'a and State," especially 371ff.

42. Sami' al-Haqq, *Iqtidar*, 41f.

43. Mufti Muhammad Shafi', "Pakistan main dini islahat," in Taqi 'Uthmani, *Nifaz-i shari'at*, 79–94: quotation is from 85 (emphasis added).

44. Muhammad Taqi 'Uthmani, *Taqlid ki shar'i haythiyyat* (Karachi: Maktaba-i Dar al-'Ulum, 1413 A.H.), 85–108.

45. Ibid., 100ff. Taqi 'Uthmani characterizes this as *ijtihad fi'l-masa'il*, that is, ijtihad in particular legal questions: cf. ibid., 140f. This is the equivalent of certain forms of *ijtihad fi'l-hukm* as described by Vogel with reference to the contemporary Saudi legal system. See Vogel, *Islamic Law*, 118–37. As Vogel notes, even when a judge does not claim to be a mujtahid, there is considerable scope for flexibility in the application of the law, as well as for new articulations of the law

in particular cases. Indeed, as Vogel suggests, such flexibility might paradoxically be greater for a judge who claims only to be following the existing rulings than for one who self-consciously sets out to undertake ijtihad on the basis of the foundational texts; for the former's "doctrinal advances can be shielded behind combinations of existing views," whereas the latter "may be constrained by the intendment of particular revealed texts" (136).

46. Cf. Muhammad Taqi 'Uthmani, "Bunyad-parasti aik gali ban chuki hai," *al-Banuriyya* (October 1993): 8–18, especially 17.

47. For instance: Taqi 'Uthmani, *Nifaz-i shari'at*, 41f.; Sami' al-Haqq, *Iqtidar*, 53f.; idem, *Islam awr 'asr-i hadir*, 2d ed. (Akora Khattak: Mu'tamar al-musannifin, 1409 A.H.), 418; Also cf. Starrett, *Putting Islam to Work*, 175f., 231. The Islamist ideologue Mawdudi concurred with the 'ulama on the necessity of religious experts, though what he and they seem to mean by that differed. Cf. Mawdudi, *Islamic Law and Constitution*, 223–25.

48. See Messick, *The Calligraphic State*, 152–66.

49. Note that the idea of disciplinary specialization is also of relatively recent origin in institutions of higher learning in the West. As Jon Roberts and James Turner have argued in tracing the history of the humanities in American colleges and universities, training in specialized disciplines or the expectation that college and university professors would be "specialists" in their respective fields began to gain ground only towards the end of the nineteenth century. See Jon H. Roberts and James Turner, *The Sacred and the Secular University* (Princeton: Princeton University Press, 2000), 83–93. In speaking of themselves as religious specialists or experts in matters Islamic, the 'ulama, of course, are speaking not of disciplinary specialization within their madrasas—though that too has increasingly occurred in these institutions—but rather of the expert and specialized knowledge that alone qualifies one to deal with or represent particular areas or fields.

50. Cf. Brown, "Shari'a and State," 369. Also cf. the anecdote recounted by Mawlana Yusuf Ludhianawi in the previous chapter.

51. On the fragmentation of religious authority, its context and consequences, see Eickelman and Piscatori, *Muslim Politics*, 37ff., 131ff. and passim.

52. See, for instance, Jackson, *Islamic Law and the State*, especially xiii–xlii, 185–229.

53. Baber Johansen, "Sacred and Religious Elements in Hanafite Law—Function and Limits of the Absolute Character of Government Authority," in *Contingency*, 189–218; quotation is from 214. A notable example of the juristic concern to circumscribe governmental authority and the scope of its intervention in the life of private individuals, and especially of the schools of law, is provided by the work of the medieval Maliki jurist al-Qarafi (d. 1285). For a detailed discussion of his legal and constitutional thought, see Jackson, *Islamic Law and the State*, especially 185–229.

54. Johansen, *Contingency*, 214.

55. Ibn 'Abidin, *Radd al-muhtar 'ala al-durr al-mukhtar* (Cairo, 1307 A.H.), 2: 156, quoted in Johansen, *Contingency*, 214. Johansen also notes that while the jurists were prepared to countenance the rulers' transgression of the sphere the former had demarcated for them, such transgression was also a source of continuing tension between the jurists and the ruling elite (216f.).

56. Talal Asad, "Religion, Nation-State, Secularism," in *Nation and Religion*, ed. van der Veer and Lehmann, 178–96; the quotations are from 192.

57. For instances where the judges of Pakistan's higher courts have arrogated to themselves the authority for ijtihad by basing their decision directly on the Qur'an and hadith, see Lucy Carroll, "Qur'an 2.229: 'A Charter Granted to the Wife'? Judicial *Khul*' in Pakistan," *Islamic Law and Society* 3/1 (1996): 91–126, esp. 107f. Carroll does not, however, discuss the 'ulama's reaction to such ijtihad. For an example of the 'ulama's reaction, taking issue with the Supreme Court's handling of *khul*' (divorce at the instance of the wife), see Muhammad Taqi 'Uthmani, "Islam main khul' ki haqiqat," in *Fiqhi maqalat* (Karachi: Memon Islamic Publishers, 1996), 2: 135–92.

58. *Pakistan Legal Decisions 1959*, Lahore 566, 581, cited in Carroll, "Qur'an 2.229," 107; emphasis added.

59. Malik, *Colonialization of Islam*. Also see Nasr, *Islamic Leviathan*.

60. For Mawdudi's life and thought, see Charles J. Adams, "Mawdudi and the Islamic State," in *Voices of Resurgent Islam*, ed. John L. Esposito, 99–133; Nasr, *Mawdudi*. Some of Mawdudi's most important statements on Islamic law and the state are brought together in translation in his *Islamic Law and Constitution*.

61. For an interpretation of Mawdudi's relations with the 'ulama that differs in certain respects from mine, see Nasr, *Mawdudi*, 107–25.

62. Mawdudi, *Islamic Law and Constitution*, 111.

63. See ibid., 112. Among the modern works he mentions, suggesting that they be translated from Arabic into Urdu, are the *Fath al-Mulhim* of Mawlana Shabbir Ahmad 'Uthmani, which is a commentary on the *Sahih* of Muslim (on this work, see chapter 3, in the present volume); Khalil Ahmad Saharanpuri's *Badhl al-majhud*, a commentary on the *Sunan* of Abu Dawud; and the *Awjaz al-masalik*, a commentary on Malik b. Anas' *Muwatta'* by Muhammad Yahya Kandahlawi.

64. Ibid., 104.

65. Nasr, *Mawdudi*, 69–79.

66. Ibid., 78.

67. For a detailed history of Mawdudi's Islamist organization, see Nasr, *The Vanguard of the Islamic Revolution*.

68. Mawdudi, *Islamic Law and Constitution*, 177.

69. Sayyid Abu'l-A'la Mawdudi, *Let Us be Muslims* (Leicester: The Islamic Foundation, 1985), 295f., cited in Nasr, *Mawdudi*, 82; emphasis added.

70. Nasr, *Mawdudi*, 82.

71. Taqi 'Uthmani, *Takmila*, 3:271. Compare al-Qarafi's firm exclusion of liturgical rituals from any tampering by the state: "Know that all of the *'ibadat*, without exception, are absolutely immune to the decisions of government officials. Rather, these may be treated only by legal opinions (*fatwas*). Thus, every pronouncement we encounter concerning a matter of the *'ibadat* is no more than a legal opinion. It is thus not the right of an official to rule that the prayer of a certain individual is invalid. . . . Rather, everything that is said concerning these matters constitutes no more than a [nonbinding] legal opinion. If these statements comport with the view of one who hears them, he may follow them; if not he may ignore them and follow his own *madhhab* [school of law]." Al-Qarafi, *al-Furuq* (Beirut: 'Alam al-kitab, n.d.), 4: 48, quoted in Jackson, *Islamic Law and the State*, 198.

72. Taqi 'Uthmani, *Takmila*, 3: 271. Taqi 'Uthmani also quotes the critique of the noted Indian scholar Sayyid Abu'l-Hasan 'Ali Nadwi that an exclusive focus on politics makes Islam formalistic, arid, worldly, narrow, and "devoid of inner sensibilities." Ibid., 271, citing Abu'l-Hasan 'Ali Nadwi, *al-Tafsir al-siyasi li'l-Islam* (Lucknow, 1399 A.H.), 107. On Nadwi's critique of Mawdudi's political thought, see Christian W. Troll, "The Meaning of Din: Recent Views of Three Eminent Indian Ulama," in *Islam in India: Studies and Commentaries*, ed. Christian W. Troll (New Delhi: Vikas Publishing House, 1982), 168–77.

73. Taqi 'Uthmani, *Takmila*, 3: 270. It is significant that Mawdudi's position is critiqued in the context of a commentary on a classical collection of hadith. This affords us one more example of how this supposedly arcane genre continues to be used to settle contemporary scores, as noted in chapter 2.

74. Ibid., 3: 272.

75. See "Islamic Government" in Algar, *Islam and Revolution*, 27–166.

76. Cf. Arjomand, *The Turban for the Crown*, 147–88.

77. *Summary of World Broadcasts: Middle East and Africa* (London), January 8, 1988; quoted in Eickelman and Piscatori, *Muslim Politics*, 50. For an illuminating discussion of this remarkable development and its context—a discussion to which I am much indebted—see Chibli Mallat, *The Renewal of Islamic Law: Muhammad Baqer as-Sadr, Najaf and the Shi'i International* (Cambridge: Cambridge University Press, 1998), 79–107.

78. Algar, *Islam and Revolution*, 79.

79. Ibid., 80.

80. On the signification of the *wilayat al-faqih* here as the authority of the government rather than only of the leading jurist, cf. Mallat, *Renewal of Islamic Law*, 92.

81. For the range of such debates as they pertain to women but with implications that extend to all facets of the relationship between religious and political authority, see Ziba Mir-Hosseini, *Islam and Gender: The Religious Debate in Contemporary Iran* (Princeton: Princeton University Press, 1999).

82. The ambivalence of 'ulama like Taqi 'Uthmani towards the Islamic state is not rooted, however, in a "pluralistic" view of the world, which, according to Robert Hefner, is what underlies the opposition of many Indonesian Muslim intellectuals to the idea of the Islamic state. Cf. Hefner, *Civil Islam*, 218, 220. The 'ulama's view of the autonomy of the Islamic tradition, or the flexibility of their discourses in invoking and variously mobilizing this tradition, does not usually amount to what might be understood as liberal pluralism.

83. Just such a portrayal comes across strongly in the otherwise highly sophisticated work of Leonard Binder on constitutional debates in Pakistan during its first decade. See Binder, *Religion and Politics*, 22, 27, 33, 98 n. 59, 141f., and passim; but contrast 336f.

84. Mufti Muhammad Rafi' 'Uthmani, *Dini jama'atain awr mawjuda siyasat* (Karachi: Idarat al-ma'arif, 1996), 7–9.

85. "The Renewer of the Second Millennium" is the title by which the great Naqshbandi Sufi and scholar of Mughal India, Shaykh Ahmad Sirhindi (d. 1624), is best known. On Sirhindi, see Yohanan Friedmann, *Shaykh Ahmad Sirhindi: An*

Outline of His Thought and a Study of His Image in the Eyes of Posterity (Montreal: McGill University Press, 1971).

86. Rafi' 'Uthmani, *Dini jama'atain*, 22f.

CHAPTER 5. REFASHIONING IDENTITIES

1. Roy, *The Failure of Political Islam*, 75–88.

2. On the history of the emergence, growth, and crystallization of Sunni and Shi'i Islam, see, *inter alia*, W. Montgomery Watt, *The Formative Period of Islamic Thought* (Edinburgh: Edinburgh University Press, 1973); Moojan Momen, *An Introduction to Shi'i Islam* (New Haven: Yale University Press, 1985); Zaman, *Religion and Politics under the Early 'Abbasids.*

3. J. N. Hollister, *The Shi'a of India* (London: Luzac, 1953), 177ff; Sandria B. Freitag, *Collective Action and Community: Public Arenas and the Emergence of Communalism in North India* (Berkeley: University of California Press, 1989), 249–79; Juan R. I. Cole, *Roots of North Indian Shi'ism in Iran and Iraq: Religion and State in Awadh, 1722–1859* (Berkeley: University of California Press, 1988), 229ff.

4. Cole, *Roots of North Indian Shi'ism*, 223–50.

5. Ibid., 240f.

6. Ibid., 241f.

7. Freitag, *Collective Action and Community*, 263–79.

8. Cf. Etan Kohlberg, "Some Imami Shi'ite Views on the Sahaba," *Jerusalem Studies in Arabic and Islam* 5 (1984), 143–75. On 'A'isha as a figure of intense contestation between the Shi'is and the Sunnis through the ages, see D. A. Spellberg, *Politics, Gender, and the Islamic Past: The Legacy of 'A'isha bint Abi Bakr* (New York: Columbia University Press, 1994).

9. The lower figure is given in an anonymous, polemically motivated pamphlet published at a time of increasing tensions between the Sunnis and the Shi'a: *Pakistan main mawjuda Shi'a abadi*, (n.p., [1980?]), 16 pp.) Moojan Momen estimates the Twelver Shi'i population of Pakistan to have been about 12,000,000 in 1980, i.e., about 14.5 percent of the population (82,952,000). See Momen, *Shi'i Islam*, 278, 282. All discussion of the Shi'a in this chapter refers to the Ithna 'ashari, or "Twelver" Shi'a.

10. The phrase comes from Bryan Wilson, *The Social Dimensions of Sectarianism* (Oxford: Clarendon Press, 1990), 180.

11. On the Ahmadis, see Friedmann, *Prophecy Continuous.*

12. See *Report of the Court of Inquiry [into] . . . the Punjab Disturbances of 1953* (Lahore: Government Printing, 1954).

13. On these developments, see Friedmann, *Prophecy Continuous*, 40–46.

14. Cf. Paula R. Newburg, *Judging the State: Courts and Constitutional Politics in Pakistan* (Cambridge: Cambridge University Press, 1995), 184 n. 26.

15. See Muhammad Ilyas Balakoti, *Amir-i 'azimat: Hadrat Mawlana Haqq Nawaz Jhangawi Shahid* (Jhang: Jami'a 'Uthmania [1990]), 29–31; *Khilafat-i Rashida* 4/7 (December 1993): 5.

16. On the differences between the Sunni and Shi'i schools of law, see Coulson, *History of Islamic Law*, 113–19.

17. See Andreas Rieck, "The Struggle for Equal Rights as a Minority: Shia Communal Organizations in Pakistan, 1948–68," in *The Twelver Shia in Modern Times*, ed. Brunner and Ende, 268–83.

18. Formative developments in Shi'i law are believed to have taken place in the time, and under the guidance, of Ja'far al-Sadiq (d. 765), the sixth imam in the reckoning of the Twelver Shi'a. Shi'i law (fiqh) is therefore often designated as "Ja'fari."

19. The demand for "adequate" or "effective" representation in the political system, irrespective of the actual numerical strength of the people on whose behalf that demand was made, was of course a familiar theme of Muslim political discourse in British India. See Shaikh, *Community and Consensus*.

20. See the anonymous Persian biography, *'Allama Shahid Sayyid 'Arif Husayn al-Husayni; Az wiladat ta shahadat* (Qumm: Sazman-i tablighat-i Islami, 1369 A.H.), 36ff. and passim.

21. Interview with 'Allama Sajid Naqwi, chief of the Tahrik-i Ja'fariyya Pakistan, in *Takbir* (March 30, 1995), 27–35.

22. On the TNFJ/TJP, see *'Allama Shahid*; Munir D. Ahmed, "The Shi'is of Pakistan," in *Shi'ism, Resistance, and Revolution*, ed. M. Kramer (Boulder: Westview Press, 1987), 275–87; Maleeha Lodhi, "Pakistan's Shia Movement: An Interview with Arif Hussaini," *Third World Quarterly* (1988), 806–17.

23. On institutionalized Shi'i learning in Najaf, see Mallat, *Renewal of Islamic Law*.

24. On Mufti Ja'far Husayn, see Sayyid 'Arif Husayn Naqwi, *Tadhkira-i 'ulama-i Imamiyya-i Pakistan* (Islamabad: Markaz-i tahqiqat-i Farsi-yi Iran wa Pakistan, 1984), 73–76; *'Allama shahid*, 43ff.

25. Mufti Ja'far Husayn had, however, remained active in defending Shi'i causes in earlier decades. Notably, he had served as the president of the Organization for Safeguarding Shi'i Rights in Pakistan from 1948 to 1953. See Rieck, "Struggle for Equal Rights," 272.

26. Mallat, *Renewal of Islamic Law*, 1–58 and passim.

27. *'Allama Shahid*, 24–25.

28. Mallat, *Renewal of Islamic Law*, 4ff. and passim.

29. *'Allama Shahid*, 25.

30. Michael M. J. Fischer, *Iran: From Religious Dispute to Revolution* (Cambridge: Harvard University Press, 1980).

31. On the life and career of al-Husayni, see *'Allama Shahid*, passim; Naqwi, *Tadhkira-i 'ulama*, 483–91; Lodhi, "Pakistan's Shia Movement," 806–17. Also cf. Mallat, *Renewal of Islamic Law*, 188f.

32. For the text of this manifesto, entitled "Hamara rasta" (Our path), see Muhammad 'Uthman and Mas'ud Ash'ar, eds., *Pakistan ki siyasi jama'atain* (Lahore: Sang-i mil Publications, 1988), 774–811.

33. Ibid., 783.

34. Ibid., 786.

35. Ibid., 805.

36. Ibid., 802–4.

37. Biographical notices of the Shi'i 'ulama of Pakistan are replete with claims of successful proselytizing: see Naqwi, *Tadhkira-i 'ulama*, 7, 9, 24, 26, 28, 33,

34, 38, 39, 41, 45–46, 48, 51, 53, 55, 56, 65, 69–70, 71, 94, 109, 118, 122, 123, 125, 131, 135, 150, 156, 159, 164, 170, 173, 199, 206, 209, 211, 213, 218, 222, 232–33, 246, 252, 262, 265, 278, 291, 298, 299, 305, 306, 310, 323, 324, 330, 343, 346, 349, 371, 400, 420, 422, 449, 463, 474–75.

38. See Syed Hussain Arif Naqvi, "The Controversy about the Shaikhiyya Tendency among Shia 'Ulama' in Pakistan," in *The Twelver Shia in Modern Times*, ed. Brunner and Ende, 135–49. On the Shaykhiyya, so named after a prominent Twelver Shi'i thinker and mystic of eastern Arabia, Shaykh Ahmad al-Ahsa'i (d. 1826), see *Encyclopaedia of Islam*, 9: 403–5, s.v. "Shaykhiyya" (D. MacEoin).

39. For continuing dissensions within the ranks of the TJP, cf. *Dawn*, November 5, 1999.

40. On the Sipah-i Muhammad, see Aamer A. Khan, "The Rise of Sectarian Mafias," *The Herald* (June 1994): 27–37; M. Hanif et al., "In the Name of Religion," *Newsline* (September 1994): 24–41; *Zindagi* (May 25, 1995), interview with 'Allama Murid 'Abbas Yazdani, "Chief Commander" (*salar-i a'la*) of the Sipah-i Muhammad Pakistan, 35–38.

41. Cf. Zaigham Khan, "Losing Control," *The Herald* (May 2000): 53–56, especially 54. In August 2001, the Pakistani government banned the Sipah-i Muhammad as well as the Lashkar-i Jhangawi, a radical offshoot of the Sunni Sipah-i Sahaba. In January 2002, the Sipah-i Sahaba itself and the TJP were banned as well. See *Dawn*, August 15–16, 2001; ibid., January 13, 2002. Because of infighting, external threat (including government regulation), and strategy, Pakistan's militant sectarian organizations have often been prone to structural instability, fragmentation, and metamorphosis. This has especially been so with the Shi'i organizations. It is often difficult to know whether a particular organization has ceased to exist, has adopted a different form, or is merely keeping a low profile. And an organization's activities can, of course, continue even when it has formally been banned. I will therefore speak of these organizations in the present tense to bring out their overall position in the sectarian landscape of Pakistan.

42. Ghulam Riza Naqvi of the Sipah-i Muhammad claimed in July 1995 that nearly two thousand Pakistani Shi'a were studying in the madrasas of Qumm alone: see his interview in *Zindagi* (July 20, 1995): 21.

43. On the career of Sayyid Ghulam Riza Naqvi, see M. Zaidi, "The Godfather," *Newsline* (February 1995): 52–53; and the interview with Naqwi in *Zindagi* (July 20, 1995): 20–23.

44. *The Herald* (June 1994): 37; *Newsline* (February 1995): 50–54.

45. On the Jam'iyyat 'Ulama'-i Islam, see Sayyid A. S. Pirzada, *The Politics of the Jamiat Ulema-i-Islam Pakistan, 1971–1977* (Karachi: Oxford University Press, 2000). For a concise but broader overview, see Charles Kennedy, "Jam'iyatul 'Ulama'-i Islam" in *The Oxford Encyclopaedia of the Modern Islamic World*, ed. John L. Esposito (New York: Oxford University Press, 1995), 2: 364–65. For the relationship of the Jam'iyya with Sunni sectarianism in Pakistan, see S.V.R. Nasr, "The Rise of Sunni Militancy in Pakistan: The Changing Role of Islamism and the Ulama in Society and Politics," *Modern Asian Studies* 34/1 (2000): 139–80, especially 169ff.

46. According to the census of 1981, the total population of Jhang district was 1,978,263, of which 22.6 percent lived in urban areas. The city of Jhang had a

population of 195,558. Government of Pakistan, Population Census Organization, *1981 District Census Report of Jhang* (Islamabad: Statistics Division, 1984), 5, 19. The 1998 census reported the district's total population to be 2,834,545 (an increase of 43.8% since 1981), of which 23.4 percent lived in urban areas; the population of the city of Jhang in 1998 was 293,366. See Government of Pakistan, Population Census Organization, *1998 District Census Report of Jhang* (Islamabad: Statistics Division, 2000), 25, 58.

47. See Balakoti, *Amir-i 'azimat.* The author of this book has served as the editor of the Sipah-i Sahaba's monthly journal, the *Khilafat-i Rashida,* and is the brother of Mawlana Zia al-Rahman Faruqi, the former head of the organization. The book may therefore be considered the Sipah-i Sahaba's "official" biography of its founder.

48. Balakoti, *Amir-i 'azimat,* 20–23 (abbreviated in translation). The "life of pleasure and libertinism" refers here to the institution of *mut'a,* or temporary marriage. A distinctively Shi'i institution, it allows a man and a woman to enter into a sexual relationship for a specified period of time (ranging from a few hours to many years) and for a clearly stipulated amount of money, which is paid to the woman specifically for sex. On the insitution of mut'a, see Shahla Haeri, *Law of Desire: Temporary Marriage in Shi'i Iran* (Syracuse: Syracuse University Press, 1989). As Cole notes, many of the Muslim courtesans in British India (and presumably later as well) were, or became Shi'is, because mut'a "provided limited legal protection to the courtesan, which simple prostitution did not." Cole, *Roots of North Indian Shi'ism,* 87f. Rural landholders were also known to give landed property to courtesans: ibid., 88.

49. Cf. Metcalf, *Islamic Revival,* 68ff., 252ff. and passim; this theme is strikingly conspicuous in the speeches delivered at the early conventions of the Nadwat al-'Ulama'. See, for instance, the speeches given at the Nadwa's second annual convention in Lucknow in 1895: *Madamin-i thalatha* (Kanpur: Intizami Press [1895?]), 25ff. and passim.

50. Cf. Malcolm Darling, *The Punjab Peasant in Prosperity and Debt* (London: Oxford University Press, 1925); some of the themes in this description of the peasant's plight in the early twentieth century continue to resonate in the Sipah-i Sahaba's rhetoric.

51. There were only 13 Shi'i madrasas in the Punjab in 1971, but 100 in 1994. On the other hand, Deobandi madrasas grew from 173 in 1971, to 972 in 1994, and Barelawi madrasas from 93 in 1971, to 1216 in 1994. I have compiled these figures from: Nadhr Ahmad, *Ja'izah-i madaris-i 'arabiyya,* 693; *The News* (March 7, 1995): 11; *Zindagi* (February 17, 1995): 38–39. Also see table 1, in this chapter.

52. On "the structure of rural Islam" in the Punjab see Gilmartin, *Empire and Islam,* especially 39–72. On the importance of the attitude towards the Sufi pirs as a critical marker of one's credentials as a "true" Muslim in *urban* Punjab, see Katherine P. Ewing, *Arguing Sainthood: Modernity, Psychoanalysis, and Islam* (Durham, N.C.: Duke University Press, 1997), 93–127. As Ewing observes, "Even among neighbours whose relationships are close and complex and whose goals in interaction are usually quite removed from and more diverse than contests for political dominance, the pir as a topic of conversation readily generates ideological discourse" (93).

53. Cf. Nasr, "Rise of Sunni Militancy," 176f.

54. Cf. W. C. Smith, *Islam in Modern History* (Princeton: Princeton University Press, 1957), 245–56, on the fascination with this ideal polity especially in Pakistan's early years.

55. For the goals of the Sipah-i Sahaba see Balakoti, *Amir-i 'azimat*, 139–52; Ziya al-Rahman Faruqi, *Sipah-i Sahaba kiya hai, kiya chahati hai?* (n.p., n.d.); idem, *Sipah-i Sahaba ka nasb al-'ayn awr taqade* (Faisalabad: Idara-yi isha'at al-ma'arif, 1994). Also see the following collection of speeches by the organization's founder: Haqq Nawaz Jhangawi, *Mawlana Nawaz Jhangawi ki pandara ta' rikh-saz taqrirain* (Lahore: Idara-i nashriyyat-i Islam, 1991), passim.

56. Jhangawi, *Ta'rikh-saz taqrirain*, 272f. The speech was delivered at the Jami'a 'Ilmiyya madrasa in Shuja'-abad in the Punjab on June 1, 1989. .

57. Ibid., 273. Jhangawi goes on: "This is the time to act in the practical sphere (*maydan-i 'amal*) and to challenge the cruel and oppressive ruler" (ibid.). This speech was delivered during the first premiership of Benazir Bhutto, who was widely perceived as hostile to the 'ulama and the religious parties. The opposition to her on the part of many 'ulama was also because she was a Shi'i and a woman.

58. Following his assassination, Mawlana Haqq Nawaz has himself been given something of a saintly image: see Balakoti, *Amir-i 'azimat*, especially 317–18, for dreams in which he is seen in heaven in the company of the sahaba.

59. Four of the stars have the names of the four Rashidun caliphs written on them, and on the fifth appear the names of Hasan and Husayn (two sons of 'Ali) and Mu'awiya. The last, also a Companion of the Prophet, was the founder of the Umayyad dynasty (661–750), which the Shi'a hold responsible for the tribulations of no fewer than six of their twelve imams (including 'Ali, Hasan, and Husayn). Conjoining Hasan, Husayn, and Mu'awiya is of course not an initiative towards sectarian harmony, but only a vivid reminder that Mu'awiya is no less venerable to Sunnis than Hasan and Husayn, and that the latter two, as well as 'Ali, belong properly with other figures revered by the Sunnis, not with the later imams of the Shi'a. For the Sipah-i Sahaba's flag as well as other symbolism, see Balakoti, *Amir-i 'azimat*, 147–52; also cf. the title page of Faruqi, *Sipah-i sahaba kiya hai?*

60. Catherine Bell, *Ritual: Perspectives and Dimensions* (New York: Oxford University Press, 1997), 223–42, especially 231; quotation is from 231.

61. Emmanuel Sivan, "Sunni Radicalism in the Middle East and the Iranian Revolution," *International Journal of Middle East Studies*, 21 (1989): 1–30; Werner Ende, "Sunni Polemical Writings on the Shi'a and the Iranian Revolution," in *The Iranian Revolution and the Muslim World*, ed. D. Menashri (Boulder: The Westview Press, 1990), 219–32.

62. Such centers have consequently been targeted for sectarian attacks. In December 1990, an Iranian diplomat who was the director of the Iranian Cultural Center in Lahore was assassinated by militants from the Sipah-i Sahaba. *Newsline* (April 1991): 44. Also cf. Balakoti, *Amir-i 'azimat*, 144–45; and see table 3, in this chapter.

63. Balakoti, *Amir-i 'azimat*, 69.

64. Jhangawi would often lace his fiery speeches with detailed quotations from Shi'i books to document such sacrileges. For some instances, see Jhangawi, *Ta'rikh-saz taqrirain*, 99ff., 122ff., 278–94. These speeches are also available on cassette.

65. The Sipah-i Sahaba, as well as Shi'i organizations, have, or have had, branches in the Middle East and even in Europe and North America. Cf. *Khilafat-i Rashida*, 3/4 (April 1992): 50, 52.

66. *Khilafat-i Rashida*, 5/6 (November 1994), interview with Mawlana Zia al-Rahman Faruqi (part 4), 30.

67. Mawlana Zia al-Rahman Faruqi, the former head of the Sipah-i Sahaba, stated in late 1994 that "about 14,000 party units" were then functioning in Pakistan and abroad, compared to only about 300 such units at the time of Jhangawi's assassination in February 1990. See *Khilafat-i Rashida*, 5/5 (October 1994): 6.

68. The phrase "imagined community" comes, of course, from Benedict Anderson, who uses it for the nation-state, not, as I do here, for religious communities. See Benedict Anderson, *Imagined Communities: Reflections on the Origin and Spread of Nationalism* (London: Verso, 1991).

69. Cf. *Newsline* (September 1994): 36.

70. Among the more famous and successful businessmen from Jhang are the Chiniotis, known as such by association with Chiniot, a town in the district. Chinioti business families had migrated to Calcutta and elsewhere, but returned (or migrated back) to the Punjab after the establishment of Pakistan to become one of the most important business groups in Pakistan's economy. See Stanley Kochanek, *Interest Groups and Development: Business and Politics in Pakistan* (Delhi: Oxford University Press, 1983), 23–24. For one early instance of the support of Chinioti businessmen for Sunni madrasas of Jhang (and elsewhere), see *Al-Jami'a* (the monthly journal of the Jami' Muhammadi), 1/3 (December 1948): 5.

71. *Newsline* (September 1994): 36.

72. Balakoti, *Amir-i 'azimat*, 15.

73. Mian Iqbal Husayn, a leader of the Sipah-i Sahaba who was assassinated in Jhang in August 1991, owned a textile mill in the city. *The Muslim* August 14, 1991; also cf. *The Herald* (March 1995): 57. On the Punjabi industrial bourgeoisie in general, see Anita M. Weiss, *Culture, Class, and Development: The Emergence of an Industrial Bourgeoisie in Punjab* (Boulder: Westview Press, 1991).

74. News reports about protests and strikes on the assassination of Sipah-i Sahaba leaders Haq Nawaz Jhangawi and Isar al-Haq Qasimi, both in Jhang, in February 1990 and January 1991, respectively, provide much illustrative material in this regard. See *The Muslim*, March 26, 1990; *The Nation*, April 10, 1990; *Dawn*, January 12, 1991; *The Muslim*, January 12 and February 10, 1991; *Nawa-i Waqt*, January 12, 1991; *The Frontier Post*, February 9, 1991.

75. Not all are *Twelver* Shi'is, however. The Daudi Bohras, a community of energetic and affluent businesspeople who have a considerable presence in Karachi (in addition to Bombay, and in Africa and North America), are a subsect of the Isma'ili Shi'a. On this community, see Jonah Blank, *Mullahs on the Mainframe: Islam and Modernity among the Daudi Bohras* (Chicago: University of Chicago Press, 2001).

76. Cf. Nikki R. Keddie, *Iran and the Muslim World: Resistance and Revolution* (New York: New York University Press, 1995), 208f.

77. Keddie, *Iran and the Muslim World*, 208f., exaggerates the "secular" attitudes of the middle-class Shi'a of Pakistan. Consider, for instance, Muhammad 'Ali Naqvi (d. 1995), the secretary-general of the Tahrik-i Ja'fariyya, who was assassinated in Lahore in March 1995. 'Ali Naqvi, a professor and doctor at a teaching hospital in Lahore, was not typical of other middle-class Shi'a in the extent of his involvement with Shi'i sectarian mobilization but did nevertheless typify middle-class Shi'i support for such organizations. On 'Ali Naqvi, see *The News*, March 8, 1995; *The Herald* (March 1995): 57–58. The following statement by Ghulam Riza Naqvi of the Sipah-i Muhammad is also instructive: "We do not need any [financial] assistance from other countries [read: Iran], for our own people are very generous in helping us. Indeed, if our people pay all the khums [a Shi'i wealth-tax] they are obliged to, there will be so much money as to create a new Pakistan" (*Zindagi*, July 20, 1995: 23). Compare the observations of Khumayni on the importance of *khums* as a major source of the (Shi'i) Islamic state's revenue: Algar, *Islam and Revolution*, 44f.

78. Roy, *The Failure of Political Islam*, 187ff. Also cf. Riesebrodt, *Pious Passion*, 185ff.

79. Omar Noman, "The Impact of Migration on Pakistan's Economy and Society," in *Economy and Culture in Pakistan: Migrants and Cities in a Muslim Society*, ed. H. Donnan and P. Werbner (London: Macmillan, 1991), 83.

80. Jonathan Addleton, *Undermining the Centre: The Gulf Migration and Pakistan* (Karachi: Oxford University Press, 1992), 88ff. My discussion here of overseas labor migrants is largely based on Addleton's findings.

81. Ibid., 190, 197.

82. Noman, "Impact of Migration," 90.

83. Addleton, *Undermining the Centre*, 187–201.

84. Cf. the fatwa issued by the Khayr al-madaris, an influential Deobandi madrasa of Multan, Punjab, authorizing payment of zakat and other donations to the Sipah-i Sahaba: Mufti Muhammad Anwar, comp., *Khayr al-fatawa* (Multan: Maktabat al-khayr, 1993), 3: 466.

85. One residential colony of about ten thousand people in Jhang was reported in April 1991 to have thirty-five mosques, many of them of recent origin. See *Newsline* (April 1991): 45. A survey conducted in August 1994 reported in Okara city in the Punjab 160 mosques belonging to the Barelawis alone; there had been only *one* Sunni mosque there in the early 1950s: *Newsline* (September 1994): 33. The larger towns and cities can have several thousand mosques: *The Herald* (March 1995): 71 (report on Faisalabad city in the Punjab).

86. A random sample of the monthly or fortnightly journals (each usually around 50 pages) published by madrasas, religious associations, and various sectarian organizations shows that almost all carry numerous advertisements from shopkeepers and small merchants, but sometimes also from larger businesses. My sample includes the following monthly journals: *al-Balagh* (Dar al-'Ulum, Karachi); *al-Bayyinat* (Jami'at al-'Ulum al-Islamiyya, Karachi); *al-Haqq* (Dar al-'Ulum Haqqaniyya, Peshawar); *al-Sa'id* (Jami'a Anwar al-'Ulum, Multan); *Ziya-i haram* (Lahore); *Misaq* (Tanzim-i Islami, Lahore); *Ishraq* (al-Mawrid, Lahore); *Khilafat-i Rashida* (Sipah-i Sahaba, Faisalabad); *Majallat al-da'wa* (al-Da'wa wa'l-Irshad, Lahore).

87. Cf. Anderson, *Imagined Communities*, 77; compare the "mechanisms of integration" in the making of Shiʻi fundamentalism in Iran: Riesebrodt, *Pious Passion*, 160ff.

88. See Mark Juergensmeyer, *The New Cold War? Religious Nationalism Confronts the Secular State* (Berkeley: University of California Press, 1993), 167ff. on the empowering of "marginal peoples" in religious nationalism through, *inter alia*, the sanctification of religious violence; idem, *Terror in the Mind of God: The Global Rise of Religious Violence* (Berkeley: University of California Press, 2000), 187–215.

89. *Khilafat-i Rashida* 4/1 (January 1993): 20; Jhangawi, *Ta'rikh-saz taqrirain*, 132, 136.

90. It is worth noting that one of the Zia al-Rahman Faruqi's brothers has also worked in Saudi Arabia; another has served as the editor of the Sipah-i Sahaba's journal, the *Khilafat-i Rashida*, See *Khilafat-i Rashida* 5/3 (August 1994): 6.

91. On the Sials of Jhang, see L. Griffin and C. F. Massy, *Chiefs and Families of Note in the Punjab* (Lahore: Government Printing, Punjab, 1940), 2: 365–71.

92. Jhangawi, *Ta'rikh-saz taqrirain*, 166–79.

93. This account is based on a biographical notice in *Khilafat-i Rashida* 4/1 (January 1993): 20.

94. As one example among many, see Balakoti, *Amir-i ʻazimat*, 72–74, for a list of "the martyrs of Jhang" (till 1990?).

95. The Sipah-i Sahaba, too, has a splinter group, the Lashkar-i Jhangawi (established in 1994), which has been involved in many acts of sectarian terrorism. On this and other sectarian groups, see Mariam Abou Zahab, "The Regional Dimension of Sectarian Conflicts in Pakistan," unpublished paper. (I am grateful to Ms. Abou Zahab for making a copy of this paper available to me.) Together with the radical Shiʻi Sipah-i Muhammad, the Lashkar-i Jhangawi was banned by the Pakistani government in August 2001.

96. Stanley J. Tambiah, *Leveling Crowds: Ethnonationalist Conflicts and Collective Violence in South Asia* (Berkeley: University of California Press, 1996), 192; emphasis in the original.

97. On the career of Mawlana Aʻzam Tariq, see *Khilafat-i Rashida* 3/9–10 (September-October 1992): 27–28. Also see the detailed interview with him in ibid., 4/7 (December 1993), 5–8; 4/8 (January 1994): 4–10.

98. See Zeghal, *Gardiens de l'Islam*; idem, "Religion and Politics in Egypt." I use the term "peripheral" in a somewhat broader sense than Zeghal, however. In her usage, the peripheral ʻulama are those Azhar-educated scholars and preachers who have typically not enjoyed much standing within the Azhar-establishment but have often been sympathetic to Islamist trends (see chapter 6 of the present work, especially n. 2). A similar characterization would also hold for the dissident Saudi ʻulama (see again chapter 6). In the Pakistani context, however, where there is no "official" religious establishment, the characterization "peripheral" is meant to designate those who are politically activist but lack strong credentials for intellectual or religious authority.

99. For more on Nuʻmani's life, see his autobiography, *Tahdith-i niʻmat*.

100. Ibid., 37–60.

101. Mawlana Muhammad Manzur Nu'mani, *Khumayni awr Shi'a kai bare main 'ulama-i kiram ka muttafiqa faisala*, 2 vols. (n.p. [1988?]). Both Nu'mani's *Iranian Revolution* and his treatise asking for the fatwas provide ample "proof texts" to document the charge that the Shi'a had no claim to be members of the Muslim community; as such, both are precursors of the sort of work Zia al-Rahman Faruqi later wanted compiled to damn the Shi'is with the testimony of their own writings. The Shi'i beliefs that Nu'mani singles out are the following: that the first two successors of Muhammad, Abu Bakr and 'Umar, both of whom are regarded by Sunnis as "rightly guided" caliphs, were in fact infidels; that the text of the Qur'an was corrupted after Muhammad's death to suit the anti-'Alid purposes of the caliphs; and that the Shi'i imams are the mediators of divine guidance. Sunni polemicists say that the last-mentioned belief makes the imams rivals of the Prophet Muhammad, and, as such, amounts to the Shi'i denial of the finality of Muhammad's prophethood. This belief is consequently taken to put the Shi'ia in the same league as the Ahmadis, which explains, in part, the transition from the Sunni 'ulama's anti-Ahmadi position to the anti-Shi'i one. For a discussion of these doctrines and their implications, see Manzur Nu'mani, *Muttafiqa faisala*, 1: 16ff. and passim.

102. Manzur Nu'mani, *Muttafiqa faisala*, 1: 39; also cf. 1: 5f.

103. Cf. his appeal—printed on the back cover—to all readers of the fatwas collected in his *Muttafiqa faisala*.

104. Ibid., 1: 34.

105. See ibid., 2: 75–92. On Mufti Wali Hasan, a leading jurisconsult characterized by his followers as "Pakistan's grand mufti," see Mufti Khalid Mahmud, "Mufti-i a'zam Pakistan mufti Wali Hasan Tonki ki khidmat," *al-Banuriyya*, 2/5 (March 1995): 11–13; 2/6 (April 1995): 15–18.

106. For a sampling of Sami' al-Haqq's anti-Shi'i views, see his *Islam awr 'asr-i hadir*, 323–45.

107. *Dawn*, May 19, 2000.

108. On violence as performance, see Juergensmeyer, *Terror*, 122ff. "Terrorist acts . . . can be both *performance events*, in that they make a symbolic statement, and *performative acts*, insofar as they try to change things" (124; emphasis in original).

109. Nasr, "Rise of Sunni Militancy," 169–80.

110. Cf. ibid., 170 n. 91, and 177 (a reference to Taqi 'Uthmani's Dar al-'Ulum madrasa of Karachi).

111. Also cf. Taqi 'Uthmani's discussion of jihad in *Islam awr jiddat-pasandi*, 97–109.

112. Mufti Muhammad Rafi' 'Uthmani, *Yeh tere pur-asrar bandey: Jihad-i Afghanistan ki an-kahi dastan* (Karachi: Idarat al-ma'arif, 1995).

113. Also see chapter 4, n. 33, in the present volume.

114. Nasr, "Rise of Sunni Militancy," 176 and passim.

115. On the "Iranianization" of non-Iranian Shi'ite clergy in the Middle East (but also elsewhere), see Roy, *Failure of Political Islam*, 185ff.

116. Cf. Naqvi, *Tadhkira-i 'ulama*, 291, 320, 340, 403, 411 for instances of Shi'i preachers striving to "reform" local beliefs and customs.

117. Faruqi, *Sipah-i Sahaba ka nasb al-'ayn*, 75–78.

118. Nasr, "Rise of Sunni Militancy," 179.

119. On the Taliban the most detailed work so far is that of Pakistani journalist Ahmed Rashid: *Taliban: Militant Islam, Oil, and Fundamentalism in Central Asia* (New Haven: Yale University Press, 2000). Other accounts (besides the numerous investigative and news reports by journalists in the aftermath of the September 11, 2001 terrorist attacks) include: William Maley, ed., *Fundamentalism Reborn? Afghanistan and the Taliban* (London: Hurst & Company, 1998); David B. Edwards, "Learning from the Swat Pathans: Political Leadership in Afghanistan, 1978–97," *American Ethnologist* 25/4 (1998): 712–28; Zahid Hussain et al., "Islamic Warriors," *Newsline* (February 1995): 22–49; idem, "Inside Taliban Land," *Newsline* (March 1999): 20–34. On the Soviet occupation of Afghanistan, the Afghan factions that participated in the struggle against it, and the role of Islam in this struggle, see Olivier Roy, *Islam and Resistance in Afghanistan* (Cambridge: Cambridge University Press, 1986); Barnett Rubin, *The Fragmentation of Afghanistan: State Formation and Collapse in the International System* (New Haven: Yale University Press, 1995).

120. While the number of Afghan refugees in Pakistan has fluctuated considerably since the time of the Soviet occupation, government estimates have indicated the continuing presence, even in 2001, of more than three million refugees in Pakistan (the exact figure given in November 2001 was 3,018,686): See *The News*, November 6, 2001.

121. Schools established by the major parties that were active in the jihad in Afghanistan likewise functioned as centers for the ideological molding of young Afghans. As the "education president" of one of the most powerful of these parties, the Hizb-i Islami, put it in 1986, "The educational schools serve as spiritual (*ma'nawi*) guides along [*sic*] the Islamic revolution and as a fundamental support (*takyah-gah*) for the stability and protection of the purity of the Islamic revolution. The trenches of education are the best grounds for the training of the refugee and mujahid children who cut the dirty hands of Islam's enemies." Farshad Rastegar, "Education and Revolutionary Political Mobilization: Schooling versus Uprootedness as Determinants of Islamic Political Activism among Afghan Refugee Students in Pakistan" (Ph.D. dissertation, University of California at Los Angeles, 1991), 171. Also cf. Rubin, *Fragmentation*, 215.

122. On religious education as a long-standing means of social mobility for rural Afghans, see Edwards, "Learning from the Swat Pathans," 724.

123. 'Abd al-Qayyum Haqqani, "Jihad-i Afghanistan awr Dar al-'Ulum Haqqaniyya," in *Khutbat-i Haqqani* (Akora Khattak: Mu'tamar al-musannifin, 1991), 92–108; Rafi' 'Uthmani, *Yeh tere pur-asrar bandey*, 312ff.; also cf. Rubin, *Fragmentation*, 216f.

124. Malik, *Colonialization of Islam*, 207.

125. Ibid., 207.

126. Rashid, *Taliban*, 21.

127. See ibid., 143–82 and passim.

128. On the role of the Jam'iyyat al-'Ulama'-i Islam in setting up madrasas during the Afghan war, and the party's ties with the Taliban, see ibid., 89ff. The party is presently split into two factions, led by Mawlana Fazlur Rahman and

Mawlana Samiʿ al-Haqq, respectively; both have maintained close ties with the Taliban, as also with the Sipah-i Sahaba.

129. *The New York Times*, December 5, 1998: B2.

130. For the various justifications offered by General Pervez Musharraf for Pakistan's participation in the U.S.-led coalition, see, for instance, *Dawn*, October 1, 2001; and November 9, 2001. For indications of confusion and anxiety among ordinary Pakistani people about the consequences of the new war in their part of the world, see Sarfaraz Ahmed, "People Shudder at Fallout of U.S. Action," *Dawn*, September 22, 2001. For warnings of a civil war in Pakistan as a result of this crisis, see *Dawn*, September 30, 2001; October 8, 2001; and October 27, 2001; also cf. Rahimullah Yusufzai, "Pakistan Faces Threat of Polarization in Society," *The News*, October 22, 2001. A Gallup poll sponsored by *Newsweek* also revealed something about simmering tensions (and contradictions) among Pakistanis in the wake of the U.S.-led military operations against Afghanistan: even as a small majority of those polled supported the Pakistani president, an overwhelming 83 percent said their sympathies in this war lay with the Taliban. See *Newsweek* (Atlantic edition), October 22, 2001: 45.

131. Rashid, *Taliban*, 90.

132. *Al-Haqq*, the monthly magazine of the Dar al-ʿUlum Haqqaniyya, Akora Khattak, special issue on the Taliban, 31/12 (September 1996): 2.

133. *Al-Haqq* vol. 32/9 (June 1997): 8. For another admiring view of the Taliban from a madrasa in Karachi, see Mawlana Muhammad Adam Khan, "Taliban ke Islami Afghanistan ka safar" (A Journey through the Islamic Afghanistan of the Taliban), parts 1–4, *al-Faruq*, 12/9 (January 1997): 9–12; 12/10 (February 1997): 42–46; 12/11 (March 1997): 43–45; and 12/12 (April 1997): 17–20.

134. Jeffrey Goldberg, "The Education of a Holy Warrior," *The New York Times Magazine* (June 25, 2000): 32–37, 53, 63–64, 70–71. For an account of this madrasa after the September 11, 2001 terrorist attacks, see Khaled Dawoud, "Passionate Pedagogy," *al-Ahram Weekly Online*, October 4–10, 2001. Those studying at the madrasa were reported to have not taken kindly to this spate of visits by foreign journalists (including women journalists): cf. *Dawn*, September 25, 2001.

135. Robert Fisk, "Thousands Massacred by Taliban," *The Independent*, September 4, 1998; idem, "Taliban's Secret Massacre," *The Independent*, November 29, 1998; Michael Sheridan, "How the Taliban Slaughtered 8,000," *The Sunday Times*, November 1, 1998; Rashid, *Taliban*, 72ff.

136. These camps were among those targeted by U.S. missile strikes on August 20, 1998, in retaliation for the bombing of American embassies in Kenya and Tanzania by operatives of Usama bin Laden earlier that month. See Rashid, *Taliban*, 92: "Hundreds of SSP [Sipah-i Sahaba Pakistan] militants have trained at the Khost training camp run by the Taliban and Bin Laden . . . and thousands of SSP members have fought alongside the Taliban." On the 1998 U.S. missile strikes, see *The New York Times*, August 21, 1998, and the news reports of the following days.

137. *The Pakistan Times*, August 15, 1998; quoted in Abou Zahab, "Regional Dimension," 13.

138. It is worth noting that despite their opposition to the Deobandis, and hence to the Deobandi Taliban, the Barelawi Jam'iyyat al-'Ulama'-i Pakistan also participated in public protests against the American military operations in Afghanistan. (For Barelawi participation in these protests and statements by Barelawi leaders, see *Dawn*, October 1, 2001; ibid., October 8, 2001; October 11, 2001; October 21, 2001; October 27, 2001.) This was a matter of showing solidarity with the Afghans, however, not a change of Barelawi attitude towards the Deobandi Taliban.

139. See, for instance, *The News*, November 5–6, 2001. An especially prominent role in the recruitment for jihad was played by the Tanzim-i Nifaz-i Shari'at-i Muhammadi (Organization for the implementation of Muhammad's shari'a), which is made up of Pashtun tribesmen with ties to both Islamist and Deobandi groups. This organization, led by Mawlana Sufi Muhammad, had first arisen in 1989 to demand replacement of long-standing (colonial) tribal regulations by the shari'a in at least its native home, the Malakand division of the North-West Frontier Province. It was banned, alongside several other militant groups, in January 2002. For the early history of this organization, see Rahimullah Yusufzai, "Malakand: Armed Insurrection and Political Inadequacies," *The News*, November 11, 1994. For the activities of this organization in mobilizing support for the Taliban and in fighting alongside them in Afghanistan, see Pamela Constable, " 'Jihad Is My First Obligation'," *The Washington Post*, November 6, 2001: A1. Also see *The News*, November 5–6, 2001; *Dawn*, November 18, 2001.

140. For news reports to this effect see, for instance, *Dawn*, October 24, 2001; *The News*, October 26, 2001; November 3, 2001; *Dawn*, November 12, 2001; November 18, 2001.

141. "A Letter to the Taliban Leadership from Leading 'Ulama," *al-Balagh* 31/6–7 (November 1996): 9–11. The letter was signed by Salim Allah Khan, the president of the federation of Pakistan's Deobandi madrasas and the principal of the Jami'a Faruqiyya madrasa of Karachi; Subhan Mahmud, Muhammad Rafi' 'Uthmani, and Muhammad Taqi 'Uthmani, all of the Dar al-'Ulum madrasa of Karachi; and Habib Allah Mukhtar, principal of the Jami'at al-'Ulum al-Islamiyya of Karachi.

142. "Hakumat-i Taliban: Bihtar tawaqqu'at," *al-Balagh*, 32/2 (June 1997): 3–5; quotation is from 4.

143. See Muhammad Taqi 'Uthmani, *Jahan-i dida: Bis mulkon ka safarnama* (Karachi: Idarat al-ma'arif, 1996). This is a detailed account of his travels in twenty countries in the Middle East, Southeast Asia, and Western Europe, and including Canada and the United States. Accounts of these travels first appeared, and continue to be published, in the madrasa's monthly journal, *al-Balagh*. Also cf. idem, "Harvard University ka aik safar" (A visit to Harvard University), *al-Balagh*, 32/9 (January 1998): 3–11.

144. For an account of Rafi' 'Uthmani's visit, in the company of some other 'ulama, see *al-Balagh*, 31/3 (1996): 3–16.

145. *Al-Balagh*, 31/6–7 (November 1996): 10. Note that the 'ulama and the "technical experts" are ranged side by side in this formulation, but that only underscores the former's expertise in their own "field," which is no less important than any other.

146. *Dawn*, April 10–12, 2001. For some of the speeches delivered during a related event, which was hosted for the 'ulama from India at Sami' al-Haqq's Dar al-'Ulum Haqqaniyya, see *al-Haqq*, 36/6–7 (March-April 2001): 7–24.

147. Interestingly enough, two "advisers" to the Iranian president, Muhammad Khatami, also participated in the conference; so too did a representative of the Libyan president, Muammar al-Qaddafi. See *Dawn*, April 10–11, 2001.

148. In interviews and public statements in the aftermath of the September 2001 terrorist attacks, President Pervez Musharraf repeatedly characterized the "religious extremists" opposed to his cooperation with the U.S. war effort against the Taliban as a "handful." See, for instance, *Dawn*, October 1, 2001; November 9, 2001.

149. *Dawn*, November 8, 1997.

150. At a large Friday rally in late October, 2001, attended by an estimated 50,000 people, Mawlana Sami' al-Haqq characterized Musharraf as a "traitor of Muslim nations" [*sic*]. The Taliban, he added—and not for the first time—were "a symbol of Islam." *The News*, October 27, 2001. Also see *Dawn*, October 29, 2001, where Mufti Nizam al-din Shamzai, the chief mufti of the Jami'at al-'Ulum al-Islamiyya madrasa of Karachi and a leader of the Jam'iyyat al-'Ulama'-i Islam, is quoted as follows: "Musharraf openly supports the U.S. and its allies against [the] Taliban. And under the Islamic laws if any Muslim cooperates with infidels against Muslims, he must be excommunicated from the religion." A leader of the Jaish-i Muhammad, a militant Pakistani Deobandi organization active in the Muslim insurgency in Indian-controlled Kashmir, was even reported to have announced " 'head money' on General Pervez Musharraf"—an offer he was said later to have recanted. See *Dawn*, October 21, 2001.

151. In turn, the government filed criminal charges, and charges of "treason," against some of those making threatening calls or efforts to dislodge the government: cf. *Dawn*, October 2, 2001; October 7, 2001; *The News*, October 31, 2001.

152. For declarations of jihad against the United States by leaders of the Jam'iyyat al-'Ulama'-i Islam, see *Dawn*, October 11, 2001 ("JUI Declares Jihad against US, Allies"); October 27, 2001. Also cf. ibid., September 19, 2001 (fatwa in favor of jihad in the event of a U.S. attack on Afghanistan by Mufti Nizam al-din Shamzai). For the Taliban's own threats of jihad against anyone (read: Pakistan) aiding the American war effort against Afghanistan, see ibid., September 16, 2001. One of Bin Laden's several statements during the war also specifically called upon the people of Pakistan to wage jihad against the United States: see *The News*, November 2, 2001.

153. Some others include Mawlana Abd al-Ghafur Haydari and Mufti Nizam al-din Shamzai, both of the Jam'iyyat al-'Ulama'-i Islam. (On Haydari, cf. *The New York Times*, October 8, 2001: B5; on Shamzai, see previous notes.) Ironically, Shamzai was one of those sent to Afghanistan by the Pakistani government shortly before the American attacks to persuade the Taliban to relent. While this mission of the 'ulama was reported to have failed, Shamzai's earlier and later pronouncements in favor of jihad—even as he condemned the killing of innocent people in terrorist attacks—make it hard to imagine that he would have felt very strongly about recommending an alternative course to the Taliban. On this mis-

sion, see *Dawn*, September 28–29, 2001; also cf. *The Washington Post*, September 29, 2001: A22; *The New York Times*, September 29, 2001: B6.

154. *Dawn*, September 23, 2001 ("Ulema's Advice to Afghan Gov[ernmen]t"). My account of the 'ulama's statement is a summary of this news report. Taqi 'Uthmani was also a member of the 'ulama delegation that had gone to meet the Taliban leadership shortly before the beginning of the American attacks. See *Dawn*, September 28–29, 2001.

155. The statement issued on this occasion read, in part: "If the US has an iota of justice and fair play, instead of responding to terrorism by adopting a policy of terrorism, it should examine the reasons which have been creating hatred and unrest against it in the Third World, where people are bent upon destroying it at the cost of their life." *Dawn*, October 11, 2001 ("US Attacks Termed Act of Collective Terrorism").

156. Riesebrodt, *Pious Passion*, 16 and passim.

CHAPTER 6. RELIGIOPOLITICAL ACTIVISM AND THE 'ULAMA

1. See chapter 3, of the present work.

2. Zeghal, "Religion and Politics," 371–99; quotation is from 380. Cf. 386: "Peripheral ulema usually belong to Islamic associations that specialize in *da'wa*. . . . They generally show affinities with the ideology of the Muslim Brothers, but they are scattered throughout the structure of the religious institution and are not sociologically homogeneous." For more discussion of the "peripheral" and other 'ulama, see idem, *Gardiens de l'Islam*, 165–372 and passim. My discussion of the Egyptian 'ulama is greatly indebted to Zeghal's work. Other recent studies of the contemporary 'ulama in Egypt include: Skovgaard-Petersen, *Defining Islam*; Moustafa, "Conflict and Cooperation," 3–22; Majida 'Ali Salih Rabi', *al-Dawr al-siyasi li'l-Azhar, 1952–1981* (Cairo: Kulliyat al-iqtisad wa'l-'ulum al-siyasiyya, 1992); Hala Mustafa, *al-Nizam al-siyasi wa'l-mu'arada al-Islamiyya fi Misr* (Cairo: Markaz al-mahrusa li'l-nashr wa'l-khidmat al-suhufiyya, 1995), especially 239–56. For other studies on Islam and the 'ulama in contemporary Egypt, see the following notes.

3. Starrett, *Putting Islam to Work*.

4. Rudolph Peters, "Divine Law or Man-Made Law: Egypt and the Application of the Shari'a," *Arab Law Quarterly*, 3/3 (1988): 236. For the debate on the implementation of Islamic law in Egypt, see also: Bernard Botiveau, "Contemporary Reinterpretations of Islamic Law: The Case of Egypt," in *Islam and Public Law: Classical and Contemporary Studies*, ed. C. Mallat (London: Graham and Trotman, 1993), 261–77; also see Clark Benner Lombardi, "Islamic Law as a Source of Constitutional Law in Egypt: The Constitutionalization of the Sharia in a Modern Arab State," *Columbia Journal of Transnational Law* 37 (1998): 81–123.

5. On 'Abd al-Halim Mahmud and his efforts for the implementation of the shari'a, see Zeghal, *Gardiens*, 141–64.

6. On the Azhar's advocacy of a gradualist approach in the face of Islamist calls for the immediate implementation of the shari'a, see Skovgaard-Petersen, *Defining Islam*, 206.

7. Moustafa, "Conflict and Cooperation," 3–22.

8. The then Shaykh al-Azhar, Jad al-Haqq 'Ali Jad al-Haqq, complained in 1994, for instance, that "other groups [that had taken] . . . control of the media and the arts [were working] . . . to change social thinking and the Egyptian and Islamic traditions in a way which was sometimes inconsistent with the creed of this society." Such state-sponsored challenges to "the Egyptian and Islamic traditions," he was suggesting, had prompted people to react by turning to the appeal of the Islamists. Even on his analysis, the state was responsible for the appeal of Islamist discourses, and the proper thing to do was to give the Azhar 'ulama greater access to the media. Cited in Steven Barraclough, "Al-Azhar: Between the Government and the Islamists," *Middle East Journal*, 52/2 (1998), 239f.

9. Zeghal, "Religion and Politics," 389f.

10. Moustafa, "Conflict and Cooperation," 14; Barraclough, "Al-Azhar," 241; also cf. Starrett, *Putting Islam to Work*, 210f.

11. On the 1994 United Nations conference and the public debate it generated, see Donna Lee Bowen, "Abortion, Islam, and the 1994 Cairo Population Conference," *International Journal of Middle East Studies* 29 (1997): 161–84; Barraclough, "Al-Azhar," 244f. On the 'Ulama' Front, see Zeghal, "Religion and Politics," 389ff. On Jad al-Haqq, cf. Malika Zeghal, "La guerre des fatwas—Gad al-Haqq et Tantawi: Les cheikhs à l'épreuve du pouvoir," *Les cahiers de l'orient* 45 (1997): 81–95. Also see note 8, this chapter.

12. Zeghal, "Religion and Politics," 391.

13. Moustafa, "Conflict and Cooperation," 14f.; Barraclough, "Al-Azhar," 242.

14. Moustafa, "Conflict and Cooperation," 3–22, especially 13ff.; Barraclough, "Al-Azhar," 236–49.

15. On 'Umar 'Abd al-Rahman and his ties with the Islamist groups, see Zeghal, *Gardiens*, 337ff., especially 340f.

16. Barraclough, "Al-Azhar," 245.

17. Carrie Rosefsky Wickham, "Political Mobilization under Authoritarian Rule: Explaining Islamic Activism in Mubarak's Egypt" (Ph.D. dissertation, Princeton University, 1996) 433–633 and passim. Also cf. Skovgaard-Petersen, *Defining Islam*, 221f.

18. Wickham, "Political Mobilization," 440f.

19. Ibid., 458f.

20. Ibid., 461–83 and passim. On the difficulties of regulating the "private" mosques, see Gaffney, *The Prophet's Pulpit*, 265f. On the penetration of state institutions by this parallel sector, as reflected, for example, by lawyers and judges who are sympathetic to Islamists and to the implementation of the shari'a, see Botiveau, "Contemporary Reinterpretations," 275–77. Also cf. Quintan Wiktorowicz, *The Management of Islamic Activism: Salafis, the Muslim Brotherhood, and State Power in Jordan* (Albany: State University of New York Press, 2001), 111–46 on the informal Islamist networks of the Salafis of Jordan during the 1990s.

21. Wickham, "Political Mobilization," 532.

22. Skovgaard-Petersen, *Defining Islam*, 221f.

23. Cf. the profile of the peripheral 'ulama as provided by Zeghal: "Religion and Politics," 386.

24. On the popularity of "lay" preachers (that is, those lacking formal religious training) in contemporary Egypt, see Charles Hirschkind, "Technologies of Islamic Piety: Cassette-Sermons and the Ethics of Listening" (Ph.D. dissertation, Johns Hopkins University, 1999), 77f. and passim. Also see Gaffney, *The Prophet's Pulpit.*

25. Quoted in Wickham, "Political Mobilization," 552.

26. Ibid., 552.

27. Compare Starrett, *Putting Islam to Work*, 226.

28. Hirschkind, "Technologies of Islamic Piety," 82, and cf. 79ff.

29. Zebiri (*Mahmud Shaltut and Islamic Modernism*) considers Mahmud Shaltut, who was Shaykh al-Azhar from 1958 to 1963, a "modernist." Such a characterization would be difficult to make for any leading Pakistani 'alim. Shaykh 'Abd al-Halim, for his part, had done his doctoral work with Louis Massignon at the Sorbonne (Zeghal, *Gardiens*, 144). Again, there is nothing comparable in case of the Pakistani 'ulama.

30. For a brief overview of Wahhabism, see Aziz al-Azmeh, "Wahhabite Polity," in *Islams and Modernities*, 2d ed. (London: Verso, 1996), 143–60; also see *Encyclopaedia of Islam*, 11: 39–47, s.v. "Wahhabiyya," by Esther Peskes and W. Ende; on the legal aspects of Wahhabism, see Vogel, *Islamic Law*, index, s.v. "Wahhabi" and passim.

31. Vogel, *Islamic Law*, 211.

32. Ibid., 211 and passim.

33. For instances of Saudi judges not abiding by royal decrees, see ibid., 175f.

34. On the Board, see Vogel, *Islamic Law*, index, s.v. "Board of Senior 'Ulama'."

35. See Lombardi, "Islamic Law as a Source of Constitutional Law."

36. Vogel, *Islamic Law*, 272–76; quotation is from 274.

37. On this episode, see Joseph A. Kechichian, "The Role of the Ulama in the Politics of an Islamic State: The Case of Saudi Arabia," *International Journal of Middle East Studies* 18 (1986): 53–71.

38. Cf. Eickelman and Piscatori, *Muslim Politics*, 60–63.

39. The most detailed study of the religious opposition to the Saudi state in the aftermath of the Gulf War is Fandy, *Saudi Arabia and the Politics of Dissent*. My analysis here is much indebted to him.

40. Quoted in Fandy, *Saudi Arabia*, 51.

41. For a detailed description of the demands, on which I have drawn for this summary, see Fandy, *Saudi Arabia*, 50–60.

42. See "The Sketch of an Islamic University" that Mawdudi had presented to the Saudi government in Abu'l-A'la Mawdudi, *Ta'limat* (Lahore: Islamic Publications, 1972), 165–76; also cf. the publisher's note, 3.

43. On Abu Ghudda, see chapter 2 of the present work.

44. See the title page of the published version of this Ph.D. dissertation: Safar b. 'Abd al-Rahman al-Hawali, *Zahirat al-irja fi'l-fikr al-Islami*, 2 vols. (Cairo: Maktab al-tayyib, 1996).

45. Zeghal, *Gardiens*, 339f.

46. This information comes from the official home page of the Saudi government: *http://www.mohe.gov.sa/univs/iu.html* (accessed on June 18, 1998).

47. On the Murji'a, see *The Encyclopaedia of Islam*, 7: 605–7, s.v. "Murdji'a," by W. Madelung.

48. Al-Hawali, *Zahirat al-irja*, 1: 12.

49. Ibid., 1: 9ff.

50. Ibid., 1: 11.

51. For an overview of his writings and speeches during and after the Gulf War, see Fandy, *Saudi Arabia*, 61–87.

52. Safar ibn 'Abd al-Rahman al-Hawali, *Haqa'iq hawla azmat al-khalij* (Mecca: Dar al-Makka al-mukarrama, 1991), 3.

53. Ibid., 132.

54. Ibid., 128–30.

55. Ibid., 137.

56. Ibid., 131; emphasis added.

57. Fandy, *Saudi Arabia*, 72.

58. Ibid.

59. Fandy, *Saudi Arabia*, passim; Talal Asad, "The Limits of Religious Criticism in the Middle East: Notes on Islamic Public Argument," in *Genealogies of Religion*, 200–236.

60. Cf. Eickelman and Piscatori, *Muslim Politics*, 62; Vogel, *Islamic Law*, 295–97.

61. Fandy, *Saudi Arabia*; also cf. idem, "CyberResistance."

62. For instances of the Saudi 'ulama setting the terms of discourse, cf. Vogel, *Islamic Law*, 172, 177f., 223.

63. al-Hawali, *Haqa'iq*, passim; Fandy, *Saudi Arabia*, 61–87.

64. Ibid., passim.

65. Unlike Fandy, however, who—at the cost of some analytical clarity—characterizes all religious dissidents as Islamists, we ought to note what distinguishes the 'ulama from the latter. In Saudi Arabia, as in other contemporary Muslim societies, what distinguishes them is their essential point of reference in all their discourses, viz., the Islamic tradition. For all its rhetorical effect, it is appeal to this tradition that underlies al-Hawali's insistence that *the 'ulama* ought to guide the people in their hour of adversity, and indeed that the hour of adversity would not have arrived if the 'ulama had not neglected this function. Also cf. Asad, *Genealogies of Religion*, 200–236. As Asad notes with reference to a Saudi preacher active in the wake of the Gulf War, "the Islamic tradition is the ground on which the reasoning takes place," just as the mode of offering moral criticism and advice (*nasiha*) is itself grounded in, and justified with reference to, the Islamic tradition (236).

66. Hardy, *Partners in Freedom*, 39f.

67. Ibid., 34–43. Hardy characterizes this expectation of the 'ulama as "jurisprudential apartheid" (34).

68. Cf. Thomas Blom Hansen, "Predicaments of Secularism: Muslim Identities and Politics in Mumbai," *Journal of the Royal Anthropological Institute*, n.s., 6 (2000): 255–72.

69. Friedmann, "The Jam'iyyat al-'Ulama'-i Hind in the Wake of Partition," 211. Also cf. Gregory Kozlowski, "Shah Banu's Case, Britain's Legal Legacy and Muslim Politics in Modern India," in *Boeings and Bullock Carts: Studies in Change and Continuity in Indian Civilization*, vol. 3, *Law, Politics and Society in India*, ed. Y. K. Malik and D. K. Vajpeyi (Delhi: Chanakya Publications, 1990), 88–111, especially 105; Mushirul Hasan, *Legacy of a Divided Nation*, 323.

70. Qamar al-din Khan et al., *Hindustan ki dini darsgahen*, 85. Of the remaining madrasas surveyed in this report, twenty-three were established between 1800 and 1900, two between 1650 and 1799, and three at an unknown earlier date. The survey comprises fifteen Indian states.

71. Ibid., 286f. The number of students between 1945–46 and 1970–71 at both institutions is either more or less consistent or shows a gradual increase. Annual figures for the years between 1970–71 and 1993–94 are not available.

72. Cf. Friedmann, "The Jam'iyyat al-'Ulama'-i Hind in the Wake of Partition," 190.

73. Nadwi, *Karwan*, 2: 85f.

74. All graduates of the Dar al-'Ulum of Nadwat al-'Ulama' bear "Nadwi" as the last part of their name. In the present context, the name Nadwi should be understood to refer exclusively to the person under discussion, Abu'l-Hasan 'Ali Nadwi.

75. Abu'l-Hasan 'Ali Nadwi, *Madha khasira'l-'alam bi'l-inhitat al-muslimin?* The book had been reprinted about fifteen times by 1982, besides being translated into Urdu, English, Persian, and Turkish. The English translation (by M. A. Kidwai) is entitled *Islam and the West*. All subsequent references are to the revised and enlarged Urdu translation, *Insani dunya par musalmanon ke 'uruj wa zawal ka athar* 5th ed. (Lucknow: Majlis-i tahqiqat wa nashriyyat-i Islam, 1966). For the publication history of this work, see Nadwi, *Karwan*, 1: 256–70, especially 265 n. For a critical review of this book, see G. E. von Grunebaum, "Fall and Rise of Islam: A Self-View," in *Modern Islam: The Search for Cultural Identity* (New York, 1964), 244–57.

76. Nadwi, *Insani dunya*, 163ff. and passim.

77. Ibid., 428ff.

78. Nadwi, *al-'Arab wa'l-Islam* (Lucknow: al-Majma' al-Islami al-'ilmi, 1980), especially 9ff. On nationalism as religion, and the religious opposition to nationalism, cf. Juergensmeyer, *The New Cold War?*,11–25 and passim.

79. Nadwi, *al-'Arab wa'l-Islam*, 3–16, and passim; idem, *Insani dunya*, 408ff.

80. Emmanuel Sivan credits Mawdudi with developing the theory of a modern Jahiliyya, and Nadwi with introducing it into the Arab world. See his *Radical Islam: Medieval Theology and Modern Politics* (New Haven: Yale University Press, 1985), 22–23. The theory has had many formulations, some with explicit revolutionary implications, as in the writings of Sayyid Qutb (ibid., 21ff). Despite the contribution of both Mawdudi and Nadwi to the notion of a modern jahiliyya, however, it is noteworthy that (unlike Qutb) neither advocated a politically subversive form of opposition to the state. For Mawdudi's position in this regard, cf. Nasr, *Mawdudi*, 75.

81. Cf. Nadwi, *Insani dunya*, 102–3, 109–10, and 37–99, passim.

82. Ibid., 102–3.

83. By the same token, Nadwi also speaks of a "new *ridda*," or apostasy, a term used in Islamic historiography to denote Arab tribal movements that threw off allegiance to the Islamic state of Medina, and even to Islam itself, in the wake of the Prophet Muhammad's death. On the "new *ridda*" cf. Nadwi, *Karwan*, 1: 452–53.

84. On Nasserism, see ibid., 2: 64–83.

85. On the Rabitat al-'alam al-Islami, see Reinhard Schulze, *Islamischer Internationalismus im 20. Jahrhundert: Untersuchungen zur Geschichte der islamischen Weltliga* (Leiden: Brill, 1990).

86. For an early instance of Saudi financial assistance for the Nadwa, see *Ta'rikh-i Nadwa*, 2: 438. The Saudi government seems, moreover, to have subsidized or bought large quantities of Nadwi's publications. For instance, of a print run of 100,000 copies of the 1982 edition of his *Madha khasira'l-'alam*, published in Kuwait, the Saudi Ministry of Education immediately bought 80,000 copies! See Nadwi, *Karwan*, 1: 265.

87. Nadwi, *al-'Arab wa'l-Islam*, 98–100.

88. Ibid., 100.

89. Ibid., 100–101.

90. For the proceedings of the conference and an account of other celebrations on this occasion, see Muhammad al-Hasani, *Rudad-i chaman: Nadwat al-'Ulama' key pachchasi sala jashn-i ta'limi ki mufassal rudad* (Lucknow, 1976). Also see Nadwi, *Karwan*, 2: 171–95.

91. Abu'l-Hasan 'Ali Nadwi, "Inaugural Address," in al-Hasani, *Rudad-i chaman*, 117; Nadwi, *Karwan*, 2: 188.

92. Nadwi, *al-'Arab wa'l-Islam*, p. 101.

93. On visits to Pakistan in 1978 and 1984, for instance, Nadwi repeatedly reminded his Pakistani audiences that regional, linguistic, class-based, and other conflicts among them could, by undermining Pakistan's stability, hurt Muslims elsewhere (an allusion perhaps to the Muslims of India). Abu'l-Hasan 'Ali Nadwi, *Hadith-i Pakistan* (Karachi: Majlis-i nashriyyat-i Pakistan, 1979), 20 and passim. He also spoke vaguely of the need for an Islamic political center that Muslims elsewhere could look upto: cf. 20, 74f.; idem, *Tuhfa-i Pakistan* (Karachi: Majlis-i nashriyyat-i Islam, [1985?]), 20, 25–27.

94. Abu'l-Hasan 'Ali Nadwi, *Muslims in India*, tr. from the Urdu by M. A. Kidwai (Lucknow: Academy of Islamic Research and Publications, [1960]). Note, however, that a substantial part of this book originated as talks in Arabic on All India Radio in 1951. The original audience, therefore, was the Arab Middle East, though the book under discussion here was primarily intended, Nadwi says, for non-Muslim audiences in India. See ibid., 4–5. Also idem, *The Musalman*, tr. from the Urdu by M. Ahmad (Lucknow: Academy of Islamic Research and Publications, 1972). The term "musulman" is the standard rendition of the Arabic "Muslim" in Urdu.

95. Partha Chatterjee, "History and the Nationalization of Hinduism," *Social Research* 59 (1992): 111–49; quotation is from 149.

96. Nadwi, *Muslims in India*, 65; translation modified slightly.

97. Nadwi, *The Musalman*, 25; cf. idem, *Muslims in India*, 73–75.

98. Cf. Nadwi, *The Musulman*, 6: "Islam is a universal religion rooted in the Qur'an and the *Sunnah*, and, therefore, there is hardly any difference in the basic tenets and religious observances of the Muslims of other countries. Indian Muslims have, on the other hand, adopted numerous customs and usages of the land which have been pointed out where necessary in order to identify their indigenous origin."

99. Cf. Sayyid Abu'l-Hasan 'Ali Nadwi, *Reconstruction of Indian Society: What Muslims Can Do* (Lucknow: Academy of Islamic Research and Publications, 1972).

100. Cf. Hardy, *Partners in Freedom*, 41.

101. Nadwi, *Karwan*, 2: 173–74.

102. Ibid., 2: 293–97.

103. On the establishment of this Board, see ibid., 2: 136–39.

104. For the text of the Supreme Court judgment, see Asghar Ali Engineer, ed., *The Shah Bano Controversy* (Bombay: Orient Longman, 1987), 23–34. In addition to the Supreme Court's verdict, this book also provides a broad sampling of other documents and statements pertaining to the controversy. Among other works on various aspects of the controversy, see Tahir Mahmood, *Islamic Law in the Indian Courts since Independence* (Delhi: Institute of Objective Studies, 1997); Kozlowski, "Shah Banu's Case, Britain's Legacy and Muslim Politics in Modern India," 88–111; Bruce B. Lawrence, *Shattering the Myth: Islam beyond Violence* (Karachi: Oxford University Press, 2000), 131–56; Mushirul Hasan, *Legacy of a Divided Nation*, 263ff. For Nadwi's own account, see his *Karwan*, 3: 111–57.

105. Citing various English translations of Qur'an 2.241–42, the Court stated its conviction that these verses "leave no doubt that the Quran imposes an obligation on the Muslim husband to make provision for or to provide maintenance to the divorced wife. The contrary argument does less than justice to the teachings of the Quran." Engineer, *Shah Bano Controversy*, 30.

106. *Aga Mahomed v. Koolsom Bee Bee* (1897), quoted in Fyzee, *Outlines*, 65.

107. The decision was written for the majority by the chief justice, Chandrachud.

108. For the Court's call to this effect, see Engineer, *Shah Bano Controversy*, 33.

109. Cf. Nadwi, *Karwan*, 3: 125f.

110. Ibid., 3: 131–38.

111. For the text of the bill, see Engineer, *Shah Bano Controversy*, 85–88.

112. Cf. Hasan, *Legacy of a Divided Nation*, 264f.

113. Nadwi, *Karwan*, 3: 133f.

114. Cf. Hasan, *Legacy of a Divided Nation*, 253–357 passim and especially 266. On the "secular modernists," a category in which Mushirul Hasan counts himself, see 319ff.

115. Ibid., 253–357; Zoya Hasan, *Quest for Power: Oppositional Movements and Post-Congress Politics in Uttar Pradesh* (Delhi: Oxford University Press, 1998), 175–233. It was also alleged by some that in exchange for the government's support of the Muslim Personal Law Board's demands, Nadwi himself had

tacitly agreed to let the Hindus claim the site of the contested Baburi Masjid for themselves: cf. Nadwi, *Karwan*, 5: 153f., for a refutation of this charge.

116. On Hindu nationalism, see Daniel Gold, "Organized Hinduisms: From Vedic Truth to Hindu Nation," in *Fundamentalisms Observed*, ed. Martin E. Marty and R. Scott Appleby (Chicago: University of Chicago Press, 1991), 531–93; Peter van der Veer, *Religious Nationalism: Hindus and Muslims in India* (Berkeley: University of California Press, 1994); Thomas Blom Hansen, *The Saffron Wave: Democracy and Hindu Nationalism in Modern India* (Princeton: Princeton University Press, 1999).

117. Cf. Hasan, *Legacy of a Divided Nation*, 323: "The Indian state . . . has bolstered the religio-political leadership. To swing the 'Muslim vote,' ruling and opposition parties pander to their sentiments and readily accommodate them in political structures through nomination, election and appointment. Thus Rajiv Gandhi's government ignored liberal Muslim opinion over the Shah Bano case to negotiate *with Muslim priests*. On the Masjid-Mandir impasse too, men of religion were propped up as the community's sole spokesmen on the assumption that the 'unenlightened hordes' were receptive to their *fatawa* and decrees"; emphasis added.

118. Cf. Euben, *Enemy in the Mirror*, 85ff. and passim.

119. Ibid., 85ff. and passim; the quotation is from p. 85.

120. Ibid., 123–67.

121. Ibid., 86.

122. Taqi 'Uthmani, "Bunyad-parasti aik gali ban chuki hai." Also cf. Nadwi, *Karwan*, 5: 162ff.

123. Fandy, *Saudi Arabia*, 93.

124. Zeghal, *Gardiens*, 340; translation mine.

125. Thomas M. McKenna, *Muslim Rulers and Rebels: Everyday Politics and Armed Separatism in the Southern Philippines* (Berkeley: University of California Press, 1998), 213ff.; quotation is from p. 213.

126. Ibid., 232; emphasis added. Martial law was imposed in 1972 by Ferdinand Marcos, the president of the Philippines. The Muslim rebellion in the south was precipitated by this measure. Ibid., 3.

127. My discussion of Islam and the 'ulama in the southern Philippines is largely indebted to McKenna, *Muslim Rulers and Rebels*. For other studies, see idem, "Appreciating Islam in the Muslim Philippines: Authority, Experience, and Identity in Cotabato," in *Islam in an Era of Nation-States*, ed. Hefner and Horvatich, 43–73; Michael O. Mastura, "Assessing the Madrasah as an Educational Institution: Implications for the Ummah," in *Muslim Filipino Experience* (Manila: Ministry of Muslim Affairs, 1984), 93–107; Nagasura Madale, "The Resurgence of Islam and Nationalism in the Philippines," in *Islam and Society in Southeast Asia*, ed. Taufik Abdullah and Sharon Siddique (Singapore: Institute of Southeast Asian Studies, 1986), 282–314.

128. This was part of Nasser's competition with Saudi Arabia for influence in the Islamic world. Cf. Moustafa, "Conflict and Cooperation," 7.

129. McKenna, *Muslim Rulers*, 197–233. One of the resolutions passed at the First Congress on Muslim Education at Mindanao State University in Marawi City in October 1980 was that "the existing Madaris [singular: madrasa] and

Maahads shall remain private schools and that their rapport with the local Muslim communities and the international Muslim community must not be disturbed or altered" (306).

130. McKenna, *Muslim Rulers*, 203.

131. Ibid., 215.

132. Ibid., 207.

133. On long-standing Saudi patronage, also cf. Madale, "Resurgence of Islam," 290f.; McKenna, *Muslim Rulers*, 205, 221f. More recently, there have also been suspicions of ties between al-Qa'ida, the terrorist network of the Saudi Islamist Usama bin Laden, and some of the Muslim militants involved in the insurgency in the southern Philippines. Bin Laden is said to have visited this region himself in 1987. See *The New York Times*, November 4, 2001: B4.

134. This information comes from a semi-official Saudi website: www.alqimam.com.sa/saudi_info/scholar.html. (accessed on June 18, 1998). Following the September 2001 terrorist attacks in New York and Washington, D.C., Saudi public and private patronage of various Islamic ventures throughout the world came under intense American inspection for suspicion of their possible links with terrorist organizations. See *The New York Times*, October 13, 2001: A1, B3; October 25, 2001: A1, B4; Blaine Harden, "Saudis Seek to Add U.S. Muslims to their Sect," *The New York Times*, October 20, 2001: A1, B9; David B. Ottaway and Dan Morgan, "Muslim Charities under Scrutiny," *The Washington Post*, September 29, 2001.

135. See Markazi Jami'iyyat Ahl-i Hadith *Ta'aruf Jami'a Salafiyya* ([Faysalabad: Jami'a Salafiyya, 1995?]). Also cf. Mufti Muhammad 'Abduh al-Fallah, "Tahrik-i tanzim al-madaris ahl-i hadith," *Majallat al-Jami'a al-Salafiyya* 1/2 (March-May, 1988): 10–17.

136. See Markazi Jam'iyyat Ahl-i Hadith, *Ta'aruf al-Jami'a al-Salafiyya Islamabad* (Rawalpindi: Markazi Jam'iyyat Ahl-i Hadith, n.d.).

137. Marc Gaborieau, "Mission en Inde (5 février–10 mars 1994)," in *La transmission du savoir dans le monde musulman périphérique*, lettre d'information no. 14 (June 1994): 119ff.

138. See Idarat al-ta'lim wa'l-tasnif wa'l-ta'lif, *Jami'at al-'Ulum al-Islamiyya* (Zargari, Kohat: Jami'at al-'Ulum al-Islamiyya [1990?]), 9 and passim.

139. *Al-Faruq*, 8/9 (March 1993): 57; also cf. 6/10 (April 1991): 5; 7/8 (February 1992): 49f.

140. Ibid., 7/8 (February 1992): 47. The madrasa has also received considerable assistance from Muslims of South Africa, as well as from Muslims in Britain and North America. Ibid., 6/10 (April 1991): 8.

141. Ibid., 7/8 (February 1992): 51. The Jam'ia Faruqiyya's claim (ibid.) that it is the *first* madrasa to have such technology in South Asia is exaggerated, however. The madrasas of the Daudi Bohras (a community of Isma'ili Shi'a) no doubt preceded Sunni madrasas like the Jami'a Faruqiyya in their use of computer technology. On the role of modern technology in the Daudi Bohra community, see Blank, *Mullahs on the Mainframe*, especially 174–79; on their educational institutions, 207–28.

142. *Al-Faruq*, 6/10 (April 1991): 5f.; 7/8 (February 1992): 51f.; 8/9 (March 1993): 59; 17/4 (July 2001): 13. The journals of the International Islamic Univer-

sity are published simultaneously in Arabic, Urdu, and English, but not in Pakistan's regional languages, such as Sindhi.

143. Cf. Nu'mani, *Tahdith-i ni'mat*, 115f. for his denial that this book had anything to do with Saudi prompting. In fact, he says, for many years after its publication this book was not allowed entry into the Saudi kingdom. He attributes this initial indifference to bureaucratic inefficiency.

144. Cf. Nadwi, *Karwan*, 3: 251–62.

145. On the impact of the Iranian revolution across the Muslim world, see John L. Esposito, ed., *The Iranian Revolution: Its Global Impact* (Miami: Florida International University Press, 1990). Oddly, South Asia is not one of the regions examined in this collection of essays; nor (with the exception of the Philippines) does it say much about the revolution's impact on the Sunni 'ulama.

146. Cf., *inter alia*, Fandy, *Saudi Arabia*, 82, 97, 105.

147. Cited in McKenna, *Muslim Rulers*, 249; the brackets are McKenna's. This statement was part of a radio speech by a prominent datu, Michael Mastura. The candidate against whom it was directed was Zacaria Candao, who had been associated with the Moro Islamic Liberation Front. Candao, who had already been appointed as acting governor of Maguindanao province by President Corazon Aquino, won this 1988 gubernatorial contest. On Candao, see ibid., 213ff.; on this election and other political activities in the Muslim south after the fall of the Ferdinand Marcos regime in 1986, ibid., 234–68.

148. Dale F. Eickelman and Jon W. Anderson, "Redefining Muslim Publics," in *New Media in the Muslim World*, ed. Eickelman and Anderson 1–18; quotation is from 16.

149. Ibid., 15.

150. Euben, *Enemy in the Mirror*, 88.

151. For a rather different yet related argument, compare Blank, *Mullahs on the Mainframe*. With reference to the Daudi Bohras, Blank argues that various technological, organizational, and other adjustments to the modern age have enabled the Bohra clerics to "strengthen and reinstitutionalize the fundamental core of their faith" (6). More simply put, "the Bohras have used modernity as a tool to reinvigorate their traditions" (1 and passim).

EPILOGUE

1. Wahid al-din Khan, " 'Ulama ka qa'idana kirdar," in idem, *Fikr-i Islami: Afkar-i Islami ki tashrih wa tawdih* (Delhi: al-Risala Books, 1996), 163–217, especially 194. Note that he includes the traditionally educated religious scholars and the Islamists in his critique of the 'ulama here.

2. Cf. ibid., 190.

3. Ibid., 196.

4. Ibid., 196–97; cf. Abu'l-A'la Mawdudi, *Tafhim al-Qur'an* (Lahore: Idara-i Tarjuman al-Qur'an, 1958–72), 6: 382.

5. Khan, 'Ulama ka qa'idana kirdar," 197–98.

6. Ibid.,182.

7. Wahid al-din Khan, "Fikr-i Islami ki tashkil-i jadid," in *Fikr-i Islami*, 31–95, at 32. The title of this article, "The Reconstruction of Islamic Thought," is of

course reminiscent of Muhammad Iqbal's (d. 1938) *The Reconstruction of Religious Thought in Islam* (London: Oxford University Press, 1934).

8. Though he does not say so explicitly, Wahid al-din Khan is referring here to the view of ijtihad and taqlid specifically of the Hanafi scholars. Contemporary Saudi 'ulama of the Hanbali school of law often take a much less restricted view of their ability to practice ijtihad. See Vogel, *Islamic Law*, passim; also see chapter 4 of the present work.

9. Khan, *Fikr-i Islami*, 46–49. For the argument that there never was a consensus among Sunni jurists that the "gate of ijtihad" had been closed, see Hallaq, "Was the Gate of Ijtihad Closed?"

10. Khan, *Fikr-i Islami*, 39. Cf. 51f.

11. Ibid., 38.

12. Ibid., 56f.

13. He mentions the following works: Ibn Taymiyya, *al-Sarim al-maslul 'ala shatim al-rasul*; Taqi al-din al-Subki, *al-Sayf al-maslul 'ala man sabb al-rasul*; Ibn 'Abidin, *Tanbih al-wulat wa'l-hukkam 'ala ahkam shatim khayr al-anam*. See ibid., 57f.

14. Ibid.

15. The doctrine of abrogation (*naskh*) holds that over the more than two decades during which the Qur'an was revealed to Muhammad, certain verses of the Qur'an were abrogated by other verses. Many of the "abrogated" verses have continued to be part of the scriptural text, but they cannot serve as the source of legal rulings. It is part of the jurist's training to know, therefore, which verses are the "abrogating" ones, and which the "abrogated." On this doctrine in medieval Sunni juristic thought, see Hallaq, *Islamic Legal Theories*, 68–74.

16. Khan, *Fikr-i Islami*, 59.

17. Ibid., 59.

18. The reason why efforts to implement Islamic law have failed in modern Muslim states is not, he says, "the oppression of secular rulers or the conspiracies of Islam's enemies. . . . The real reason is the folly of those carrying the banner of Islam in that they began the campaign for the implementation of Islamic law without first preparing the society for it. This is demonstrated most clearly by the case of Pakistan." Ibid., 185.

19. Wahiduddin [Wahid al-din] Khan, *Indian Muslims: The Need for a Positive Outlook*, tr. Farida Khanam (Delhi: al-Risala Books, 1994), 115–31.

20. Ibid., 27f. and passim.

21. This characterization is reported, for instance, in Sakina Yusuf Khan's interview with Wahid al-din Khan in *The Times of India*, September 3, 2000.

22. Indeed, incidents of lower-caste Hindu conversion to Islam have sometimes sparked communal riots in India. Likewise, the allegation that polygamy and the lack of the practice of birth control would eventually enable Muslims to numerically outstrip the Hindus in India is among the rallying cries of the Hindu nationalists. Cf. Hansen, *The Saffron Wave*, 151, 177ff., 195f.

23. Khan, *Indian Muslims*, 28.

24. Wahiduddin [Wahid al-din] Khan, *Uniform Civil Code: A Critical Study*, tr. Farida Khanam (Delhi: al-Risala Books, 1996). On the Hindu nationalist insis-

tence on a uniform civil code as a measure of true Indianness, cf. Hansen, *The Saffron Wave*, 177, 195.

25. Wahiduddin [Wahid al-din] Khan, *Tabligh Movement* (Delhi: The Islamic Centre, 1986).

26. Barbara Metcalf has insisted, in several of her studies of the Tablighi Jama'at, on this movement's firm refusal to engage with any political issues. See, for instance, Barbara Metcalf, "Meandering Madrasas: Knowledge and Short-term Itinerancy in the Tablighi Jama'at," in *The Transmission of Learning in South Asia*, ed. Crook, 49–61, especially 57f.; idem, "Nationalism, Modernity, and Muslim Identity in India before 1947," in *Nation and Religion*, ed. van der Veer and Lehmann, 129–43. For a contrary view, see Marc Gaborieau, "A Peaceful Jihad? Proselytism as Seen by Ahmadiyya, Tablighi Jama'at and Jama'at-i Islami," unpublished paper; *The Encyclopaedia of Islam*, 10: 38–39, s.v. "Tablighi Djama'at," by Marc Gaborieau.

27. Wahiduddin Khan, *Tabligh Movement*, 67f., especially 68.

28. Ibid., 68; emphasis added.

29. Wahid al-din Khan, *Diary* (Delhi: al-Risala Books, 1995), 165.

30. For a brief biographical sketch, see "Profile of Maulana Wahiduddin Khan," on the official website of his Delhi-based Islamic Centre: *www.alrisala.org* (accessed on March 4, 2001). He was the editor of *al-Jami'a*, the weekly journal of the Jam'iyyat al-'Ulama, from 1967 to 1974 (cf. Khan, *Mewat ka safar*, 7). There is little more than some cursory references to Wahid al-din's life and thought in the available scholarly literature on Indian Islam. See, for example, Christian W. Troll, "Sharing Islamically in the Pluralistic Nation-State of India: The Views of Some Contemporary Indian Muslim Leaders and Thinkers," in *Christian-Muslim Encounters*, ed. Yvonne Yazbeck Haddad and Wadi Zaidan Haddad (Gainesville: University Press of Florida, 1995), 257f.; Hasan, *Legacy of a Divided Nation*, 284, 307, 322f.

31. See Zebiri, *Mahmud Shaltut*, 16–31.

32. Zebiri, however, believes that "there is a degree of correspondence between the reform ideas of al-Maraghi and Shaltut and the aims of the 1961 [Azhar] Reform Law." Ibid., 28.

33. See Akhavi, *Religion and Politics in Iran*, 117–29.

34. For a discussion of Sa'idzadeh's thought, see Mir-Hosseini, *Islam and Gender*, 246–72. On Sorush, see ibid., 217–46. For a sample of some of Sorush's ideas, see Mahmoud Sadri and Ahmad Sadri, eds. and trans., *Reason, Freedom, and Democracy in Islam: Essential Writings of 'Abdolkarim Soroush* (New York: Oxford University Press, 2000).

35. Mir-Hosseini, *Islam and Gender*, 256.

36. Ibid., 257f.

37. After twenty-one months in office, Abdurrahman Wahid was removed by the Indonesian parliament on charges of mismanagement in July 2001. See *The New York Times*, July 24, 2001: A1 and A9.

38. Martin van Bruinessen, "Traditions for the Future: The Reconstruction of Traditionalist Discourse within NU," in Greg Barton and Greg Fealy, eds., *Nahdlatul Ulama, Traditional Islam and Modernity in Indonesia* (Clayton: Monash Asia Institute, 1996), 163–89; quotation is from 169. On the Nahdlutul Ulama,

besides other essays in the same collection, see Andree Feillard, "Traditionalist Islam and the State in Indonesia: The Road to Legitimacy and Renewal," in *Islam in an Era of Nation-States*, ed. Hefner and Horvatich, 129–53; Hefner, *Civil Islam*.

39. Mir-Hosseini, *Islam and Gender*, 248.

40. Ibid., 249.

41. Lindbeck, *The Nature of Doctrine*, 112–38, especially 129.

42. Ibid.,132.

43. Ibid., 132ff.

44. Ibid., 128. For a critique of Lindbeck, see Tanner, *Theories of Culture*, 156ff.

Glossary

adab — Belles lettres, literature; culture and culturally prescribed forms of comportment.

Ahl-i Hadith — "The people [or, partisans] of hadith." The Ahl-i Hadith, who emerged in late-nineteenth-century colonial India, denied the authority of all schools of Sunni law and insisted rather on the exclusive and unmediated authority of the Qur'an and hadith as the sources of all guidance.

Ahmadi — A doctrinal orientation that emerged in late-nineteenth-century India and is defined most notably by the belief of its adherents (the Ahmadis) in the prophethood of the movement's founder, Mirza Ghulam Ahmad (d. 1908). Other Muslims consider the Ahmadis heretical or non-Muslim on account of this belief, which contravenes the Islamic doctrine that Muhammad was the last of God's prophets.

amir — Leader of a group or community.

anjuman — Association or organization.

'Ashura' — The tenth day of Muharram, the first month of the Islamic calendar; the Shi'a (q.v.) commemorate the martyrdom of their third imam (q.v.), Husayn b. 'Ali, on this day.

Barelawi — The doctrinal orientation associated with Ahmad Rida Khan (d. 1921) of Bareilly, a town in Uttar Pradesh in northern India; an adherent of this orientation. The Barelawis lay special emphasis on ritualized forms of devotion to the Prophet as well as to the memory of other holy persons. Their ritual practices, which are often associated with Sufi shrines, are strongly opposed by the "reformist" Deobandis (q.v.).

dar al-'ulum — Institution of Islamic learning; madrasa (q.v.).

dars (pl. durus) — Course of study; lesson.

Deobandi — The doctrinal orientation associated with the madrasa (q.v.) of Deoband, a small town in Uttar Pradesh in northern India; an adherent of this movement. The Deobandi movement, which emerged in late-nineteenth-century colonial India, lays stress on a renewed commitment to hadith (q.v.) and sacred law as the basis of a "reformed" and reinvigorated Islamic identity. The Deobandis define themselves against other Sunni groups in the Indian subcontinent, notably the Barelawis and the Ahl-i Hadith, as well as against the Shi'a (q.v.) and the Ahmadis (q.v.).

din — Faith; religion.

faskh — Dissolution of marriage.

fatwa — A legal opinion issued by a jurisconsult (mufti [q.v.]).

fiqh — Islamic law and jurisprudence.

fitna — Disorder; chaos; the term is also used for the first civil wars in the history of Islam, which permanently divided the Muslim community into hostile factions and later into distinct sects.

fuqaha' (sing. faqih) — Scholars of law (fiqh).

hadith — Traditions attributed to the Prophet Muhammad; regarded by Muslims as second to the Qur'an as a source of religious guidance and law.

Hanafi — A school of Sunni law named after Abu Hanifa (d. 767); an adherent of this school. Most Sunni Muslims in South Asia, including the Deobandis and the Barelawis, belong to this school of law.

Hanbali — A school of Sunni law named after Ahmad b. Hanbal (d. 855); an adherent of this school. Hanbalism is the dominant school of law in Saudi Arabia.

hudud (sing. hadd) — Punishments expressly sanctioned in the Qur'an and the sunna, and (unlike many other punishments) not subject to being mitigated by the ruler or the aggrieved party.

huquq (sing. haqq) — Rights.

huquq Allah — The rights of God, regarded as non-negotiable.

hukm (pl. ahkam) — A legal ruling.

'idda — The "waiting period" following divorce or the death of the husband that must pass before a woman is allowed to remarry.

ijaza — Formal "authorization" to transmit a particular religious text or religious learning in general.

ijtihad — Systematic reflection on the foundational sources of the law to arrive at legal rulings on matters not already or explicitly determined by sacred law.

ikhtilaf — Disagreement among jurists.

'ilm (pl. 'ulum) — Knowledge; religious learning; science(s).

imam — Leader or head of the community; those descendants of 'Ali who are regarded by the Shi'a as their infallible guides; the term is also used for the person leading the ritual prayers.

isnad — Chain of transmission that forms an essential part of any report relating the words or deeds of the Prophet Muhammad (hadith).

Ithna 'ashari ("Twelver") — A sub-division of the Shi'a (q.v.), whose members regard twelve successive descendants of the Prophet Muhammad through his daughter Fatima and her husband, 'Ali, to be their infallible religious guides (imams).

Ja'fari — The school of law of the Ithna 'ashari ("Twelver") sect (q.v.) of the Shi'a; named after the sixth Shi'i imam, Ja'far al-Sadiq (d. 765).

jahiliyya — "The age of ignorance"; designation for the era before the advent of Islam; also used in the twentieth century by certain Islamist thinkers to assert that their coreligionists were living in a new age of unbelief or apostasy.

jama'at/jama'a — Group; association; community.

jihad — "Struggle," including armed struggle against unbelievers.

khilafa — "Deputyship"; the caliphate.

Khilafat al-Rashida — "The rightly guided caliphate"; designates the four caliphs (Abu Bakr, 'Umar b. al-Khattab, 'Uthman b. 'Affan, and 'Ali b. Abi Talib) who immediately succeeded Muhammad as the leaders of the Muslim community (632–61 C.E.). To the Sunnis, they are the most revered of all the Companions (sahaba [q.v.]) of Muhammad; the Shi'a recognize only 'Ali as a legitimate caliph and as their first imam.

madhhab — School of law; in Urdu, sometimes used interchangeably with religion (din [q.v.]).

madrasa — Institution of higher Islamic learning.

mahr — Dower paid or promised to the wife at the time of marriage

Maliki — A school of Sunni law named after Malik b. Anas (d. 795); an adherent of this school.

masjid — Mosque.

mawlawi/mawlana — A term used to designate a religious scholar; *see* 'ulama.

milla — A community as defined by ties of faith.

mufti — A jurisconsult; one who issues legal opinions (fatwas [q.v.]).

mujahidin — Those waging jihad (q.v.).

mujtahid — A practitioner of ijtihad (q.v.).

muqallid — A practitioner of taqlid (q.v.).

mullah — A religious scholar; *see* 'ulama.

Murji'a — A religiopolitical group in early Islam whose adherents insisted on "deferring" to God judgment on those who had committed grave sins; often associated with the doctrine of giving precedence to "faith" over "works."

pandit — Hindu religious scholar.

pir — A Sufi master.

qawm — Nation as defined by ties of ethnicity, shared territory, and language.

qadi — Muslim judge who rules according to the shari'a (q.v.).

qanun — Law as enunciated by the ruler, as distinguished from the discourses of the Muslim jurists (fiqh).

qasba — Small town.

ra'y — "Opinion"; in the early history of Islamic law, it designated a mode of argumentation based on informed personal reasoning. Critics of the Hanafi jurists have often accused them of basing their legal rulings on "mere" personal opinion rather than on the secure authority of foundational religious texts.

sahaba — The Companions of the Prophet Muhammad. For the Sunnis, they are not only the source of all information about the teachings of Muhammad but also the paragons of religious authority that is second only to the Prophet. The Shi'a recognize only some of the Companions as righteous.

Shafi'i — A school of Sunni law, named after Muhammad b. Idris al-Shafi'i (d. 820); an adherent of that school.

shari'a — The totality of Islamic legal and ethical norms; the sacred law of Islam.

shaykh — A religious scholar; a Sufi master.

Shi'a (sing. Shi'i) — Community of Muslims who, unlike the Sunnis, believe that after the death of the Prophet infallible religious guidance must continue in the person of the imams (q.v.), who are divinely designated to lead the community in religious and political matters. There are several subdivisions within the Shi'a, of which the historically most important are the Ithna 'ashariyya (q.v.) and the Isma'iliyya.

Sufi — Muslim mystic.

sunna — The normative example of the Prophet, usually expressed in the form of reports relating his teachings and conduct (hadith [q.v.]).

Sunnis — Those professing adherance to the sunna (q.v.) of the Prophet and to the agreed upon norms and practices of the universal Muslim community. The Sunnis constitute the overwhelming majority of the Muslim people worldwide.

tabligh — The preaching of Islam.

Tablighi Jama'at — A proselytizing movement that emerged in early-twentieth-century India and now has operations worldwide. Those associated with the

Tablighi Jama'at often belong to or have some affinity with the Deobandi orientation.

taqlid — "Investing with authority"; following the legal rulings of earlier scholars, or of the school of law to which one professes adherence.

'ulama (sing. 'alim) — "People of knowledge ('ilm [q.v.])"; religious scholars; those with formal training in the religious sciences, especially but not exclusively in Islamic law and hadith.

umma — The worldwide community of Muslims.

usul al-fiqh — The sources of the law; the principles of the science of jurisprudence and the methodology of legal reasoning.

Wahhabi — An adherent of the puritanical teachings of Muhammad ibn 'Abd al-Wahhab (d. 1791); Wahhabism is the official ideology of the Kingdom of Saudi Arabia.

waqf (pl. awqaf) — Pious endowments

wali — "Friend [of God]"; saint

zakat — Islamic alms-tax paid annually on one's accumulated wealth; one of the five "pillars" of the faith.

Bibliography

'Abd al-Sattar. *Ta'rikh-i madrasa-i 'aliya*. 2 vols. Dhaka: Research and Publications, Madrasa-i 'aliya, 1959.

'Abd al-Shakur. *Tadhkirat al-zafar*. Faisalabad: Matbu'at-i 'ilmi, 1977.

Abou El Fadl, Khaled. "Islamic Law and Muslim Minorities: The Juristic Discourse on Muslim Minorities from the Second/Eighth to the Eleventh/Seventeenth Centuries." *Islamic Law and Society* 1-2 (1994): 141–87.

Abou Zahab, Mariam. "The Regional Dimension of Sectarian Conflicts in Pakistan." Unpublished paper.

Abu Ghudda, 'Abd al-Fattah. *Tarajim sitta min fuqaha al-'alam al-islami fi'l-qarn al-rabi' 'ashar wa atharuhum al-fiqhiyya*. Beirut: Maktab al-matbu'at al-Islamiyya, 1997.

Adam, William. *Reports on the State of Education in Bengal (1835 and 1838)*. Ed. A. Basu. 3 vols. Calcutta: University of Calcutta Press, 1941.

Adams, Charles J. "Abu'l-A'la Mawdudi's *Tafhim al-Qur'an*." In *Approaches to the History of the Interpretation of the Qur'an*, ed. Andrew Rippin, 307–23. Oxford: Clarendon Press, 1988.

———. "Mawdudi and the Islamic State." In *Voices of Resurgent Islam*, ed. John L. Esposito, 99–133. New York: Oxford University Press, 1983.

Addleton, Jonathan. *Undermining the Centre: The Gulf Migration and Pakistan*. Karachi: Oxford University Press, 1992.

Ahmad, Aziz. *Islamic Modernism in India and Pakistan, 1857–1964*. London: Oxford University Press, 1967.

Ahmad, Muhammad Bashir. *The Administration of Justice in Medieval India*. Karachi: The Manager of Publications, 1951.

Ahmad, Mumtaz. "Islamic Fundamentalism in South Asia: The Jamaat-i-Islami and the Tablighi Jamaat of South Asia." In *Fundamentalisms Observed*, ed. Martin Marty and R. Scott Appleby, 457–530. Chicago: University of Chicago Press, 1991.

Ahmad, Nadhr. *Ja'iza-i madaris-i 'arabiyya-i Maghribi Pakistan*. Lahore: Muslim Academy, 1972.

Ahmed, K. N. *The Muslim Law of Divorce*. New Delhi: Kitab Bhavan, 1978.

Ahmed, Munir D. "The Shi'is of Pakistan." In *Shi'ism, Resistance, and Revolution*, ed. M. Kramer, 275–87. Boulder: Westview Press, 1987.

Akhavi, Shahrough. "The Dialectic in Contemporary Egyptian Social Thought: The Scripturalist and Modernist Discourses of Sayyid Qutb and Hasan Hanafi." *International Journal of Middle East Studies* 29 (1997): 377–401.

———. *Religion and Politics in Contemporary Iran: Clergy-State Relations in the Pahlavi Period*. Albany: State University of New York Press, 1980.

Alam, Muzaffar. *The Crisis of Empire in Mughal North India: Awadh and the Punjab, 1707–48*. Delhi: Oxford University Press, 1986.

———. "Shari'a and Governance in the Indo-Islamic Context." In *Beyond Turk and Hindu: Rethinking Religious Identities in Islamicate South Asia*, ed. David

Gilmartin and Bruce B. Lawrence, 216–45. Gainesville: University Press of Florida, 2000.

Algar, Hamid, ed. and trans. *Islam and Revolution: Writings and Declarations of Imam Khomeini*. Berkeley: Mizan Press, 1981.

'Allama Shahid Sayyid 'Arif Husayn al-Husayni: Az wiladat ta shahadat. Qumm: Sazman-i tablighat-i Islami, 1369 A.H.

Anderson, Benedict. *Imagined Communities: Reflections on the Origin and Spread of Nationalism*. London: Verso, 1991.

Anderson, Michael R. "Classifications and Coercions: Themes in South Asian Legal Studies in the 1980s." *South Asia Research* 10/2 (1990): 158–77.

———. "Islamic Law and the Colonial Encounter in British India." In *Institutions and Ideologies: A SOAS South Asia Reader*, ed. David Arnold and Peter Robb, 165–85. Richmond: Curzon Press, 1993.

Ansari, Muhammad Rida. *Bani-i Dars-i Nizami*. Lucknow: Nami Press, 1973.

Anwar, Mufti Muhammad, ed. *Khayr al-fatawa*. 3 vols. to date. Multan: Maktabat al-Khayr, 1987–93.

Arjomand, Said Amir. *The Shadow of God and the Hidden Imam: Religion, Political Order, and Societal Change in Shi'ite Iran from the Beginning to 1890*. Chicago: University of Chicago Press, 1984.

———. *The Turban for the Crown: The Islamic Revolution in Iran*. New York: Oxford University Press, 1988.

Asad, Talal. *Genealogies of Religion: Discipline and Reasons of Power in Christianity and Islam*. Baltimore: Johns Hopkins University Press, 1993.

———. *The Idea of an Anthropology of Islam*. Washington, D.C.: Center for Contemporary Arab Studies, Georgetown University, 1986.

———. "Religion, Nation-State, Secularism." In *Nation and Religion*, ed. van der Veer and Lehmann, 178–96.

'Atiyya, Muhy al-din, Salah al-din Hafani, and Muhammad Khayr Ramadan Yusuf. *Dalil mu'allafat al-hadith al-sharif al-matbu'a al-qadima wa'l-haditha*. 2 vols. Beirut: Dar Ibn Hazm, 1995.

al-Azmeh, Aziz. *Islams and Modernities*. 2d ed. London: Verso, 1996.

al-Baghdadi, al-Khatib. *Ta'rikh Baghdad*. 14 vols. Beirut: Dar al-kutub al-'ilmiyya, 1997.

Balakoti, Muhammad Ilyas. *Amir-i 'azimat: Hadrat Mawlana Haqq Nawaz Jhangawi*. Jhang: Jami'a 'Uthmaniyya, [1990].

Banuri, Mawlana Muhammad Yusuf. "Dars-i Nizami: Chand tawajjuh-talab pahlu." *Jaridat al-ashraf*, March-April 1994: 26–52.

———. *Ma'arif al-sunan*. 6 vols. Karachi: H. M. Sa'id Company, 1986–89.

Barraclough, Steven. "Al-Azhar: Between the Government and the Islamists." *Middle East Journal* 52/2 (1998): 236–49.

Bayly, C. A. *Empire and Information: Intelligence Gathering and Social Communication in India, 1780–1870*. Cambridge: Cambridge University Press, 1996.

Bell, Catherine. " 'A Precious Raft to Save the World': The Interaction of Scriptural Traditions and Printing in a Chinese Morality Book." *Late Imperial China* 17/1 (1996): 158–200.

———. *Ritual: Perspectives and Dimensions*. New York: Oxford University Press, 1997.

Benton, Laura. "Colonial Law and Cultural Difference: Jurisdictional Politics and the Formation of the Colonial State." *Comparative Studies in Society and History* 41/3 (1999): 563–88.

Berkey, Jonathan P. "Tradition, Innovation and the Social Construction of Knowledge in the Medieval Islamic Near East." *Past and Present* 146 (1995): 38–65.

———. *The Transmission of Knowledge in Medieval Cairo: A Social History of Islamic Education*. Princeton: Princeton University Press, 1992.

Bhatia, M. L. *Administrative History of Medieval India: A Study of Muslim Jurisprudence under Aurangzeb*. New Delhi: Radha Publications, 1992.

Bhatti, Muhammad Ishaq. *Barr-i saghir Pak wa Hind main 'ilm-i fiqh*. Lahore: Idara-i thaqafat-i Islamiyya, 1973.

Binder, Leonard. *Religion and Politics in Pakistan*. Berkeley: University of California Press, 1961.

Blank, Jonah. *Mullahs on the Mainframe: Islam and Modernity among the Daudi Bohras*. Chicago: University of Chicago Press, 2001.

Botiveau, Bernard. "Contemporary Reinterpretations of Islamic Law: The Case of Egypt." In *Islam and Public Law: Classical and Contemporary Studies*, ed. C. Mallat, 261–77. London: Graham and Trotman, 1993.

Boullata, Issa J. *Trends and Issues in Contemporary Arab Thought*. Albany: State University of New York Press, 1990.

Bowen, Donna Lee. "Abortion, Islam, and the 1994 Cairo Population Conference." *International Journal of Middle East Studies* 29 (1997): 161–84.

Bowen, John. *Muslims through Discourse: Religion and Ritual in Gayo Society*. Princeton: Princeton University Press, 1993.

Brass, Paul R. *Language, Religion, and Politics in North India*. Cambridge: Cambridge University Press, 1974.

Brockelmann, Carl. *Geschichte der arabischen Literatur*. 2d ed. 2 vols. Leiden: E. J. Brill, 1943–49.

Brown, Daniel. *Rethinking Tradition in Modern Islamic Thought*. Cambridge: Cambridge University Press, 1996.

Brown, Judith M. *Gandhi and Civil Disobedience: The Mahatma in Indian Politics, 1928–34*. Cambridge: Cambridge University Press, 1977.

Brown, Nathan J. "Shari'a and State in the Modern Middle East." *International Journal of Middle East Studies* 29/3 (1997): 359–76.

Bruinessen, Martin van. "Traditions for the Future: The Reconstruction of Traditionalist Discourse within NU." In *Nahdlatul Ulama, Traditional Islam and Modernity in Indonesia*, ed. Greg Barton and Greg Fealy, 163–89. Clayton: Monash Asia Institute, 1996.

Brunner, Rainer, and Werner Ende, eds. *The Twelver Shia in Modern Times: Religious Culture and Political History*. Leiden: Brill, 2001.

Bulliet, Richard. *The Patricians of Nishapur*. Cambridge: Harvard University Press, 1972.

Burgat, Francois, and William Dowell. *The Islamic Movement in North Africa*. 2d ed. Austin: Center for Middle Eastern Studies, University of Texas, 1997.

Cannon, Garland, ed. *The Letters of Sir William Jones*. 2 vols. Oxford: Clarendon Press, 1970.

Carroll, Lucy. "The Muslim Family Laws Ordinance, 1961: Provisions and Procedures—A Reference Paper for Current Research." *Contributions to Indian Sociology*, n.s. 13 (1979): 117–43.

———. "Nizam-i-Islam: Processes and Conflicts in Pakistan's Programme of Islamisation, with Special Reference to the Position of Women." *Journal of Commonwealth and Comparative Politics* 20 (1982): 57–95.

———. "Orphaned Grandchildren in Islamic Law of Succession: Reform and Islamization in Pakistan." *Islamic Law and Society* 5/3 (1998): 409–47.

———. "Qur'an 2.229: 'A Charter Granted to the Wife'? Judicial *Khul'* in Pakistan." *Islamic Law and Society* 3/1 (1996): 91–126.

Casanova, José. *Public Religions in the Modern World*. Chicago: University of Chicago Press, 1994.

Castells, Manuel. *The Information Age: Economy, Society and Culture*. 3 vols. Oxford: Blackwell Publishers, 1996–98.

Chamberlain, Michael. *Knowledge and Social Practice in Medieval Damascus, 1190–1350*. Cambridge: Cambridge University Press, 1994.

Chatterjee, Partha. "History and the Nationalization of Hinduism." *Social Research* 59 (1992): 111–49.

Chelkowski, Peter J., ed. *Ta'ziyeh: Ritual and Drama in Iran*. New York: New York University Press, 1979.

Cohn, Bernard S. *Colonialism and Its Forms of Knowledge: The British in India*. Princeton: Princeton University Press, 1996.

Cole, Juan R. I. *Roots of North Indian Shi'ism in Iran and Iraq: Religion and State in Awadh, 1722–1859*. Berkeley: University of California Press, 1988.

Cook, Michael. *Commanding Right and Forbidding Wrong in Islamic Thought*. Cambridge: Cambridge University Press, 2000.

Cooperson, Michael. *Classical Arabic Biography: The Heirs of the Prophets in the Age of al-Ma'mun*. Cambridge: Cambridge University Press, 2000.

Copland, Ian. *The Princes of India and the Endgame of Empire, 1917–1947*. Cambridge: Cambridge University Press, 1997.

Coulson, N. J. *A History of Islamic Law*. Edinburgh: Edinburgh University Press, 1964.

———. "Reform of Family Law in Pakistan." *Studia Islamica* 7 (1957): 135–55.

Crecelius, Daniel. "Non-Ideological Responses of the Egyptian 'Ulama' to Modernization." In *Scholars, Saints, and Sufis*, ed. Keddie, 167–209.

Crook, Nigel, ed. *The Transmission of Learning in South Asia*. Delhi: Oxford University Press, 1996.

Darling, Malcolm. *The Punjab Peasant in Prosperity and Debt*. London: Oxford University Press, 1925.

Das, S. K. *Sahibs and Munshis: An Account of the College of Fort William*. Calcutta: Orion Publications, 1978.

Derrett, J.D.M. *Religion, Law and the State in India*. New York: The Free Press, 1968.

Dhofier, Zamakhsyari. *The Pesantren Tradition: The Role of the Kyai in the Maintenance of Traditional Islam in Java*. Program for Southeast Asian Studies Monograph Series. Tempe: Arizona State University, 1999.

Donner, Fred M. *Narratives of Islamic Origins: The Beginnings of Islamic Historical Writing*. Princeton: Darwin Press, 1998.

Eccel, A. Chris. *Egypt, Islam and Social Change: Al-Azhar in Conflict and Accommodation*. Berlin: Klaus Schwarz Verlag, 1984.

Edwards, David B. "Learning from the Swat Pathans: Political Leadership in Afghanistan, 1978–97." *American Ethnologist* 25/4 (1998): 712–28.

Eickelman, Dale F. "Islam and the Languages of Modernity." *Daedalus* 129/1 (2000): 119–35.

———. "Islamic Religious Commentary and Lesson Circles: Is There a Copernican Revolution?" In *Commentaries—Kommentare*, ed. Glenn W. Most. Gottingen: Vandenhoeck & Ruprecht, 1999: 121–46.

———. *Knowledge and Power in Morocco: The Education of a Twentieth-Century Notable*. Princeton: Princeton University Press, 1985.

———. "Mass Higher Education and the Religious Imagination in Contemporary Arab Societies." *American Ethnologist* 19/4 (1992): 1–13.

Eickelman, Dale F., and Jon W. Anderson, eds. *New Media in the Muslim World: The Emerging Public Sphere*. Bloomington: Indiana University Press, 1999.

Eickelman, Dale F., and James Piscatori. *Muslim Politics*. Princeton: Princeton University Press, 1996.

Eisenstein, Elizabeth. *The Printing Press as an Agent of Change: Communications and Cultural Transformation in Early-Modern Europe*. 2 vols. Cambridge: Cambridge University Press, 1979.

El-Nahal, Galai. *See* Nahal, Galal El-.

Enayat, Hamid. *Modern Islamic Political Thought*. Austin: University of Texas Press, 1982.

The Encyclopaedia of Islam. 2d ed. Leiden: E. J. Brill, 1960–.

Ende, Werner. "Sunni Polemical Writings on the Shi'a and the Iranian Revolution." In *The Iranian Revolution and the Muslim World*, ed. D. Menashri, 219–32. Boulder: The Westview Press, 1990.

Engineer, Asghar Ali, ed. *The Shah Bano Controversy*. Bombay: Orient Longman, 1987.

Esposito, John L., ed. *The Iranian Revolution: Its Global Impact*. Miami: Florida International University Press, 1990.

———. *The Oxford Encyclopedia of the Modern Islamic World*. 4 vols. New York: Oxford University Press, 1995.

Esposito, John L., and John O. Voll. *Makers of Contemporary Islam*. New York: Oxford University Press, 2001.

Euben, Roxanne L. *Enemy in the Mirror: Islamic Fundamentalism and the Limits of Modern Rationalism*. Princeton: Princeton University Press, 1999.

Ewing, Katherine Pratt. *Arguing Sainthood: Modernity, Psychoanalysis, and Islam*. Durham, N.C.: Duke University Press, 1997.

al-Fallah, Mufti Muhammad 'Abduh. "Tahrik-i-tanzim al-madaris ahl-i hadith." *Majallat al-Jami'a al-Salafiyya* 1/2 (March-May, 1988): 10–17.

Fandy, Mamoun. "CyberResistance: Saudi Opposition between Globalization and Localization." *Comparative Studies in Society and History* 41 (1999): 124–47.

Fandy, Mamoun. *Saudi Arabia and the Politics of Dissent*. New York: St. Martin's Press, 1999.

Farani, M. *The Shariat Application Laws (1935–1968)*. Lahore: Pakistan Legal Publications, 1968.

Faruqi, Ziya al-Rahman. *Islam main sahaba-i kiram ki 'a'ini haythiyyat*. Faisalabad: Idara-yi isha'at al-ma'arif, 1993.

———. *Sipah-i Sahaba ka nasb al-'ayn awr taqade*. Faisalabad: Idara-yi isha'at al-ma'arif, 1994.

———. *Sipah-i Sahaba kiya hai, kiya chahati hai?* n.p., n.d.

———. *What is Islam?* Faisalabad: Asha'at ul Ma'arif, 1995.

Faruqi, Ziya-ul-Hasan. *The Deoband School and the Demand for Pakistan*. Bombay: Asia Publishing House, 1963.

Fatawa Dar al-'Ulum Deoband. See 'Uthmani, Mufti 'Aziz al-Rahman.

al-Fatawa al-Hindiyya fi madhhab al-imam al-a'zam Abi Hanifa al-Nu'man. 6 vols. Beirut: Dar al-ma'rifa, 1393 A.H. (reprint of the Bulaq edition.: al-Matba'a al-amiriyya, 1310 A.H.).

Fatawa Qadi-khan, printed on the margins of *Al-Fatawa al-Hindiyya fi madhhab al-imam al-a'zam Abi Hanifa al-Nu'man*. 6 vols. Beirut: Dar al-ma'rifa, 1393 A.H. (reprint of the Bulaq edition: al-Matba'a al-amiriyya, 1310 A.H.).

Feillard, Andree. "Traditionalist Islam and the State in Indonesia: The Road to Legitimacy and Renewal." In *Islam in an Era of Nation-States*, ed. Hefner and Horvatich, 129–53.

Fischer, Michael M. J. *Iran: From Religious Dispute to Revolution*. Cambridge: Harvard University Press, 1980.

Fischer, Michael M. J., and Mehdi Abedi. *Debating Muslims: Cultural Dialogues in Postmodernity and Tradition*. Madison: University of Wisconsin Press, 1990.

Freitag, Sandria. *Collective Action and Community: Public Arenas and the Emergence of Communalism in North India*. Berkeley: University of California Press, 1989.

Friedmann, Yohanan. "The Attitude of the Jam'iyyat-i 'Ulama'-i Hind to the Indian National Movement and the Establishment of Pakistan." *Asian and African Studies* 7 (1971): 157–80.

———. "The Jam'iyyat al-'Ulama'-i Hind in the Wake of Partition." *Asian and African Studies* 11 (1976): 181–211.

———. *Prophecy Continuous: Aspects of Ahmadi Religious Thought and Its Medieval Background*. Berkeley: University of California Press, 1989.

———. *Shaykh Ahmad Sirhindi: An Outline of His Thought and a Study of His Image in the Eyes of Posterity*. Montreal: McGill University Press, 1971.

Fyzee, Asaf A. A. *Outlines of Muhammadan Law*. London: Oxford University Press, 1955.

Gaborieau, Marc. "Mission en Inde (5 février–10 mars 1994)." In *La transmission du savoir dans le monde musulman périphérique*, lettre d'information no. 14 (June 1994): 113–27.

———. "A Peaceful Jihad? Proselytism as Seen by Ahmadiyya, Tablighi Jama'at and Jama'at-i Islami." Unpublished paper.

Gaffney, Patrick D. *The Prophet's Pulpit: Islamic Preaching in Contemporary Egypt*. Berkeley: University of California Press, 1994.

Gangohi, Rashid Ahmad. *Al-Kawkab al-durri 'ala Jami' al-Tirmidhi*. Compiled by Muhammad Yahya Kandahlawi; with glosses by Muhammad Zakariyya Kandahlawi. 1st ed., 2 vols., Saharanpur: al-Maktaba al-Yahyawiyya, 1933–35; 2d ed., 3 vols., Karachi: Idarat al-Qur'an wa'l-'ulum al-Islamiyya, 1987.

———. *Lami' al-darari 'ala jami' al-Bukhari*. 2 vols. Saharanpur: al-Maktaba al-Yahyawiyya, Mazahir al-'ulum, Saharanpur, 1959. New ed., 10 vols. Mecca: al-Maktaba al-Imdadiyya, 1395–98 A.H.

Gardner, Daniel K. "Confucian Commentary and Chinese Intellectual History." *Journal of Asian Studies* 57/2 (1998): 397–422.

Gerber, Haim. *Islamic Law and Culture, 1600–1840*. Leiden: Brill, 1999.

Gesink, Indira Falk. "Beyond Modernisms: Opposition and Negotiation in the Azhar Reform Debate in Egypt, 1870–1911." Ph.D. dissertation, Washington University, St. Louis, Missouri, 2000.

Gibbon, Edward. *The History of the Decline and Fall of the Roman Empire*. Ed. David Womersley. 3 vols. London: Allen Lane, 1994.

Giddens, Anthony. *The Consequences of Modernity*. Stanford: Stanford University Press, 1990.

Gilani, Manazir Ahsan. *Ihata-i dar al-'ulum main bitai huwe din*. Ed. I'jaz Ahmad A'zami. Deoband: Maktaba-i Tayyiba, n.d.

———. *Pak wa Hind main musalmanon ka nizam-i ta'lim wa tarbiyyat*. 2 vols. Lahore: Maktaba-i Rahmaniyya, n.d.

Gilmartin, David. "Customary Law and Shari'at in British Punjab." In *Shari'at and Ambiguity in South Asian Islam*, ed. Katherine P. Ewing, 43–62. Berkeley: University of California Press, 1988.

———. *Empire and Islam: Punjab and the Making of Pakistan*. Berkeley: University of California Press, 1988.

———. "A Magnificent Gift: Muslim Nationalism and the Election Process in Colonial Punjab." *Comparative Studies in Society and History* 40/2 (1998): 415–36.

Gold, Daniel. "Organized Hinduisms: From Vedic Truth to Hindu Nation." In *Fundamentalisms Observed*, ed. Martin E. Marty and R. Scott Appleby, 531–93. Chicago: University of Chicago Press, 1991.

Gonzalez-Quijano, Yves. "Crise du livre ou nouvelles pratiques culturelles? Editeurs et edition dans l'Egypte contemporaine." In *Bulletin du CEDEJ* 25 (1989): 91–109.

Government of Pakistan, Ministry of Education. *Pakistan ke dini madaris ke 'ulama-i kiram ki directory, 1986*. Islamabad: Islamic Education Research Cell, [1987].

Government of Pakistan. Population Census Organization. *1981 District Census Report of Jhang*. Islamabad: Statistics Division, 1984.

———. *1998 District Census Report of Jhang*. Islamabad: Statistics Division, 2000. For other governmental documents, see under Report.

Graham, William A. "Traditionalism in Islam: An Essay in Interpretation." *Journal of Interdisciplinary History* 23/3 (1993): 495–522.

Grandin, Nicole, and Marc Gaborieau, eds. *Madrasa: La transmission du savoir dans le monde musulman*. Paris: Editions Arguments, 1997.

Grewal, J. S. *In the By-Lanes of History: Some Persian Documents from a Punjab Town*. Simla: Indian Institute of Advanced Study, 1975.

———. "The Qazi in the Pargana." In *Studies in Local and Regional History*, ed. J. S. Grewal, 1–36. Amritsar: Guru Nanak University, 1974.

Griffin, L., and C. F. Massy. *Chiefs and Families of Note in the Punjab*. 2 vols. Lahore: Government Printing, Punjab, 1940.

Grunebaum, G. E. von. "Fall and Rise of Islam: A Self-View." In *Modern Islam: The Search for Cultural Identity*, 244–57. New York, 1964.

Gutas, Dimitri. "Aspects of Literary Form and Genre in Arabic Logical Works." In *Glosses and Commentaries on Aristotelian Logical Texts: The Syriac, Arabic and Medieval Latin Traditions*, ed. Charles Burnett, 28–76. London: The Warburg Institute, 1993.

Haeri, Shahla. *Law of Desire: Temporary Marriage in Shi'i Iran*. Syracuse: Syracuse University Press, 1989.

Hallaq, Wael B. *Authority, Continuity, and Change in Islamic Law*. Cambridge: Cambridge University Press, 2001.

———. "From Fatwas to Furu': Growth and Change in Islamic Substantive Law." *Islamic Law and Society* 1 (1994): 17–56.

———. *A History of Islamic Legal Theories: An Introduction to Sunni Usul al-Fiqh*. Cambridge: Cambridge University Press, 1997.

———. *Law and Legal Theory in Classical and Medieval Islam*. London: Variorum, 1995.

———. "Model Shurut Works and the Dialectic of Doctrine and Practice." *Islamic Law and Society* 2/2 (1995): 109–34.

———. "Notes on the Term Qarina in Islamic Legal Discourse." *Journal of the American Oriental Society* 108 (1988): 475–80. Reprinted in *Law and Legal Theory*, by Wael B. Hallaq.

———. "Was the Gate of Ijtihad Closed?" *International Journal of Middle East Studies* 16 (1984): 3–41. Reprinted in *Law and Legal Theory*, by Wael B. Hallaq.

Hansen, Thomas Blom. "Predicaments of Secularism: Muslim Identities and Politics in Mumbai." *Journal of the Royal Anthropological Institute*, n. s. 6 (2000): 255–72.

———. *The Saffron Wave: Democracy and Hindu Nationalism in Modern India*. Princeton: Princeton University Press, 1999.

al-Haqq. Special issue on Dar al-'Ulum Haqqaniyya, Akora Khattak, Peshawar. 32/2 (November 1996).

———. Special issue on the Taliban. 31/12 (September 1996).

al-Haqq, Sami'. *Iqtidar ke iwanon main shari'at bill ka ma'rika*. Akora Khattak: Mu'tamar al-musannifin, 1991.

———. *Islam awr 'asr-i hadir*. 2d ed. Akora Khattak: Mu'tamar al-musannifin, 1409 A.H.

Haqqani, 'Abd al-Qayyum. *Khutbat-i Haqqani*. Akora Khattak: Mu'tamar al-musannifin, 1988.

Hardy, Peter. *The Muslims of British India*. Cambridge: Cambridge University Press, 1972.

————. *Partners in Freedom—and True Muslims: The Political Thought of Some Muslim Scholars in British India 1912–1947.* Lund: Scandinavian Institute of Asian Studies, 1971.

Harrison, Peter. *"Religion" and the Religions in the English Enlightenment.* Cambridge: Cambridge University Press, 1990.

Hasan, Mushirul. *Legacy of a Divided Nation: India's Muslims since Independence.* Boulder: Westview Press, 1997.

Hasan, Zoya. *Quest for Power: Oppositional Movements and Post-Congress Politics in Uttar Pradesh.* Delhi: Oxford University Press, 1998.

al-Hasani, 'Abd al-Hayy. *Al-Thaqafa al-Islamiyya fi'l-Hind.* 2d edition. Damascus: Majma' al-lugha al-'Arabiyya bi-Dimashq, 1983.

al-Hasani, Muhammad. *Rudad-i chaman: Nadwat al-'ulama key pachchasi sala jashn-i ta'limi ki mufassal rudad.* Lucknow, n.p., 1976.

al-Hasani, Sayyid Muhammad. *Sirat-i Mawlana Sayyid Muhammad 'Ali Mongiri, bani-yi nadwat al-'ulama.* Lucknow: Maktabat Dar al-'Ulum Nadwat al-'Ulama, 1964.

Hasani, Sayyid Muhammad Thani. *Sawanih hadrat mawlana Muhammad Yusuf Kandahlawi.* Lucknow: Maktaba-yi Islam, 1967.

al-Hawali, Safar ibn 'Abd al-Rahman. *Haqa'iq hawl azmat al-khalij.* Mecca: Dar al-Makka al-mukarrama, 1991.

————. *Zahirat al-irja fi'l-fikr al-Islami.* 2 vols. Cairo: Maktabat al-tayyib, 1996.

Hefner, Robert W., *Civil Islam: Muslims and Democratization in Indonesia.* Princeton: Princeton University Press, 2000.

Hefner, Robert W., and Patricia Horvatich, eds. *Islam in an Era of Nation-States: Politics and Religious Renewal in Muslim Southeast Asia.* Honolulu: University of Hawaii Press, 1997.

Henderson, John B. *Scripture, Canon, and Commentary: A Comparison of Confucian and Western Exegesis.* Princeton: Princeton University Press, 1991.

Heyworth-Dunne, J. *An Introduction to the History of Education in Modern Egypt.* London: Luzac, 1938.

Hirschkind, Charles. "Technologies of Islamic Piety: Cassette-Sermons and the Ethics of Listening." Ph.D. dissertation, Johns Hopkins University, 1999.

Hobsbawm, Eric, and Terence Ranger, eds. *The Invention of Tradition.* Cambridge: Cambridge University Press, 1983.

Hodgson, Marshall G. S. *The Venture of Islam.* 3 vols. Chicago: University of Chicago Press, 1974.

Hollister, J. N. *The Shi'a of India.* London: Luzac, 1953.

Holmes, Stephen. *The Anatomy of Antiliberalism.* Cambridge: Harvard University Press, 1993.

Horton, John, and Susan Mendus, eds. *After MacIntyre: Critical Perspectives on the Work of Alasdair MacIntyre.* Notre Dame: University of Notre Dame Press, 1994.

Hourani, Albert. *Arabic Thought in the Liberal Age, 1798–1939.* Oxford: Oxford University Press, 1983.

Hussain, Aftab. *Status of Women in Islam.* Lahore: Law Publishing Company, 1987.

Hussain, Fayyaz. "An Ethnographic Study of Jamia Ashrafia, a Religious School at Lahore, with Special Reference on Socio-Practical Relevance of Its Objectives." M.S. thesis, Quaid-i-Azam University, Islamabad, 1994.

Ibn ʿAbidin, Muhammad Amin. *Nashr al-ʿurf fi bina baʿd al-ahkam ʿala'l-ʿurf.* In *Rasaʾil,* Damascus: Matbaʿat al-maʿarif, 1301 A.H.

———. *Sharh al-manzuma al-musammat bi-ʿuqud rasm al-mufti.* In *Rasaʾil,* Damascus: Matbaʿat al-maʿarif, 1301 A.H.

Ibn Hajar. *Fath al-bari.* Cairo, n.p., 1319–20 A.H.

Ibn Khaldun. *The Muqaddimah: An Introduction to History.* Tr. F. Rosenthal. 3 vols. New York: Pantheon Books, 1958.

Ibn Taymiyya. *Iqtida al-sirat al-mustaqim mukhalifat ashab al-jahim.* Ed. Muhammad Hamid al-Fiqi, Lahore: al-Maktaba al-salafiyya, 1978. Also see Memon, Muhammad Umar.

Ibrahimy, M.S.A. *Reports on Islamic Education and Madrasah Education in Bengal (1861–1977).* 5 vols. Dhaka: Islamic Foundation Bangladesh, 1987.

Idarat al-taʿlim waʾl-tasnif waʾl-taʾlif. *Jamiʿat al-ʿUlum al-Islamiyya.* Zargari, Kohat: Jamiʿat al-ʿUlum al-Islamiyya, [1990?].

ʿInayat Allah. *ʿUlama-i Firangi mahall.* Lucknow: Nizami Press, 1988.

Iqbal, Muhammad. *The Reconstruction of Religious Thought in Islam.* London: Oxford University Press, 1934.

———. *Speeches, Writings and Statements of Iqbal.* Ed. Latif Ahmed Sherwani. Lahore: Iqbal Academy, 1977.

al-Isfahani, Abu Nuʿaym. *Hilyat al-awliyaʾ wa tabaqat al-asfiyaʾ.* 12 vols. Beirut: Dar al-kutub al-ʿilmiyya, 1997.

Ishaq, Muhammad. *India's Contribution to the Study of Hadith Literature.* Dacca: University of Dacca, 1955.

al-Jabri, Mohammed ʿAbed [Muhammad ʿAbid al-Jabiri]. *Arab-Islamic Philosophy: A Contemporary Critique.* Tr. from the French by Aziz Abbassi. Austin: University of Texas Press, 1999.

Jackson, Sherman A. *Islamic Law and the State: The Constitutional Jurisprudence of Shihab al-Din al-Qarafi.* Leiden: E. J. Brill, 1996.

Jalal, Ayesha. *Self and Sovereignty: Individual and Community in South Asian Islam since 1850.* London: Routledge, 2000.

Jallundhari, Rashid Ahmad. *Bartanawi hind main musulmanon ka nizam-i taʿlim: Aik naqidana jaʾiza.* Vol. 1, *Dar al-ʿulum Deoband.* Islamabad: National Book Foundation, 1989.

Jamiʿa taʿlim al-Islam, Mamun Kanjan . . . : taʾsisuha, manahijuha, asalib al-tadris fiha. Mamun Kanjan, Faysalabad: Jamiʿa Taʿlim al-Islam, n.d.

Jansen, Johannes J. G. *The Dual Nature of Islamic Fundamentalism.* Ithaca: Cornell University Press, 1997.

Jennings, R. C. "Kadi, Court, and Legal Procedure in Seventeenth-Century Ottoman Kayseri." *Studia Islamica* 48 (1978): 136–62.

———. "Limitations on the Judicial Powers of the Kadi in Seventeenth-Century Ottoman Kayseri." *Studia Islamica* 50 (1979): 151–84.

Jhangawi, Haqq Nawaz. *Mawlana Haqq Nawaz Jhangawi ki pandara taʾrikh-saz taqrirain.* Lahore: Idara-yi nashriyyat-i Islam, 1991.

Johansen, Baber. *Contingency in a Sacred Law: Legal and Ethical Norms in the Muslim Fiqh*. Leiden: Brill, 1999.

Juergensmeyer, Mark. *The New Cold War? Religious Nationalism Confronts the Secular State*. Berkeley: University of California Press, 1993.

———. *Terror in the Mind of God: The Global Rise of Religious Violence*. Berkeley: University of California Press, 2000.

Kashmiri, Anwar Shah. *Fayd al-bari 'ala Sahih al-Bukhari*. Compiled by Badr-i 'Alam Mirathi. Lahore: al-Matba'a al-Islamiyya al-Sa'udiyya, 1978.

Kaur, Kuldip. *Madrasa Education in India: A Study of Its Past and Present*. Chandigarh: Centre for Research in Rural and Industrial Development, 1990.

Kechichian, Joseph A. "The Role of the Ulama in the Politics of an Islamic State: The Case of Saudi Arabia." *International Journal of Middle East Studies* 18 (1986): 53–71.

Keddie, Nikki R. *Iran and the Muslim World: Resistance and Revolution*. New York: New York University Press, 1995.

———, ed. *Scholars, Saints, and Sufis: Muslim Religious Institutions in the Middle East since 1500*. Berkeley: University of California Press, 1972.

Kelly, Paul. "MacIntyre's Critique of Utilitarianism." In *After MacIntyre*, ed. Horton and Mendus, 127–45.

Kennedy, Charles. "Repugnancy to Islam—Who Decides?" *International and Comparative Law Quarterly* 41 (October 1992): 769–88.

Kepel, Gilles. *Jihad: Expansion et declin de l'Islamisme*. Paris: Gallimard, 2000.

———. *Muslim Extremism in Egypt: The Prophet and the Pharaoh*. Tr. John Rothschild. Berkeley: University of California Press, 1986.

Kerr, Malcolm. *Islamic Reform: The Political and Legal Theories of Muhammad Abduh and Rashid Rida*. Berkeley: University of California Press, 1966.

Khadduri, Majid. *The Islamic Conception of Justice*. Baltimore: Johns Hopkins University Press, 1984.

Khafaji, Muhammad 'Abd al-Mun'im. *Al-Azhar fi alf 'am*. 3 vols. Cairo: Maktabat al-kulliyyat al-Azhariyya, 1987.

Khalid, Adeeb. *The Politics of Muslim Cultural Reform: Jadidism in Central Asia*. Berkeley: University of California Press, 1998.

———. Printing, Publishing, and Reform in Tsarist Central Asia. *International Journal of Middle East Studies* 26 (1994): 187–200.

Khalidi, Tarif. *Arabic Historical Thought in the Classical Period*. Cambridge: Cambridge University Press, 1994.

Khalifa, Hajji. *Kashf al-zunun 'an asami al-kutub wa'l-funun*. 7 vols. Ed. G. Fluegel. Leipzig: Oriental Translation Fund, 1835.

Khan, Qamar al-din, et al. *Hindustan ki dini darsgahen: kull Hind survey*. Delhi: Hamdard Education Society, 1996.

Khan, Saqi Musta'ad. *Maasir-i-'Alamgiri*. Tr. Jadunath Sarkar. Calcutta: Royal Asiatic Society of Bengal, 1947.

Khan, Wahid al-din. *Diary*. Delhi: al-Risala Books, 1995.

———. *Fikr-i Islami: Afkar-i islami ki tashrih wa tawdih*. Delhi: al-Risala Books, 1996.

———. *Indian Muslims: The Need for a Positive Outlook*. Tr. Farida Khanam. Delhi: al-Risala Books, 1994.

Khan, Wahid al-din. *Madamin-i Islam: Islam ke mukhtalif pahlu'on par maqalat.* Delhi: al-Risala Books, 1998.

———. *Mewat ka safar.* Delhi: Maktaba-i risala, 1988.

Khan, Wahiduddin [Wahid-al-din]. *Tabligh Movement.* Delhi: The Islamic Centre, 1986.

———. *Uniform Civil Code: A Critical Study.* Tr. Farida Khanam. Delhi: al-Risala Books, 1996.

Khumayni. *See* Algar, Hamid.

Kister, M. J. " 'Do Not Assimilate Yourselves . . .' *La tashabbahu.*" *Jerusalem Studies in Arabic and Islam* 12 (1989): 321–71.

Kochanek, Stanley. *Interest Groups and Development: Business and Politics in Pakistan.* Delhi: Oxford University Press, 1983.

Kohlberg, Etan. "Some Imami Shi'ite Views on the Sahaba." *Jerusalem Studies in Arabic and Islam* 5 (1984): 143–75.

Kopf, David. *British Orientalism and the Bengal Renaissance: The Dynamics of Indian Modernization 1773–1835.* Berkeley: University of California Press, 1969.

Kozlowski, Gregory C. "Loyalty, Locality and Authority in Several Opinions (fatawa) delivered by the Mufti of the Jami'ah Nizamiyyah Madrasah, Hyderabad, India." *Modern Asian Studies* 29 (1995): 893–927.

———. *Muslim Endowments and Society in British India.* Cambridge: Cambridge University Press, 1985.

———. "Shah Banu's Case, Britain's Legal Legacy and Muslim Politics in Modern India." In *Boeings and Bullock Carts: Studies in Change and Continuity in Indian Civilization*, vol. 3, *Law, Politics and Society in India*, ed. Y. K. Malik and D. K. Vajpeyi, 88–111. Delhi: Chanakya Publications, 1990.

———. "When the 'Way' Becomes the 'Law': Modern States and the Transformation of *Halakhah* and *Shari'a*." In *Studies in Islamic and Judaic Traditions*, ed. William M. Brinner and Stephen D. Ricks, 2:97–112. Atlanta: Scholars Press, 1989.

Kugle, Scott Alan. "Framed, Blamed and Renamed: The Recasting of Islamic Jurisprudence in Colonial South Asia." *Modern Asian Studies* 35 (2001): 257–313.

al-Laknawi, Muhammad 'Abd al-Hayy. *Fatawa-i 'Abd al-Hayy.* Tr. Khurshid 'Alam. Karachi: Muhammad Sa'id and Sons, 1964.

———. *Al-Fawa'id al-bahiyya fi tarajim al-Hanafiyya.* Beirut: Shirkat Dar al-Arqam, 1998.

Lambton, A. K. S. *State and Government in Medieval Islam.* Oxford: Oxford University Press, 1981.

Lapidus, Ira M. "The Evolution of Muslim Urban Society." *Comparative Studies in Society and History* 15 (1973): 21–50.

———. *A History of Islamic Societies.* Cambridge: Cambridge University Press, 1988.

———. "The Separation of State and Religion in the Development of Early Islamic Society." *International Journal of Middle East Studies* 6 (1975): 363–85.

Lawrence, Bruce B. *Defenders of God: The Fundamentalist Revolt against the Modern Age.* 2d ed. Columbia: University of South Carolina Press, 1995.

———. *Shattering the Myth: Islam beyond Violence*. Karachi: Oxford University Press, 2000.

Leitner, G. W. *History of Indigenous Education in the Panjab since Annexation and in 1882*. 1883; Patiala: Languages Department Punjab, 1971.

Lerner, Daniel. *The Passing of Traditional Society: Modernizing the Middle East*. Glencoe, Ill.: The Free Press, 1958.

Lindbeck, George A. *The Nature of Doctrine: Religion and Theology in a Postliberal Age*. Philadelphia: The Westminster Press, 1984.

Lodhi, Maleeha. "Pakistan's Shia Movement: An Interview with Arif Hussaini." *Third World Quarterly* 10 (1988): 806–17.

Lombardi, Clark Benner. "Islamic Law as a Source of Constitutional Law in Egypt: The Constitutionalization of the Sharia in a Modern Arab State." *Columbia Journal of Transnational Law* 37 (1998): 81–123.

Ludhianawi, Muhammad Yusuf. *Apke masa'il awr unka hall*. 7 vols. Karachi: Maktaba-i bayyinat,1989–97.

———. *'Awrat ki sarbarahi*. Karachi: Maktaba-i Bayyinat, n.d.

MacIntyre, Alasdair. *After Virtue: A Study in Moral Theory*. Notre Dame: University of Notre Dame Press, 1981.

———. "Incommensurability, Truth, and the Conversation between Confucians and Aristotelians about the Virtues." In *Culture and Modernity: East-West Philosophic Perspectives*, ed. Eliot Deutsch, 104–22. Honolulu: University of Hawaii Press, 1991.

———. "A Partial Response to My Critics." In *After MacIntyre*, ed. Horton and Mendus, 283–304.

———. *Three Rival Versions of Moral Enquiry: Encyclopaedia, Genealogy, and Tradition*. Notre Dame: University of Notre Dame Press, 1990.

———. *Whose Justice? Which Rationality?* Notre Dame: University of Notre Dame Press, 1988.

Madale, Nagasura. "The Resurgence of Islam and Nationalism in the Philippines." In *Islam and Society in Southeast Asia*, ed. Taufik Abdullah and Sharon Siddique, 282–314. Singapore: Institute of Southeast Asian Studies, 1986.

Madani, Husayn Ahmad. *Khutbat-i Madani*. Ed. Ahmad Salim. Lahore: Nigarishat, 1990.

———. *Mawdudi dastur awr aqa'id ki haqiqat*. Deoband: Maktaba-i diniyya, n.d.

———. *Muttahida qawmiyyat awr Islam*. [1938?] Delhi: Qawmi aikta trust, [1972].

Mahdi, Muhsin. "From the Manuscript Age to the Age of Printed Books." In *The Book in the Islamic World: The Written Word and Communication in the Middle East*, ed. George N. Atiyeh. Albany: State University of New York Press, 1995.

Mahmood, Tahir. *Islamic Law in the Indian Courts since Independence*. Delhi: Institute of Objective Studies, 1997.

Majeed, Javed. *Ungoverned Imaginings: James Mill's The History of British India and Orientalism*. Oxford: Clarendon Press, 1992.

Makdisi, George. *The Rise of Colleges: Institutions of Learning in Islam and the West*. Edinburgh: Edinburgh University Press, 1981.

Maley, William, ed. *Fundamentalism Reborn? Afghanistan and the Taliban*. London: Hurst & Company, 1998.

Malik, Jamal. *Colonialization of Islam: Dissolution of Traditional Institutions in Pakistan*. Delhi: Manohar, 1996.

————. *Islamische Gelehrtenkultur in Nordindien: Entwicklungsgeschichte und Tendenzen am Beispiel von Lucknow*. Leiden: E. J. Brill, 1997.

————."The Making of a Council: The Nadwat al-'Ulama.' " *Zeitschrift der deutschen morgenländischen Gesellschaft* 144 (1994): 60–90.

Mallat, Chibli. *The Renewal of Islamic Law: Muhammad Baqer as-Sadr, Najaf and the Shi'i International*. Cambridge: Cambridge University Press, 1993.

Mani, Lata. *Contentious Traditions: The Debate on Sati in Colonial India*. Berkeley: University of California Press, 1998.

Markazi Jam'iyyat Ahl-i Hadith. *Ta'aruf al-Jami'a al-Salafiyya Islamabad*. Rawalpindi: Markazi Jam'iyyat Ahl-i Hadith, n.d.

————. *Ta'aruf Jami'a Salafiyya*. [Faysalabad: Jami'a Salafiyya, 1995?].

Marsot, A.F.L. al-Sayyid. "The Beginnings of Modernization among the Rectors of al-Azhar, 1798–1879." In *Beginnings of Modernization in the Middle East*, ed. Polk and Chambers, 267–80.

Mason, Andrew. "MacIntyre on Liberalism and Its Critics: Tradition, Incommensurability and Disagreement." In *After MacIntyre*, ed. Horton and Mendus, 225–44.

Mastura, Michael O. "Assessing the Madrasah as an Educational Institution: Implications for the Ummah." In *Muslim Filipino Experience*, 93–107. Manila: Ministry of Muslim Affairs, 1984.

Masud, Muhammad Khalid. "Apostasy and Judicial Separation in British India." In *Islamic Legal Interpretation: Muftis and their Fatwas*, ed. Masud, Messick, and Powers, 193–203.

————. *Iqbal's Reconstruction of Ijtihad*. Lahore: Iqbal Academy Pakistan, 1995.

————, ed. *Travellers in Faith: Studies of the Tablighi Jama'at as a Transnational Islamic Movement for Faith Renewal*. Leiden: Brill, 2000.

Masud, Muhammad Khalid, Brinkley Messick, and David S. Powers, eds. *Islamic Legal Interpretation: Muftis and their Fatwas*. Cambridge: Harvard University Press, 1996.

Mas'udi, Anzar Shah. *Naqsh-i dawam*. Deoband: Shah Book Depot, n.d.

Mawdudi, Sayyid Abu'l-A'la. *Islamic Law and Constitution*. Tr. and ed. Khurshid Ahmad. Lahore: Islamic Publications, 1967.

————. *Tafhim al-Qur'an*. 6 vols. Lahore: Idara-i Tarjuman al-Qur'an, 1958–72.

————. *Tahrik-i azadi-i Hind awr musalman*. 2 vols. Lahore: Islamic Publications, 1964.

————. *Ta'limat*. Lahore: Islamic Publications, 1972.

Mayaram, Shail. *Resisting Regimes: Myth, Memory and the Shaping of a Muslim Identity*. Delhi: Oxford University Press, 1997.

McKenna, Thomas M. "Appreciating Islam in the Muslim Philippines: Authority, Experience, and Identity in Cotabato." In *Islam in an Era of Nation-States*, ed. Hefner and Horvatich, 43–73.

————. *Muslim Rulers and Rebels: Everyday Politics and Armed Separatism in the Southern Philippines*. Berkeley: University of California Press, 1998.

Memon, Muhammad Umar. *Ibn Taimiya's Struggle against Popular Religion*. The Hague: Mouton, 1976.

Messick, Brinkley. *The Calligraphic State: Textual Domination and History in a Muslim Society*. Berkeley: University of California Press, 1993.

———. "Media Muftis: Radio Fatwas in Yemen." In *Islamic Legal Interpretation*, ed. Masud, Messick, and Powers, 310–20.

Metcalf, Barbara D. *Islamic Revival in British India: Deoband, 1860–1900*. Princeton: Princeton University Press, 1982.

———. "Living Hadith in the Tablighi Jama'at." *Journal of Asian Studies* 52 (1993): 584–608.

———. "Meandering Madrasas: Knowledge and Short-Term Itinerancy in the Tablighi Jama'at." In *The Transmission of Knowledge in South Asia*, ed. Crook, 49–61.

———. "Nationalism, Modernity, and Muslim Identity in India before 1947." In *Nation and Religion*, ed. van der Veer and Lehmann, 129–43.

———. *Perfecting Women: Maulana Ashraf 'Ali Thanawi's* Bihishti Zewar. Berkeley: University of California Press, 1990.

———. " 'Remaking Ourselves': Islamic Self-Fashioning in a Global Movement of Spiritual Renewal." In *Accounting for Fundamentalisms*, ed. Martin Marty and R. Scott Appleby, 706–25. Chicago: University of Chicago Press, 1994.

Metcalf, Thomas R. *Ideologies of the Raj*. Cambridge: Cambridge University Press, 1994.

Mill, James. *The History of British India*. 5th ed. 1858; New York: Chelsea House Publishers, 1968.

Mir-Hosseini, Ziba. *Islam and Gender: The Religious Debate in Contemporary Iran*. Princeton: Princeton University Press, 1999.

Misra, B. B. *The Central Administration of the East India Company, 1773–1834*. Manchester: Manchester University Press, 1959.

Mitchell, Timothy. *Colonising Egypt*. Berkeley: University of California Press, 1991.

Momen, Moojan. *An Introduction to Shi'i Islam*. New Haven: Yale University Press, 1985.

Moosa, Ebrahim. "The Sufaha' in Qur'an Literature: A Problem in Semiosis." *Der Islam* 75 (1998): 1–27.

Morley, William H. *The Administration of Justice in British India: Its Past History and Present State*. London: Williams and Norgate, 1858.

Moustafa, Tamir. "Conflict and Cooperation between the State and Religious Institutions in Contemporary Egypt." *International Journal of Middle East Studies* 32/2 (2000): 3–22.

———. *Tuhfat al-ahwadhi fi sharh jami' al-Tirmidhi*. 4 vols. Delhi: Idarat al-hakim, 1927–35.

Mubarakfuri [Mubarakpuri], 'Abd al-Rahman. *Muqaddimat Tuhfat al-ahwadhi*. Beirut: Dar al-kitab al-'Arabi, n.d.

Mudzhar, Mohamad Atho. "The Council of Indonesian 'Ulama' on Muslims' Attendance at Christmas Celebrations." In *Islamic Legal Interpretation*, ed. Masud, Messick, and Powers, 230–41.

Mustafa, Hala. *Al-Nizam al-siyasi wa'l-mu'arada al-islamiyya fi misr.* Cairo: Markaz al-mahrusa li'l-nashr wa'l-khidmat al-suhufiyya, 1995.

Nadhir Husayn, Muhammad. *Fatawa-i Nadhiriyya.* 3 vols. 1913; Lahore: Ahl-i Hadith Academy, 1971.

Nadwi, Muhammad Ishaq, and Shams Tabriz Khan. *Ta'rikh-i nadwat al-'ulama'.* 2 vols. Lucknow: Nizamat-i Nadwat al-'Ulama', 1983–84.

Nadwi, Sayyid Abu'l-Hasan 'Ali. *Hadith-i Pakistan.* Karachi: Majlis-i nashriyyat-i Pakistan, 1979.

———. *Insani dunya par musalmanon ke 'uruj wa zawal ka athar.* 5th ed. Lucknow: Majlis-i tahqiqat wa nashriyyat-i Islam, 1966.

———. *Al-Islam wa'l-mustashriqun.* Lucknow, [1983?].

———. *Karwan-i zindagi.* 6 vols. Karachi: Majlis-i nashriyyat-i Islam; Lucknow: Maktaba-i Islam,1983–97.

———. *The Musalman.* Tr. from the Urdu by M. Ahmad. Lucknow, 1972.

———. *Muslims in India.* Tr. from the Urdu by M. A. Kidwai. Lucknow, [1960].

———. *Reconstruction of Indian Society: What Muslims Can Do.* Lucknow, 1972.

———. *Tuhfa-i Pakistan.* Karachi: Majlis-i nashriyyat-i Islam, [1985?]

Nahal, Galal El-. *The Judicial Administration of Egypt in the Seventeenth Century.* Minneapolis: Bibliotheca Islamica, 1979.

Naqwi, Sayyid 'Arif Husayn. *Tadhkira-i 'ulama-i Imamiyya Pakistan.* Islamabad: Markaz-i tahqiqat-i Farsi-yi Iran wa Pakistan, 1984.

Naqvi, Syed Hussain Arif. "The Controversy about the Shaikhiyya Tendency among Shia 'Ulama in Pakistan." In *The Twelver Shia in Modern Times*, ed. Brunner and Ende, 135–49.

Nasr, S.V.R. *Islamic Leviathan: Islam and the Making of State Power.* New York: Oxford University Press, 2001.

———.*Mawdudi and the Making of Islamic Revivalism.* New York: Oxford University Press, 1996.

———. "The Rise of Sunni Militancy in Pakistan: The Changing Role of Islamism and the Ulama in Society and Politics." *Modern Asian Studies* 34/1 (2000): 139–80.

———. *The Vanguard of the Islamic Revolution: The Jama'at-i Islami of Pakistan.* Berkeley: University of California Press, 1994.

Nawshahrawi, Abu Yahya Imam Khan. *Tarajim-i 'ulama-i Ahl-i Hadith-i Hind.* Lahore: Riyad Brothers, n.d.

Newburg, Paula R. *Judging the State: Courts and Constitutional Politics in Pakistan.* Cambridge: Cambridge University Press, 1995.

Nizami, Farhan A. "Madrasahs, Scholars and Saints: Muslim Response to the British Presence in Delhi and the Upper Doab 1803–1857." Ph.D. dissertation, University of Oxford, 1983.

Noman, Omar. "The Impact of Migration on Pakistan's Economy and Society." In *Economy and Culture in Pakistan: Migrants and Cities in a Muslim Society*, ed. H. Donnan and P. Werbner. London: Macmillan, 1991.

Nu'mani, Muhammad Manzur. *Islam kiya hai?* Lahore: Maktaba-yi madaniyya, n.d.

———. *Khumayni awr Shi'a kai bare main 'ulama-i kiram ka muttafiqa faisala.* 2 vols. N.p., [1988?].

————. *Ma'arif al-hadith*. Lucknow: Kutub khana-i al-furqan, [1954].

————. *Tahdith-i ni'mat*. Ed. 'Atiq al-Rahman Sanbhali Nu'mani. Lucknow: al-Furqan Book Depot, 1997.

Nu'mani, Shibli. *Khutbat-i Shibli*. Ed. Sayyid Sulayman Nadwi. A'zamgarh: Dar al-Musannifin, 1941.

————. *Maqalat-i Shibli*. Ed. Sayyid Sulayman Nadwi. 8 vols. Lahore: National Book Foundation, 1989.

————. *Safarnama-i rum wa misr wa sham*. Lucknow: Anwar al-matabi', n.d.

Nussbaum, Martha. "Recoiling from Reason." *New York Review of Books*, 7 December 1989: 36–41.

Pakistan main mawjuda Shi'a abadi, N.p., [1980?].

Peters, Rudolph. "Divine Law or Man-Made Law? Egypt and the Application of the Shari'a." *Arab Law Quarterly* 3/3 (1988): 231–53.

————. "Ijtihad and Taqlid in Eighteenth and Nineteenth Century Islam." *Die Welt des Islams* 20 (1980): 131–45.

————. "The Islamization of Criminal Law: A Comparative Analysis." *Die Welt des Islams* 34 (1994): 246–74.

Philips, C. H., ed. *The Correspondence of Lord William Cavendish Bentinck*. Oxford: Oxford University Press, 1977.

Pirzada, Sayyid A. S. *The Politics of the Jamiat Ulema-i-Islam Pakistan, 1971–1977*. Karachi: Oxford University Press, 2000.

Polk, W. R., and R. L. Chambers, eds. *The Beginnings of Modernization in the Middle East*. Chicago: University of Chicago Press, 1968.

Porter, Jean. "Openness and Constraint: Moral Reflection as Tradition-Guided Inquiry in Alasdair MacIntyre's Recent Works." *Journal of Religion* 73/4 (1993): 514–36.

Powers, David S. "Fatwas as Sources for Legal and Social History: A Dispute over Endowment Revenues from Fourteenth-Century Fez." *al-Qantara* 11/2 (1990): 295–341.

————. "Kadijustiz or Qadi-Justice? A Paternity Dispute from Fourteenth-Century Morocco." *Islamic Law and Society* 1/3 (1994): 332–66.

————. "Orientalism, Colonialism, and Legal History: The Attack on Muslim Family Endowments in Algeria and India." *Comparative Studies in Society and History* 31/3 (1989): 535–71.

Qureshi, Ishtiaq Husain. *Ulema in Politics: A Study Relating to the Political Activities of the Ulema in the South Asian Subcontinent from 1556 to 1947*. Karachi: Maaref, 1972.

Qureshi, M. Naeem. *Pan-Islam in British Indian Politics: A Study of the Khilafat Movement, 1918–1924*. Leiden: Brill, 1999.

Qutb, Sayyid. *Social Justice in Islam*. Tr. by William E. Shepard as *Sayyid Qutb and Islamic Activism: A Translation and Critical Analysis of Social Justice in Islam*. Leiden: Brill, 1996.

Rabi', Majida 'Ali Salih. *Al-Dawr al-siyasi li'l-Azhar, 1952–1981*. Cairo: Kulliyat al-iqtisad wa'l-'ulum al-siyasiyya, 1992.

Rahi, Akhtar. *Tadhkira-i musannifin-i dars-i nizami*. Lahore: Maktaba-yi Rahmaniyya, 1978.

al-Rahman, 'Aziz. *Ta'aruf Dar al-'Ulum Karachi*. Karachi: Shu'ba-yi nashr wa isha'at, Dar al-'Ulum, 1417 A.H.

Rahman, Fazlur. *Islam and Modernity: Transformation of an Intellectual Tradition*. Chicago: University of Chicago Press, 1982.

al-Rahman, Fuyuz. *Mashahir 'Ulama'*. 3 vols. Lahore: Frontier Publishing Company, n.d.

Ranjha, Muhammad Nazir. *Ahadith key Urdu tarajim*. Islamabad: Muqtadara Qawmi Zaban, 1995.

Rashid, Ahmed. *Taliban: Militant Islam, Oil, and Fundamentalism in Central Asia*. New Haven: Yale University Press, 2000.

al-Rashid, Muhammad ibn 'Abdallah. *Imdad al-fattah bi-asanid wa marwiyyat al-shaykh 'Abd al-Fattah*. Riyadh: Maktabat al-imam al-Shafi'i, 1999.

Rastegar, Farshad. "Education and Revolutionary Political Mobilization: Schooling versus Uprootedness as Determinants of Islamic Political Activism among Afghan Refugee Students in Pakistan." Ph.D. dissertation. University of California at Los Angeles, 1991.

Reichmuth, Stefan. "Murtada az-Zabidi (d. 1791) in Biographical and Autobiographical Accounts: Glimpses of Islamic Scholarship in the Eighteenth Century." *Die Welt des Islams* 39/1 (1999): 64–102.

Report by the Panjab Provincial Committee with evidence taken before the committee and memorials addressed to the education commission. Calcutta: Superintendent of Government Printing, India, 1884.

Report of the Committee Set Up by the Governor of West Pakistan for Recommending Improved Syllabus for the Various Darul Ulooms and Arabic Madrasas in West Pakistan. Lahore: Superintendent of Government Printing, West Pakistan, 1962.

Report of the Court of Inquiry [into] . . . the Punjab Disturbances of 1953. Lahore: Government Printing, 1954.

Report Qawmi Committee bara'i dini madaris-i Pakistan. Islamabad: Ministry of Religious Affairs, 1979.

Repp, R. C. *The Mufti of Istanbul: A Study in the Development of the Ottoman Learned Hierarchy*. London: Ithaca Press, 1986.

Rida, Muhammad Rashid. *Ta'rikh al-ustadh al-imam al-shaykh Muhammad 'Abduh*. 3 vols. Cairo: Matba'at al-Manar, 1931.

Rieck, Andreas. "The Struggle for Equal Rights as a Minority: Shia Communal Organizations in Pakistan, 1948–68." In *The Twelver Shia in Modern Times*, ed. Brunner and Ende, 268–83.

Riesebrodt, Martin. *Pious Passion: The Emergence of Modern Fundamentalism in the United States and Iran*. Berkeley: University of California Press, 1993.

Rizvi, S.A.A. *Shah Wali-Allah and his Times*. Canberra: Ma'rifat Publishing House, 1980.

Roald, Anne Sofie. *Tarbiya: Education and Politics in Islamic Movements in Jordan and Malaysia*. Lund: Lunds Universitet, 1994.

Roberts, Jon H., and James Turner. *The Sacred and the Secular University*. Princeton: Princeton University Press, 2000.

Robinson, Francis. "Islam and the Impact of Print in South Asia." In *The Transmission of Learning in South Asia*, ed. Crook, 62–97.

———. "Perso-Islamic Culture in India from the Seventeenth to the Early Twentieth Century." In *Turko-Persia in Historical Perspective*, ed. Robert L. Canfield, 104–31. Cambridge: Cambridge University Press, 1991.

———. "Problems in the History of the Farangi Mahall Family of Learned and Holy Men." *Oxford University Papers on India*. Vol. 1, pt. 2. Delhi: Oxford University Press, 1987: 1–27.

———. "Technology and Religious Change: Islam and the Impact of Print." *Modern Asian Studies* 27 (1993): 229–51.

Rosenthal, Franz. *Knowledge Triumphant: The Concept of Knowledge in Medieval Islam*. Leiden: E. J. Brill, 1970.

Roy, Olivier. *The Failure of Political Islam*. Cambridge: Harvard University Press, 1994.

———. *Islam and Resistance in Afghanistan*. Cambridge: Cambridge University Press, 1986.

Rubin, Barnett. *The Fragmentation of Afghanistan: State Formation and Collapse in the International System*. New Haven: Yale University Press, 1995.

Sadri, Mahmoud, and Ahmad Sadri, eds. and trans. *Reason, Freedom, and Democracy in Islam: Essential Writings of 'Abdolkarim Soroush*. New York: Oxford University Press, 2000.

Saeedullah. *The Life and Works of Muhammad Siddiq Hasan Khan, Nawwab of Bhopal*. Lahore: Sh. Muhammad Ashraf, 1973.

Saharanpuri, Khalil Ahmad. *Badhl al-majhud fi sharh sunan Abi Dawud*. 20 vols. Beirut, 1980.

Sajjad, Muslim, and Salim Mansur, eds. *Dini madaris ka nizam-i ta'lim*. Islamabad: Institute of Policy Studies, 1987 (reprint, 1993).

Salafi, Muhammad Mustaqim. *Jama'at-i Ahl-i Hadith ki tasnifi khidmat*. Banaras: Idarat al-buhuth al-Islamiyya wa'l-da'wa wa'l-ifta bi'l-jami'a al-Salafiyya, 1992.

Sanyal, Usha. *Devotional Islam and Politics in British India: Ahmad Riza Khan Barelwi and His Movement, 1870–1920*. Delhi: Oxford University Press, 1996.

———. "Generational Changes in the Leadership of the Ahl-e Sunnat Movement in North India during the Twentieth Century." *Modern Asian Studies* 32 (1998): 635–56.

Saran, P. *The Provincial Government of the Mughals, 1526–1658*. 1941; Lahore: Faran Academy, 1976.

Sarkar, Jadunath. *Mughal Administration*. Calcutta: M. C. Sarkar & Sons, 1952.

Saudi Arabian Cultural Mission to the USA. *Education in Saudi Arabia*, rev. Hamad I. Al-Salloom. Beltsville, Md.: Amana Publications, 1991.

al-Sayyid Marsot, A. L. "The Beginnings of Modernization among the Rectors of al-Azhar, 1798–1879." In *The Beginnings of Modernization in the Middle East*, ed. Polk and Chambers, 267–80.

Schulze, Reinhard. *Islamischer Internationalismus im 20. Jahrhundert: Untersuchungen zur Geschichte der islamischen Weltliga*. Leiden: Brill, 1990.

Selections from Educational Records of the Government of India. Vol. 1, *Educational Reports, 1859–71*. Delhi: National Archives of India, 1960.

Serjeant, R. B. "The Sunnah Jami'ah Pacts with the Yathrib Jews, and the Tahrim of Yathrib: Analysis and Translation of the Documents Comprised in the So-

Called 'Constitution of Medina.' " *Bulletin of the School of Oriental and African Studies* 41 (1978): 1–42.

Sezgin, Fuat. *Geschichte des arabischen Schrifttums*. Vol. 1, Leiden: E. J. Brill, 1967.

Shafi', Mufti Muhammad. *Jawahir al-fiqh*. 2 vols. Karachi: Maktaba-i Dar al-'Ulum, 1975.

———. *Ma'arif al-Qur'an*. 8 vols. Karachi: Idarat al-ma'arif, 1969–73.

Shahrur, Muhammad. *Al-Kitab wa'l-Qur'an*. Cairo: Sina li'l-nashr, 1992.

Shaikh, Farzana. *Community and Consensus in Islam: Muslim Representation in Colonial India, 1860–1947*. Cambridge: Cambridge University Press, 1989.

Sherkoti, Anwar al-Hasan. *Anwar-i 'Uthmani*. Karachi: Maktaba-i Islamiyya, [1966].

Sherwani, Latif Ahmed. *See* Iqbal, Muhammad.

Siddiqi, Zameeruddin. "The Institution of the Qazi under the Mughals." In *Medieval India: A Miscellany*. Bombay: Asia Publishing House, 1969, 1: 240–59.

Singha, Radhika. *A Despotism of Law: Crime and Justice in Early Colonial India*. Delhi: Oxford University Press, 1998.

Sivan, E. *Radical Islam: Medieval Theology and Modern Politics*. New Haven: Yale University Press, 1985.

———. "Sunni Radicalism in the Middle East and the Iranian Revolution." *International Journal of Middle East Studies* 21 (1989): 1–30.

Skovgaard-Petersen, Jakob. *Defining Islam for the Egyptian State: Muftis and Fatwas of the Dar al-Ifta*. Leiden: E. J. Brill, 1997.

Skuy, David. "Macaulay and the Indian Penal Code of 1862: The Myth of the Inherent Superiority and Modernity of the English Legal System Compared to India's Legal System in the Nineteenth Century." *Modern Asian Studies* 32 (1998): 513–57.

Smith, Wilfred Cantwell. *Islam in Modern History*. Princeton: Princeton University Press, 1957.

———. *The Meaning and End of Religion*. San Francisco: Harper & Row, 1978.

Soroush, 'Abdolkarim. *See* Sadri, Mahmoud, and Ahmad Sadri.

Spellberg, D. A. *Politics, Gender, and the Islamic Past: The Legacy of 'A'isha bint Abi Bakr*. New York: Columbia University Press, 1994.

Starrett, Gregory. *Putting Islam to Work: Education, Politics, and Religious Transformation in Egypt*. Berkeley: University of California Press, 1998.

Stout, Jeffrey. "Commitments and Traditions in the Study of Religious Ethics." *Journal of Religious Ethics* 25 (1998): 23–56.

———. *Ethics after Babel: The Languages of Morals and their Discontents*. 2d ed. Princeton: Princeton University Press, 2001.

Tambiah, Stanley J. *Leveling Crowds: Ethnonationalist Conflicts and Collective Violence in South Asia*. Berkeley: University of California Press, 1996.

Tanner, Kathryn. *Theories of Culture: A New Agenda for Theology*. Minneapolis: Fortress Press, 1997.

Tanzim al-madaris al-'Arabiyyah. *Nisab-i ta'lim-i tanzim al-madaris (Ahl-i Sunnat) Pakistan*. Lahore: Markazi daftar tanzim al-madaris Pakistan, 1412 A.H.

Tayob, Abdulkader. *Islamic Resurgence in South Africa: The Muslim Youth Movement*. Cape Town: UCT Press, 1995.

Thanawi, Ashraf 'Ali. *Al-Hila al-najiza li'l-halilat al-'ajiza.* Karachi: Qur'an ma-hall, n.d. [first published in 1931]; another edition, with rearranged contents, published as *Ahkam-i talaq wa nizam-i shar'i 'adalat, ya'ni al-hila al-najiza jadid,* ed. Khurshid Hasan Qasimi, Lahore: al-Faysal, 1996.

————. *Imdad al-fatawa.* Ed. Mufti Muhammad Shafi'. 2 vols. Deoband: Idarat ta'lifat-i awliya', [1394 A.H.].

Thanawi, Jamil Ahmad. *Nisab wa nizam-i dini madaris.* Lahore: Nashiran-i Qur'an Limited, n.d.

Troll, Christian W. "The Meaning of Din: Recent Views of Three Eminent Indian Ulama." In *Islam in India: Studies and Commentaries,* ed. Christian W. Troll, 168–77. New Delhi: Vikas Publishing House, 1982.

————. "Muhammad Shibli Nu'mani (1857–1914) and the Reform of Muslim Religious Education." In *Madrasa: La transmission du savoir dans le monde musulman,* ed. Grandin and Gaborieau, 145–57.

————. *Sayyid Ahmad Khan: A Reinterpretation of Muslim Theology.* Delhi: Vikas Publishing House, 1978.

————. "Sharing Islamically in the Pluralistic Nation-State of India: The Views of Some Contemporary Indian Muslim Leaders and Thinkers." In *Christian-Muslim Encounters,* ed. Yvonne Yazbeck Haddad and Wadi Zaidan Haddad, 245–62. Gainesville: University Press of Florida, 1995.

Tucker, Judith. *In the House of the Law: Gender and Islamic Law in Ottoman Syria and Palestine.* Berkeley: University of California Press, 1998.

'Uthman, Muhammad, and Mas'ud Ash'ar, eds. *Pakistan ki siyasi jama'attain.* Lahore: Sang-i mil Publications, 1988.

'Uthmani, 'Aziz al-Rahman. *Fatawa Dar al-'Ulum Deoband.* 12 vols. Compiled by Mufti Muhammad Zafir al-din. Deoband: Dar al-'Ulum, 1970–.

'Uthmani, Muhammad Rafi'. *'Awrat ki sarbarahi ki shar'i haythiyyat.* Karachi: Idarat al-ma'arif, 1994.

————. *Dini jama'atain awr mawjuda siyasat.* Karachi: Idarat al-ma'arif, 1996.

————. *Hayat-i mufti-yi a'zam.* Karachi: Idarat al-ma'arif, 1994.

————. "Jami'a Dar al-'Ulum Karachi ke ta'limi sal, 1417–18, ke aghaz par sadr-i jami'a hadrat mawlana mufti Muhammad Rafi' 'Uthmani sahib ka iftitahi khi-tab." Parts 1 and 2, *al-Balagh,* March 1997, 11–18; May 1997, 17–38.

————. *Yeh tere pur-asrar bandey: Jihad-i Afghanistan ki an-kahi dastan.* Kara-chi: Idarat al-ma'arif, 1995.

'Uthmani, Muhammad Taqi. *'Asr-i hadir main Islam kaise nafiz ho?* Karachi: Maktaba-i Dar al-'ulum, 1397 A.H.

————. *Buhuth fi qadaya fiqhiyya mu'asira.* Damascus: Dar al-qalam, 1998.

————. "Bunyad-parasti aik gali ban chuki hai." *Al-Banuriyya* (October 1993): 8–18.

————. *Dars-i Tirmidhi.* 3 vols. Karachi: Maktabat al-rushd, 1414 A.H.

————. *Fiqhi maqalat.* 2 vols. Karachi: Memon Islamic Publishers, 1996.

————. "Hakim al-ummat ke siyasi afkar." *Al-Balagh* (Karachi, March 1990): 23–53.

————. *Hamara ma'ashi nizam.* Karachi: Maktaba-i Dar al-'Ulum, 1415 A.H.

————. *Hamara ta'limi nizam.* Karachi: Maktaba-i Dar al-'Ulum, n.d.

————. *Hamare 'a'ili masa'il.* Karachi: Dar al-isha'at, 1963.

'Uthmani, Muhammad Taqi. *Islah-i mu'ashara*. Karachi: Maktaba-i Dar al-'Ulum, 1415 A.H.

———. *Islam awr jiddat-pasandi*. Karachi: Maktaba-i Dar al-'Ulum, 1419 A.H.

———. *Jahan-i dida: Bis mulkon ka safarnama*. Karachi: Idarat al-ma'arif, 1996.

———. *Nifaz-i shari'at awr uske masa'il*. Karachi: Maktaba-i Dar al-'Ulum, 1413 A.H.

———. *Nuqush-i raftagan*. Deoband: Maktaba-i Jawid, 1994.

———. *Takmilat fath al-mulhim*. 3 vols. Karachi: Maktabat Dar al-'Ulum, 1407 A.H.

———. *Taqlid ki shar'i haythiyyat*. Karachi: Maktaba-i Dar al-'Ulum, 1413 A.H.

'Uthmani, Shabbir Ahmad. *Fath al-mulhim bi-sharh Sahih al-imam Muslim*. 2 vols. Karachi: Maktabat al-Hijaz, n.d.

'Uthmani, Zafar Ahmad. *I'la al-sunan*. 21 vols. Karachi: Idarat al-Qur'an wa'l-'ulum al-Islamiyya, 1415 A.H.

'Uthmani, Zafar Ahmad, with 'Abd al-Karim Gumthallawi. *Imdad al-fatawa*. Karachi: Maktaba-i Dar al-'Ulum, 1400 A.H.

van der, Veer, Peter, *Religious Nationalism: Hindus and Muslims in India*. Berkeley: University of California Press, 1994.

van der, Veer, Peter and Hartmut Lehmann, eds. *Nation and Religion: Perspectives on Europe and Asia*. Princeton: Princeton University Press, 1999.

Viswanathan, Gauri. *Masks of Conquest: Literary Study and British Rule in India*. New York: Columbia University Press, 1989.

———. *Outside the Fold: Conversion, Modernity, and Belief*. Princeton: Princeton University Press, 1998.

Vogel, Frank E. *Islamic Law and Legal System: Studies of Saudi Arabia*. Leiden: Brill, 2000.

Voll, John. "Hadith Scholars and Tariqahs: An Ulama Group in the Eighteenth Century Haramayn and Their Impact in the Islamic World." *Journal of Asian and African Studies* 15/3–4 (1980): 264–73.

———. "Muhammad Hayya al-Sindi and Muhammad ibn 'Abd al-Wahhab: An Analysis of an Intellectual Group in Eighteenth-Century Madina." *Bulletin of the School of Oriental and African Studies* 38/1 (1975): 32–39.

Waldman, Marilyn Robinson. "Tradition as a Modality of Change: Islamic Examples." *History of Religions* 25 (1986): 318–40.

Wali Allah, Shah. *The Conclusive Argument from God*. Tr. Marcia K. Hermansen, Leiden: E. J. Brill, 1996.

Washbrook, D. A. "Law, State and Agrarian Society in Colonial India." *Modern Asian Studies* 15/3 (1981): 649–721.

Watt, W. Montgomery. *The Formative Period of Islamic Thought*. Edinburgh: Edinburgh University Press, 1973.

Weiss, Anita M. *Culture, Class, and Development: The Emergence of an Industrial Bourgeoisie in Punjab*. Boulder: Westview Press, 1991.

———, ed. *Islamic Reassertion in Pakistan: The Application of Islamic Laws in a Modern State*. Lahore: Vanguard, 1987.

Weiss, Bernard. *The Spirit of Islamic Law*. Athens: University of Georgia Press, 1998.

Wensinck, A. J., et al. *Concordances et indices de la tradition musulmane.* 8 vols. Leiden: E. J. Brill, 1936–88.

Wickham, Carrie Rosefsky. "Political Mobilization under Authoritarian Rule: Explaining Islamic Activism in Mubarak's Egypt." Ph.D. dissertation. Princeton University, 1996.

Wiktorowicz, Quintan. *The Management of Islamic Activism: Salafis, the Muslim Brotherhood, and State Power in Jordan.* Albany: State University of New York Press, 2001.

Wifaq al-madaris al-'Arabiyyah Pakistan. *Solah sala nisab-i ta'lim.* N.p., 1983.

Wilson, Bryan. *The Social Dimensions of Sectarianism.* Oxford: Clarendon Press, 1990.

Zakariyya, Mawlana Muhammad. *Hadrat-i shaykh awr unki ap-biti.* New Delhi: Idara-yi isha'at-i diniyyat, n.d.

———. *Ta'rikh-i Mazahir.* 2 vols. Saharanpur: Kutub khana-i isha'at al-'ulum, 1972.

Zaman, Muhammad Qasim. "Arabic, the Arab Middle East, and the Definition of Muslim Identity in Twentieth Century India." *Journal of the Royal Asiatic Society* ser. 3, 8/1 (1998): 59–81.

———. "Commentaries, Print, and Patronage: Hadith and the Madrasas in Modern South Asia." *Bulletin of the School of Oriental and African Studies* 62 (1999): 60–81.

———. *Religion and Politics under the Early 'Abbasids.* Leiden: Brill, 1997.

———. "Religious Education and the Rhetoric of Reform: The Madrasa in British India and Pakistan." *Comparative Studies in Society and History* 41/2 (1999): 294–323.

———. Review of *Rethinking Tradition in Modern Islamic Thought,* by Daniel Brown. *Islamic Law and Society,* 5/2 (1998): 266–69.

———. "Sectarianism in Pakistan: The Radicalization of Shi'i and Sunni Identities." *Modern Asian Studies* 32/3 (1998): 689–716.

Zastoupil, Lynn. *John Stuart Mill and India.* Stanford: Stanford University Press, 1994.

Zebiri, Kate. *Mahmud Shaltut and Islamic Modernism.* Oxford: Clarendon Press, 1993.

Zeghal, Malika. *Gardiens de l'Islam: Les ulama d'al-Azhar dans l'Egypte contemporaine.* Paris: Presses de la fondation nationale des sciences politiques, 1995.

———. "La guerre des fatwas—Gad al-Haqq et Tantawi: Les cheikhs à l'épreuve du pouvoir." *Les cahiers de l'orient* 45 (1997): 81–95.

———. "Religion and Politics in Egypt: The Ulema of al-Azhar, Radical Islam, and the State (1952–94)." *International Journal of Middle East Studies* 31/3 (1999): 401–27.

Newspapers and Magazines Cited

Al-Ahram Weekly (Cairo)
Al-Balagh (Karachi)
Bayyinat (Karachi)
Dawn (Karachi)

Al-Faruq (Karachi)
The Frontier Post (Lahore)
Al-Haqq (Akora Khattak)
The Herald (Karachi)
The Independent (London)
Ishraq (Lahore)
Al-Jami'a (Jhang)
Jaridat al-Ashraf (Sukkur)
Al-Khayr (Multan)
Khilafat-i Rashida (Faisalabad)
Majallat al-da'wa (Lahore)
Misaq (Lahore)
The Muslim (Islamabad)
The Nation (Islamabad and Lahore)
Nawa-i Waqt (Lahore)
The New York Times (New York)
The News (Islamabad)
Newsline (Karachi)
Newsweek (New York)
The Pakistan Times (Islamabad and Lahore)
Al-Sa'id (Multan)
The Sunday Times (London)
The Times of India (Delhi)
The Washington Post (Washington, D.C.)
Zindagi (Lahore)
Ziya-i haram (Lahore)

Index

'Abd al-Rahman, 'Umar, 148, 156, 173
'Abd al-Sattar, 83–84
'Abduh, Muhammad, 10, 185–86
Abu Ghudda, 'Abd al-Fattah, 52, 55–56, 156
Abu Zayd, Nasr Hamid, 147
Afghanistan: the Northern Alliance in, 139; refugees from, in Pakistan, 137, 241 n. 120; Soviet occupation of, 136–37, 151; students from, in Pakistani madrasas, 137–38; under the Taliban, 137–40. *See also* Taliban
Ahl-i Hadith, 11, 23–24, 39–42, 46, 49, 79, 175, 205 n. 55
Ahmad, Mirza Ghulam, 11, 35, 113
Ahmadis, 11, 35, 55, 119, 131–33, 240 n. 101; and constitutional definitions of a Muslim in Pakistan, 113–14, 119; as non-Muslim minority in Pakistan, 113–14; and the Shi'a, 113–14, 119, 240 n. 101; and Sunni radicalism, 113, 119
'Alamgir, Aurangzeb, 20
'Ali ibn Abi Talib, 112
'Ali, Muhammad, 60
Anglo-Muhammadan law, 23, 25
apostasy, 29–31, 250 n. 83
Arab socialism, 162
Arendt, Hannah, 172
Arya Samaj, 132
Asad, Talal, 4–7, 48, 62, 101
authority. *See* religious authority
Awadh, 112
al-Azhar, 2, 10, 40, 55, 72, 85–86, 131, 153, 174–75; and censorship in Egypt, 147–49; growth of, 85–86; and the implementation of the shari'a, 146–47; and Islamists, 107, 146–51, 198 n. 46; and Muslims in the southern Philippines, 174–75; reform of, and its effects, 60–61, 81, 145–51, 171, 185–86, 222 n. 92

Baburi Masjid, 169–70, 183, 184
Banuri, Muhammad Yusuf: on madrasa reform, 81–82; on the study of hadith in South Asia, 53
Barelawis, 11, 79, 121, 132, 235 n. 51, 243 n. 138

Bharatiya Janata Party (BJP), 184
Bhutto, Benazir, 89, 90, 236 n. 57
Bhutto, Zulfiqar 'Ali, 113, 119
Bin Baz, 'Abd al-'Aziz, 155, 157
Bin Laden, Usama, 138, 141–42, 242 n. 136, 244 n. 152, 253 n. 133
Board of Senior 'Ulama (Saudi Arabia), 153–155, 157
Bourguiba, Habib, 61
al-Bukhari, Muhammad ibn Isma'il, 40–41, 50–52

Colebrooke, H. T., 22
colonialism: conceptions of knowledge under, 64–67; conceptions of religion shaped by, 62–86; ideas of cultural authenticity under, 46–47; impact of, on the shari'a, 17, 21–37; and madrasa reform, 60–74; Muslim responses to, 11–13; 'ulama's claims to leadership under, 31, 53–54
commentaries: as discursive tradition, 37–38, 49, 59; Islamist, on the Qur'an, 39; modern examples of, on hadith, 50 (*Fath al-mulhim*), 52–53 (*Fayd al-bari*), 41–49 (*I'la al-sunan*), 50–51 (*Lami' al-darari*), 41, 210 n. 23 (*Tuhfat al-ahwadhi*); modernist, on the Qur'an, 9–10, 198–99 n. 52. *See also* hadith; Qur'an
Companions of the Prophet (sahaba), 44–46, 57, 112–13, 117, 121, 236 n. 59, 240 n. 101
conversion, 120–21, 132, 205–6 n. 63, 255 n. 22
Council of Islamic Ideology (Pakistan), 89, 96, 115–16

Dars-i Nizami, 67–68, 72, 76, 82–83
Deoband, Deobandi Islam. *See* hadith; madrasas; madrasas, sectarian affiliation of; 'ulama, Deobandi

Egypt, 2, 131; grassroots activism of 'ulama in, 149–50; impact of expatriate labor remittances on, 148–49; implementation of shari'a in, 146–48; and Pakistan compared, 148, 150–51, 185–86,

Egypt (cont)
239 n. 98; "peripheral" 'ulama in, 145–
50, 170-71, 172–73, 239 n. 98, 245 n.
2; reform of the Azhar and its impact on,
60–61, 81, 145–51, 171, 185–86, 222 n.
92; 'ulama and Islamists in, 145–51,
170–73

Fahd ibn 'Abd al-'Aziz, King, 153
Faruqi, Zia al-Rahman, 123, 127, 235 n.
47, 237 n. 67, 239 n. 90, 240 n. 101
al-Fatawa al-'Alamgiriyya (al-Fatawa al-
Hindiyya), 20–22
fatwas, 2, 25–27, 30–32, 38, 204 nn. 49–
50, 212 n. 58, 238 n. 84; on dissolution
of marriage (faskh), 26; on heresy, 92;
on jihad, 244 n. 152; on menstruation,
26–27; on the Shi'a, 123, 132, 240 n.
101
Faysal ibn 'Abd al-'Aziz, King, 167
Federal Shari'at Court (Pakistan), 89, 92,
94
fiqh, 20, 149, 152; texts of, in use in India,
22–23, 26, 27, 220 n. 65
Fuda, Faraj, 147

Gad al-Haqq, 147, 246 n. 8
Gandhi, Mohandas, 45, 211 n. 42
Gandhi, Rajiv, 168, 169, 252 n. 117
Gangohi, Rashid Ahmad, 50, 52, 213 n.
67
al-Ghannouchi, Rached, 61
al-Ghazali, Muhammad, 147
Gibbon, Edward, 38
Gulf War (1991), 154; impact of, on Saudi
Arabia, 154–59

hadith, 3, 11, 33, 39, 45, 48, 55–57, 76,
99; commentaries on, 13, 24, 37, 40–
53, 56, 81, 94–95, 103, 132, 134–35,
210 nn. 23–24, 213 n. 67, 215 n. 98,
230 n. 63, 231 n. 73; and Islamic reform, 12, 69, 70, 174; scholarship on,
in South Asia, 53; study of, in madrasas
and Islamic universities, 12–13, 68, 174,
209 n. 14, 213 n. 67. See also commentaries
Hanafi, Hasan, 9, 198 n. 50
Hanafis, 19–21, 36, 39, 41, 48, 55, 58, 97,
205 n. 55, 253 n. 8; attitudes of, towards the government, 100; borrowings
of, from Maliki law, 30–31; under colo-

nial rule, 26-31; Deobandis as, 26, 29–
31, 39, 41, 48–49; and mechanisms of
legal change, 39, 98–99; predominance
of, in Pakistan, 113–14
Hanbalis, 43, 97–98, 152, 255 n. 8
Hasan, Mufti Wali, 132
Hastings, Warren, 66
al-Hawali, Safar, 155–59
Hodgson, Marshall, 7
hudud, 50, 96, 228 n. 34
Husayn ibn 'Ali (Shi'i imam), 112
al-Husayni, 'Arif Husayn, 115–17

Ibn 'Abd al-Wahhab, Muhammad, 53, 152
Ibn 'Abidin, 19, 100, 205 n. 60
Ibn Hajar, 40–41
Ibn Taymiyya, 40, 43–44, 48
ijtihad, 17–18, 20, 40, 182, 187; and the
Deobandi 'ulama, 29–31, 98–99, 172;
Muslim modernists and 101, 230 n. 57;
and the Saudi 'ulama, 97, 152–54
imam, Shi'i, 4, 112, 236 n. 59, 240 n. 101;
juristic authority in the absence of, 105–
7
India: growth of madrasas in, 160; Hindu
nationalism in, 35, 169–70; Muslim identity in, 160–70; Shah Bano controversy
in, 167–70; 'ulama in, 159–70. See also
colonialism
Indian National Congress, 32, 34–35, 44
Indonesia, 187–88
Iqbal, Muhammad, 36; critique of Husayn
Ahmad Madani, 34–35, 47, 48
Iran, 1, 2, 102; impact of 1979 revolution
in, on Sunni 'ulama, 177–78, 254 n.
145; and Khumayni's vision of the Islamic state, 105–7; revolution of 1979
in, 2, 105, 114; and sectarian conflict in
Pakistan, 114, 115, 117, 123, 132, 176–
77
Isar al-Qasimi, 127–28, 131
Islamic universities, 155–56, 171, 175–76,
209 n. 14, 253–54 n. 142; Imam Mu-
hammad ibn Sa'ud (Riyadh), 55, 175; of
Malaysia, 155; of Medina, 156, 175–76;
of Pakistan, 155, 176; Umm al-Qura
(Mecca), 156, 175
Islami Jumhuri Ittihad, 90
Islamists, 1, 8, 100; attitudes towards the
Islamic tradition, 9–10, 102–3; and
grassroots activism, 111, 148–50; and
the Islamic state, 102–5; and modern-

ists, 7–10; and the 'ulama, 102–5, 107–8, 145–51, 154–59, 170–73, 178–80, 190, 198 n. 46

al-Jabiri, Muhammad 'Abid, 9
Ja'far Husayn, Mufti, 115–16, 233 n. 25
jahiliyya: Mawdudi on, 249 n. 80; Nadwi on, 162–64; nationalism as, 164; Sayyid Qutb on, 8, 249 n. 80; varieties of, 164
Jaish-i Muhammad, 244 n. 150
Jama'a Islamiyya (Egypt), 148
Jama'at-i Islami, 102–3, 136, 139, 141
Jam'iyyat al-'Ulama-i Hind, 30, 32, 37, 53, 102, 119, 160, 185
Jam'iyyat al-'Ulama-i Islam, 37, 42, 118–19, 133–34, 138–39, 141, 241–42 n. 128, 244 nn. 152–53; ties of, with the Taliban, 138, 244 n. 150
Jam'iyyat al-'Ulama-i Pakistan, 243 n. 138
Jam'iyyat al-'Ulama Johannesberg, 53
Jhang, 119, 124–25, 127–28, 234–35 n. 46
Jhangawi, Haqq Nawaz, 119–21, 125, 127, 131, 135, 236 nn. 57–58; and foundation of the Sipah-i Sahaba, 119–20
jihad, 137, 139, 141, 142, 227–28 n. 33, 243 n. 139, 244 nn. 152–53
al-Jihad (radical Egyptian group), 148
Jones, William, 21, 25

Kandhlawi, Muhammad Yahya, 50, 52
Kashmir, 142, 221 n. 74
Kashmiri, Anwarshah, 52–53, 55
Khalid ibn 'Abd al-'Aziz, King, 153
Khamene'i, 'Ali
Khan, Ayub, 77, 115
Khan, Muhammad Zafrullah, 113
Khan, Siddiq Hasan, 40–41
Khan, Wahid al-din: critique of the 'ulama, 181–86, 189–90; and the Tablighi Jama'at, 184–85
al-khulafa al-rashidun (Rashidun caliphate), 112, 121, 138, 240 n. 101
Khumayni, Ayatollah Ruhollah, 39, 116, 172, 177; and the Islamic state, 105–7

Laknawi, 'Abd al-Hayy, 55, 204 n. 50
language: Arabic, 40–41, 44–48, 66, 71, 161–62, 209 n. 17; and authority, 40, 49; and cultural authenticity, 71; Hindi/Hindustani, 44; and identity, 44–45, 184; Persian, 44, 65–66; Urdu, 44, 47, 49, 65, 184

Lashkar-i Jhangawi, 234 n. 41, 239 n. 95
Leitner, G. W., 46, 64, 65
Lindbeck, George, 190, 195 n. 20
Lucknow, 112–13, 115
Ludhianawi, Muhammad Yusuf, 57–58, 135; on madrasa reform, 78–80, 84; as sectarian polemicist, 132–33

Macaulay, Thomas Babington, 22
MacIntyre, Alasdair, 4–5, 7, 172
Madani, Husayn Ahmad: as advocate of "united nationalism," 32–37; compared with Nadwi, 166–67; criticism of, by Mawdudi, 34–35, 102; criticism of, by Muhammad Iqbal, 34–35; criticism of, by Zafar Ahmad 'Uthmani, 42–47; on the flexibility of Islam, 32–34; and the Islamic juristic tradition, 33–34, 36–37, 48–49, 187, 212 n. 58; and opposition to the demand for Pakistan, 32–33, 118, 133, 160, 212 n. 61
madrasas: Calcutta Madrasa (Madrasa-i 'aliyya), 66–67, 74–75, 80, 83; Dar al-'Ulum (Deoband), 11, 94, 132, 150, 175; Dar al-'Ulum (Karachi), 50, 56, 82–83, 87, 94, 98, 134, 139–40, 243 n. 141; Dar al-'Ulum Haqqaniyya (North-West Frontier Province), 132, 137–39, 228 n. 33, 242 n. 134; Dar al-'Ulum Nadwat al-'Ulama (Lucknow), 69, 72, 73, 160; Farangi Mahall (Lucknow), 68, 204 n. 50; Jami'a Ashrafiyya (Lahore), 81; Jami'a Banuriyya (Karachi), 132; Jami'a Faruqiyya (Karachi), 175–76, 253 nn. 140–41; Jami'a Islamiyya (Dabhel), 52; Jami'a Salafiyya (Banaras), 175; Jami'a Salafiyya (Faisalabad), 175; Jami'a Salafiyya (Islamabad), 175; Jam'iat al-'Ulum al-Islamiyya (Karachi), 57–58, 81, 141, 243 n. 141; Madrasa-i A'zam (Madras), 66, 68; Mazahir al-'Ulum (Saharanpur), 56; Qarawiyyin (Morocco), 61; Yusufiyya (Morocco), 61; Zaytuna (Tunisia), 61. See also al-Azhar; Islamic universities
madrasas, growth of: in India, 160; in Pakistan, 2, 85, 120, 235 n. 51; in the Punjab, 2, 235 n. 51;
madrasas, reform of, 60–86; British colonial discourses on, 62–68; in colonial Bengal, 66–68; and Deobandi 'ulama, 68–69, 78–83, 190–91; in Egypt, 60–61,

madrasas, reform of (*cont*)
144–51, 171; in Iran, 186; in Morocco, 61; and Nadwat al-'Ulama, 69–73; in Pakistan, 74–78, 144–45, 221 nn. 74, 75; in Tunisia, 61

madrasas, sectarian affiliation of: Ahl-i Hadith, 175; Barelawi, 235 n. 51; Deobandi, 11, 50, 52–53, 56, 58–59, 81–83, 87, 94, 98, 132, 134, 137–43, 150, 160, 175–76, 235 n. 51, 238 n. 84, 243 n. 141; Isma'ili Da'udi Bohra, 253 n. 141; and sectarian organizations, 118–19, 135–36; Twelver Shi'i, 115, 118, 120, 125, 136, 235 n. 51

Mahmud, 'Abd al-Halim, 146, 247 n. 29

Malikis, 18–19, 26–27, 30–32, 36, 48

Maraghi, Muhammad Mustafa, 185

Mawdudi, Abu'l-A'la, 9, 34–35, 47, 56, 156, 167, 171, 249 n. 80; collaboration of, with the 'ulama, 102–3, 171; commentary on the Qur'an by, 39, 56, 102, 181; critique of Husayn Ahmad Madani by, 34–35; and the Islamic state, 102–5; 'ulama's critique of, 104–5, 207 n. 85

mawlawis, 21–22, 47, 67

Metcalf, Barbara D., 12–14, 39–40, 256 n. 26

Mill, James, 64, 65

minorities: Muslim, 36–37, 43, 48–49, 212 n. 61; non-Muslim, 43; sectarian, 113–14

modernists, Muslim, 3, 7–8, 34–35, 67, 132, 168, 186–91; attitudes of, towards the Islamic tradition, 9–10, 39, 76–77; attitudes of, towards the 'ulama, 92, 100; and conceptions of the Islamic state, 88–93; and ijtihad, 101, 230 n. 57; reified views of Islam of, 36, 77;

Mongiri, Muhammad 'Ali, 69, 70

Morley, William, 22

Moro Islamic Liberation Front, 174

Moro National Liberation Front, 174

Mubarak, Hosni, 146

Mubarakpuri, 'Abd al-Rahman, 41

muftis, 18, 20, 27, 31, 149, 204 n. 42; changing position of, in colonial India, 25; under the East India Company, 21; Ibn 'Abidin on, 19; and print, 25, 58; and sectarian identities, 123; Wahid al-din Khan's criticism of, 183

Mughals, 19–20

Muhammad, Prophet, 3, 11, 35, 44, 45, 46, 48, 57, 112, 113, 183, 240 n. 101

Muharram, 112, 114, 117, 121–22

Mukhtar, Habib Allah, 141

Murji'a, 156–57

Musharraf, General Pervez, 75, 138; ban on sectarian organizations by, 142, 221 n. 74; and madrasa reform, 75, 221 n. 75; and September 11, 2001, 221 n. 74, 242 n. 130, 244 n. 148; 'ulama challenges to, 141, 244 n. 150

Muslim Brotherhood, 55–56, 148–49, 156

Muslim ibn al-Hajjaj, 50

Muslim League: All India, 47, 70, 102, 212 n. 55; Pakistan, 90

Muslim Personal Law Board, 167–69

Muslim public sphere, 3, 56, 146; 'ulama in, 178–80

Mustafa, Shukri, 9, 198 n. 46

mut'a, 235 n. 48

Mutahhari, Murtada, 186

Nadwat al-'Ulama (Lucknow), 52, 160–62, 165, 167, 175; and colonial discourses, 71; and Deoband, 69, 73, 161; and madrasa reform, 69–73

Nadwi, Abu'l-Hasan 'Ali, 52, 57, 70, 73, 132, 161–70, 175–77, 250 nn.86, 93; on Arabs, 162–65; compared with Husayn Ahmad Madani, 167; and Hindu nationalism, 169–70; and Islamists, 171, 249 n. 80; and modernists, 169; on Pakistan, 250 n. 93; on political activism in India, 161; Saudi patronage of, 163, 175, 250 n. 86; and the Shah Bano controversy, 167–70, 251–52 n. 115

Nahdlatul Ulama (Indonesia), 187–88

Najaf, 105; madrasas of, 115–16

Naqwi, Sayyid Ghulam Riza, 118, 238 n. 77

naskh (doctrine of abrogation), 183, 255 n. 15

Nasser, Gamal Abdel, 145–46, 156, 162, 174, 176

Nasserism, 162, 176

nationalism: Arab, 162–65, 166; Hindu, 35, 169–70; "united," in India, 32–37, 41–49, 102. See also Madani, Husayn Ahmad; Nadwi, Abu'l-Hasan 'Ali

Natsir, Muhammad, 167

Nizam al-din Muhammad, Mulla, 68

Nu'mani, Muhammad Manzur, 56–58, 132, 135; as sectarian polemicist, 132, 176–77, 240 n. 101

Nu'mani, Shibli: conception of religion of, 69–70; on Indian madrasas, 70, 185; on madrasas in Constantinople and Egypt, 72–73; vision of, for the Nadwat al-'Ulama, 69–70

Pakistan: constitutions of, 88, 90–91, 93; and Egypt compared, 148, 150–51, 185–86, 239 n. 98; and the fall of the Taliban, 138–43, 242 n. 130; growth of madrasas in, 2, 85, 120, 235 n. 51; impact of expatriate labor remittances on, 126, 148; implementation of the shari'a in, 87–102, 255 n. 18; Islamization of, 77, 89, 94, 113–15; madrasa reform in, 74–78, 144–45, 221 nn. 74–75; modernist discourses in, 75–78, 88–93, 101; relations between 'ulama and Islamists in, 102–5, 171; and the rise of the Taliban, 136–38, 151; 'ulama activism in, 109–10, 111–43. See also madrasas; madrasas, sectarian affiliation of; sectarianism in Pakistan; 'ulama; 'ulama, Deobandi; 'ulama, "peripheral"

Pakistan Peoples Party, 90

Pan-Arabism, 162, 176

pandits, 21–22, 25, 47

Philippines, 2, 254 n. 147; Muslim separatism in, 174; Saudi patronage of Muslims in, 174–75; 'ulama in, 173–75

pirs, 120–21, 125, 135, 235 n. 52;

print: and commentaries, 40–41, 51–52; and fatwas, 25, 123; impact of, on 'ulama's religious authority, 1, 13, 54–58; and sectarian identities in Pakistan, 123–24, 238 n. 86

public sphere. See Muslim public sphere

Punjab: customary law in, 23; madrasas in, 2, 235 n. 51; riots of 1953 in, 113; Shi'i proselytism in, 117, 120, 135; women's apostasy in, 29. See also sectarianism in Pakistan

qadis, 19, 20; consequences of absence of, in colonial India, 25–31, 205 n. 53; under the East India Company, 21; al-Fatawa al-'Alamgiriyya on, 19–21; in Saudi Arabia, 152–53

Qumm, 116, 188; Pakistanis studying in madrasas of, 234 n. 42

Qur'an (Koran), 8–10, 23, 33–35, 38–39, 46, 48, 56–57, 70, 88, 90–91, 93–94, 98, 101, 109, 116, 165, 174; commentaries on, 39, 56, 102, 181; and constitutions of Pakistan, 88–91; interpretation of, and the Shah Bano controversy in India, 168, 251 n. 105; the Privy Council on, 23

Qutb, Muhammad, 156

Qutb, Sayyid, 8, 9, 156, 162, 172, 180, 249 n. 80; commentary on the Qur'an of, 39, 56

Rabitat al-'alam al-Islami, 132, 163, 176

Rahman, Fazlur, 9, 39, 189

Rahman, Mawlana Fazlur, 138

reform: contention over meaning of, 15, 80–81; and sectarian identities in Pakistan, 119-24, 135–36; through study of hadith, 12, 39, 68–70, 174. See also madrasas, reform of; 'ulama, Deobandi

religion: and colonial discourses, 62–64; and the Islamist state, 102–5; objectification of, 57, 145–46; and secularization, 84; and the secular nation-state, 101; 'ulama as experts in, 86, 98–102, 140, 144, 155, 189, 229 n. 49, 243 n. 145; 'ulama's changing conceptions of, 15, 62, 66, 69–70, 79, 81, 83–86

religious authority, 8; challenges to 'ulama's claims to, 1–2, 10, 34–35, 54–55, 85, 92, 102–4, 179, 181–86; constituted through commentaries, 13, 14, 42, 49, 55; and fixed texts, 21–23; fragmentation of, 2, 85, 100; and invariant law, 24; language and, 40, 49; and madrasa reform, 78–83; and new religious intellectuals, 1, 55–58, 85, 186, 189; sectarian conceptions of, in South Asia, 11; tradition as basis of 'ulama's claims to, 170, 178–80, 189–91

Roy, Olivier, 2, 111

Rushdie, Salman, 183

al-Sadat, Anwar, 146, 148, 156, 173

sahaba. See Companions of the Prophet

Sa'idzadeh, Sayyid Muhsin, 186, 188–90

Sami' al-Haqq, 132, 135, 141; and the implementation of the shari'a, 227–28

Sami' al-Haqq (cont)
   n. 33; madrasa of, 137–39; and the Taliban, 138–39, 141, 244 n. 150
Sati, 28
al-Sa'ud, Muhammad, 152
Saudi Arabia: impact of 1991 Gulf War on,
   154–59; and Muslims in the Philippines,
   174-76; as patron of Islamists, 56, 171;
   as patron of 'ulama, 56, 132, 163, 171,
   174–77, 250 n. 86; scope of 'ulama authority in, 152–54; 'ulama and Islamists
   in, 154–59, 170–73, 248 n. 65
sectarianism in Pakistan: as grassroots activism, 110, 114–36; and the middle
   classes, 124–25, 136, 238 nn. 77, 86;
   Shi'i, 112–118; Sunni, 112–14, 118–36;
   support base of, 124–31; as vehicle of religious change, 135–36; and violence,
   13, 116–18, 124, 127–31, 133. See also
   under individual sectarian organizations:
   Lashkar-i Jhangawi; Sipah-i Muhammad
   Pakistan; Sipah-i Sahaba Pakistan; Tahrik-i Ja'fariyya Pakistan; Tahrik-i Nifaz-i
   Fiqh-i Ja'fariyya (TNFJ)
September 11, 2001: 75, 138, 139, 143,
   171, 221 n. 74, 244 n. 148, 253 n. 134
Shafi', Mufti Muhammad, 56, 83, 94, 98
Shafi'is, 19, 36
Shah Bano Controversy (India), 167–70,
   184, 251–52 n. 115, 252, n. 117. See
   also Nadwi, Abu'l-Hasan 'Ali
Shahrur, Muhammad, 9, 39, 189, 198–99
   n. 52
Shaltut, Mahmud, 10, 185, 247 n. 29
Shamzai, Mufti Nizam al-din, 244 nn. 150,
   152, 153
shari'a, 14, 15, 17, 20, 23, 31, 76; administration of, in colonial India, 24–31; codification of, 22, 25, 95–98, 152–53; as discursive tradition, 6, 97; flexibility of, in
   colonial India, 32–34; flexibility of, in
   pre-modern Islam, 17–21; implementation of, in Egypt, 146–48; implementation of, in Pakistan, 87–102, 227–28 n.
   33; inflexibility of, in colonial India, 24–
   25; modern 'ulama's changing conceptions of, 23–25, 96- 98, 182–83, 186;
   and the Saudi 'ulama, 152–54; and the
   Taliban, 96
Sharif, Nawaz, 90–93, 101
al-Shawkani, 40
Shaykhiyya, 117, 121

Shi'a (Twelvers), 11, 79; and the Ahmadi
   controversy in Pakistan, 113–14, 119,
   240 n. 101; beliefs and practices of, 4,
   105–7, 112, 235 n. 48, 240 n. 101; numbers of, in Pakistan, 113, 232 n. 9; and
   sectarian radicalism, 112–118. See also
   sectarianism in Pakistan
Shirbini, 'Abd al-Rahman, 81
al-Sindi, Muhammad Hayat, 53
Sipah-i Muhammad Pakistan, 118, 128;
   ban on, 234 n. 41, 239 n. 95; leadership
   of, 118
Sipah-i Sahaba Pakistan, 114, 118–31,
   135, 178, 237 nn. 65, 67, 238 n. 84,
   239 n. 95; ban on, 142, 234 n. 41; goals
   of, 119–23; rituals of, 121–23, 236 n.
   59; and the Taliban, 139, 141, 242 n.
   136
socialism. See Arab socialism
Society of Muslims (Society of Excommunication and Emigration), 9, 198 n. 46
Sorush, 'Abdolkarim, 186, 189
Sufi Muhammad, 243 n. 139
Sufis (Sufism), 4, 122, 135
sunna, 9, 20, 24, 33, 45–46, 93–94, 98,
   116, 165, 168; and constitutions of Pakistan, 88–91. See also hadith
Sunni/Sunnis, 1, 11, 15, 39, 40, 61, 79, 97,
   100, 102, 105, 107, 111–36, 143, 144–
   145, 152, 156, 161, 170, 172, 174, 176–
   78, 190

Tablighi Jama'at, 57–58, 73, 132, 184–85,
   256 n. 26; and the Deobandi 'ulama,
   185
Tahrik-i Ja'fariyya Pakistan, 115, 117–18,
   128, 238 n. 77; ban on, 142, 234 n. 41;
   and the Sipah-i Muhammad Pakistan,
   117–18
Tahrik-i Nifaz-i Fiqh-i Ja'fariyya (TNFJ),
   115–17; leadership of, 115–16; manifesto of, 116–17
Taliban, 15, 136–43, 151, 176, 242 n. 130;
   and Deobandi madrasas, 13, 137–38,
   227–28 n. 33; and implementation of Islamic law, 96, 138–39; and Pakistani
   'ulama, 96, 135, 137–43, 151
Tanzim-i Nifaz-i Shari'at-i Muhammadi,
   243 n. 139
taqlid, 17–18, 31, 152, 228 n. 39, 255 n.
   8; and Deobandi 'ulama, 23–24, 26–27,

39, 97-99; and Indonesian 'ulama, 187–88; modernist characterization of, 92

Tariq, A'zam, 131, 139

Taylor, Charles, 172

Thanawi, Ashraf 'Ali: and Husayn Ahmad Madani, 32; and pro-Pakistan 'ulama of Deoband, 133–34; and the shari'a in colonial India, 29–31, 36, 205–6 n. 63; and Zafar Ahmad 'Uthmani, 42, 52

Thanawi, Jamil Ahmad, 81

al-Tirmidhi, 41

tradition, 3, 4, 28, 194 n. 11, 203 n. 41; Asad on, 5–6, 196 n. 29; discursive, 5–7; Hodgson on, 7; MacIntyre on, 4–5

tradition, Islamic: as basis of 'ulama authority, 170, 178–80, 189–91; and Islamists, 9–10, 102–3; and modernists, 9–10, 39, 76–77; 'ulama and, 3–11, 37, 108, 231 n. 82, 248 n. 65, 254 n. 151

traditionalism, 3–4, 194 n. 6

'ulama, 1, 2, 7, 10, 14; ambivalence of, towards the state, 99–110, 187, 229 nn. 53, 55, 230 n. 71; and changing conceptions of the shari'a, 23–25; and grassroots activism in Egypt, 149–50; and grassroots activism in Pakistan, 109–10, 111, 114–36, 143, 188; impact of print on, 54–58; in India, 159–70; in Indonesia, 187–88; and the Islamic tradition, 3–11, 37, 108, 231 n. 82, 248 n. 65, 254 n. 151; laments on decline of, 83–85; in the Muslim public sphere, 178–80; in the Philippines, 173-74; as religious experts, 86, 98–102, 140, 144, 155, 189, 229 n. 49, 243 n. 145; Shi'i, 1, 102, 105–7, 112, 115–16, 135, 143, 144. See also under individual countries: Egypt, India, Pakistan, Saudi Arabia

'ulama, Deobandi:11–14; and apostasy, 29–31, 205–6 n. 63; commentaries on hadith by, 40, 41–54; differences among, 42–49, 133–35, 138–42; differences with other sectarian groups in India, 11, 79; as Hanafis, 26, 29–31, 39, 41, 48–49; Metcalf on, 12–13, 39–40; "nationalists" among, 33, 45, 47, 54, 118, 135, 160, 167, 212 n. 61; and polemics with Ahl-i Hadith, 24, 41–42, 46; and polemics with fellow Deobandis, 42–49; responses of, to colonial challenges, 12, 23–37; and the Taliban, 137–43, 151,

242 nn. 133–34, 136, 243 nn. 139, 141, 244 nn. 150–53, 245 nn. 154–55; and women, 26–31

'ulama, "peripheral": in Egypt, 145–50, 170–71, 172–73, 239 n. 98, 245 n. 2; in Pakistan, 131–33, 136, 239–98; in Saudi Arabia, 155–59, 170–71, 173; ties of, with high ranking 'ulama, 131–33, 172–73

'Ulama Front (Egypt), 147

United States, 138, 139, 140, 141, 142, 154, 244 nn. 150, 152, 245 n. 155

"useful" knowledge, conceptions of, 64–66, 67, 71–72, 74, 76, 81, 189, 218 n. 27, 220 n. 58

'Uthmani, Muhammad Rafi', 87, 135; on position of madrasas in society, 87, 108, 134; and the Taliban, 140, 142; on 'ulama's grassroots activism, 108–10, 134

'Uthmani, Muhammad Taqi, 134–35, 227 n. 24, 227–28 n. 33, 231 n. 82, 243 n. 143; commentary of, on hadith, 50; on the implementation of Islamic law, 94–96; and Islamists, 104–5, 172; on madrasa reform, 82–83; on secularism, 172; and the Taliban, 140, 142, 245 n. 154

'Uthmani, Shabbir Ahmad: commentary of, on hadith, 49–50; and the demand for Pakistan, 133–34

'Uthmani, Zafar Ahmad: commentary of, on hadith, 41–49, 52, 54–56, 134–35; critique of Husayn Ahmad Madani and the nationalist 'ulama, 42–49; and the Islamic juristic tradition, 48–49, 54, 212 n 58

Wahhabis, 40, 53, 152, 154, 156–57, 175

Wahid, Abdurrahman, 188

Wali Allah, Shah, 40

War on Terrorism, 75, 143, 242 n. 130

wilayat al-faqih, 105–7, 144, 231 n. 80

al-Zabidi, Murtada, 53

Zakariyya, Muhammad: as author of the Tablighi Jama'at's reformist texts, 56–58, 185; as scholar of hadith, 50–52

zakat, 89, 91–92, 114–15

Zia al-Haqq, General Muhammad, 90, 119, 151, 171; Islamization of Pakistan under, 77, 89, 94, 113–15; and madrasa reform, 77